W9-BWD-262

The Anti-Communist
Manifestos

FOUR BOOKS THAT SHAPED THE COLD WAR

JOHN V. FLEMING

W. W. NORTON & COMPANY

NEW YORK   LONDON

Copyright © 2009 by John V. Fleming

All rights reserved
Printed in the United States of America
First Edition

For information about permission to reproduce selections from this book,
write to Permissions, W. W. Norton & Company, Inc.,
500 Fifth Avenue, New York, NY 10110

For information about special discounts for bulk purchases, please contact
W. W. Norton Special Sales at specialsales@wwnorton.com or 800-233-4830

Manufacturing by RR Donnelley, Harrisonburg, VA
Book design by Ellen Cipriano
Production manager:Andrew Marasia

Library of Congress Cataloging-in-Publication Data

Fleming, John V.
The anti-communist manifestos : four books that shaped
the Cold War / John V. Fleming. — 1st ed.
p. cm.
Includes bibliographical references.
ISBN 978-0-393-06925-9 (hardcover)
1. Anti-communist movements. 2. Ex-communists—Biography.
3. Koestler, Arthur, 1905–1983. Darkness at noon. 4. Valtin, Jan, 1904–1951.
Out of the night. 5. Kravchenko, Victor, 1905–1966. I chose freedom.
6. Chambers, Whittaker. Witness. I. Title.
HX40.F572 2009
335.43092'2—dc22

2009007113

W. W. Norton & Company, Inc.
500 Fifth Avenue, New York, N.Y. 10110
www.wwnorton.com

W. W. Norton & Company Ltd.
Castle House, 75/76 Wells Street, London W1T 3QT

1 2 3 4 5 6 7 8 9 0

For Katherine and Zvi

CONTENTS

INTRODUCTION

THE SUBJECT OF *The Anti-Communist Manifestos* is the role played by four unusually influential books in the great political struggle, usually called the Cold War, that dominated much of the second half of the twentieth century. Hence one could say that the protagonists of this book are themselves books.

The struggle of the Cold War had many aspects, or "fronts," as Communists sometimes called them, but at its heart it was a conflict of competing social and political visions. At the level of abstraction the conflict was never resolved, and it probably will never be resolved. At the pragmatic level, however, there was a decisive victory for anti-Communism. Communism, the specter that according to Marx and Engels's *Communist Manifesto* was haunting Europe in 1848, and quite truly was haunting Europe still, or again, in 1948, has in 2009 become a mere ghost, which is something altogether different.

Amidst the complex history of which the practical defeat of Communism was the outcome, there are a few thick strands that seem comparatively easy to grasp. One of these is that for explicable though not inevitable historical reasons the concept of Marxist Communism became inextricably linked with the Bolshevik *coup d'état* of 1917 and with the Union of Soviet Socialist Republics, which claimed to be the Revolution's implementation or continuation. We can go even further and say that the idea of Communism became localized in the Soviet Union of Joseph Stalin, who came to power in the 1920s and stayed there until his death in 1953. For this reason the critique of Communism at the practical level was an interpretation of Soviet history and, in particular, an assessment of the degree to which the abstract theories of Marxist socialism were vindicated or repudiated in their concrete expressions within Soviet life.

From its inception, the Soviet State was the object of great and often sympathetic interest in the West: but it was also beleaguered, remote, and difficult of access. Hence what Westerners knew of it came almost exclusively from "literary" sources, that is, from the dispatches of newspaper correspondents and the reports of travelers. We say that seeing is believing; in fact, it is just as true that believing is seeing. Many early reporters and visitors were partisans of the socialist ideal who filtered what they saw through the fine mesh of their own hopes and desires.

There are numerous scholarly books about the early reporters of Soviet life. Their relationship with their hosts tended to be the relationship of tourists to guides. Of course, the Soviet authorities ran the real tourist agency—the famous Intourist—that organized all aspects of a visitor's sojourn: transportation, lodging, meals, sightseeing; visits to the newly invented or radically reformed institutions of communal life: the factory, the school, the prison, the hospital, the farm.

Many early visitors to the USSR are aptly called "pilgrims." The traveler and the pilgrim cannot always be distinguished, but the salient difference between them is this: the pilgrim knows in advance what he is to see, knows and desires it, and even as he views it, is planning how he will tell the folks back home. Toward the end of the *Divine Comedy*, Dante captures pilgrim psychology in a lovely simile meant to convey his astonishment at having been transported from time to eternity, from the human to the divine, and "from Florence to a people just and sane . . . and, as a pilgrim, in the temple of his vow, content within himself, looks lovingly about and expects to tell his tale when he gets home." (Hollander trans.)

The thought crimes of Sidney and Beatrice Webb have been so efficiently prosecuted by earlier writers that there is little need to rehearse them here. The Webbs were pioneering British Socialists, the founders of the Fabians, who in scholarly collaboration produced important work of a progressive tendency. Like so many other socialists, their enthusiasm for collectivist theory apparently blinded them to its actual practice in the Soviet Union of the 1930s, at that time the world's only "workers' state." In the run-up to the Stalin Constitution in 1936, they published a very large, laudatory, and influential book called *Soviet Communism: A New Civilization?* A few years later, they brought out a second edition that benefited from the large increment in our knowledge of the Soviet realities only by removing the question mark from their title.

There were of course from the very start some dissenters, but on the whole Western intellectuals bought into a fictive history of their heavenly city that was vulnerable to an authoritative empirical refutation exemplified in different ways by the four anti-Communist manifestos that occupy the ensuing pages. It is one of the striking features of anti-Communist literature that its great writers are all former Communists. We can appreciate how peculiar this is if we consider a few other "antis." It will not be easily assumed that most anti-Semites, anti-racists, anti-vivisectionists, or anti-Americans are former Semites, racists, vivisectionists, or Americans. Surely the adepts of that spelling bee chestnut of my childhood—antidisestablishmentarianism—cannot mostly have been disgruntled disestablishmentarians?

But all four of these anti-Communist authors were Communist renegades, Party members whose deep disillusionment led them to turn upon their former allegiance in literary fury. One (Arthur Koestler) was a Hungarian journalist of German speech and culture, a polymath intellectual. Another (Richard Krebs, aka Jan Valtin) was a German sailor and labor agitator. The third (Victor Kravchenko) was a Soviet engineer of Ukrainian background. And the fourth (Whittaker Chambers) was an American journalist. Three of them had been, to a greater or lesser degree, underground espionage agents of the Comintern. All of them seemed to speak with great knowledge and authority about the nature of Communism and the international Communist movement, and what they had to say was not pretty. Each had a dramatic impact on an unusually wide readership.

Though they wrote very important books, they were not necessarily therefore wholly attractive or admirable men. The moral relationship between an author's life and work is a question with a troubled history going back at least to Plato. Very few of us today would agree with Sir Philip Sidney that to be a good writer you must first be a good person. All four of the authors dealt with in this book attract my full attention but only at best my partial admiration. The life experience of each, which included that special form of purgatorial fire Communism orchestrated for its apostates, would have been enough to test even the strongest character. Arthur Koestler I regard as a modern genius; he appears also to have been a "serial rapist," or "a hell of a raper," in the words of his friend Richard Crossman, MP, the editor of *The God That Failed*. Richard Krebs (Jan Valtin) was by his own testimony a professional thug for half his adult life. He was probably a murderer, though his time spent in San Quentin was only for attempted murder. His first American wife left him when, in her words, she became unable to endure his further "violence."

Like many former Soviet citizens, Victor Kravchenko never entirely succeeded in leaving behind him the evidences of dishonest servility and self-preserving self-centeredness that the experience of the 1930s required of so many Soviet bureaucrats. Though he was not a spy, Kravchenko was forced to live like one in America, acting out a fiction even before his own children. And Whittaker Chambers has to have been among the most divisively controversial Americans of the twentieth century. That was not entirely his fault, of course, but he lacked any kind of public graciousness that might counteract the fierce attacks and smears unleashed upon him. He combined, unpleasingly, an unconvincing Quaker meekness with the grumpiness of the prophet without honor in his own land. The adjective normally applied to such people is "tortured." All four men contemplated suicide, and two of them achieved it.

Quite naturally, we now tend to look back at the Cold War from the perspective of the 1970s and the 1980s. We shall understand it more fully, however, by also trying in imagination to look forward to it from the perspective of the 1930s and the 1940s. In the blighted moral and political landscape of post–World War I Europe, there emerged a broad consensus among intellectuals that "capitalism" and "imperialism" were bankrupt, and that the sole political hope of the human race was "socialism." The quotation marks do not here intend to demean but to draw attention to a tricky vocabulary of capacious and shifting implication. By "intellectuals," I mean politically minded academics, artists, writers, and important sections of the Protestant clergy and governmental civil service.

The Russian Revolution of 1917, achieved amid the chaos of a disastrous war, created the first "socialist" country on earth—the geographically huge Soviet Union. By and large progressive thinkers everywhere welcomed the Russian Revolution, watched the birth pangs of the new socialist society with sympathy, hope, and admiration, and were prepared to be indulgent of obvious shortcomings and imperfections believed to be transitory. Marxism, the ostensible political and economic "science" that guided the creation of the new order, enjoyed an enormous prestige in intellectual circles. Part of the theory of Lenin's interpretation of Marx was that the Communist Party was the small "vanguard" or leadership group destined to lead the nation to full socialism. In like manner the Communist parties of every nation, and the International Communist Party (the Comintern), had similar roles. Their task was to lead the working class through violent revolution to socialism.

The great economic depression of the 1930s, which most Marxist commentators declared to be "the final crisis of capitalism," seemed yet another proof positive of the inevitability of a radically new social order. George Orwell, as firm an anti-Communist as any writer of his age, would declare that "whatever else happens, laissez-faire capitalism is dead." In every nation of the West at the beginning of the 1930s there were Communist parties closely linked to Moscow. The German Party was huge, the French Party significant. The Communist parties of Great Britain and the United States were quite small, though not without influence. Wherever they were, Western Communists amplified their presence in various ways. They found more or less moral support from other socialists, especially from those who came to be known as "fellow travelers"— meaning that they thought they shared the historical "socialist" goal of the Communists, but were approaching it by a different route or at a different pace. (One complimentary definition of an American Communist was "a liberal in a hurry.") Furthermore, it was Communist policy to project influence through "front" groups whose membership might be largely non-Communist but whose political agenda was more or less controlled by Communists. Especially during the 1930s, large numbers of Western "pilgrims" made cultural visits to the Soviet Union, many of them returning home to write glowing reports of what they had seen.

Original Marxist orthodoxy of revolutionary days held that the worldwide socialist revolution must be and would in fact be *worldwide*. When world revolution failed to occur, Stalin evolved a new theory, that of "Socialism in One Country." This theory postponed rather than abandoned the ambition of world revolution. While the capitalist countries continued to decline, the single socialist bastion would grow in strength. In Communist theory, Germany had seemed the most likely site of the Revolution's spread, but the rise of Hitler destroyed the Communist movement in Germany. Although the Communists actually played an ambiguous and duplicitous role in the Spanish Civil War, generally regarded as a "rehearsal" for World War II, they emerged from it on the whole enhanced in their reputation among Western intellectuals. (There were, of course, major exceptions to the general rule, such as George Orwell and Arthur Koestler.) Western Communist stock fell dramatically with the announcement of the Stalin-Hitler Pact in August 1939, but when Hitler betrayed his Communist allies and invaded Russia in June 1941, all was (mostly) forgiven as Western progressives rushed to support the Allied effort against the Nazis. In Nazi-occupied France (1940–44) the Communists played a major role in the Resistance, and they emerged in the immediate postwar period as a numerically large and politically and culturally prestigious party.

Three of the anti-Communist manifestos whose histories form the core of this book helped define the popular reputation of Communism in France and the United States in the period just before America's entry into World War II, and then in the years after the defeat of Germany and Japan, as the reality of a second war, a Cold War, emerged with frightening clarity on the exhausted nations of the West. The fourth had a special significance in America at a time when the contours of the Cold War seemed to have become fixed and articulate. Almost immediately following Hitler's collapse the victorious Soviet Union moved successfully to create a capacious buffer of satellite "socialist" states in Eastern Europe. The question then was whether in the rest of Europe the political arrangements of Soviet "socialism" would prevail over those of Western "democracy."

The Cold War, of course, was in many ways a global phenomenon. *The Anti-Communist Manifestos* focuses on America and to a lesser extent France. The obvious significance of the United States is that it was at the time the only power that could conceivably contain Soviet expansion in a military challenge. The anti-Communist consensus that emerged in America, though it became hegemonic, was not inevitable. It was the result of complex factors that included the persuasive power of anti-Communist literature. The significance of France is very different. France became the "new Germany." That is to say that in the years immediately following the second war, France seemed to have become what Germany had been in the years immediately following the first, the possible or even likely site of a Communist expansion achieved through indigenous revolution or even electoral means. In retrospect, the possibility of a Communist France may seem improbable or even fantastic, but the intellectuals of the late forties were not living retrospectively. They were living "existentially," in a world of books. Their book world, too, witnessed great battles between Communists and anti-Communists.

The term "anti-Communist" naturally suffers from the imprecision of the word "Communist" itself. "Anti-Communist" as I use it in this book seldom refers to a negative assessment of Marxist economic theory. Even less does it indict all liberal, progressive, or socialist thought. It denotes objection to, and rejection of, the principles, procedures, and ambitions of the organized Communist parties of the Soviet Union, Germany, France, and the United States, and of the International Communist Party or Comintern. Given the central role of the Communist Party in the Soviet Union, and the tight linkages between all Communist parties and Moscow, the term is often nearly synonymous with "anti-Soviet."

I have said that the protagonists of this book are themselves books. A book can have many lives. Its first life usually belongs to its author—the author's conception, opportunities, and constraints, the actual physical and spiritual circumstances of its writing. The process of a book's publication, usually invisible to its eventual readers, may be another life altogether. Then, again, there is the individual reader's experience of the book, so often influenced by local and arbitrary personal circumstance. Many books, indeed, owe nearly as much to their readers as to their writers. Most books, like most of those who write or read them, have, in the sad words of the Sage, "perished as though they had never been." Few of them outlive their authors. But those that do, for greater or shorter season, have a life in history. Such are the four books discussed in the following pages.

The curious vicissitudes of book life could be illustrated by almost any book, even this one. I have been a professional scholar for nearly half a century, long enough to know that the paths of scholarship are seldom straight or well lighted. I have never yet arrived at the end of a project without finding there a large surprise. But the project of *The Anti-Communist Manifestos* actually *began* with one. I am an amateur bookbinder. Large sheets of binder's board having become expensive and not always easily available, I adopted an unconventional strategy. A secondhand book dealer of my acquaintance sells off in bulk, very cheaply, books that he regards as unmerchantable. I buy, butcher, and recycle the covers of such books. In picking my materials my only concern is the size—the bigger the better—and condition of the boards. I seldom even note the titles.

One day, for no good reason whatsoever, I picked up one such book in my workshop and instead of dismembering I started reading it. After two or three pages, I couldn't put it down. *Out of the Night*, by Jan Valtin. I had never heard of it, or of him. My ignorance rather embarrassed me when I learned that it had been the best-selling American book of its year. As I was learning something of its history and resolving perhaps to write something about it, I recalled a conversation I had had thirty years earlier. At a rather dreadful academic reception I found myself chatting with a colleague I had never before laid eyes on—Nina Berberova, of the university's Slavic Department. She appeared to have known personally every Russian writer of the twentieth century, but the one she talked about that day was a very colorful character, a Russian political defector, who had written an important book that caused a big stink in Paris. Thirty years later I could remember neither the defector nor his book, but it was the work of two minutes to recover them: Victor Kravchenko, author of *I Chose Freedom*. Meanwhile, I had for several years been teaching Arthur Koestler's *Darkness at Noon* in a course called "Masterworks of European Literature."

Thus, *The Anti-Communist Manifestos* had already sought me out before I had well begun the extensive reading necessary to achieve it. In writing about four books I have naturally had to read some hundreds of others, for the "battle of the books" between Communists and anti-Communists in the wars—hot and cold—was protracted on many fronts. Writing a book so different in its subject from any I had written before encouraged me also to write in a different manner. *The Anti-Communist Manifestos* seeks to address a general educated audience rather than the guild of professional scholars or specialists. I have accordingly suppressed the apparatus of note citations and bibliographies required in specialized monographs, though I from time to time cite a few particularly helpful or even indispensable sources.

On December 15, 1950, the following exchange took place in a Paris courtroom.

M. GÉRARD ROSENTHAL: I declare that Mr. Czapski is the author of a book entitled *The Inhuman Land*.

M. VIENNEY: But all your witnesses have a book; nothing new
there!

Gérard Rosenthal was a lawyer representing the plaintiff, David Rousset, in a civil action for slander against a journal called *Les Lettres françaises*, its publisher Claude Morgan, and Pierre Daix, a famous art critic
and cultural commentator, and the author of an article attacking Rousset
as a fraud, a liar, and a purveyor of reactionary anti-Soviet propaganda.
Specifically, Rousset had said in print that there existed, in Soviet Russia, concentration camps to which people could be sent without trial, by
administrative police action alone. Paul Vienney was one of the lawyers
for the defense. The claim that *all* of Rousset's witnesses had published
books was rhetorical exaggeration, but they had indeed produced among
themselves a small library of classic memoirs of the Soviet Gulag, including *Conspiracy of Silence* (Alex Weissberg), *Tell the West* (Jerzy Gliksman),
Eleven Years in a Soviet Concentration Camp (Elinor Lipper), *Under Two
Dictators* (Margarete Buber-Neumann), and *La Condition inhumaine: Five
Years in Soviet Prison Camps* (Jules Margolin).

Had I taken as my task a general literary history of the Cold War I
would have had to say quite a bit about these books, and especially about
Czapski's *The Inhuman Land*. I do touch upon it, briefly, in the essay on
Victor Kravchenko. A work more elegiac than shrill, it at once exposed
the nearly unimaginable brutality of the Soviet regime and the cultivated
blindness that kept Western leaders and "opinion makers" from seeing
it. Its author, a cosmopolitan painter of international reputation, a Polish
patriot, a highly competent military officer and diplomat, was also a writer
of rare power. As we shall see, *The Inhuman Land* is a memoir falling into a
small but notable historical genre that itself needs fuller study: what might
be called the documented fool's errand.

In the case of *David Rousset v. Les Lettres françaises* all personal defendants and their lawyers were members of the French Communsit Party, a
fact that can help us hear the scornful impatience in the lawyer Vienney's
remark: "But all your witnesses have a book." Its implication was that we
have heard all this before—all this being a pack of lies about some allegedly brutal system of forced labor in the international paradise of the workers. Whether Vienney actually believed what he was defending I cannot
say, but he was undoubtedly right that there was no news here. By 1950,

allegedly eyewitness accounts of the Soviet police state had been appearing for about twenty years. It would not be easy for a person who had read *The Inhuman Land* to be a comfortable Communist, and at this trial the Communist fear of the power of books was a central motive of the legal strategy.

But it is one thing to be afraid to *read* a book, and quite another to be afraid to *touch* it. The four books to which we are about to turn became for the Communist cause metaphorically untouchable; but the literature reveals a phenomenon yet more dramatic, literal untouchability. Walter Ciszek was an American Jesuit of Polish ancestry who spent a quarter century of persecuted religious ministry in various Soviet prisons, labor camps, and those remote provincial towns and cities with unfamiliar names that were the KGB's favorite sites of exile for liberated prisoners. In every one of these places Ciszek found a hunger for his sacramental ministrations, and surprising opportunities to supply them. In several Siberian outposts there were more or less permanent Roman Catholic congregations.

Father Ciszek recounts the following anecdote. One day (this was in his post-Gulag period of exiled "freedom") he decided to visit another priest of his acquaintance. With nearly supernaturally awful timing he arrived at his friend's lodgings at a moment when the priest himself was out but the NKVD was in. That is, the police were in the very act of conducting a search of the man's quarters. They detained Ciszek and made him stand by along with the two dragooned neighborhood "witnesses" required by Soviet law. He was there for hours. "The agents were going through everything, examining things thoroughly, then replacing them carefully. The search dragged on until almost 1 a.m., with one very curious incident: among the bookshelves they found a missal and a prayer book; one of the young agents was afraid even to touch them."

That would have been about 1959, and suggests that the incidence of Soviet bibliophobia had not greatly decreased in two decades. For twenty years earlier, in Moscow, Markoosha Fischer was trying to take her mind off the purges by renewing her lapsed career as an expert translator of Western books into Russian. She went to the head of the State Publishing House with several possible works she had brought back from a recent trip abroad. These included Arthur Koestler's account of his experiences in the Spanish Civil War and I. J. Singer's *Brothers Ashkenazi*, which had appeared to considerable applause in 1936. Speaking of the Singer book,

Fischer mentioned in a matter-of-fact way that a part that was "anti-Soviet" would have to be edited out. "He was paging through the book while I talked. When I said 'anti-Soviet,' he literally dropped the book as if it burned him." It is perhaps only meet that book-burners should themselves be burned by books, such as the four anti-Communist manifestos to which we now turn.

The French sculptor Jean-Louis Faure entitled this witty construction *Jean-Paul Sartre and Simone de Beauvoir Refusing to Shake the Hand of Arthur Koestler*. The operation of a mechanical device causes Sartre and de Beauvoir to turn their backs as Koestler extends his right hand. The "event" commemorated is imaginary, but the concept accurately reflects Sartre's opinion that "Every anti-Communist is a dog." From *La Bétise de l'intelligence* by Jean-Louis Faure and Pierre Pachet (Paris: Editions Joca Sena, 1995).

Arthur Koestler posed at a hotel desk for this publicity shot. In the first decade following the war he became an international literary superstar. The lighted cigarette was a nearly obligatory iconographic attribute for "candid" shots of male writers and intellectuals until the 1960s. Koestler settled in England and adopted various self-conscious British props, such as heavy Harris tweed jackets.

DARKNESS AT NOON

do the sense justice: *qui vive la pietà quando è ben morta*: "Here piety lives, when pity is quite dead."

Dante is playing on the ambiguity of the Latin *pietas* as it descended into his own and other Romance vernaculars. His guide in hell is Virgil, and he himself is the living antitype of Virgil's epic hero, *pius Æneas*. The phrase that has amused modern schoolboys had a profound meaning for Virgil. *Pietas* was both a social and a personal virtue. It meant a due respect for civic and religious duty on the one hand, and deference to personal and humane instinct on the other. In the twentieth *canto* of the *Inferno*, Dante encounters the ancient diviners and soothsayers, Amphiaraus and Tiresias among them, who tried to appropriate for human ends the inscrutable judgments of God. Than them, says Virgil, no one could be more criminal. Their punishment is terrible. Their bodies have been contorted, turned back to front on their legs. "Because he would see too far ahead," Virgil says of Amphiaraus, "he looks behind and makes his way backwards." And when Dante sheds a tear for their hideous deformity, Virgil scolds him: *qui vive la pietà quando è ben morta*. (*Inferno*, 20.28) The point, frequently made by Dante but only this once with such verbal brilliance, is that a correct theological perspective forbids in this circumstance the sentimental feeling of pity. To "feel sorry" for the damned souls is to reveal an imperfect understanding of God's justice—the sin of the diviners, indeed. Something of the breadth of the Latin word is remembered in the Italian art historical term *Pietà*—a *Pietà* being of course a depiction of the Virgin sorrowing over the dead body of her Son.

One of Koestler's major themes in the book is the opposition between the individual and the social—or in the particular Marxist terms here developed the "grammatical fiction" of the first-person singular and the "masses." Koestler early introduces the idea of *pietà* in an obvious but effective way with regard to the betrayal of the German Communists. The imprisoned Rubashov has a constricted field of vision—it is limited to what he can see from the judas, or peephole, of the door of his cell, Cell 404. One of the first things he sees is a warder delivering bread to his neighbor in Cell 407. "Rubashov could only see his forearms and hands. . . . The palms of the Invisible No. 407 were turned upwards, curved in the shape of a bowl." (p. 18) A little later, "He remembered with a slight feeling of uneasiness those thin arms and the curved hands; they reminded him vaguely of something he could not define . . . familiar and yet gone from his memory like an old tune or the smell of a narrow street in a harbor." (p. 19) Another prisoner, this one a long-incarcerated ex-Tsarist officer in Cell 402, communicates with Rubashov by using the Morse code pipe-tapping method familiar to any reader of Gulag literature. This man is desperate for some vicarious sexual experience, a pornographic account of Rubashov's most recent sexual congress with a woman. The man begs for more details, and Rubashov imagines him, "perhaps . . . kneeling in the bunk with his hands folded. . . . And now at last Rubashov knew of what experience this gesture had reminded him—the imploring gesture of the meager, stretched-out hands. *Pietà*. . . ." (p. 31)

The episode Rubashov here recalls, the first of three morally significant "flashbacks," is a clandestine meeting with a young German Communist, "Richard," in one of the galleries of an unnamed art museum. The meeting features the usual drama of underground Comintern work. The man has no last name. He is able to identify Rubashov because the latter carried a copy of "Goethe's *Faust* in Reclam's Universal Edition." But the circumstances are by no means usual. It is 1933. Hitler has come to power. The anti-Communist Terror is in full swing. "The Party was no longer a political organization; it was nothing but a thousand-armed and thousand-headed mass of bleeding flesh." Rubashov has come with the authority of the Central Committee to dash Richard's last hopes, to scold him for utterly irrelevant "deviationism," and, indeed, to convey to him a sentence of expulsion and abandonment. Rubashov, unflustered, utterly unfeeling, carries out his Party duty with calm efficiency; Richard stammers, pleads, begins to panic. "To Richard's left hung a pen drawing by a German master; Rubashov could only see a part of it—the rest was hidden by the plush back of the sofa and by Richard's head: the Madonna's thin hand, curved upward, hollowed to the shape of a bowl. . . ." (p. 35)

In the episode of "Richard," Koestler gives a local habitation and a name to what the historians now generally call "Stalin's betrayal of the KPD."*

* The German Communist Party (*Kommunistische Partei Deustchlands*) was widely known by its German initials throughout Europe. On the eve of Hitler's rise to power the KPD was very large and powerful. So also was the German Social-Democratic Party. Many commentators then and later believed that Communists and Socialists in concert could have defeated Nazism. Far from cooperating with the Social Democrats, however, the Communists, following the Moscow line, confronted them with a bitter enmity. Once Hitler was in power Stalin's foreign policy was directed far more toward reaching an accommodation with Hitler than with supporting the now beleaguered KPD. Many leftists eventually saw this as a clear betrayal of socialist internationalism for the sake of narrow Russian nationalist interests. *Darkness at Noon* touches on this betrayal in several different ways.

The larger betrayal of revolutionary internationalism is the theme of the second flashback, the suicide of "Little Loewy." The image of the folded hands of the sorrowing Virgin is in the book connected with another— "familiar and yet gone from his memory like an old tune or the smell of a narrow street in a harbour." The harbor is Antwerp. We can construct from Rubashov's musings and the remarks of his interrogator Ivanov an historical trajectory. The episode with Richard took place in 1933. Shortly after it, Rubashov was captured by the Gestapo. In their jails he was terribly mistreated, but he never broke. After two years he was released and returned to Russia, to something of a hero's welcome. But it is now 1935, and the effects of the Terror of which the Kirov assassination was the initiation are everywhere to be seen.* Rubashov immediately seeks another foreign assignment. Mussolini has carried through the conquest of Ethiopia, and even the League of Nations has called for an economic boycott of Italy. Radical maritime unions throughout Europe have been enforcing the boycott. Rubashov's assignment from the Central Committee is to convey orders to the Communist section of the Antwerp longshoremen that they are to cooperate in unloading a shipment of Russian oil eventually destined for Italy. The necessities of Soviet economic development outweigh futile and "sentimental" political posturing.

"Little Loewy" is one of the Communist leaders on the docks of the town, where the narrow streets smell of seaweed and of petrol. The life story of this simple, noble proletarian, which in certain respects closely resembles the experiences of Jan Valtin on the same waterfront, dramatizes the betrayal of its own rank-and-file by a sclerotic Party bureaucracy. In a larger sense it exemplifies the degree to which the "international Communist movement" has become nothing more than the tool of a mercurial Soviet foreign policy. When Little Loewy and his friends stick to their anti-Fascist principles, Rubashov's superiors throw them to the wolves.

The third betrayal is personal. One of the tragic themes of much anti-Communist literature is the power of a hateful ideology to corrupt

---

* Sergei Kirov (1886–1934), an Old Bolshevik, was a close aide of Stalin's and the Communist Party Secretary in Leningrad. He was shot to death while in his place of work in 1934. The crime was committed by a conventional "lone assassin," but as with many other high-profile political murders of the twentieth century, there has been much scholarly speculation concerning a "wider conspiracy." What is certain is that the assassination was at least ostensibly the instigating event that triggered Stalin's Great Purge. A recent well-balanced discussion is by Amy Knight, *Who Killed Kirov?: The Kremlin's Greatest Mystery* (New York, 1999).

all frank and loving personal relationships. Rubashov, now a high-ranking bureaucrat back in Moscow, takes as his lover one of his secretaries, Arlova. When Arlova is arrested on a baseless charge of "deviationism"—soon to be executed—he does nothing to defend her. Moral cowardice indeed eventually leads him to make a statement of loyalty to the regime. He now in prison remembers her, recalling "the folded hands of the *Pietà*, and the smell of sea-weed in the harbour town."

The Purge Trials and the West

History is retrospective, to be viewed only through a rear-vision mirror. One of the hardest of historical tasks is to negotiate justly between what we see in the mirror and "what we know now." No intelligent person today believes that the Moscow defendants were literally guilty of the crimes for which they were so crudely arraigned. Things were very different in 1936 or 1938, and left-wing intellectuals in the West spent an amazing amount of time, energy, and ingenuity debating whether or not, or how, or in what manner they were in fact guilty. *Darkness at Noon*, of course, hardly engages with this crude fiction. On the other hand, most Communists, and many others, with varying degrees of uneasiness, accepted the defendants' guilt as a fact beyond debate. As to the *why* of it, developments in the Spanish Civil War provided many with a rationale and a metaphor: that of the "fifth column."* Stalin was prudently cleansing the Soviet State of a potential fifth column—those traitors prepared to collaborate with Hitler or the imperial powers of the West. The extraordinary early history of *Darkness at Noon* cannot be understood without some awareness of some other modes in which American and European leftists reacted to the Moscow Trials.

The so-called Moscow Trials ("Purge Trials," "Show Trials"), which took place in the second half of the 1930s, effectively destroyed all the veteran Bolsheviks who had been prominent during Lenin's reign, more than half of the delegates to the 1934 Party Congress, much of the top

---

*As the rebel general Emilio Mola in 1936 advanced on Madrid at the head of four military columns, he announced in propaganda broadcasts that once within the city he would be joined by a metaphoric "fifth column" of secret supporters. Fifth columns are ecumenical. American anti-Communists would later use the same image for members of the CPUSA.

brass in the Red Army, and three quarters of the sitting members of the Central Committee of the Communist Party. The first trial (August 1936) convicted and executed Zinoviev, Kamenev, and fourteen of the other most prominent Old Bolsheviks. They were called "the Sixteen." In January 1937 followed "the Seventeen," including Radek and Pyatakov. In June 1937 secret military tribunals bloodily purged the army, executing Marshal Tukhachevsky among scores of others. A final trial of "Right Deviationists" in March 1938 caught Bukharin and Rykov, among many other notables.

All of the civilian trials were public and, indeed, widely publicized in the Russian and international press. They had several remarkable characteristics. The first was the extravagance of the charges. The defendants, practically all of whom were grizzled Marxist revolutionaries, were accused of such crimes as conspiring with Leon Trotsky to reintroduce capitalism into Russia, or colluding with Nazi generals to sell out their country, or planning the assassination of important political leaders, or with purposely impeding or sabotaging the national industrial life, and so on. The nature of the evidence was likewise extraordinary. Almost all the charges depended upon confessions made by the defendants in which they accused themselves and often their co-defendants of such terrible crimes as those enumerated. One after another the defendants rose in open court and, without obvious signs of coercion or "brainwashing," confessed to crimes nearly certain to merit the "extreme measure of social defense," as the Communists called capital punishment. Indeed, many of them said they merited death.

The Moscow Trials were mimes or simulacra of ethical judicial processes, and they called into being another such process. To some Western observers many of the charges seemed, literally, fantastic, and the confessions to them even more so. As a very great deal of the crime was attributed directly to Trotsky, or consisted in nefarious meetings or communications with him, some non-Stalinist leftists established what they called an independent fact-finding commission to look into the question of Trotsky's guilt or innocence. The chair of its American branch, which conducted hearings in Coyoacán, the Mexican suburb in which Trotsky had taken up residence, was the philosopher John Dewey, a man of radiant intellectual integrity, and a man nearly universally admired. The venue had been chosen to accommodate not Trotsky himself but the Mexican government.

The proceedings were public, except for occasional *in camera* deliberations on such highly sensitive questions as the current whereabouts of Trotsky's archives, and the commissioners had taken care to send formal invitations to a wide cross section of left-wing opinion makers. Some, like the Soviet ambassador to Mexico, declined to attend, but several others accepted. Trotsky himself was treated with the correct civility due to a defendant presumed innocent until proven guilty, but still rather standoffishly. Trotsky had been the absent defendant in Moscow. In Cayoacán, where he was present as the ostensible "defendant," the real defendant was the authority of the Moscow Trials.

This commission was naturally not without a certain agenda of its own. Its driving force was George Novack, perhaps the principal American disciple of Trotsky and certainly one of the best minds produced by American Communism. Among the other members was Benjamin Stolberg, the labor historian and the aphorist who first defined "an expert" as "a person who avoids small error as he sweeps on to the grand fallacy." Stolberg's good friend was the journalist Carleton Beals, a maverick leftist of a kind that was becoming increasingly rare in America as competing versions of "scientific" Marxism swept the intellectual field in the early 1930s. He was not a Marxist at all, but he was an expert on Latin American revolutionary movements, and in particular the Mexican Revolution, which he regarded as a "natural" and indigenous political movement of far greater relevance to the future happiness of Latin America than anything that had happened in Russia. He had had an adventurous life as a journalist. His biographer published a photograph of him being led by masked revolutionary riders deep into the Nicaraguan jungle to interview César Augusto Sandino, the rebel leader being hunted by U.S. Marines. Stolberg nominated Beals for the commission, and Dewey was keen on the idea. They both lived to regret it.

For a variety of reasons Beals was the odd man out on the commission, and he immediately caused anxiety among his colleagues by asking Trotsky hard questions. One of the charges against the Moscow "Trotskyites" was that they were conspiring to turn over Soviet territories to the Japanese in exchange for political advantages. Beals asked Trotsky about the Treaty of Brest-Litovsk. Was it not true that at Brest-Litovsk, Lenin and Trotsky had made exactly that kind of deal with the Germans? Could he imagine circumstances under which he would do it again? Then there was the very sticky question of the Communist role in the Spanish Civil

War, at that point still uncertain of outcome. Could not the Communists best serve the Spanish Republic by joining the government (as they eventually did)? Trotsky, an utter dogmatist, stuck to his dogmatic theory. Then Beals asked whether it was true, as he had heard, that "around 1920," the Bolsheviks were attempting to meddle in the Mexican political sphere? This was extremely touchy, since of course Trotsky's Mexican exile was based in an understanding that he would remain entirely aloof from any local political activity. Here the Apostle of World Revolution became rather huffy. He knew nothing of any revolutionary designs on Mexico. On what documents could Beals justify his question? In executive session, Dewey and others chided Beals for his "antagonistic" attitude toward Trotsky. Beals decided that he didn't want to be part of a show trial, even if it was a different show than that playing in Moscow, and he resigned from the commission after the seventh sitting.

The proceedings of Dewey's subcommission were published under the title *The Case of Leon Trotsky* in the form recorded by an official court stenographer. While they are not entirely free of the risible self-importance characteristic of some of the pseudolegal tribunals of "people's justice" of later decades, they were extraordinarily effective up-market anti-Communist propaganda. They provided Trotsky himself with a bully pulpit, or at least a prissy lectern, from which he delivered his apothegms of Spartan revolutionary rectitude. In the scrupulosity of their fairness, which manifested itself in the theatrical fashion of a mock courtroom, they contrasted tellingly with the very different theater of the Moscow Trials themselves.

They also demolished various pieces of the material evidences that the Moscow defendants had offered to inculpate Trotsky. Public Prosecutor Andrei Vyshinsky and his henchmen had done a good though not quite perfect job of "softening up" and preparing the defendants for their courtroom appearances. They had been much less thorough in conducting what an American prosecutor would think of as a preliminary criminal investigation. As it turns out, it is probably more important to conduct such an investigation when it is known in advance that no crime has actually been committed.

It is perhaps not surprising that some of the Moscow defendants, being Russians, appeared to have been prepared in the Stanislavsky Method of acting. As Method actors, their job was less to memorize the lines of a conspiratorial script than to make themselves in their histrionic imaginations *become* and therefore naturally *behave like* Trotskyist conspirators. The minimum requirement for a Trotskyist conspirator was of course to have conspired with Trotsky, and several defendants confessed in detail to having done so. As always, the devil was in the details. One man flew from Berlin to Sweden to conspire with Trotsky on a day when there had been no flights from Berlin to Sweden. Another testified to a clandestine meeting with Trotsky in a Copenhagen hotel that had been razed before the time of meeting. A third conspirator testified to a foreign tryst with Trotsky at a time when he, the conspirator, was under lock and key in a prison of the GPU (state security police). These complicating facts were easily available in the public domain, having been almost immediately brought to light by investigative reports in the bourgeois European press. They yielded to the most elementary and distant detective work. Trotsky had been under considerable restraints and often enough under competing surveillance in all his various places of exile. He was able to give a good account of nearly every minute of his time, and of his movements.

The final report of the whole commission was published in English under the banner title *Not Guilty!*, and its publication had an impact on the surprisingly large number of leftists for whom it appeared still to be an open question whether or not Leon Trotsky had conspired with the German High Command with the aim of reestablishing the market economy in Russia. Of course if Trotsky were innocent of anti-Soviet conspiracy with the Old Bolsheviks, what was one to conclude about the Old Bolsheviks themselves? They were now all in their graves, to which they had been dispatched for the confessed crimes of having entered into anti-Soviet conspiracy with Leon Trotsky. Anastas Mikoyan was given the task of defusing this potential embarrassment in public relations. (Anastas Mikoyan was one of the few Old Bolsheviks to die in his bed. He was an early ally of Stalin. In the fifties and sixties he became well known on the international scene as the first deputy premier of the Soviet Union and later the chairman of the Presidium of the Supreme Soviet. During the Purge Trials he played various roles as a kind of legal utility infielder.) So perfidious were the traitors, said Mikoyan, that even in the act of confessing the capital crimes that it was no longer possible for them to deny, they managed to insert cunning and inconsequential untruths that, as they hoped, might yet be seized upon by the malicious bourgeois press or even sow seeds of doubt in the minds of the innocent but unwary.

The *why* question naturally arose. *Why* had all these men stood up in open court and, with straight faces, confessed to lurid political crimes subject to capital punishment? Orthodox Party-line Communists were able to say, and perhaps even to believe, that they had simply spoken the truth, and that that was the end of the matter. Many nervous Western leftists, unsettled by the preposterousness of many of the charges and the strange affect of the defendants, thought that something was fishy, though they knew not exactly what. Among this group a theory grew up that the defendants were indeed guilty, but that the presentation of their guilt in the courtroom had been orchestrated, simplified, and allegorized, as it were, for the benefit of the Soviet "masses," who were incapable of subtle or nuanced adjudication. The whole "vanguard" theory of the Communist Party, embraced by the Bolsheviks and their Western admirers alike, held that the peasant population of Old Russia was pretty poor revolutionary material and needed a great deal of guidance indeed. This interpretation tended to skirt the specifics of the evidence in favor of the more certain terrain of moral guilt.

But to the very large number of the skeptical, from the slack-jawed to the amused, the question of the confessions presented a considerable conundrum. Why did these men willingly cooperate in their own destruction? Why did they confess? Robert Conquest, in his scholarly study *The Great Terror: Stalin's Purge of the Thirties* (1968), examined in considerable detail a number of possible reasons. He noted in the first place that not *all* of the defendants did in fact confess. Most did, but some whose names appeared in the indictments never appeared in court, the implication being that the court could not depend upon their cooperation. One other man briefly recanted a written confession already revealed to the court. After a day's adjournment during which he would have had the opportunity to think things over in consultation with his interrogators, he returned to the public arena to confess.

Though the defendants declared their confessions voluntary, there was the strongest possible suspicion of coercion. This could have been fairly crude physical torture, which was routinely used by the NKVD interrogators. It could have been the technique, hardly less crude, called the "conveyor." Here the suspect was subjected to cruel periods of sleep deprivation through repeated and repetitious interrogations that followed endlessly one upon the other. The very length of the period of interrogation, during which the tag-teams of investigators would say quite openly that there could be no end to the process except through confession, might have been a powerful motive. Even the most fearless or reckless defendant, a man able to endure frightful tortures and the certainty of his own execution, might be moved to a false confession if he could believe that it might spare his family members or other hostages subject to the power of his tormentors.

We now know that all physical and metaphysical methods of coercion will be used by interrogators who regard themselves as authorized by transcendent purpose. Koestler's suggestion, which was brilliantly original at the time he advanced it in *Darkness at Noon*, was to look for an internal compulsion within the psychology of Bolshevism itself. In this he anticipated the approach taken by Nathan Leites and Elsa Bernaut in the more speculative parts of their study of the trials, *Ritual of Liquidation*. The Moscow Trials were called "trials." In their iconography we shall find some of the themes and accoutrements of Western or "bourgeois" jurisprudence. Under these circumstances, it is nearly impossible to remember that they were so little like a "trial" as we know it that they should be thought of in another category—that of drama, ritual, spectacle, auto-da-fé, or perhaps pedagogical demonstration.

Leites reminds us that most of the defendants were longtime members of the Bolshevik Party. Their view of justice was a Marxist view in which "individual rights" played no part. Justice was what the Party defined as justice as, like a meandering stream, it moved through history. The individual was nothing; the collective was all. Such people could concern themselves with the truth or falsity of the charges brought against them, the validity or fraudulence of the evidence adduced, only to the degree that they lapsed from revolutionary into bourgeois and individualistic modes of thought. We may imagine that in those extreme circumstances such lapses were not unknown, but they must have been comparatively rare. In this analysis the motives for confession and acquiescence, whatever physical or psychological pressures might have been the midwives, were Bolshevik motives.

Here Leites followed the lead of one of the most prominent and intellectually subtle of the victims, Nikolai Bukharin. Many knowledgeable readers of *Darkness at Noon* have seen that the central character, Rubashov, in the words of Conquest, "is modeled on Bukharin in his thinking and Trotsky and Radek in his personality and physical appearance."

According to Walter Krivitsky, Stalin had predicted that "Europe will swallow the whole thing."* Still, the Soviet government was not entirely indifferent to the reaction caused by the Purge Trials abroad. It addressed them in a rather ingenious way in the published record of the last of the great trials, that of the "Bloc of Rights and Trotskyists," which took place in March 1938. The biggest fish caught in this net was Nikolai Bukharin. Bukharin was perhaps the most brilliant man ever to sit in the Politburo—a group that included over the years its share of brilliant men. He was indeed an "oppositionist" and a "right deviationist" in the special jargon used by the Stalinists. An "oppositionist" was anyone who had disagreed with what became the Stalin line. The past tense is of importance here. In the earliest days of Bolshevism there was sometimes lively debate within Party conclaves. However, Stalin forced upon the Politburo the policy that all decisions must be unanimous. Communist Party discipline, furthermore, required every Party member to fall in line behind decisions announced by the Politburo. Hence real oppositionism—that is, public disagreement with Stalin's policies—was by now an historical memory. "Left deviationism," as sensationally exemplified by Trotsky, had insisted on the world proletarian revolution as the fundamental and necessary task of Marxism while Stalin moved toward the policy, eventually canonized, of "Socialism in One Country." "Right deviationism" had been in favor of moderating the drive for heavy industries with some attention to consumer goods and the amelioration of living standards, and of approaching the question of the collectivization of agriculture in a somewhat gradualist manner. During the first Five Year Plan, Stalin of course gave an absolute priority to the development of heavy industry, and imposed agricultural collectivization with utter savagery.

---

* Krivitsky was the nom de guerre taken by Walter Ginzburg, a high-ranking Soviet espionage agent in Western Europe in the middle and late thirties. He necessarily makes several appearances in this book. Disgusted by what he regarded as Stalin's betrayal of Communist principle, particularly in his Spanish policy, Krivitsky defected in 1938. Suspicious Western intelligence departments undervalued his testimony. Whether or not he was in fact "General" Krivitsky and the "head" of Soviet operations was a matter of dispute; but he was very far from being an imposter, as claimed by European and American Communists. In America he came into contact with Isaac Don Levine, through whose instigation he published the sensational book *In Stalin's Secret Service: An Exposé of Russia's Secret Policies by the Former Chief of the Soviet Intelligence in Western Europe* (1939). He became a friend of Whittaker Chambers and played an indirect role in Chambers's own "defection." In what many inevitably suspected was an NKVD operation, Krivitsky died of a gunshot wound to the head, apparently self-inflicted, in a seedy hotel in Washington in 1940. For a full treatment, see Gary Kern's excellent book, *A Death in Washington: Walter G. Krivitsky and the Stalin Terror* (New York, 2004).

The records of each of the public trials were published in Moscow in several languages immediately upon their conclusion, and it seems obvious that Arthur Koestler had access to the *Report of the Court Proceedings in the Case of the Anti-Soviet "Bloc of Rights and Trotskyites"* in its English edition. This volume of nearly 800 pages of often drifting and desultory colloquy between Vyshinsky and the defendants contains, almost at the very end, a long and remarkable statement by Bukharin. In it he approaches directly the motives of his confession, or "repentance," and addresses and anticipates the presumed skepticism of Western intellectuals. That under his circumstances he should be concerned about the misprisions of Western intellectuals is a curiosity that demands some explanation, and the explanation leads us to another battle of the books.

LION FEUCHTWANGER

Koestler was of course not the only important writer to engage with the Moscow Trials, though in its unique "success" *Darkness at Noon* has long since left behind a literary context highly relevant to its creation. Much of the horror of the early Stalin years was, if not invisible to Western eyes, sufficiently hidden to require for its detection a degree of inquisitiveness few socialists cared to exercise. The invisibility of the Ukrainian famine of 1932–33 was nearly complete. Few commentators noted the considerable expansion of the Gulag system even before the assassination of Sergei Kirov in 1934. The daily misery of working life during the first Five Year Plan was generally overlooked by enthusiasts of the production statistics. But the Moscow Trials were, and were meant to be, highly visible international events.

Furthermore, the Russians were extremely concerned as to what others thought, and would think. "As a matter of fact," wrote the famous French writer André Gide, "though they do take some interest in what is happening in foreign parts, they are far more concerned about what the foreigner thinks of them. What really interests them is to know whether we admire them enough. What they are afraid of is that we should be ill-informed as to their merits. What they want from us is not information but praise." The little book in which he wrote these words was called *Retour de l'URSS* (*Back from the USSR*), a brief account of his trip to Moscow to deliver a eulogy at the funeral of Maxim Gorky, who died in June 1936. Gide had been a fellow traveler with the best of them, but now, distancing himself from the mode of Sovietolatry demanded of the French literary left, he was very critical of the direction that Soviet life had taken under Stalin, particularly in its drift toward a stultifying intellectual conformism and toward bureaucracy.

The publication of this little book brought down upon Gide's head a thunderstorm of political execration, to which he replied immediately with a slightly longer sequel entitled *Afterthoughts*. This was less constrained. Much of it is a wickedly funny tormenting of his would-be tormentors, but there are also many more specific criticisms of the Stalin regime. And by now the question of the trials was prominent in his mind. To the army of literary true believers he offered the following prophetic challenge: "Comrades, confess that you are beginning to get uneasy; and you ask yourselves with increasing anxiety (in face of the Moscow trials, for instance), 'To what lengths shall we have to carry our approval?' Sooner or later, your eyes will be obliged to open. Then you will ask yourselves—you, the honest ones—'How could we have kept them shut so long?'"

Gide returns to the trials several more times in the latter part of *Afterthoughts*, which is a collection of letters sent and received. He copies a letter of his to Jean Guéhenno, a prominent academic leftist of the day. Guéhenno had written, "It seems impossible to question the guilt of the accused, of the condemned. . . . These men are guilty." But he had gone on to try to maintain peace among French socialists by saying: "It is not our business to be either Stalinists or Trotskyists; these questions are specifically Russian." Gide agreed with Guéhenno—after a fashion. ". . . I maintain that it is possible not to approve Stalin without for that reason instantly becoming a Trotskyist." The greater danger, Gide maintained, was in linking Stalin's "compromising policy" with the idea of the Revolution itself. "Trotsky, for having denounced this compromising policy, is declared to be a public enemy, whereas he is only the enemy of Stalin's compromises, and is thus identified with fascism—which is really a bit too simple. He is far more the enemy of fascism than is Stalin himself, and it is as a revolutionary and anti-fascist that he denounces Stalin's compromises. But just try to make a deluded people grasp this!"

That was strong stuff, but there was even stronger. He includes a letter from a certain Kléber Legay, the assistant secretary of the French National

Federation of Miners. This man was part of a five-man delegation—four mining union officers and one Communist deputy—whose visit to Moscow happened to coincide with the Radek trial. These mining experts had been perplexed by the evidence on which Pyatakov and others had been convicted of sabotaging mining operations. The accusation, to which the defendants solemnly declared themselves guilty, was that they had intentionally allowed explosive concentrations of methane gas to build up in the mines, maintaining the hazard without interruption over a two-year period as they awaited the command to detonate! This was from the technological point of view an impossibility. But if anything even vaguely like it was true, it could only mean either that there were none of the safety precautions boasted of in the Soviet industrial protocols in which they had been instructed, or that a vast army of mine inspectors, still undetected, must have conspired with the defendants. Kléber Legay had published an essay on this subject in the French press in December 1936. Legay had noted that any of his fellow mining experts would confirm his view, but that it was probably best not to ask Quinet, the Communist deputy. "I do not mention the fifth, for he can do nothing to annoy his Moscow idols—those who are masters today, but will perhaps be shot tomorrow."

The historical obligation of objectivity, always taxing, sometimes seems to ask too much. Gide no doubt demanded to be "answered," yet how is one to account for the remarkable book published by Lion Feuchtwanger in 1937? *Moscow—1937* ostensibly concerns his protracted visit to Moscow in January and February of that year, but it is in fact the fellow travelers' answer to Gide. "In Moscow," wrote Feuchtwanger, "one could quite easily be led to an unjustifiably adverse opinion by the many minor discomforts which make daily life difficult there and be blinded to the important things. Very soon I realized than even so eminent a writer as André Gide had had his judgment warped by petty annoyances of this kind." As a matter of fact, Gide had said very little about "petty" matters. He did give the impression that at a practical level nothing in Soviet Russia worked except for the police apparatus, which worked overtime. But his concerns seemed more spiritual and philosophical.

Literary reputation, like truth, is a daughter of time. Gide is now remembered among the great writers of the twentieth century. Feuchtwanger is an unremembered and unread "once popular author." Things were very different at the time of the Spanish Civil War, when they were contemporary titans—the one a leftist hero, the other a disturbing apostate and probable crypto-Fascist. Feuchtwanger was an able, prolific, and widely read novelist. *The Jew Seuss* was one of the great best-sellers of an era that loved the panoramic historical novel like *Anthony Adverse* and *Gone With the Wind*. He was a man of very considerable culture and learning. His name is chiefly remembered today in the title of an academic library at the University of Southern California.

Like Thomas Mann, whom many of their contemporaries regarded as the lesser writer, Feuchtwanger was actively persecuted by the Nazis, and, as he was a Jew, with the most deadly intentions. His name was also very near the top of the list, compiled by Goebbels, of natives of the Reich to be stripped of their citizenship for anti-German activities and attitudes. Goebbels crowned the insult by commissioning a hideously anti-Semitic caricature of *The Jew Seuss*. Feuchtwanger fled Hitler to France, where at Sanary-sur-Mer, a small Mediterranean watering place, he established a kind of *salon* of exiled German leftists. One eminent visitor was Arthur Koestler. It was from Sanary that Feuchtwanger made his famous trip to Moscow, where he was able to conduct two high-profile interviews with Stalin. After the fall of France he was for a time interned in a camp by the Vichy authorities. He escaped death partly by luck and partly through the active intervention of American Unitarian human rights activists, who, in a dramatic episode, smuggled him to safety through the port of Lisbon. But all this came after the publication, throughout the world, of *Moscow—1937: My Visit Described for My Friends*. The tenor of this baffling book may be suggested by the fact that in England it was published in a large edition through the Left Book Club. The American edition came out from Viking in August 1937.

Moscow—1937 has been called the "most nauseating" of all the Western defenses of the show trials—a considerable insult, given the strength of the competition. Some scholars have concluded that Feuchtwanger was an actual Soviet agent. The most benign interpretation invokes the author's consciousness as a Jew in Hitler's Germany, to which Stalin's Russia was at any rate the rhetorical antithesis. Whatever the case, it unquestionably achieved the apogee, from the Communist point of view, of useful idiocy. According to Feuchtwanger, all liberal criticisms of the Stalin regime were pettifogging and irrelevant. They reflected an inability to appreciate the grandeur of the forest on account of a few inconveniently placed saplings.

His aspersions on "bourgeois" liberty were typical of a certain kind of 1930s leftist discourse. They might be characterized as the lament of Harold Laski. The only "freedom" offered by capitalism was the freedom to exploit and be exploited, the freedom to be unemployed.

Feuchtwanger cites with full approval the Soviet self-realization of its own superiority. "One of the leaders of the Union"—meaning of course the Soviet Union—says, "We are a battalion on the march. First we must conquer, and then we can consider whether the buttons on our uniforms would be better a little higher or a little lower." The buttons referred to are such decorative inessentials as civil liberties. He was outraged by the moral equation, increasingly offered, especially by ex-Communists, between the Soviet and the Nazi states. He preferred another, stranger equivalence proposed to him by a Soviet philologist. "Democracy is government by the people, dictatorship government by an individual. But if this individual represents the people as ideally as is the case with us here, do not democracy and dictatorship become one and the same thing."

The real heart of the book is in two fascinating chapters devoted to Trotsky and the Trotskyite trials. Feuchtwanger's benign attitude toward Stalin in no way vitiates the elegance of his deployment of the nature of the dispute between the two men. Trotsky is the smooth talker and risk taker who, however, cannot really get things done. Placid, undramatic, modest Stalin, though a lackluster orator, is an expert at getting things done. For example, he "organized the peasants"—a truly remarkable summary of the collectivization of agriculture under Stalin. The trials, Feuchtwanger realizes, have dealt a terrible blow to the prestige of Russian Communism among Western intellectuals. "Many who had before been friends of the Soviet Union have become its opponents as a result of these trials." Feuchtwanger himself was dubious so long as he was at a distance, but as it happened he was in Moscow and attended all sessions of the second trial (Radek-Pyatakov). The experience of his own eyes removed all doubts. Of the confessions of the principal defendants, he says this: "I was forced to accept the evidence of my senses, and my doubts melted away as naturally as salt dissolves in water. If that was lying or prearranged, then I don't know what truth is." Indeed.

And just as he was convinced of the guilt of the defendants, he was certain of the greater guilt of their remote manipulator, Leon Trotsky. Those who thought it improbable that Trotsky, the dogmatist of the world socialist revolution, would enter into secret concord with Fascism, knew neither their history nor their literature. "If Alcibiades went to the Persians, why not Trotsky to the Fascists?" Had not Shakespeare's Coriolanus, banished from Rome, sought to make alliance with the Volscians, Rome's enemies?

Moscow—1937 may be regarded today as one of the curious aberrations of literature. It had a wide circulation in several European languages during the immediate prewar period, and Koestler certainly knew it. But both the book and its author were soon overtaken by terrible events. First, the gentle Stalin and not the violent Trotsky made an alliance with Fascism. Soon thereafter the gentle Stalin finally succeeded in having the violent Trotsky murdered with what is usually called an "ice ax" but looks much more to me like a shingling hatchet. Feuchtwanger, having escaped Hitler to the South of France, was incarcerated in a concentration camp by the Vichy authorities. He made a most providential escape to the United States, eventually taking up residence in Southern California. There, under the desultory surveillance of the FBI, he became part of a community, half exiles, half lotus-eaters. Hollywood was very far from Moscow, concerning which Feuchtwanger had little more to say except for a few embarrassed half-apologies.

The relevance of Feuchtwanger to Koestler's *Darkness at Noon* is tangential but telling. Among the curious details in Nikolai Bukharin's *apologia* or death speech is a bibliographical detail. Although the NKVD interrogation prisons were not conspicuous for their library holdings, Bukharin tells us that "I happened by chance to get Feuchtwanger's book from the prison library. There he refers to the trials of the Trotskyites. It produced a profound impression on me. . . ." Presumably *Moscow—1937* came into Bukharin's hands by the same kind of chance that put a copy of Augustine's *Confessions* in Petrarch's pocket as he set out to climb Mont Ventoux.

"I have been in prison for over a year," Bukharin tells us at the beginning of his carefully worded statement, "and I therefore do not know what is going on in the world. But, judging from those fragments of real life that sometimes reached me by chance, I see, feel and understand that the interests which we so criminally betrayed are entering a new phase of gigantic development, are now appearing in the international arena as a great and mighty factor of the international proletarian phase." The book had not even been written at the time Bukharin was thrown into jail, but it has come into his hands in a most timely fashion. His admission that he knows nothing of what is going on in the world admits the very general exception of his sense of a huge progress in the Soviet Union. It admits as well one international fact. Bukharin is aware, and made aware by Feuchtwanger, that some Western intellectuals have cast doubts upon the reliability of the confessions brought forward in the trials of the Trotskyites. This doubt he seeks to remove at the very brink of his grave.

True complexity of character is perhaps the rarest of the novelist's achievements. Koestler's Nicholas Rubashov is brilliant in his complexity. There are few greater monuments to the genius of the historical novel. Several of Stalin's victims may seem to us rather attractive and sympathetic fellows. Zinoviev was the author of numerous accessible essays in which it is not hard to detect a familiar and uplifting humanistic spirit. Radek, who was quite a wit, often seems a kind of Frenchman *manqué* among the more dour bearded theoreticians. Bukharin combined acute intelligence with an attractive vision of the betterment of humankind, and he emerges from his semi-hagiographical biographer not merely as a man Margaret Thatcher could do business with, but as someone you yourself might enjoy having lunch with. Even Trotsky—or perhaps especially Trotsky, if the dialectic of history forces us to a choice between him and Stalin—had some redeeming human qualities, well disguised though they often were. But all these men were Bolsheviks. A corollary of their political choice was that they were by principle committed to mass murder. Not a one of those men would have escaped hanging if judged according to the canons invoked for the German war criminals at Nuremberg. They lived by the sword of historical inevitability, and by that same sword they died.

Furthermore, they were indeed guilty of the great crime of which all the small fictitious crimes to which they confessed were mere allegories. That crime was "oppositionism." Every one of them had at some point or another opposed Stalin, his ideas, his policies, or his programs. Most of them probably opposed him still—*in pectore*! Who knows? It is not at all impossible that the long friendships among them might have on occasion allowed them, in groups of two or three, in guarded terms and hushed tones, to talk about their opposition. In other words, they may have been actual as well as virtual conspirators. Stalin doubtless sought to clear the ground of all possible opposition, but the personal element in his action, the element founded in his jealousy, his insecurities, or his vindictiveness, has probably been exaggerated. The Purge Trials were after all simply a small but highly visible part of a huge process by which he sought to rid the country of all possible sources of opposition.

Nor is the fact that the Moscow Trials lacked the transparency expected by Western judicial standards of much relevance in understanding them. The Sovietologist George Katkov, who devoted a thoughtful book to the Bukharin trial, puts it thus: "Law, being, like the state, only a superstructure in the organization of human society, was interpreted as one of the instruments of the class struggle, an instrument which in the hands of the property-owning classes served to maintain their privileges but which in the hands of a proletarian dictatorship . . . was to be a revolutionary weapon to bring about the desired historical changes. . . . It would be self-contradictory, un-Marxist and counter-revolutionary for a Marxist to object to the use of legal procedures for political ends." Radek had been the editor of *Pravda*. Bukharin had been the editor of *Izvestia*. What could be more absurd than that such men should suddenly appeal to the norms of bourgeois as opposed to proletarian "justice"?

BUKHARIN, KOESTLER, AND THE SPANISH WAR

George Katkov characterized *Moscow—1937* as "perhaps the most nauseating of the Western apologists for the Moscow trials." Though the competition is large, I shall not gainsay him. Several scholars have been of the opinion that Feuchtwanger was an actual Soviet agent; he was certainly an informal one. For any foreign journalist a one-on-one interview with Stalin was a kind of Holy Grail that even the most internationally eminent of correspondents might regard as a career goal. During his relatively short sojourn in Russia, Feuchtwanger actualy conducted *two* interviews with the dictator. They were widely reported both within the USSR and in the West. The extraordinary circumstances encourage a suspicion of political collusion.

It is probable that Feuchtwanger, like Koestler, was a "secret" Communist—that is, one more useful to the Party if he would adopt the pose of the neutral, objective, foreign observer of the Soviet scene. It has been suggested that Stalin actually used him to convey to Karl Radek, whose historical ties to the German Communists were particularly close, the message that his life would be spared in exchange for full cooperation. At the end of January 1937, Feuchtwanger made a statement concerning the conduct of the trials that was published at length in *Izvestia*. It said in part: "Abusive epithets and noisy indignation, however understandable they are, cannot explain in the end what is going on in the souls of these people. Only the pen of a great Soviet writer could explain to Western Europeans the crimes and the punishment of the defendants."

In the published version of *Moscow—1937*, Feuchtwanger expressed these somewhat cryptic sentiments in a slightly different way. "Immediately after the trial, I summarized my impressions in a commentary for the Soviet press: 'West Europeans are experiencing some difficulty in arriving at the fundamental causes of the procedure adopted by the accused, and, above all, the ultimate reason for their behaviour before the court. It may be that the deeds of most of these men deserved death; but invective and outbursts of indignation, understandable though these may be, will not give an explanation of the psychology of these men. It would take a great Soviet poet to make their guilt and their sin comprehensible to Western minds.'"

Katkov and others point out that this was probably meant as advice concerning the courtroom techniques that would be most palatable to Western observers. We may note the syntactic surprise of the first sentence. The understandable "abusive epithets and noisy indignation," though misguidedly intended to explain what was going on in the souls of the defendants, were coming not from their mouths but from those of the judge and prosecutor, before being amplified by the press. In other words, go easy with the *public* browbeating. But the reference to "a great Soviet writer," who alone could explain the defendants' "crimes" and "punishment," took matters further.

This was clearly a reference to Dostoyevsky as author of *Crime and Punishment*; and it is very likely that Bukharin in referring to Feuchtwanger's "book" is actually referring to the statement in *Izvestia*. Bukharin began his final statement to the court in the evening session of March 12, 1938, by alluding to his isolation. "I have been in prison for over a year, and I therefore do not know what is going on the world." Certain rumors had reached him, rumors of "a new phase of gigantic development . . . appearing in the international arena as a great and mighty factor of the international proletarian phase." The point of this obscure remark seems to have been a "confession" that Stalin's course in the Five Year Plans was correct while his own was incorrect. But it seems highly likely that Bukharin had in fact been briefed on certain other developments—including the problematic Western response to the earlier trials. The explicit reference to Feuchtwanger's book, in the implicit reference to his earlier "report," must reflect the "assignment" he was given for his court appearance.

At the end of the statement Bukharin recognized the solemnity of the situation: "I am perhaps speaking for the last time in my life." It may seem curious under such circumstances that he would spend so many of his last words in an effort to correct the mistaken notions of Western intellectuals concerning the confessions of earlier defendants. "It seems to me that when some of the West European and American intellectuals begin to entertain doubts and vacillations in connection with the trials taking place in the U.S.S.R., this is primarily due to the fact that these people do not understand the radical distinction, namely, that in our country the antagonist, the enemy, has at the same time a divided, a dual mind. And I think that is the first thing to be understood."

He had already defined this "dual mind" with deep obscurity as "an incomplete faith in his counter-revolutionary cause." The dichotomy was to be seen in "the eulogies I wrote of socialist construction, although on the morrow I repudiated this by practical actions of a criminal character." Bukharin says that he is suffering from "what in Hegel's philosophy is called a most unhappy mind. This unhappy mind differed from the ordinary unhappy mind only by the fact that it was also a criminal mind." This Hegelian concept is usually translated in English as unhappy "consciousness," meaning the incomplete stage that must be passed through in order to achieve full self-consciousness. The implication, never made explicit, is that the conspirators confessed when they came to their right minds or unified consciousness. "I take the liberty of dwelling on these questions because I had considerable contacts with these upper intellectuals abroad, especially among scientists, and I must explain to them what every Young Pioneer in the Soviet Union knows." Bukharin ridicules such suggestions from Western intellectuals as "Tibetan powders" and "hypnotism"—that is, psychotropic agents of any sort. He then moves on to Dostoyevsky. "Repentance is often attributed to the Dostoyevsky mind, to the specific properties of the soul ('*l'âme slave*' as it is called), and this can be said of types like Alyosha Karamazov, the heroes of the 'Idiot' and other Dostoyevsky characters, who are prepared to stand up in the public square and cry: 'Beat me, Orthodox Christians, I am a villain!'"

Of course what Bukharin is in effect saying, as most of the defendants before him had said, was "Punish me, Orthodox Bolsheviks. I am an oppositionist!" Hence the following disclaimer is at the literal level meaningless, and must have been intended to be so. "But that is not the case here at all," said Bukharin. "L'âme slave and the psychology of Dostoyevsky characters are a thing of the remote past in our country, the pluperfect tense. Such types do not exist in our country, or exist perhaps only on the outskirts of small provincial towns, if they do even there. On the contrary, such a psychology is to be found in Western Europe." Now cracks a noble heart.

The impact of the Spanish Civil War on the European Communist consciousness was complex and various. It was not a single discrete event, like the Hitler-Stalin Pact of 1939 or the suppressed Hungarian Revolution of 1956—other events that had a dramatic and clarifying impact on the thinking of individual Communists. It was a long, complex process, deeply ambiguous in all the hidden interstices behind its bold facade of a conflict between black and white, political virtue and political evil. It was a process requiring analysis, interpretation, and indeed meditation. In some ways it witnessed the apogee of prewar Soviet foreign policy triumph. The conspiratorial double-dealing of the Communists in Spain was for the most part highly successful. Some of the historians of the Spanish war are still in plausible denial concerning it. But for many individual leftists, including Koestler, it was *the* event that turned them against Soviet Communism.

There were many aspects of Soviet perfidy in Spain, and they have been laid out with a somewhat stolid irrefutabilty in a long book by B. Bolletin. They boil down to a single fact. Beneath the guise of revolutionary international proletarian solidarity, Stalin was pursuing a policy of Soviet nationalism and expansionism. The military aid he offered the Spanish Republic was carefully delimited and attached to so many political strings as nearly to guarantee its actual inefficacy. Among his chief aims were getting his hands on the vast gold reserves of the Republic and using the chaotic military situation to pursue in an international arena his bloody purge of "Trotskyites."

This latter pursuit was most clearly exposed by George Orwell in *Homage to Catalonia*, perhaps the single most famous book to come out of the Spanish Civil War. At the outbreak of the rebellion in the summer of 1936, the Spanish Communist Party was so small as to be practically insignificant as either a political or a military force in the large and largely united Spanish left. A small but valiant military part of the left, which was particularly strong in the industrial northeast, was the POUM (the Partido Obrero de Unificación Marxista). The official political doctrine of the POUM was classical anarchy in the tradition of Kropotkin, Goldman, and Berkman; but its members were also explicit Marxists who believed in the world proletariat and the world revolution. Its principal leader, Andrés Nin, held the old doctrine of the Comintern, of which he had been a prominent member. This was not the doctrine of Soviet exceptionalism or "Socialism in One Country." It could legitimately be said to be the doctrine of "Trotskyism," though it was shared with Trotsky rather than derived from him.

The Soviet military agents operating openly in Spain, some members of the burgeoning Spanish Communist Party, a substantial number of covert GPU agents, and a significant number of the Communists openly or covertly attached to the International Brigades, joined in slandering, demonizing, and actually liquidating the POUM. Andrés Nin was kidnapped by the GPU, which undoubtedly executed him. Hundreds, and probably thousands of other revolutionary Marxists were murdered by Communists, many of them in the NKVD prisons that were established wherever the Party got the upper hand. All this was done under the preposterous pretext of combating Franco and "Fascism."

Since the narrative content of *Darkness at Noon* deals with the Moscow Trials, it is necessary perhaps to make one other point that, while it would have been obvious to Koestler, might elude today's reader. The crimes of the Communists in Spain were of the same origin as the crimes of the Moscow courtroom. That is, they were part and parcel of one huge process of "purgation," the aim of which was to secure an absolute Stalinist hegemony.

We can trace Koestler's spiritual withdrawal from his Communist allegiance through at least two sources. The most immediate and explicit consists of his actual letters of resignation from the Party in April 1938. The other primary source is his body of autobiographical writings, and particularly his two books about his Spanish experiences—*Spanish Testament* and *Dialogue with Death* (both 1937). I call them separate books because Koestler himself came to regard them as such. In their original publication, in 1937, they formed an apparently single work entitled *Spanish Testament*. The bibliographical history of this diptych is complex and confused, but a single attentive reading is sufficient to detect the profound spiritual differences between its two parts. Oversimplifying only slightly, one can say that the first part is an able but eventually unexceptional work of Communist propaganda, while the second is a profoundly authentic and introspective personal document.

The explanation of the startling disparity will be found in the famous apothegm of Dr. Johnson concerning the unfortunate Dr. Dodd: the prospect of hanging wonderfully concentrates the mind. The aptly named *Dialogue with Death* is a record of Koestler's experience as a condemned prisoner in a Nationalist prison in Málaga for three months in the later winter of 1937. The death he faced was by bullet rather than by rope, but the mental clarity it induced was no different.

In January 1937, six months into the war, Koestler arrived in Barcelona. His overt role was that of a "liberal" journalist covering the Republican side for a British newspaper, the *News Chronicle*. He had also a covert role. He had been a secret member of the German Communist Party since 1932, and he took with him to Spain a secret assignment from the Comintern. He was captured by Nationalist troops in Málaga when that city was overrun by Queipo de Llano in the general collapse of the Republican front in Andalusia in December 1936 and January 1937.

The most obvious significance of this experience for the eventual composition of *Darkness at Noon* is, of course, the shared setting of the condemned cell. Rubashov is technically being confined during a prolonged investigation and interrogation preliminary to a trial, but he knows from the outset that he is a man condemned by the dialectic of history. One of the curiosities of Koestler's situation, in military circumstances somewhat less settled, was that he had already been condemned to death *before* his criminal investigation began. But many of the details of Rubashov's experience surely gain their vivacity from the author's own experience—for example, the prisoner's heightened physical awareness of the most trivial aspects of his surroundings and his quotidian regime, or the effect of his awareness of the gradual disappearance of his fellow prisoners as they go, one by one, to their individual executions.

Some historical connections become clearer with the passage of time, others more obscure. One connection that arose naturally and spontaneously in the minds of men like Koestler and Krivitsky and Orwell, though we must dig for it, was the connection between the Moscow Trials and the Russian double-dealing with the Republic in the Spanish War. The overarching theme was the consolidation of Stalin's power. Of these three anti-Communists, Walter Krivitsky alone was sufficiently privy to the thinking within the Kremlin to be able to predict to his absolutely unbelieving auditors that Stalin was more interested in finding an accommodation with Hitler than in countering him in Spain or elsewhere. But for Koestler and some others, the Spain of 1937 was the end of a road that others would reach only in August of 1939. The Hitler-Stalin Pact would make him an *anti*-Communist, but he had for more than a year been a *non*-Communist.

Arthur Koestler resigned from the German Communist Party on April 22, 1938. On that date he was a non-Communist rather than an anti-Communist, but a careful consideration of the context of the resignation can greatly advance our understanding of the plan of *Darkness at Noon*, which even then was beginning to form in his mind. A common thread of reflection among many literary ex-Communists is the difficulty in identifying a particular moment or event leading to the break. The process was frequently gradual, indeed hardly perceptible, often involving a slow and painful victory of empirical evidence over the powerful will to deny. Koestler writes about the phenomenon in several of his works, perhaps most fully in his essay in *The God That Failed*, an anthology of essays by lapsed Communists and fellow travelers.

By then of course the "God" had failed. What was going through Koestler's mind when it was only failing? Koestler had been on the whole successful in denying the meaning of the horrors he had witnessed in the Soviet Union in 1932 and 1933. They had been trumped by the horrors of Hitler's ascent to power in Berlin. For most German leftists, and certainly all German Communists, no greater horror could be imagined, and now it was as a German Communist among German Communist exiles in France that he lived and moved and had his being. But there was a growing list of grievances. Some were local and personal as, we are told, all politics must be. He was rather vaguely aware of the growing unhappiness of his friend and mentor Willi Münzenberg. He was further shocked and moved to action by the persecution by purge, in Russia, of his friend Alex Weissberg.

We shall come to know Weissberg a little in a later essay. He was a distinguished Austrian Communist scientist, a pioneer in the field of low-temperature physics; his wife, Eva, was one of Koestler's oldest school chums. At the time when many other German-speaking Communists found exile in Paris, the Weissbergs had gone to Russia, where they lived and worked. Eventually they both were overtaken by the Purge. Weissberg's "case" was not unlike that of thousands of others caught up in the Terror, but Koestler, animated by the personal connection, set out to organize an international campaign to save Weissberg. Remarkably, it worked. The Soviet authorities expelled rather than executed Alex Weissberg. Even Homer nods, and the GPU did occasionally make mistakes bitterly regretted later. Returned to the West, Weissberg eventually wrote one of the important exposé books, for which Koestler provided a preface.

But that was still in the future. He regarded the charges against Weissberg as patently absurd, of course, but Koestler himself was still at that stage, frequently encountered in the memoirs of Russian political prisoners themselves, in which he thought he was dealing with an individual abberant "mistake" rather than a systematic norm. What disturbed him more than a bureaucratic miscarriage of justice, however gross, was the dogmatic ease with which his German comrades were able to believe that if a man had been charged by an NKVD court, that man was guilty—even if he were a distinguished scientist, an old personal friend, and a Party colleague of long standing. Here, the matter of confession of guilt seemed very important. Weissberg had after all "confessed." In fact, he confessed repeatedly between his retractions—whenever the coercion became unbearable. Rare was the Communist willing to express public doubt about the nature of such confessions. In 1950, the Czech government hanged the poet Zavis Kalendra, whom several of the more prominent French intellectuals had known before the war. When André Breton invited the Communist poet Paul Eluard to join in the campaign to save their old friend, Eluard said in an open letter, "I am too busy with the innocent who proclaim their innocence to be concerned with the guilty who proclaim their guilt."

Spain and the Moscow Trials coalesced in Koestler's consciousness in the following way: Koestler had been in Spain while working as a journalist for a British paper, and it was in Britain that the effective campaign to save him from execution had been chiefly conducted. His Spanish book was adopted and promoted by Victor Gollancz's Left Book Club. In this connection he undertook, at the beginning of 1938, a month-long promotional book tour that covered most of England. His audiences of leftists always contained numerous Communists and Communist sympathizers. In the question-and-answer period following one of his first lectures, someone asked him a question about the POUM—the Catalan anarchists. The Communists had succeeded in getting the party outlawed in 1937. Orwell's *Homage to Catalonia* was at this time only in the process of preparation for publication (it appeared in April), but its general contents as regarded the POUM were already well known in leftist circles. Nin had been prominent in the earlier Comintern, and he had many admirers among the older revolutionaries. The matter of the POUM was becoming a major propaganda problem for the Communists.

In retrospect Koestler would claim that the question took him by surprise, and that his honest response to it was a subliminal attempt at Communist "suicide." He answered that although he disagreed with some of the POUM principles, he regarded the Communist Party persecution of its members as a mistake that had the "objective" effect of aiding Fascism. He knew that this was anything but the Party line, and he expected a swift retribution. The worst he got was some low-grade grumbling. He attributed the circumstance to the unserious nature of British Communists, who were hopelessly tarred by bourgeois civility and even good humor. (One of the amusing leitmotifs encountered in the research for this book is the patronizing scorn of "real" Communists for the members of the Communist Party of Great Britain.) The same question, to which he gave his same reply, was raised following several other lectures.

This lecture tour fell in January and February 1938. In March occurred the event of the greatest immediate and genetic significance for the composition of *Darkness at Noon*. That was the trial in Moscow in the first two weeks of March of the "Bloc of Rightists and Trotskyites," often called the Bukharin trial on account of its most celebrated victim.

The dialectical ax never fell in England, but it would appear that news of Koestler's deportment reached the Communist leadership in the German exile community in Paris. Returned there, Koestler was invited to give a talk about Spain to a conference of exiled German writers, many of whom were Communists. He was visited in advance of the scheduled event by an authoritative Party member who wanted to "chat" about the upcoming talk. This man told Koestler that, in the talk, he should attack the POUM. In fact, this was a *Parteibefehl*, a "Party order," an imposition of the notorious and vaunted Communist discipline. The man also asked to review a copy of the talk in advance, a condition to which Koestler did not agree, despite the fact that, altering his usual practice of talking extemporaneously or from a few notes, he worked long and hard on a polished written text.

From the displeasure with which his corrector terminated the interview, Koestler must have known that his contemplated political suicide would be easier to commit among the dour Germans than among the genial Britons. Koestler's talk repeated much of the material he had prepared for the Left Book Club tour, but with the defense of the POUM now occupying a prominent position in the body of the text. In his autobiography, Koestler described its conclusion: "I finally decided on three simple phrases with which to conclude the speech, each in itself a pious platitude, and yet a capital heresy for a Stalinist. The first was 'No movement, party or person can claim the privilege of infallibility.' The second was 'It is as foolish to appease the enemy, as it is to persecute the friend who pursues the same end as you by a different road.' The third was a quotation from Thomas Mann: 'In the long run, a harmful truth is better than a useful lie.'" There was some applause, but not from the Communists, some of whom scowled ostentatiously, with clasped, crossed arms.

This had not been an active initiative of resignation, but a passive exposure to expulsion. He returned to his rooms to brood and await his punishment. In his autobiography, Koestler tells us that it was in that inert state of mind that the idea of resignation came upon him suddenly, as a novel and exhilarating thought, and that almost at once, without any agony of indecision, he sat down and addressed a letter to the Writers' Caucus of the German Communist Party, the group most scandalized by his lecture about Spain. "I worked on my letter of resignation all night," wrote Koestler. "It was, I believe, a good letter, and I am sorry I have no copy of it." There are at least two confusions here. The first is that by the time he published *The Invisible Writing* he would appear to have forgotten that he wrote *two* resignation letters. And although he could find no copies, his biographer Michael Scammell did. They were in an archive first impounded and sent to Berlin at the time of the fall of France, and thence taken again by the Russian secret police back to Moscow, where they still were at the dawn of *perestroika*.

The first letter, dated April 22, is temporizing. Its main task is to announce the fact of resignation and to promise a fuller explanation soon to come. The letter itself begins, "After long thought and reflection I have decided to resign from the German Communist Party." It probably would have been impossible even for Koestler to reconcile the dramatic divergence in the degree of premeditation. Elsewhere in his writings he several times refers to the Communist's necessity constantly to deny, submerge, or contain doubts about Communism. Perhaps the premeditation, though deep and probing, had been of a subconscious sort. There certainly would be fruitful postmeditation.

The letter of April 22 is brief. It gives no "cause" or explanation for the resignation. Its tone is conciliatory if not apologetic. It touches on two issues only. The first is his continuing sympathy with the political aims of the Communists, his lack of intention of joining any opposition or splinter group, and his continuing belief that "the existence of the Soviet Union is a decisively positive factor in the political balance of our time, and that nothing is further from my mind than to abandon this conviction." The second issue is that of secrecy. Just as his membership in the Party was a secret, he would like his severance from it to be secret. The motive for this request is conspiratorial. The international campaign to free Koestler from captivity in Spain had been spearheaded by British left liberals who did not know that he was a Communist and who had repeatedly insisted in public that he was not. In this useful untruth, knowledgeable Party members had acquiesced. It could harm the fruitful alliance with such innocents if the truth were to come out.

It is no doubt the second and much longer piece of April 29 that Koestler remembered as "a good letter." It provides an excellent analysis of his thinking at the time, but also exposes his characteristic self-absorbed egoism. One has the impression that he really believed that the comrades were going to read the letter carefully, with penitential sympathy. It is five single-spaced pages long, covered by a brief personal note to Egon Kisch, the head of the Writers' Caucus and something of a father figure to Koestler.

An Ex-Communist Novelist

Koestler's defection from Communism in 1938 coincided with another life change. He now began to think of himself as a professional *writer* rather than as a *journalist*—a distinction that greatly enlarged his possible fields of inquiry. He sold his unfinished novel about Spartacus (*The Gladiators*) to Jonathan Cape in London. Cape also wanted an option on a "next book." A small advance allowed him to return to Paris to finish *The Gladiators*, and finish it he did, in July. He immediately began work on what would be *Darkness at Noon*. The book's very somber tone reflected not merely the author's political apostasy but also a kind of depression with the outcome of the Spanish War and, as he got into the book, with Hitler's early and stupendous victories. World War II would drown out its English publication, and even in America, where it had a large distribution, its impact was blunted by war's distractions and exigencies. During the war years it lay shallowly buried in the political topsoil of the Western consciousness to emerge, cicadalike, in the tense climate of postwar France. The book's gestation was hardly less dramatic than its postwar reception. Koestler was a European, a *Continental* European, and he came to live in Britain only through historical duress. As he planned *Darkness at Noon*, beginning even in 1938, his intention had probably been to publish the book in Paris, and in French. Quite apart from his arrangement with Jonathan Cape, developments both in world events and in his personal life would alter that plan.

In the prewar months of 1939 he met in Paris a young British artist, Daphne Hardy. (She was twenty-two, he thirty-four.) He soon took up with her, and they for a time set up a household in the South of France, in the Alpes-Maritimes. There he worked away at his novel, and she at her sculpting. After a brief time they returned to Paris, where he continued to work on the book under increasingly difficult circumstances. England and France declared war on Germany on September 3, and while during the several months of "Phony War" there was little military action, the French authorities did move against "enemy aliens" like Koestler. He has written about this period of his life in that part of his autobiography entitled *Scum of the Earth*. In that book he refers to Daphne Hardy, whom he shields in various ways, as "G."

Arthur Koestler, born in Budapest, of course knew Hungarian, but German was his native "cultural" language. He had lived for several years in Germany, where he had worked as a journalist in the German language. German—not Russian—was also the international language of European Communism. Although by 1938 his French was excellent and his English good, he was keenly aware of not being a native speaker of either. He naturally composed most easily in German. Daphne Hardy, the daughter of a British diplomat, was of course a native English speaker. She also knew both French and German with near-native fluency, having had parts of her early schooling in both languages.

Koestler was fully aware of the importance of the translator's contribution to his project. On the title page of the New York 1941 edition of *Darkness at Noon*, over which he exercised supervision, her name is given an unusual typographical prominence. The original German sheets of Koestler's composition did not survive. Hence, all translations—and the book was translated into most known tongues—were done from Hardy's English text, including even the eventual German-language translation. The situation raises the issue of "authorial indeterminacy" that fascinates some literary critics. We may conclude that *Darkness at Noon* is, among other things, the product or offspring of a remarkable love affair.

By the time they returned to Paris, the plan was definite that Hardy would translate Koestler's German into English for publication in London. That is what happened, but not without much difficulty and drama. One collateral effect of the nearly incredible collapse of the French defensive forces before the German *Blitzkrieg* of May 1940 was to put the substantial number of leftist German refugees in France, many of them Communists, into a desperate position. In occupied France they would be seized by the Gestapo, but their fate in the semi-Fascist Vichy territories was not a great deal better. Here they became the "scum of the earth" of Koestler's title. Koestler was in and out of police and military detention. He spent time in the notorious concentration camp at Le Vernet. His actual Hungarian citizenship sometimes complicated but seldom eased his difficulties.

Several prominent exiles, including the now famous literary theorist Walter Benjamin, elected suicide as being preferable to the untender mercies they expected upon repatriation to Hitler's Germany. (Koestler dedicated *Scum of the Earth* to a number of them.) In the autumn following the fall of France some hunters found hanging from a tree in an isolated copse a horribly decayed corpse. It turned out to be that of Koestler's old friend and mentor, Willi Münzenberg, the genius propagandist of the German Communist Party. Willi had become rather wobbly on Stalin, and there is reason to believe that Comintern agents may have assisted this particular suicide.

It was under these circumstances that in June 1940, Koestler and Hardy, clutching the finished translation of *Darkness at Noon*, took desperate flight toward the Atlantic ports of the coast between Bordeaux and the Spanish border. It was rumored that there one might find a British military ship. In fact, Hardy did gain passage on a ship, said to be the last before a complete German clamp down, from the port of Saint-Jean-de-Luz. Koestler later heard a report (false, though he had no reason to doubt it at the time) that her ship had been destroyed by the Germans, with the loss of life of all on board. This was for him the last full measure of despair, and he attempted suicide. Only the inefficacy of his poison spared this latter-day Piramus. Hardy was able to get the manuscript to the publisher, Jonathan Cape, and the rest is history.

DARKNESS AT NOON—LE ZÉRO ET L'INFINI

And to that history we must address ourselves. Koestler eventually made it to England himself. Everything about him was now suspicious to the British authorities, and he was incarcerated in Pentonville. He could rightly regard himself as a connoisseur of the jails of Europe, and this stretch was brief and comparatively tolerable. It was apparently in Pentonville Prison that he saw his first printed copy of *Darkness at Noon*. The book made as much of a splash, in that brief period of prelude to the Battle of Britain, as a cobblestone dropped into the gale-tossed sea. That is, it was born obsolete. The shock of the Hitler-Stalin Pact, which might have instantly given the book a large and sympathetic British audience earlier, was yesterday's news, overtaken by the fall of France and the strange narcissism of Britain's isolated defiance. From the political point of view, what were the options for a classical European leftist? *Scum of the Earth* concludes with an appendix of two supposed letters to the author—one from "Colonel Blimp" (the caricature voice of the Tory reactionary), the other from "Comrade Blump" (Koestler's imagined voice of the doctrinaire British left). Blimp encourages a crusade to defend the Empire; Blump insisted that resistance to Hitler depends upon a prior "clarification of the war aims"—meaning the front-loaded promise of the dissolution of the Empire and the commitment to a planned economy. Arthur Koestler joined the British army.

Darkness at Noon received in the preoccupied British press what is usually called a respectful reception. That word "respectful" can strike an author's ear as more cruel than invective or calumny, very little of which Koestler's book at first excited. America was a different matter, at least to the degree that the country had not yet fully fixated on Hitler. In America there was a more robust and slightly less distracted anti-Communist clientele. There was also an expectant audience. There had been a buzz about the book in New York, and the edition brought out by Macmillan in March 1941 had been adopted as a Book-of-the-Month Club selection, guaranteeing a certain financial success. In the American literary press there was mostly praise, but also at least a suggestion of the controversy to come later. However, in June Hitler unleashed Operation Barbarossa, the *Blitzkrieg* against Russia, an event that had, perhaps toward the bottom of a lengthy hierarchy of consequences, a significant if so far unstudied impact on Anglo-American literary history. America, Britain, the Soviet Union—these were now "the Allies." Such topics as the bad manners of the NKVD or Commissar Rubashov's toothache became for a time utterly unimportant, and also perhaps indecent. Now *Darkness at Noon* took on another metaphoric career. It became like a message in a tightly corked bottle, bobbing without notice in the choppy waters of the English Channel. One day, when the storms of war subsided, it would drift back on a tide to the French shores of its origins, whence in desperation Daphne Hardy had removed it in 1940.

The publication in France of Koestler's novel must be regarded as a major factor in clarifying the political situation in a way unfavorable to the Soviet Union and its friends, among the more slavish of whom were the members of the Communist Party of France. It was not that Communists in large numbers read the book and converted *sur le champ* to pro-American free marketeers, though in fact references to the book can be found in a surprisingly wide range of contemporaneous French political discourse. In the immediate postwar years, a burgeoning French Communist Party was active and fairly effective in the creation of its own mythical version of recent French history. This version camouflaged the actual postures and positions of the Party in the immediate prewar years and during the period of the "Phoney War" before the German invasion, during which time Stalin and Hitler were still in formal alliance. It considerably aggrandized the nature of the anti-Nazi Resistance during the occupation, and aggrandized the role of the Communists within it.

The book had been written in France. Paris was the center—self-appointed, but not vigorously contested—of Western intellectual life. Koestler's was a name well known among French intellectuals. His return to Paris in the fall of 1946 would have been inevitable regardless of what publishing arrangements he had made there. In Paris, Koestler found an immediate entrée to "leading intellectual circles," the most leading of all being of course the *salon* of Jean-Paul Sartre and Simone de Beauvoir. Theirs was a friendship, though initially animated, destined to crash on the shoals of Koestler's anti-Communism.

The powerful English title, *Darkness at Noon*, is actually rather mysterious. There is no echo of it in the text of the novel. Koestler said that the title "sounded good"—as it indeed does. Later scholars have derived it from a striking line in Milton's *Samson Agonistes* that defines the state of the blinded hero—"O dark, dark, dark, amid the blaze of noon." Thus it may allude to the metaphoric blindness that has for so many years distorted Rubashov's moral vision, or that of Stalinist collaborators generally. That is possibly correct, but I rather doubt it, given the usual standard of clarity and aptness in the author's literary allusions.

The French translation was given a new title: *Le Zéro et l'infini*. Here there is rich suggestiveness, but little mystery. The mathematical contrast between zero and infinity has very clear connections with the themes and language of the book. In one of its most famous passages—and one most execrated by his Communist detractors—Koestler puts the following speech into the mouth of the NKVD interrogator Ivanov: "There are only two conceptions of human ethics, and they are at opposite poles. One of them is Christian and humane, declares the individual to be sacrosanct, and asserts that the rules of arithmetic are not to be applied to human units. The other starts from the basic principle that a collective aim justifies all means, and not only allows, but demands, that the individual should in every way be subordinated and sacrificed to the community—which may dispose of it as an experimentation rabbit or a sacrificial lamb. The first conception could be called anti-vivisection morality, the second vivisection morality." (p. 157) Elsewhere the individual, as denoted by the first-person pronoun—*I, Ego, Ich, Je*—is said to be a "grammatical fiction."

The theme of "the individual and society" is among the great themes of world literature. It is not the only major theme of Koestler's book, but his French title emphasizes it in a special way. One of the criticisms made by the book's detractors is that Koestler's binary is too brittle and simplistic to command conviction. They say the same of the contrast between the Yogi and the Commissar in his famous essay of that title. The criticism is by no means negligible, but Koestler is dealing in poetic language, and he is certainly taking up a familiar theme in Marxist and even pre-Marxist political discourse. One of the most famous books of the French Revolution, *What Is the Third Estate?* by the abbé Sieyès, begins thus:

What is the Third Estate: Nothing.
What is it to become: Everything.

PARIS READS KOESTLER

A professional librarian in France, Martine Poulain, has written a scholarly study of the history of the publication and reception of *Le Zéro et l'infini* in France.* French publishing, centered in the capital, naturally suffered marked dislocations during the German occupation. Identifiably "Jewish" publishing houses were shut down. In the postwar period some of these were scrambling to get back into the game, including the house of Calmann-Lévy, which was actively trying to construct a list. Even during the suspension of their operations Robert Calmann-Lévy was scouting around against a possible brighter future, and Koestler was one of the writers who most interested him. His interest in the project went beyond the commercial. Wherever in free countries there were Communists there were also voluble anti-Communists and ex-Communists, sometimes the same people. Among those quiet but principled anti-Communist intellectuals in Paris was Calmann-Lévy himself.

Even before the end of the war, Allen Lane at Penguin Books had made arrangements for a paperback edition of *Darkness at Noon*. Soon after the liberation, Calmann-Lévy negotiated the French-language rights to this edition, commissioned a translation, and awaited it with impatience during the months of the war's end and its immediate aftermath. At the very end of 1945, almost exactly five years after its first English publication in London, *Le Zéro et l'infini* appeared in Paris.

Whatever spiritual struggles or political battles might face a French publisher of the immediate postwar period were exacerbated by a problem wholly practical and material: there was a chronic shortage of suitable

---

* Martine Poulain, "A Cold War Best-Seller: The Reaction to Arthur Koestler's *Darkness at Noon* in France from 1945 to 1950," in the journal *Libraries and Culture*, 36 (2001): 172–184. The publication statistics cited come from this essay.

printing paper. Anyone who has worked with the printed documents of the period is familiar with the little piles of dusty confetti that are the unavoidable residue of consulting books perhaps immortal in their aspirations but printed on an acidic pulp paper as humble as newsprint, and now as brown and brittle as the shattered leaves of the Sibyl.

The effects of the paper shortage on the huge publication of *Le Zéro et l'infini*—more than 300,000 copies were sold in France between 1945 and 1948, according to Poulain—were complex. The publishers were able to reprint only on a somewhat arbitrary and opportunistic basis. Successive early runs—an initial 20,000, then 44,000 more, then 30,000, then 20,000 more—sold out in short order, sometimes in a single day. A phenomenon later made familiar in the planned economies of Eastern Europe now came into play—you first joined the forming queue, and only later learned what it was you were queuing to buy. Consumers bought not what they wanted when they wanted it but whatever they could get whenever they could get it. Calmann-Lévy bought paper when he could, and his customers bought his books when they could. Parisian purchasers of *Le Zéro et l'infini* knew what they were buying, of course, but they might not know when or even if they would have another chance. The book was an attack on totalitarian Communism, not an encomium of the free market. But the free market took care of itself in its dramatic demonstration that the law of supply and demand still operated. *Le Zéro et l'infini* became a very hot item on the black market, commanding sums far in excess of its list price.

Though in fact it was already five years old, practically nobody in France knew anything about the earlier English edition, and readers greeted the book as newborn. After all, it took up world events of 1938, just before the lights went out. It was as though power had returned after a prolonged electrical outage.

Jacques Fauvet gave a subtitle to the second volume of his history of the French Communist Party, the one dealing with the period from 1939 to 1965. He called it *Twenty-Five Years of Drama*. Drama there was aplenty, as French Communist policy bobbed about in the wake of the great Soviet ship of state. It is an ill wind that blows no good. The French Communists, comparatively feeble in the 1930s, had emerged from the war with a greatly heightened prestige based largely on their reputation as the "heart of the Resistance." Their numbers grew rapidly and the number of votes they could attract in elections even more rapidly. Their strategy in the immediate postwar period was one of cooperation and collaboration with other "progressives" in the spirit of the old anti-Fascist "Popular Front." The party continued to hold out its "open hand" to Catholics.

If this policy seemed good for the Communists, it seemed also good to General de Gaulle, whose political hopes depended upon an ecumenical coalition of all the forces that had found unity in a common opposition to the German occupation. Charles de Gaulle cooperated in the rehabilitation of the Communist leader, Maurice Thorez, who had fled to Moscow and been condemned as a traitor *in absentia*. Though de Gaulle refused the Communist demand for one of the major cabinet posts in his government of 1945, there were no fewer than five Communists in lesser positions. Relations were to all appearances semi-amicable. The party now commanded something approaching a third of the French electorate. By the beginning of 1947 there was a Communist minister of defense! But all that changed a few months later when, in circumstances described more fully in a later section, the Socialist premier Ramadier expelled the Communists from his government.

Now the French Communist Party took an openly adversarial stance consistent with the "Zhdanov doctrine,"* announced in 1946, which divided the world into two camps: peace-loving democrats and war-mongering imperialists. In September 1947, Zhdanov made a second speech. Now he held another war to be inevitable, and he announced the formation of the Kominform, the reincarnation of the old Comintern that Stalin had abolished during the war as a gesture to his capitalist allies. "The further we get from the end of the War, the clearer become the two principal tendencies of postwar international politics. . . . The United States is the principal force leading the imperialist camp. . . . Anti-imperialists and anti-fascists form the other camp. The USSR and the new democratic countries are its foundation." The "new democratic countries" were of course what anti-Communists called "the enslaved nations of Eastern Europe." Zhdanov also scolded the Communist parties of France and Italy for their earlier footling flirtations with the bourgeoisie. The left-wing reception of *Le Zéro et l'infini* in general reflected the trajectory of the rapidly shifting

---

* Andrei Zhdanov (1896–1948) was one of Stalin's most powerful lieutenants and the father-in-law of his daughter Svetlana. At various times he had been charged with the defense of Leningrad, with the formulation and enforcement of Soviet cultural policy, and with the articulation of the doctrine ("Zhdanovism"), according to which the world was divided into two irreconcilable camps, the one democratic and socialist, the other capitalist and war-mongering. Hence, for the West, Zhdanov became the voice of the "hard-line" Kremlin orthodoxy of the early Cold War.

political scene into which it was thrust—roughly from a reluctant coexistence to a frank confrontation.

EARLY SKIRMISHES OF A LITERARY WAR

The reviews in the "bourgeois" press were almost all highly positive, and many were extravagant in their praise. The review in *Le Figaro* (February 9, 1946) was highly laudatory, but it makes for odd reading today because it treats Koestler's book as what it is, a work of imaginative fiction. It fully recognizes the important political themes, but it expends its efforts in discussing formal and literary matters, such as character and psychological mood. It does not treat it as political argument pure and simple. Even the early left-wing reviews were comparatively respectful. That *Le Zéro* was anti-something was apparent. That it was anti-Communist had to be determined by the Communists themselves, and they were at first somewhat equivocal in coming up with a line. Robert Calmann-Lévy noted with surprise the balanced tone of the review in *Les Lettres françaises*. The Communist takeover of that journal was not yet complete, but it was nonetheless the literary voice of the far left. It was still possible for reputable leftists to read the book from a "Rubashovian" perspective and to take Koestler for some kind of Trotskyite—that is, a Marxist revolutionary who happened to be anti-Stalinist. (Such a perception, indeed, would have approached accuracy.) The initial instinct of the left-wing press may have been to ignore the book as something unworthy of notice. Then, instead of direct confrontation with the book, there was a small flurry of scorn directed at the "bourgeois" organs, such as the *Figaro*, that had printed positive notices.

But in the Communist *Action*, Claude Roy gave an adumbration of things to come: namely, an attack on the *historical inappropriateness* of the book. "In this book written in 1939 and published in 1940, it could be said that there is no national-socialist menace, no Wehrmacht, that Munich had never been, that Mussolini was never born, that Hitler is inconceivable, that Soviet Russia reigns without peril, alone in the world, its existence concerning only itself."

It would be very hard indeed to miss either Hitler or Mussolini in Koestler's book, though it is true neither is mentioned by name. Yet Roy's point is unassailable, granted the peculiar Communist point of view. This held that the defeat of the Axis powers and the destruction of Hitler and Mussolini had only *increased,* by masking it, the Fascist threat in the world, which was indeed so current and so acute as to render obsolete and probably obscene any qualifications whatsoever about any possible minor discomforts of Soviet history. Roy's obscure phrase about Soviet Russia reigning without peril, "its existence concerning only itself," makes sense if one believes that Soviet Russia is the sole guarantor of safety in a world actively threatened by the successors of the Third Reich. Still, there was no personal invective or explicit charge of fraud or treason.

Just as the book itself appeared as it were incrementally on the public stage, by the fits and starts determined by the paper supply, so also did a kind of running literary skirmish grow in intensity. The organized Communist attack on Koestler came only when the Party had absorbed a second blow, that from *The Yogi and the Commissar,* the French version of which also appeared in late 1945. The anti-Communism of its powerful essays was not oblique or novelistic. Koestler debunked the "Stalingrad syndrome"— the idea popular among Western leftists that the Russians had won a nearly supernatural victory at Stalingrad not on the basis of actual military realities but through the unique inspiration of their love of Communism. He ridiculed the "fifth column" interpretation of the Purge Trials. Most painful of all, perhaps was his diagnosis of the psychological pathologies that allowed Western Communists and fellow travelers to maintain their "belief." A kind of morbid fascination with the creedal mechanisms of their abandoned political commitments might be said to be typical among ex-Communist writers. A metaphoric, political meaning seems now to be the primary sense of the French word *aveuglement,* blindness.

Much cruder forms of personal abuse were by no means lacking. Pierre Courtade, a Communist writer of talent constrained by his vocation of hack's hack, attacked Koestler violently on January 31, 1947. Courtade spearheaded a campaign of long duration to convict Koestler of a scabrous anti-French prejudice. (The Communists presented themselves as *the* French patriots par excellence, and the defenders of French culture.) Apart from that, Koestler had associated himself with the *Carrefour Paris,* a bourgeois publication that the far left loved to hate. Courtade's essay—which is called "The Venus of the *Carrefour*"—is full of odd sexual imagery. Koestler has set out "to conquer with a single stroke the battalions of French neo-fascism, who have just rushed to associate themselves with that little band who daily masturbate their brains over his analytical review of the Moscow trials. People have sometimes smiled at the expression 'Hitlero-Trotskyite.' Read *Carrefour*, and you'll now know what it means. . . ."

In the February 1946 issue of the *Cahiers du communisme* there appeared an article entitled "A Dangerous Weapon of Anti-Communism" by Jean Gacon. (The dangerous weapon was, of course, Koestler's novel.) An editor's note introduces Koestler to the journal's readers: "M. Koestler is the type of the adventurer and provocateur. Born in Hungary of German parents, he has obtained British citizenship on condition that he do his best to impede the spread of democracy in his native country. When his role of provocateur was discovered, he was forced to leave the Hungarian Communist Party. He also reneged on his Jewish origins to join forces with the anti-semites and pogromistes. . . ."

This analysis demonstrates rather more than Communist spleen and prevarication. The slur against the British government is also revealing. Britain's prewar alliance with France had in theory been renewed. In practice, relations were touchy in the extreme. In British popular opinion, France was a nation of poltroons who had collapsed before Hitler in ten days. The French had their own resentments, acknowledged and unacknowledged. The scuttling of the French fleet, the endless humiliations of de Gaulle in his British exile, a hundred other wounds, pained their *amour propre*. The French Communists were particularly aggrieved. Churchill regarded their Party as a "fifth column" and didn't mince words about it. They, in turn, rarely spoke of "the English" or "the British"; the preferred appellation was "the Anglo-Saxons," a term that linked them with the despised Americans and dismissed their claim to be Europeans. It was widely rumored in the Communist press that the British foreign minister, Ernest Bevin, had subsidized the publication of *Le Zéro* in France. So far as I know, this was a rumor without foundation, though certainly Bevin, as a most rare specimen of an actual proletarian Socialist of international eminence, was interested in the book's "message."

Roger Garaudy, a Communist deputy in the National Assembly and all-purpose intellectual gadfly, wrote a pamphlet attacking the three superstars of French letters at the time—Jean-Paul Sartre, François Mauriac, and André Malraux—and threw in Arthur Koestler for good measure. The American Communist Party thought it worthy of translation and brought it out under the title *Literature of the Graveyard* (1948). The attack on Koestler entitled "The Lie in its Pure State" is particularly crude. Koestler suggests that Rubashov was innocent of the charges against him, but everybody knows that the Moscow defendants were guilty. Did not the American ambassador, Davies, explain that the trials were Stalin's means of ridding his land of a fifth column of potential traitors? And did not Bukharin himself not merely confess his guilt but actually praise Stalin while doing so?

Saint Augustine, greatest of the exegetes, stated as an interpretive rule that a sacred author never said anything in a figurative, allegorical, or oblique manner that was not elsewhere to be found in the Scriptures in plain and open language. This principle is useful, *mutatis mutandis*, for certain secular authors as well, including Arthur Koestler. He was a prolific writer who left a large body of work, a good deal of it explicitly political journalism. His autobiographies (or autobiography in many parts) deal extensively with his engagement with Communism. In the essays of *The Yogi and the Commissar* he takes a very direct approach to questions raised sometimes obliquely in the musings and browbeatings of Nicholas Rubashov. His luminous contribution to *The God That Failed* is justly regarded as a modern masterpiece of the confessional mode. All of these works, and many more, can be helpful guides to today's reader of *Darkness at Noon*, but they are mostly after-the-fact. They were unavailable to the readers of 1940 and 1941—which is one of the reasons for the extraordinary delayed reaction to the book, to which we must next turn.

What They Believed

The history of our times has moved very rapidly, and it may require an act of the sympathetic historical imagination to approach some events even in living memory. To appreciate the nature of the French debate about Koestler's novel requires the reconstruction of some modes of thought nearly vanished from the earth. There is a very large body of autobiography and memoir written by former Communists, and in it the psychological mechanism of *belief* is often a prominent topic. In this literature the Communist "belief system" is very frequently compared with the "belief systems" of organized religions. Koestler himself made important contributions to such discussion. The most famous anthology of essays by ex-Communists explicitly writing about their political evolution is called *The God That Failed*. Douglas Hyde, a British journalist who was one of several thoughtful and idealistic Communists who moved from Communism to Roman Catholicism, entitled his memoir of his Communist life simply *I Believed* (1950).

Even though the words get muddled in our daily usage, "belief" is not the same thing as "opinion." We all have opinions, perhaps even strongly held or dogmatic opinions. But that "two plus two make four" or that "on the third day He arose again according to the Scriptures" are not opinions. They are beliefs—the one of nearly universal credit, the other of more limited credit, but beliefs. It is important to try to understand what Western Communists of the postwar period believed, for it was on the basis of belief that they acted and wrote.

They believed that capitalism was immoral, indeed criminal, in its "exploitation of man by man." From its very nature capitalism was the cause of conflict, slavery, oppression, and human misery of every kind. The remedy was for them as certain as was the nature of the pathology and its diagnosis. The remedy was "socialism." Just as in the seventeenth century Isaac Newton had for the first time in human history understood and explained the laws of the physical world, so also for the first time in human history had Karl Marx understood and explained the laws of the social world. "Nature, and Nature's laws, lay hid in night," wrote Alexander Pope. "God said, *Let Newton be!* and all was light." The Marxists did not believe in God, in fact vigorously disbelieved in God; but they believed that History had brought forth Karl Marx, and that Marx had explained it "all."

In a very famous formulation, Marx had written: "The philosophers have only *interpreted* the world in various ways; the point is to *change* it." Lenin had, through the Russian Revolution, translated theoretical understanding into practice. He had changed the world. Joseph Stalin, the current and charismatic leader of "the socialist sixth of the globe," was continuing the historical mission of Marx and Lenin. He was going to change the world even more.

Such were the foundational beliefs of French Communists around 1945, and to them must be added a number of subsidiary or local beliefs. They believed that French Communism had been the only effective opposition to the Nazi occupation, and that the struggles that the Party now faced were a continuation of their successful anti-Fascism. They believed that the Red Army had defeated Hitler and that the United States and Britain, having been sluggish and unreliable allies, had then rushed into Germany with Nazi collusion to claim far more than the modest spoils justly theirs. They believed that the USSR was a shining beacon, and the harbinger of socialism in the world. They believed the Western democracies were rotten to the core. They believed that the Sovietization of Eastern Europe was the historical equivalent of proletarian revolution, and that it was bringing the blessings of socialism to millions. Imperialist forces, headed by the United States, were actively preparing to initiate a war against the Soviet Union. Their body of belief thus embraced historical truth, historical falsehood, and much debatable opinion, but it provided a firm grounding for actions and attitudes that, peculiar though they might seem to outsiders, were from the Communists' point of view coherent, principled, and moral.

A feature of exclusive belief—perhaps a necessary feature—is to criminalize non-belief or wrong belief. In the Christian Church, this was done in the opening lines of one of the important creedal statements, the Athanasian Creed: "Whosoever will be saved, before all things it is necessary that he hold the Catholic faith, which faith except every one do keep whole and undefiled, without doubt he shall perish everlastingly."

In these circumstances belief itself is a virtue to be nourished, cultivated, and practiced like other virtues. Belief leads to more belief. "Lord, I believe. Help Thou my unbelief!" The examination of midcentury French Communism—or rather, Communisms, plural, as one has come to speak of Catholicisms or masculinities, plural—is now a large scholarly undertaking. Some of the autobiographical literature—such as Dominique Desanti's *Les Staliniens* (1975)—is particularly helpful in recapturing the vanished mind-set that confronted *Le Zéro*. Among the literally dozens of memoirs of ex-Communists of the period, several speak more or less explicitly of the conflicts and psychology of their Communist belief in terms that, were the subject religion rather than politics, one might call "spiritual exercises."

There are two French phrases that take on a special significance in the literature of political casuistry: *for intérieure* and *remise de soi*. The obsolete word *for* meant a judicial tribunal. In modern French, *for intérieure* means "conscience" or "heart of hearts," that inmost place where in reflection you hold yourself accountable. There is no English equivalent of *remise de soi*. It means something like the "reduction of self," or the principled submission of individual judgment or belief to the authority of the collective of the Communist Party. The parallel with the demands of religious orthodoxy is nearly exact. Was Karl Radek guilty as charged in 1938, or Laszlo Rajk in 1949? How to move from a judgment of possibility or plausibility to certain conviction? The necessity to discipline the *for intérieure* with the *remise de soi* was frequent amid the sometimes high-speed alterations of the Party line.

Another way of describing the *remise de soi* is as a kind of self-censorship or voluntary ignorance. Communist intellectuals were often quite literally ignorant of challenging or opposing points of view, since by the self-censorship of the *remise de soi* they would not read them. Whittaker Chambers tells us that he was actually *afraid* to read an anti-Soviet book that had fallen into his hands. There was among Communists a large pamphlet literature which allowed its readers off-the-rack refutations of anti-Communist arguments with which they were unfamiliar from any primary source. This was of the genre of booklets I have seen in some Catholic parish churches offering aid in "what to say when your friends ask you about *The Da Vinci Code*." True believers held that criticism of the Soviet Union could be ruled illegitimate on two grounds: it was against history, and it was an incitement to war. In their view, criticism of the Soviet Union was actually conspiratorial. One of the most widely read books among French Communists of the forties was a translation of *The Great Conspiracy: The Secret War Against the Soviet Union*. This book, armed with an impressive-looking apparatus of learned notes, was the work of two Americans, Michael Sayers and Albert E. Kahn. Its title tells its tale. We shall meet this pseudoscholarly work, which Sidney Hook once dismissed as "plain propaganda," in upcoming sections. In the episode of *Le Zéro*, it was repeatedly invoked by adversaries who argued that Koestler's novel was just one element in a concerted conspiracy of untruths about Russia. So far as *Le Zéro* was concerned, the conspiracy worked in an opposite direction, with a great deal of boilerplate rhetoric issuing from central headquarters. The volume of attack was huge. In the scholarly bibliography of "Koestler studies," a surprisingly large number of the items date from this controversy.

French intellectuals! Their immense contribution to the way we think, or at least to what we talk about at cocktail parties, is staggering. French intellectuals make up a kind of guild, and an ancient one at that. It is with justice that contemporary French intellectuals consider themselves matriculated in a direct and continuing conversation that goes back to Montesquieu and Babeuf, Ernst Renan and Marc Bloch. All American imitations of the guild—such as the "New York Intellectuals" of the thirties and forties, or the think tank cultures and Sunday round tables of today—are simply that: imitations, pale ones.

French intellectuals have been rewarded for their enormous contributions to our literature with a significant literature devoted to *them*. But to the degree that this literature focuses on politics, it may be problematical. "The past is never dead," Faulkner famously said. "In fact, it's not even past." Certainly, there is a vivacity in the current historiography of twentieth-century Communism. Some of our history of old political struggles is not content with description. It chooses to reenact the battles. All historians have a point of view, but history actually founded in distortion and erasure is, to say the least, suspect.* There are at least a dozen good books devoted to French intellectuals of the twentieth century. The best in English is Tony Judt's *Past Imperfect* (1992). Judt's scholarship is meticulous, but his title does of course announce a certain point of view. It suggests a certain imperfection in the historical record of French intellectuals when it came to recognizing and addressing the political realities of postwar Europe. In particular, there was a kind of generalized intellectual myopia in their assessment of the realities of Soviet society and the intentions of Soviet foreign policy. The nature of the attack on Arthur Koestler is one small evidence of that myopia.

KOESTLER AMONG THE FRENCH INTELLECTUALS

French culture, which can treat its intellectuals like rock stars, may seem attractive to marginalized American college professors. But along with the respectful adulation went a line of gossip not unlike that of the fan

---

* Thus a book about the historiography of American Communism by two leading experts in the field is entitled *In Denial*—the reference being to the stance taken by certain contemporary left-wing historians. In France there is a similar book entitled *Du Passé faisons une table rase!: Histoire et mémoire du Communisme en Europe* (*Let Us Make a Blank Slate of the Past: The History and Memory of Communism in Europe*), a quotation of a line from the French text of the *Internationale*, meaning that the Revolution will erase all previous history. This book was put together by the principal editor of *The Black Book of Communism*.

magazines or supermarket tabloids. There was a great deal of chatter about who was in and who out, who was or was not welcome in the pages of *Les Temps modernes*, who was or was not speaking to whom. The tone was anything but blithe or lighthearted. The intense nastiness of religious debate in earlier periods had a name. It was called *odium theologicum*— hatred of the divines. The old *odium theologicum* was transferred from the old theologians to the new ones, the political theorists. The friendly difference of opinion scarcely existed in these circles—not when the stakes were transcendental in importance. Serious political disagreement was dramatic and violent, and invoked a vocabulary of drama and of violence. There were intellectual "preludes" and "denouements." There were literary "attacks" and "counterattacks." One of the leading journals was called simply *Combat*. Former friends and colleagues didn't have a parting of the ways. They *broke*. Breaks were of several kinds—initial, partial, complete, and definitive. Sartre broke with Camus, initially, then definitively. Sartre and Merleau-Ponty had together edited a journal of great intellectual authority and influence. They broke.

"The Yogi and the Commissar" was published as an independent essay in the journal *Horizon*, in London, in June 1942. Koestler put it into a book with some other essays, some old and some new, and published the collection under the same title in 1945. By that time, immersed in an English setting, he had nearly perfected the fluid and powerful English style that characterizes his later work. The book of essays appeared in its French version in Paris at the end of that year, just about the same time as *Le Zéro*. The title essay is highly literary and playful, though its political aim is entirely serious. The "Yogi" and the "Commissar" exemplify two very different ways of thinking about the world.

The Commissar, who is of course a Marxist, naturally thinks about *changing* the world: "The Commissar believes in Change from Without. He believes that all the pests of humanity, including constipation and the Oedipus complex, can and will be cured by Revolution, that is, by a radical reorganization of the system of production and distribution of goods; that this end justifies the use of all means, including violence, ruse, treachery and poison; that logical reasoning is an unfailing compass and the Universe a kind of very large clockwork in which a very large number of electrons once set in motion will forever revolve in their predictable orbits; and that whosoever believes in anything else is an escapist."

The Yogi, on the other hand, "has no objection to calling the universe a clockwork, but he thinks that it could be called, with about the same amount of truth, a music-box or a fishpond. He believes that the End is unpredictable and that the Means alone count. He rejects violence under any circumstances. He believes that logical reasoning gradually loses its compass value as the mind approaches the magnetic pole of Truth or the Absolute, which alone matters. He believes that nothing can be improved by exterior organization and everything by the individual effort from within; and that whoever believes anything else is an escapist."

These brief excerpts do justice to Koestler's main thesis, though not to the elegance and range of the whole essay. In their sprightly irreverence—seen from another point of view as triviality or even blasphemy—they also suggest what most threatened and infuriated his Communist readers. In another longer, much more sober essay ("Soviet Myth and Reality"), Koestler turns his attention from theory to practice—the actual social and political practice of the USSR. There is a shorter supplement to this essay called "The End of an Illusion." It begins thus: "Soviet Russia is a State-capitalistic totalitarian autocracy. It is progressive in its economic structure and regressive in every other respect. Politically, culturally, in the relations between rulers and ruled, it is reactionary compared with most capitalist democracies. It pursues an expansionist policy which, though operating with new methods, reflects the old historic aims of Imperial Russia." That was quite a lot to say in 1945, but he added a further sentence virtually designed to infuriate French Communists: "To the working classes and the progressive forces in other parts of the world Russia has no more special significance than any other great Power."

Few noticed that Koestler was still speaking as a socialist. Russia "is progressive in its economic structure." The sting of his final sentence erased whatever left-wing *bona fides* might be his due. For it was near dogma not merely for Communists but for almost the entire French left that the USSR was exceptional, unique, and priceless. The first law of the revolutionary must be to defend at all costs the unique home of the Revolution. The image was that of parturition. The Soviet Union was like a pregnant woman, soon to give birth to utopian socialism. She must be nourished, protected, coddled. She was also to be forgiven any temporary peevishness, such as the suppression of civil liberties, for instance, or eccentricity of appetites, as for pickles and ice cream, for example. To carp about such details was, according to Merleau-Ponty, "propaganda" that ignored a necessary "context." The intellectuals' investment in the USSR was enormous and improvident. In time, it would lead to intellectual bankruptcy.

Maurice Merleau-Ponty (1908–1961) was a brilliant academic philosopher whose influence is still lively in several fields. He was a phenomenologist—meaning that his philosophical work centered on the nature and mechanisms of perception in a way that involved both hard science, in physiology and psychology, and theoretical speculation.

He was never a member of the Communist Party, which indeed he sometimes criticized both implicitly and explicitly. But he was a serious Marxist, and although he never surrendered his intellectual independence, there was no qualification in his commitment to the "proletarian revolution." In late 1945—just a few weeks before the publication of *Le Zéro*—he and Jean-Paul Sartre founded *Les Temps modernes*, perhaps the premier "thought" journal within a wide and distinguished field. Merleau-Ponty was, specifically, the journal's "political editor" until his resignation in 1952 over what he called Sartre's "ultra-Bolshevism." His book *Humanism and Terror: An Essay on the Communist Problem* (1947) was in one sense a monument to his role at *Les Temps modernes*. In a more important sense, the "essay" was an attempt to refute and check the obviously burgeoning influence of two books by Arthur Koestler: *Darkness at Noon* and *The Yogi and the Commissar.*

To read *Darkness at Noon* today may require a refresher course in European history of the late 1930s; but once a little "background" is in place, the book is as profound and stimulating as it was on the day it was published. *Humanism and Terror,* on the other hand, has been so overwhelmed by history that it takes a strenuous effort to appreciate its many good qualities. Merleau-Ponty is an altruist imbued with Marx's own longing for social justice and also with an explicit appreciation of Marx's ironic humanism—a quality by no means universally present in all his disciples. He was demanding a kind of even-handedness. Merleau-Ponty rather casually posits that "all regimes are criminal." And since there is no ethical distance between a judicial murder in Moscow and the lynching of a Negro in Louisiana, Western liberals like Koestler needed to abandon their "fundamental hypocrisy." The author made two pleas that seem as noble today as they did then. He added his voice to those who were calling for a European "third force" spiritually independent of the two great powers. That was at the time a fantasy, but a benign one. Merleau-Ponty was also advancing a plea for peace, and advancing it in terms obviously more examined and sincere than those of the worldwide Communist "peace offensive."

Merleau-Ponty's book is today regarded in some academic circles as an important contribution to "evolutionary Marxism." But Merleau-Ponty did not intend a work of high theory. He was aiming for a general audience; yet in terms of its ability to challenge Koestler in the middlebrow press, the book was a signal failure, as he himself almost immediately recognized. (The work began as a series of periodical essays, so that he was made aware of strong negative reactions even before the argument was complete.) Although one of its conclusions was that criticism of the Soviet Union was, in the totality of the circumstances, morally equivalent to an act of war, it was full of criticisms of the Soviet Union, which it claimed was weak and defensive. This infuriated the Communists and some of their friends.

The anti-Communists didn't like the book, either. Merleau-Ponty accused Koestler of being a very bad Marxist and of structuring his arguments around simplistic moral and political binaries (Yogi/Commissar; anti-vivisectionist ethics/vivisectionist ethics; etc.). That criticism, which has also been made by others, is by no means without force. But the remedial subtleties with which Merleau-Ponty sought to cure his patient struck most readers as worse than the illness. Since Koestler's subject was the Moscow Trials, he spent many pages talking about, or at least around them. Though Merleau-Ponty denied that he was "justifying" them, his "explaining" was not greatly different from that of Feuchtwanger a decade earlier. He held, for example, that Radek and Bukharin and the rest might have been "objectively innocent" yet "subjectively guilty." Koestler might have been a bad Marxist, but if so, he created two very good ones in Rubashov and his interrogator Ivanov, who in different ways embrace Merleau-Ponty's unity of "objective innocence" and "subjective guilt." So Merleau-Ponty, who set out to create a philosophical "third way," ended instead falling between two stools. One of the larger ironies of the attack on *Le Zéro* was that in attempting to demolish it, so many of its pro-Communist critics seemed to be exemplifying in "real life" the patterns of its fictional double-think.

His own argument is clogged with stark if selective binaries of a different sort. Merleau-Ponty the Marxist subscribed to the orthodox theories of the proletariat and its necessary role in a violent revolution. Hence his articulation of a distinction between "good" and "bad" violence. Good violence is violence tending toward socialism. Bad violence is the other kind. But though he was comfortable with two shades of violence, anti-Communism was another matter. Here there is no room for distinctions between legitimate and illegitimate. Koestler's essays and the persecutions of the House Un-American Activities Committee came from the same bolt of cloth. Between insisting on distinctions that most of his readers could not see while denying those they could, he muddled his apologetic purpose. Though he claimed that there was no such thing as "pure" morality, that all morality had to be examined within its concrete historical circumstances, he repeatedly makes moral equivalencies that are difficult to maintain except in the "purest" of ethical forms or by accepting a very dubious Marxist analysis. It is true that one and a thousand are "equivalents" in the sense that they are both numbers. From other points of view they are very different.

One of the harder dialectical pills to swallow was the following comparison: "Within the U.S.S.R. violence and deception have official status while humanity is to be found in daily life. On the contrary, in democracies the principles are humane but deception and violence rule daily life." Here the famed author of *The Phenomenology of Perception* learned that many of his readers by no means shared his perceptions. What his contrast meant, according to one liberal reviewer, could be summarized thus: If I go into my corner shop in Dreux and purchase from a shop assistant working for wages a pint of milk which the shopowner is selling retail for three or four centimes more than he paid for it wholesale to the dairyman, I am experiencing deception and violence. Whereas if I go into a state shop in Tomsk, where there has been no milk for weeks, and am told with a wink by the state employee there that rumor has it there might be some milk next Thursday for those who can join the queue by five in the morning, then I have experienced humanity in daily life. "When it comes to dialectical materialism, most of us would prefer the material as the main course, with the dialectic for dessert."

There were literally dozens of "answers" to Koestler in the French press, most of which were formulaic in content and ephemeral in impact. Only two are weighty enough to examine here. The first was the thick pamphlet published by Roger Garaudy under the title *Littérature des fossoyeurs*

(*Gravediggers' Literature*). As we have seen, the American Communist Party thought it of sufficient significance to bring out an English translation (*Literature of the Graveyard*) in 1948.

Garaudy was a ubiquitous French Communist politician and intellectual gadfly with considerable skill as a writer. He was an idealistic seeker after truth, who briefly thought in his youth he had found it in Protestant Christianity before joining the Communist Party about the time of the rise of Hitler. At the time of the French publication of *Le Zéro* he was an elected deputy in the National Assembly.

Garaudy is not lacking in ambition or gall, depending upon how you view it. His pamphlet is a brief arraignment of four very famous and admired writers: Jean-Paul Sartre; François Mauriac; André Malraux; and Arthur Koestler. These writers are all "gravediggers," according to Garaudy, because they have turned their backs on "the joy of life" that the Communist future alone can bring. They wallow in pessimism or nihilism. Sartre is a "false prophet," unable to engage in his fiction with characters other than the deranged, the dissolute, or the disintegrating. Mauriac offers a brilliant picture of the moral obscenities of bourgeois life, but spoils it all by offering as a diagnosis feeble Catholic bromides rather than any sound class analysis. Malraux is a talented but hopelessly muddled moral relativist who fails to grasp the unique nobility of the Communists of whom he writes. Furthermore, a certain passage in his novel *Man's Hope* is a clear adumbration of Koestler. But Koestler is the worst of them all, for he is simply a liar.

From a certain perspective, Koestler would have had grounds for self-congratulation to have been included in such a group. To be called scum like Sartre, Malraux, or Mauriac is after all a humbling compliment. And he enjoys among them a certain unique distinction. Garaudy claims to be writing "in defense of French culture." His chief criticism of Sartre regards the *kind* of Frenchmen Sartre chooses to write about: degenerates sipping their alcohol in the cafés rather than bold youths in the Resistance. But Koestler's book is not about Frenchmen, nor was it even written in French. Garaudy has specially imported Koestler for his own abusive purpose.

And when compared with the quality of Garaudy's remarks about his three French writers, which while highly negative nonetheless have plausible connections with the work under discussion, the nature of the abuse heaped upon Koestler seems particularly coarse. The title of the brief chapter devoted to Koestler is "The Lie in its Pure State." The lie in its pure state concerns Rubashov's innocence of the charges to which he eventually confesses and for which he is shot. The Moscow defendants were, in fact, all guilty. For did not the darling of wishy-washy Westerners, Bukharin, confess to his own guilt? (So, one might point out, did Rubashov.) The other evidence adduced, equally preposterous, comes from Joseph Davies's *Mission to Moscow*, one of the most conspicuous literary monuments of American diplomatic naïveté.

Davies was a Roosevelt crony, and the head of his presidential campaign of 1936, to which Davies's heiress wife, it was hoped, might make substantial contributions. Roosevelt appointed him ambassador to the Soviet Union, and he was an eyewitness to some of the trials. Stalin is supposed to have said, "Europe will swallow the whole thing." So far as Davies was concerned, Stalin might have added "and America." Although he was not really a pro-Communist, he had a vested interest in justifying the Roosevelt pro-Soviet policy at a time when there was still grumbling from some Republicans about Roosevelt's diplomatic recognition of "the Reds." The distinguished diplomat Chip Bohlen, who was a junior officer in Moscow under Davies, later wrote that "Ambassador Davies was not noted for an acute understanding of the Soviet system, and he had an unfortunate tendency to take what was presented at the trial as the honest and gospel truth." Davies's ambassadorial memoir, *Mission to Moscow*, was a publishing success. It was the basis of the propaganda movie of the same name made during the war.

According to Davies, the larger meaning of the Moscow Trials was that Stalin was astutely cleaning house, purging his "administration" (as Davies called it) of his potential "fifth column." This was the reason that there were no Russian traitors or collaborators—as there had been in all the other countries invaded by Hitler. This was the first and irrefutable evidence that Garaudy cited against the "liar" Koestler, and he waxed indignant over other lies: "Nor does he shrink from tales of madmen when he coldly narrates the story of the thirty agronomists shot because they asserted that nitrates were superior to potash as fertilizers. Has anti-communism paralyzed the critical faculties to such an extent that these zoological forms of anti-Bolshevik hatred are accepted without the batting of an eye?"

The other proof came from the confession of Bukharin, and from the passage in it, already discussed earlier, which unquestionably does find a presence in *Darkness at Noon.* "I am explaining how I came to realize the necessity of capitulating to the investigating authorities and to you, Citizen Judges" (thus the transcript). "We came out against the joy of the new life with the most criminal methods of struggle." According to Garaudy, practically all of modern literature, whether in its pessimistic subject matter or in its aesthetic escapism, has come out against the joy of the new life. By the end, Garaudy's attack seems to achieve incoherence and approach within hailing distance of hysteria. "[Koestler's] articles blatantly reveal to us his ultimate aim: destruction of the Soviet Union, of communism, of democracy in general, and that of France in particular. His open contempt for our country fits in with the declaration of Field-Marshal Jan Smuts concerning France's irremediable decadence."

Garaudy's little book at first presents its subject as the state of contemporary *fiction*, and the novel in particular, but his mention of Koestler's articles shows that he regards *Le Zéro* and *The Yogi and the Commissar* as a continuous piece of work. That is, he erases altogether the fictional nature of *Darkness at Noon.* That is typical of the attacks on Koestler. Also formulaic was Garaudy's charge that, in contrast to the modulated subtleties of correct Marxist thought, Koestler's gross either-ors were puerile simplisms. The true Communist was *ni zéro ni l'infini*—neither nothing nor everything. This had become a catch phrase among French Communists, following the lead of a fellow-traveling Parisian bookseller who famously refused to sell the book. If asked for the book—as he and every other bookseller in France was continually—he would pretend that he thought he was being asked for two books, and would answer, "No, I have neither the *Zéro* nor the *Infini.*"

If such was the tone of a self-advertised blithe spirit of the Party, a man luxuriating in the anticipation of the joy of the new life, what could be expected of a real hard-core Stalinist, a dour Russian Bolshevik trapped in the body of a French banker? That would be Jean Kanapa, who served for many years as Commissar of Foreign Affairs in the Politburo of the French Communist Party, and who never departed from the Stalinist line even long after the death of Stalin and Khrushchev's speech denouncing him. Some indication of Kanapa's character and reputation are to be found in Dominique Desanti's *Les Staliniens.* He spent a good deal of time in Moscow, and a certain amount of time in Havana, where the proletarian revolution that seemed dormant elsewhere was active and vibrant.

Kanapa had the plenary credentials of an intellectual—meaning that in addition to a capacious intelligence, a broad education, and a mastery of the political dialect, he held the editorship of a journal. In this instance it was *La Nouvelle Critique*, with a wide readership, especially among Party members.

In 1950 he published *his* pamphlet, *Le Traître et le prolétaire, ou l'entreprise Arthur Koestler & Co. Ltd.* (*The Traitor and the Proletarian, or the Business of Arthur Koestler & Co. Ltd.*). It is instructive to note the date, which suggests that even after four years Koestler's books were still troubling the political waters. Nobody would have missed the dubious homage to the title of *The Yogi and the Commissar*, even had Kanapa omitted the specific name of Koestler, who was, obviously, the "Traitor." In the same way that "traitor" is perhaps a harsher word than "liar," Kanapa's essay is perhaps even more violent and *ad hominem* than Garaudy's. Apostasy from the Communist Party brought, if possible, even more reprobation than expulsion from the Party. Kanapa's pamphlet is also much less literary and much more "political." Garaudy's argument was dialectical materialism, but he was capable of the engaging literary flourish, as in his final line: "A good book is a book that teaches us how to live and how to die." Kanapa was much less poetic. A good book was a book that advanced the aims of the revolutionary working class. Kanapa was among French Communists a tough enforcer of the Party line. In this role he spoke frequently of the "ideological front" in which books were "tools" or "weapons." Except for the members of the choir to which he was preaching, however, *The Traitor and the Proletarian* seemed a dull and rusty old butcher's knife when set alongside the gleaming, razor-sharp scimitar that was *Le Zéro*. Nor was Kanapa alone in thinking of books as "weapons."

Of course Koestler gained powerfully effective political *friends* in Paris as well. Robert Calmann-Lévy and Koestler gradually became fast friends during the adventure of *Le Zéro et l'infini*, which was in different ways thrilling for them both. Koestler had such trust in the publisher that he gave him a kind of informal power-of-attorney for business matters. His other great Parisian friend and ally was Raymond Aron. One is tempted to write "the great" Aron—one of the finest and most influential public intellectuals of the twentieth century. In retrospect, it was Aron among all the political scribblers of the capital who had the sanest and most responsible understanding of the meaning of the conflict between Moscow and Washington, a struggle "in which peace is impossible but war improbable."

As the improbability of "hot"war was a major heresy, comparatively few people had spent much time thinking about to how to conduct a "cold" one. In the socialist camp, the "Zhdanov doctrine," both law and gospel, held war to be inevitable. This also was the view of many conservatives in the United States. In this view two fixed and immutable systems—the one "socialist," the other "capitalist"—were locked in an historically inevitable struggle. But in 1948, amidst the continuing drama of *Le Zéro et l'infini*, Aron published his brilliant and prophetic book *The Great Schism*, which, taking a pragmatic view expressed in a tone of moderation and reflection, predicted that the battle would most likely be determined on two fronts: the economic and the ideological. The decisive factor on the economic front was the Marshall Plan—in his opinion absurdly libeled by many leftists as "imperialist" but actually likely to produce in Western Europe levels of political independence, economic vigor, and personal prosperity against which the socialism of the East could inveigh but with which it could never compete.

What he meant by "ideological" was, in shorthand terms, meeting Soviet propaganda head-on. This meant on the one hand telling the truth about the actual conditions of life in the Soviet sphere, and on the other boldly confronting the "myths" around which "the intellectuals" organized their peculiar worldview. Karl Marx had famously called religion "the opium of the people." Aron was concerned to expose the cryptoreligious nature of the widespread belief in a socialist utopia. It was clear, he said, that "the intellectuals" could live without God. But could they live without "idols"? His masterpiece *The Opium of the Intellectuals* appeared only in the fifties, but already in *The Great Schism* he was busily delapidating the Heavenly City of the Parisian Communists. For Aron, Koestler's *Le Zéro et l'infini* was the very model of the kind of "ideological weapon" with which the Cold War—a battle of ideas and of "science"—would be fought and won.

Aron undertook a little ideological warfare himself. Whether this would better be called an offensive or defensive damage control would be hard to say. Unfortunately, Koestler could be and often was a rather beastly fellow. It is impossible to have an uncomplicated opinion about his personal morality and deportment. Unpleasant rumors about him spread immediately. But Aron was eager to show his better side. There is in the *Carrefour Paris*—one of the "bourgeois" papers Communist writers most loved to hate—under the date of October 17, 1946, a kind of gossip column about a recent party given in Koestler's honor at Raymond Aron's place. The author of this revealing piece of fluff signs himself "Le Magot Solitaire," the *magot* on his own. Witticisms that can be reclaimed from the tight grip of oblivion only with the aid of learned footnotes lose their sparkle, but this one is perhaps worthy of an attempt at explanation. A *magot* is among other things an imposing bibelot, a Chinese wooden or porcelain figurine. The café called the Deux Magots, originally named for two such tchotchkes that grace its interior, on the Boulevard Saint-Germain, was among the most famous artists' hangouts in the city. Here the greatest writers and painters of the first half of the twentieth century took refreshment, usually liquid. Gide, Janet Flanner, Hemingway, Malraux, Picasso—you name them, they had hung out at the Café des Deux Magots. For a time, before they had been driven away by an incipient army of fame-chasers, Sartre and de Beauvoir had made the place their social headquarters.

So the Solitary Magot is poking a little fun at the intellectually chic, creators of "the legend of Arthur Koestler." The legend of Arthur Koestler is that this newly arrived literary superstar is vain, haughty, and aloof, choosing to isolate himself in the bar of the Hôtel Pont-Royal, where he writes, rudely refusing communication from anyone who might dare approach his greatness, "even by telephone." But the Solitary Magot has just met Koestler and found him to be warm, approachable, modest, and very likable. "He is a man unfaithful to his legend, and a man one will not forget." He reports the following touching incident designed to counter the slander that Koestler was un-French or anti-French. The elderly Monsieur Calmann-Lévy, father of his publishers, was at the party. According to the Solitary Magot, "I saw M. Arthur Koestler, with emotion, place his hand on that of M. Calmann-Lévy, the father of Robert and Pierre, and say, 'He knew Emile Zola and Anatole France!'"

KOESTLER AND SARTRE

The iconic intellectual of the period, and probably of twentieth-century France, was the philosopher and writer Jean-Paul Sartre. His prestige was enormous. In its evidences of a broad national esteem, his funeral in 1980 was in some ways reminiscent of that of Victor Hugo in 1885. Sartre was not a Communist. He was not even during the period under consideration the hard-core fellow traveler he later became. He had had his share of abuse in the Communist press, which liked to link him with such bourgeois scum as the antinomian Camus or the Catholic Mauriac. But he held and acted upon several of the left-wing dogmas that Koestler's book was likely to disturb. Though he was not a systematic Marxist, he expressed many familiar Marxist ideas in a familiar Marxist language. These included the absolute necessity of socialism achieved through revolution by and in the name of the working class or "proletariat." The Soviet Union was the one place on earth where the socialist revolution had occurred, in however infantile and unfinished form, and the Soviet Union must be protected and nourished. The Soviet Union was on the side of History, the side of the Future. Anti-Communism might pretend to address certain infelicities and aberrations of the Stalin regime, but it was at bottom an attack on socialism itself, and as such inadmissible.

Koestler's colorful and stormy relations with Jean-Paul Sartre and Simone de Beauvoir have been documented by so many interested people, both principals and their seconds, and from so many points of view, that it is doubtless impossible to reconstruct their truth with any confidence. Koestler went to Paris in the autumn of 1946 and immediately presented his credentials at the Sartre–de Beauvoir *salon*. She had read his book, in its English version, before *Le Zéro* appeared, and she had praised it. De Beauvoir had a habit of reading and liking books, only later to discover that she was supposed *not* to like them. (She did something very similar with Kravchenko's *I Chose Freedom*). Koestler was at first welcomed warmly— so warmly that he and de Beauvoir fell into a drunken mini-fling, the retrospective embarrassment of which possibly explains why they later said such nasty things about each other in print. In her novel *The Mandarins*, de Beauvoir has a thinly disguised version of Koestler, who according to his biographer David Cesarani "represents the ex-Communist, anti-Soviet lobby which pressed Sartre to adopt either a pro-American stance or a neutralist, 'Third Force,' position."

Once again the circumstances of a precise moment may explain the puzzling nature of certain aspects of a relationship. Sartre was just at that moment achieving the superstar status in which he would bask for the next several decades. His play *Huis clos* was a huge success, and *Les Temps modernes* was rapidly becoming the indispensable trophy of the coffee tables of the progressive elite. Koestler was energized by a strong current of self-confidence. Put in less oblique terms, he was on an ego trip. He had now passed forty, and he was bent on "conquering" Paris and recapturing the vanished "paradise" of the prewar city. He discovered that in the circles into which he now plunged—a kind of intellectuals' supercollider—there was plenty of competing ego to brush up against.

Sartre immediately introduced Koestler to the other stars in his constellation, including Malraux and Camus. Koestler had his own friends in Paris, especially his fellow ex-Communist writer Manes Sperber, who has now fallen into an unjust neglect but for whom he always had the highest intellectual regard. For a brief time all, or some subgroup of them, held nightly seminars in the cafés, nightclubs, and dance halls in which Parisians were trying, sometimes desperately, to recapture a prewar gaiety amidst postwar exhaustion and privation. Koestler was being a bit of a self-conscious bad boy. They did a great deal of drinking. (This was still in the days when, in intellectual circles, alcohol abuse was regarded as a possible sign of talent and a probable requirement of genius.)

Koestler and Sartre seem genuinely to have liked each other. According to Koestler, Sartre several times offered him "unconditional friendship," using those very words. But Koestler had conditions, ones that very shortly turned out to be unacceptable to Sartre. Essentially, Koestler wanted to "convert" Sartre, and Sartre soon took a dim view of his political evangelism. The issue was anti-Communism. Sartre had by no means as yet entered his "ultra-Bolshevik" period, nor had he uttered his famous declaration that "Every anti-Communist is a dog." But he had an unshakable allegiance to "the working class," whose interests the Soviet Union served—perhaps imperfectly but nonetheless nobly. He was unwilling to engage in criticism that was not "even-handed," that seemed to single out the Soviets for some special disapprobation. Koestler took the point of view that it was difficult to be "even-handed" in discussing vast enterprises of slave labor, since the only one he knew of was in Soviet Russia. Koestler warned Sartre, perhaps pompously but also prophetically, that history would judge those who, at a crucial moment, would not condemn what deserved condemnation. That was also, of course, the view taken by Camus.

Sartre's attitude was very widely shared throughout the European—and even to some extent the American—left. It is easy to understand, but no longer very easy to justify, if indeed it ever was. His view was simply that Communism was, categorically, to be preferred to anti-Communism. To be silent about shortcomings in the Soviet system was to be preferred to speaking out in alliance with the despicable forces of reaction. For anti-Communism was always "objectively" reactionary. The Americans who harped on the want of civil liberties in the Soviet Union were not really interested in civil liberties, but in weakening or destroying socialism in the world's first "workers' state." To thwart or discourage the aspirations of "the working class" was a cardinal sin, in relation to which a well-chosen taciturnity was at most a small peccadillo.

There now seems to be some doubt as to whether Sartre ever actually articulated one of his most famous "quotations." He is supposed to have said that the reason to refrain from a vehement condemnation of the Soviet slave labor system—of which he and Merleau-Ponty were aware, though its existence was denied absolutely by French Communists—was that to do so might dishearten the auto workers: *Il ne faut pas désésperer Billancourt*, Billancourt being a Parisian suburb in which many Renault factory workers lived. A tactful silence concerning the gross malfeasance of states and their leaders is employed regularly in international diplomacy. The state always has reasons to trump commonplace ethics. The United Nations Organization could hardly operate without such silences. But for a great public intellectual and apostle of ethical "engagement" to adopt the sullied expediencies of the state was perhaps not wise from the long view of history. Koestler has been proved right. The darkest of the several shadows falling across Sartre's reputation today is his reluctance to condemn what deserved condemnation.

An intellectual can weather being embattled, scorned, detested, or perhaps even proved wrong; but an intellectual trembles at the prospect of being exposed as ridiculous. French Communist discourse of the early Cold War often fell into the narrow ditch separating the high serious from the terminally humorless. There is probably more sparkle and wit in the funeral orations of Bishop Bossuet than in any of the voluminous utterances of Maurice Thorez or Jacques Duclos. But there was something actually *funny* about the frenzy of the left-wing reaction to *Darkness at Noon*.

Some years ago, the French sculptor Jean-Louis Faure—whose works are perhaps a combination of Barbara Hepworth and Woody Allen—produced an extraordinary construction entitled *Jean-Paul Sartre and Simone de Beauvoir Refusing to Shake the Hand of Arthur Koestler*. Later, Pierre Pachet wrote a little book giving the historical background of this remarkable work of art. The book is entitled *The Stupidity of Intelligence* (*La Bêtise de l'intelligence*).

Arthur Koestler, his neck like those of the two others a column of bright metal tubing, stands enveloped in a long trench coat, his left hand in his pocket, his right hand beginning to reach out in greeting toward Sartre and de Beauvoir, who face him. Koestler wears a devilish, horned dark mask. Sliding out from the platform on which the construction is mounted is a thin panel with drawer pulls. On this panel is one of the more familiar and heroic Socialist-Realist portraits of the head of Joseph Stalin. The space housing this pull-out portrait separates the two figures. For though there are three people, there are only two bodies. The shared trunk of the lower bodies of the two intellectual eminences, suggesting a lockstep of political attitude, looks something like a barber's pole, though with colors of dark blue and dark green. When activated by a mechanical device, it revolves on its circular base so that Sartre and de Beauvoir turn their backs (and prominent rumps) toward Koestler.

There are some not entirely funny details. The visible body parts of the French couple approximate flesh tones, but those of Koestler—the part of the head left uncovered by the mask and the right hand in the process of being raised to shake hands—are a bright yellow, the color of the excluded or the untouchable, the color of the Tsarist passport for prostitutes and the Nazi star of David for Jews. (The "Jewish question" had been inserted into the anti-Koestler campaign by some Communists—though not so far as I know by Sartre—through a curious argument. *Darkness at Noon* was particularly insulting and ingrate since it was the Red Army that had rescued the Jew Koestler and had allowed the Jews Calmann-Lévy to operate their publishing house.)

The implicit condemnation of Koestler's Jewishness was ambivalent.

Whether too Jewish or insufficiently Jewish, there was something wrong with his Jewishness. In May 1946, the following item appeared in a Communist paper: "The Zionists at *Notre Patrie* have a great deal of admiration for Arthur Koestler, the author of the too famous *Le Zéro et l'Infini*. They are very proud to know that Koestler is a Jew. And they are very offended by the fact that 'no commentator on Koestler has mentioned his Jewish origins.' What's more they say that Rubashov, Koestler's hero, is a Jew-type.* Well, we say, first, Koestler's hero is, when you get right down to it, a traitor; and, second, Arthur Koestler, being a Trotskyist, serves the interests of reaction and Fascism . . . Reaction, treason, Fascism—this is death for the Jews."

Perennial Themes of *Darkness at Noon*

One learns a great deal about a book from careful and repeated readings. One learns also from what others have written, reviewers and literary critics, sometimes from the author in person, writing from a perspective detached in time or situation. But a single experience is unique in its depth: to teach a book over a period of many years in engaged discussion with bright undergraduates. In this context even the cultural deficit of a youthful generation is not without its benefits. Very few of today's students have heard of Bukharin or the Comintern; not all that many can identify Leon Trotsky. The Spanish Civil War has no particular meaning. The history that dominated discussion of *Darkness at Noon* in the 1940s, vivid and importunate, now needs to be filled in with a few oversimplifying footnotes. With many works of fiction this becomes a difficult and distracting problem.

It is hardly a problem at all with *Darkness at Noon*. That is because the moral questions it raises are enduring and profound. Any good book will offer an invitation to serious thought and discussion; a few great ones demand it on every page. It was this aspect of the book that guaranteed its powerful intervention in the French national political conversation of the immediate postwar years, and maintains its relevance today. Recall the form of the often-cited distinction advanced in the book. "There are only two conceptions of human ethics, and they are at opposite poles." The speaker

---

* In fact, Rubashov's Jewishness is a seldom noticed but significant detail signaled by a single and seemingly irrelevant mention of his patronymic.

is Ivanov, the first of Rubashov's interrogators. "One of them is Christian and humane, declares the individual to be sacrosanct, and asserts that the rules of arithmetic are not to be applied to human units. The other starts from the basic principle that a collective aim justifies all means, and not only allows, but demands, that the individual should in every way be subordinated and sacrificed to the community—which may dispose of it as an experimentation rabbit or a sacrificial lamb. The first conception could be called anti-vivisection morality, the second vivisection morality." (p. 157)

It is dubious, possibly absurd, that there are only two conceptions of human ethics; but the way Ivanov has posed the issue forces an immediate confrontation with the question of the relationship between ends and means. That is a question always raised by the audacity of revolution and the defense of its results. The famous journalist Walter Duranty, known in his day as "Stalin's man at the *New York Times*," famously addressed it with the apothegm, "You can't make an omelette without breaking eggs." Maurice Merleau-Ponty says the same thing, though at greater length and in serious philosophical language. In *Darkness at Noon*, the place is Moscow and the time 1938. But there are other places, other times. Koestler's book cannot be relevant for the Lubyanka prison or the old Fortress of Peter and Paul in Leningrad without also being relevant for the old naval base at Guantánamo Bay.

In Soviet Russia, the "organs" of state security underwent morphogenesis and an evolution of nomenclature along with evolution of size and power. What had been the Cheka became the GPU; the OGPU the NKVD, and then the KGB. The English translation of the abbreviation KGB is "Committee for State Security." In the United States, there is now a Department of Homeland Security. Between a Department of Homeland Security and a Committee for State Security there is little lexical distance. Koestler's novel poses a question about ethical distance.

In his final interview with Rubashov, which ends in the prisoner's capitulation, the inquisitor Gletkin seems more the lecturer than the interrogator. He reviews the history of the Party since the Revolution: its disappointment that Revolution was not greeted with international imitation but with international reaction; the tensions within the Party between an errant group of internationalists (Trotskyites) and the clearsighted leader who knew that the only correct path was the building of "Socialism in One Country." Gletkin does not use the word "homeland." His word is "bastion."

[Stalin] realized that everything depended on surviving the period of world reaction and keeping the bastion. He had realized that it might last ten, perhaps twenty, perhaps fifty years, until the world was ripe for a fresh wave of revolution. Until then we stand alone. Until then we have only one duty: not to perish. . . . The bulwark must be held, at any price and with any sacrifice. . . . The policy of the International had to be subordinated to our national policy. Whoever did not understand this necessity had to be destroyed. Whole sets of our best functionaries in Europe had to be physically liquidated. We did not recoil from crushing our own organizations abroad when the interests of the Bastion required it. We did not recoil from co-operation with the police of reactionary countries in order to suppress revolutionary movements which came at the wrong moment. We did not recoil from betraying our friends and compromising with our enemies, in order to preserve the Bastion. (p. 236)

In two or three pages of *Darkness at Noon* there is a plausible, coherent, comprehensive elucidation of a decade of Soviet history, including the mystifying public trials, that had baffled most of the world's "experts."

What if Lincoln had lived? The "what-ifs" of history are always imponderable, but some a little more ponderable than others. Arthur Koestler had been a committed revolutionary member of the *German* Communist Party. As he now looked back at history, he believed, with many others, that in the early 1930s a working coalition of German Communists and German Socialists could have blocked Hitler's rise to power. Instead Party policy, forged in Moscow, had been totally hostile to the Social Democrats. Indeed, the official slur used by German Communists for the Social Democrats was "Social Fascists." Koestler also believed, again in company with many others, that Stalin viewed Hitler's crushing of the German Communist Party with, to say no more, a rather muted sense of international socialist solidarity. Koestler had seen all this firsthand. "The Party was no longer a political organization," he wrote in the episode of Richard, the first of the flashbacks in *Darkness at Noon*; "it was nothing but a thousand-armed and thousand-headed mass of bleeding flesh." These are the circumstances under which Rubashov lectures to Richard: "The last congress of the Party stated in a resolution that the Party has not suffered a defeat and has merely carried out a strategic retreat; and that there is no reason whatever for changing its previous policy." (pp. 42–43)

Gletkin is a torturer. Rubashov knows he is a torturer, for he has seen the results of torture on the bodies of some of his fellow prisoners, including the young man Kieffer (Hare-Lip) who is his alleged co-conspirator. Rubashov knows also from Ivanov, his first interrogator—who he tardily learns has been shot by "administrative action" for his failure to produce the required results—that Gletkin has proposed using torture on him, too. "'I was told [says Rubashov to Gletkin] that you were a partisan of certain drastic methods—the so called "hard method." Why have you never used direct physical pressure on me?' 'You mean physical torture,' said Gletkin in a matter-of-fact tone. 'As you know, that is forbidden by our criminal code.'"

Obviously a regime that is prepared to do *anything* to preserve the Bastion is prepared both to torture and then to lie about its use of torture. In the next sentence, Gletkin demonstrates as much. But the decision to use physical torture or to refrain from it is to be made on a case-by-case basis, and on pragmatic rather than ethical grounds. ("There is a certain type of accused who confess under pressure, but recant at the public trial." They are to be shot in cellars without first parading them through the public court.) Furthermore, he is speaking truth when he says that torture was forbidden by statute. The Soviet Union had a written constitution, the famous Stalin Constitution of 1936. It was on the basis of this document that Ambassador Davies could declare the Soviet Union "the most democratic nation on earth." The theme of means and ends, already so capacious, is supplemented by another perhaps as vast: the theme of letter and spirit. The lawful state is not the state that has the most laws on the books, but the state that lives by the letter and the spirit of the laws it has.

KOESTLER'S TRILOGY: SOME CRITICISMS

Few readers of *Darkness at Noon* (1940) are aware that it is the centerpiece of a trilogy. It was preceded by *The Gladiators* (1939) and followed by *Arrival and Departure* (1943). This is a fact largely unobserved because largely unnecessary to our reading of the novel. But it was of considerable importance to Koestler, who mentions it frequently. These are two pretty good novels, but a pretty good novel is not a great or a brilliant novel, and they have been lost sight of in the dazzle of *Darkness at Noon*. Yet even the more modest successes are most useful in illuminating Koestler's larger design.

As thinker and writer, Koestler was drawn to large and consequential designs. That appetite had drawn him in his youth first to Zionism and then to Communism. Later it drew him to his lifelong engagement with science. The consequential design of the trilogy with which he began his career as a novelist was, in his formulation, "the examination of the relation between means and ends."

The subject of *The Gladiators* is the slave revolt led by Spartacus in classical Antiquity. Long before Koestler, this revolt was seen as a revolutionary prototype, and, in Communist circles, a prototype of the proletarian revolution. That is certainly how Koestler treated it. The connection was particularly articulate in Germany, where the Spartacist *Bund*, or brotherhood, had been a kind of precursor of the German Communist Party.

Howard Fast, an American Communist novelist, dealt with the same historical material in his *Spartacus*, the source of a popular American film. Indeed Fast, who remained a Party loyalist long after Koestler's defection, was perhaps attempting to "save" the historical Spartacus for more orthodox radical history. For Koestler had presented Spartacus as a man whose noble pragmatic purpose of human liberation had shipwrecked on the rocks of a utopian theory. It is hardly necessary to inquire what kind of theory he might have had in mind, but the specific form of utopianism in *The Gladiators* may strike the reader as more appropriate for science fiction than for socialist realism.

Arrival and Departure, which was the first Koestler book actually composed in English, is at least superficially more obviously "autobiographical." The novel's hero, Peter Slavek, is a young ex-Communist from somewhere in Central Europe. Like Rubashov, he is a hero of resistance. He was captured and tortured by Fascists without breaking, only later to find himself succumbing to something inward and obscure. Like Koestler, he has fled westward from Fascist oppression and reached Neutralia (!)—i.e., Portugal. Now he must decide whether to go to America, leaving Europe and its rottenness behind, or to join the British army and continue the fight against Nazis. That is the novel's external "problem." The inner problem is this. In intensive psychotherapy with a remorseless therapist, Slavek comes to see that the entire basis of his political idealism and personal heroism has been neurotic, an attempt to redress long-hidden guilts accrued in early childhood. Hence, to the troubled relationship between ends and means, Koestler adds the complication of integrity of motivation.

All three are "historical" novels, but for the reader the advantage of *Darkness at Noon* was clear. Most people had perhaps heard of Spartacus, but didn't know much about him. Readers of *The Gladiators* would be largely dependent upon Koestler's thin, underresearched Roman history for the "context." Readers of *Scum of the Earth* might see some of the easy external parallels between the recent biographies of Peter Slavek and Arthur Koestler, but again the parallels had little depth. On the other hand, everybody knew about the Purge Trials. They knew their motivation was at least a supposed mystery, though one perhaps not so great as the preposterous confessions of the defendants. The Purge Trials were a subject that had already to some extent split the European left, and had required of believing Communists an adherence to a brittle catechism sharply challenged by Koestler's book. Furthermore, in the second half of the forties, the challenge was one raised from the grave. The onset of the war in 1939, and more particularly Hitler's invasion of Russia in 1941, had granted a kind of intellectual amnesty to the more questionable aspects of Soviet policy in the late thirties. But now here came *Le Zéro* to raise the most fundamental doubts about the Soviet system precisely at the time French people were being told that the Soviet system alone held hope for mankind.

With too few exceptions, neither the book's admirers nor its detractors have let the book be a novel before it is a philosophical tract, but a novel it is, and in the old etymological sense. It brings *news*. It insists on the *story* that is in history. The reader who meets Rubashov on page 1 has little doubt what is to become of him on page 267; yet it is the kind of book one is likely to read at a single sitting, or perhaps two, impelled by a finely honed suspense and captured by a crafted desire to know what is to happen next. A very great deal happens considering that, for the most part, the reader is cooped up with the hero in a prison cell a few meters square.

Such "aesthetic" criticism as the book has received has seldom strayed far from the political or the cryptopolitical. *Darkness at Noon*, with its obvious sympathy for "Old" Bolshevik ideas, was hardly directed toward political conservatives, whom Koestler to his dying day usually called "reactionaries." It was addressed to the "left" very broadly conceived, and during the period of its most intense discussion in France Koestler had settled in, more or less comfortably, with the soft socialism of the British Labour Party, decolonization, and the welfare state. He formed a close friendship with Richard Crossman, one of the most eminent socialist intellectuals of postwar Britain, the editor of *The New Statesman* and of the essays in *The God That Failed*.

At least two impressive left-wing critics of *Darkness at Noon* do engage seriously with the book in a way that cannot easily be dismissed: the American Irving Howe and the Englishman John Strachey. Howe, one of the "New York Intellectuals" in capital letters, was a professor of literature who in 1957 published a book, *Politics and the Novel*, that enjoyed considerable authority in its time. Its chapter on Koestler's novel offers a mixed but on the whole negative judgment. Howe accuses Koestler of authorial manipulation, moral simplism, and the reduction of very complicated ideas and events to a predetermined and shallow formula. John O'Neill, introducing his translation of Merleau-Ponty's *Humanism and Terror*, echoes and summarizes Howe as follows: "Koestler's novel fails to come to grips with its central problem: to create characters who inhabit their own history and live through choices within it rather than to present characters who operate by means of simplistic moral alternatives, decided on before their story begins." But the judgment of a critic should be confronted with the judgment of a novelist. "Whatever single criticisms may be made of him," wrote Saul Bellow in a book review, "Arthur Koestler is one of the very few living novelists who attacks the most difficult and troubling issues of private and political morality and who, having raised serious questions, never tries to satisfy us with ready-made answers or evasions."

Very few readers have found *Darkness at Noon* "shallow," but the criticism cannot be refuted save by recourse to one's own reading experience. I find little difference in quality between Rubashov's "inhabited history" and that of Anna Karenina, Quentin Compson, Clyde Griffiths, or the central character of any other novel informed by some responsible sense of the relationship of individuals to history. Novels create characters, but they also create history. A fictional character who lives in "real" history is no more possible than a "real" person who lives in a fictional history. As for Rubashov, he repeatedly chooses. He chooses to serve the Central Committee. He chooses to persecute Richard. He chooses to allow Arlova to go to her death undefended. By the time we encounter him in the interrogation prison, his habitable space has been reduced to a few square meters and his moral alternatives rendered stark indeed. He perhaps can choose to live or to die, though it seems much more probable that his only choice will be the mood, within narrow parameters, in which he will in fact die. Even then he manages to engage and perhaps astonish us.

Howe's real complaint is that the Russian Revolution didn't turn out better than it did—a disappointment shared by millions, though seldom with his elegiac urgency. Howe saw the Russian Revolution as the central event of the twentieth century. "For a moment, one of the most fervent in all history, it stirred the hope among millions of people that mankind had at last begun to lift itself, however painfully, from the realm of necessity to the realm of freedom." But he continues, more morosely: "That hope, like the heroic phase of the revolution from which it sprang, did not long survive, and in the literature of our time there are few direct reflections of its original intensity." What Howe is saying in terms of literary production, I take it, is that there are no photographs of beaming bride and groom because divorce proceedings had begun even before the developed prints could be fetched from the shop. He can think of only two "direct reflections of its [the Revolution's] original intensity"—a phrase apparently meaning "glowing reports." Those two are John Reed's *Ten Days That Shook the World* and Trotsky's *History of the Russian Revolution*. John Reed died in 1920, before, as his friend Max Eastman put it, he had time to be disillusioned with Communism. Leon Trotsky, after a long persecution by the Revolution, was finally murdered by it in 1940.

The Golden Age of the October Revolution becomes ever briefer with each revision of Russian revolutionary history. For a while indulgent historians used to reckon that the honeymoon extended at least until the brutal suppression of the Kronstadt naval base mutiny in 1921. Now many suggest that there never was a honeymoon at all, merely a noisy, bibulous wedding reception, the essential horrors of "Stalinism," though of course not its manifold Linnaean varieties, having been present in the heart and mind of Lenin. The truly radical feature of *Darkness at Noon* is that it questions the legitimacy of the revolutionary ideal in and of itself. What precisely, if indeed anything at all, did the Bolshevik Revolution have to do with moving humanity "from the realm of necessity to the realm of freedom"? It is unpleasant to contemplate that the foundational ideas of the Russian Revolution could lead logically or even necessarily to the execution cellar in the Lubyanka. That does seem to be the conclusion at which Rubashov arrives.

Howe was a literary critic with an interest in left-wing politics. John Strachey (1901–1963), an even more impressive intellect, was a left-wing politician with an interest in literature. He was that kind of British socialist likely to have several Christian names (Evelyn John St Loe) and to have been educated in the lap of privilege (Eton and Oxford). He became an anti-Stalinist Marxist perched on the extreme left of the British Labour Party. He was for a time an MP and a Privy Councilor. He knew Koestler personally. The memory of Strachey has dimmed with the waning of his cause, but for much of the period dealt with in this book he was a prominent public intellectual, one of the animators of the influential Left Book Club (which had, incidentally, sponsored Koestler's books), and one of the mainstays of *The Spectator*. He had an American as well as a British following.

In 1962, Strachey published a remarkable book called *The Strangled Cry*—the "strangled cry" being, in effect, a lament for the lost socialist hopes of the 1930s. In it he has an essay on Koestler and Whittaker Chambers, who had by then joined Koestler in a competition for the prize for the world's most famous literary ex-Communist. Strachey makes no attempt to rescue Stalin or Soviet Communism. His central criticism of the two men is that they exemplify a retreat from pure rationality and a defection from the progressive line of thought born of the Enlightenment.

This is a very interesting argument, and with regard to Whittaker Chambers it seems eminently just. Chambers's *Witness* is at its core a conversion narrative and a religious *apologia*. But Strachey probably misses the mark with Koestler.

It is perhaps Koestler's invocation of an attractive "Christian and humane" ethics, together with several scriptural allusions and his prominent use of images from a sacred lexicon (such as the *Pietà*), that have misled some readers in the direction of an explicitly "religious" reading of *Darkness at Noon*. A surprising number of prominent Communist renegades did in fact convert or return to Roman Catholicism; some returned to Jewish religious obsevance. Koestler is by no means to be grouped among them. When he told Whittaker Chambers that there were parts of *Witness* he simply could not understand, he almost certainly alluded to its religious ideas. His own humanism derived from neither law nor gospel; it was the rich and indignant humanism of Karl Marx himself. He remained to the end of his life what he had been at least since his early youth: a Jew wholly secular, and a convinced materialist.

Yet to call him a materialist is insufficient, and this, perhaps, is what Strachey wanted to get at. When not long after the war Koestler made an (unkept) vow to write no more about "politics" and to concentrate thenceforth on "science," his materialist conception, always capacious, expanded yet more. He wrote several ambitious, risky books that attempted to expand the boundaries of the explicable world. These included *The Ghost in the Machine*, *The Roots of Coincidence*, and *The Creative Ac*t. They were by no means always applauded by real scientists. He might get a more sympathetic hearing today, for his agenda was compatible with some trends in contemporary neuroscience. He had a special contempt for the manner in which a commitment to Communism could and did compromise, in specific instances, the sacred objectivity of science. In *The Case of the Midwife Toad*, he examines a famous episode in the history of Soviet biology in which the dogma had taken precedence over the data, just as papal astronomy had once trumped the observations of Galileo. Koestler left a considerable sum of money in his will for the establishment of academic research in what was once called "parapsychology" or "extrasensory perception." In all this he was embracing, not fleeing, the Enlightenment. He was pursuing in his own modern and Marxist fashion what thinkers of the eighteenth century once thought of as "natural religion" and a famous scholar has called "natural supernaturalism." Such a thin transcendentalism could hardly be called an opiate. A truly committed materialist would have to regard it at worst as the marijuana, or perhaps the pep pills, of the intellectuals.

Despite such criticisms, *Darkness at Noon* is unlikely to be deconsecrated or decanonized by future cultural developments. Soviet Communism in the specific historical form known to Koestler has probably vanished, never to return, but the book's moral power is no more dependent on transient historical circumstance than is that of *Moby-Dick* on the briskness of trade in sperm-oil lamps. Secondly, the book is a "classic." Except in book jacket blurbs it is quite difficult for a book really to become a classic; and classical status, once achieved, is not easily lost. Koestler's novel has become, along with Orwell's *Animal Farm* and *1984*, one of the cultural indices of the Cold War.

By the end of 1947, a year of disasters for the French Communist Party, *Le Zéro* had already "won." The story was no longer the story of Rubashov, but the story of the impotent rage of French Communists. On

August 3, 1947, there appeared in the *France-Dimanche* a gossipy squib with the following lurid title: "For Having Betrayed Stalin, Three Men Are Being Hunted Down (Kravchenko, Koestler, Gouzenko)." It reads in part: "The publication in this country of the book in which the novelist Koestler paints the USSR in somber colors—*Le Zéro et l'infini*—has already resulted for its publishers in numerous pressures ranging from attempted persuasion to threat. The printing of another book by Koestler, *The Yogi and the Commissar*, was for a time suspended by the French government on the grounds of 'political awkwardness' [*inopportunisme politique*]. Koestler must constantly change his places of habitation and travel under false identities, with the aid of the police in major countries. . . ."

That is the kind of thing, true or untrue, likely to increase a book's sales. Most of it is in fact untrue. What is most interesting is that Koestler has now become the leader or symbolic representative of a band of literary Communist defectors which includes Victor Kravchenko, author of *I Chose Freedom* (1946), and Igor Gouzenko, the Russian intelligence technician whose defection exposed the Soviet "atom spies." Gouzenko had not yet published the book he was known to be writing (*This Was My Choice*, 1948), but the world awaited it eagerly. Gouzenko *was* hunted by NKVD agents, briefly. For a time Kravchenko *did* have to keep on the move, traveling with disguised identity. *France-Dimanche* has created and assigned to Arthur Koestler a kind of composite biography for the generic author of a now recognized genre: the anti-Communist manifesto. In this genre, *Darkness at Noon* could claim a preeminence and a scant temporal priority. Yet Koestler was by no means without colleagues, nor his book without competitors.

BEFORE ENTERING... know the truth

'DAS ISS GÜT, HERR VALTIN!'

BEWARE OF VALTIN'S POSE - HE IS NOT WHAT HE SEEMS.

"HITLER SANCTIONS "OUT OF THE NIGHT"
Hitler likes Valtin's book, because it is still
being read and liked by the Nazis (New York Times)

Jan Valtin maliciously and repeatedly slandered the
Jewish people in court where he was convicted of robbery.

JAN VALTIN, AN UNDESIRABLE ALIEN, IS SUBJECT TO DEPORTA-
TION BY THE DEPARTMENT OF JUSTICE. G. MEN CONSIDER
HIM A MENACE TO THE AMERICAN WAY OF LIFE.

Hearst and Valtin schemed up the promotion for "Out
of the Night" Hearst is a notorious reactionary.

ALL COMPETENT AUTHORITIES RIDICULE VALTIN'S AUTO-
BIOGRAPHY AS AN OBVIOUS FAKE.

On some occasions, American Communists picketed Jan Valtin's lectures. This crudely mimeographed sheet was distributed among the audience at one of his numerous appearances in Chicago in November 1941. The Communists had still not fixed their line concerning Valtin's book, so they attributed it to the nearly supernatural evil powers of their default villain, William Randolph Hearst. The actual geniuses behind the book's promotion were Henry Koppell and Isaac Don Levine. [Reproduced from the Levine Papers with the permission of the Emory University Library.]

Life Magazine's unprecedented two-part preview of *Out of the Night* achieved both vast publicity for the book and a teasing mystification concerning its author. The caption to this photo in the first installment (February 24, 1941) read: "Jan Valtin, author of 'Out of the Night,' plays with his 200-lb watchdog. He hides his face from the Secret Police of Russia and Germany." He actually had more to fear from the U.S. Immigration and Naturalization Service.

OUT OF THE NIGHT

WRITING IN 1941, an American historian who was a frank admirer of Mexican president Lázaro Cárdenas said of his policy in the oil workers' crisis of September 1940 that "it dramatized the final break of Cárdenas with the Communists. Its aftermath came months later during his illness at Jiquilpan, when reporters found him reading the strongest denunciation of communism in our time—*Out of the Night*." As the man who made that judgment can hardly have been ignorant of *Darkness at Noon*, that is high praise indeed. Of course, "our time" is a moving target. Though few of either, there may be more Americans today who would recognize the name of Lázaro Cárdenas than would recognize the title *Out of the Night*. Yet it remains one of the most remarkable books in the library of anti-Communism, and the history of its publication and impact dramatize in a unique manner an important but imperfectly understood moment in the spiritual life of America on the brink of World War II.

Out of the Night was published in New York at the beginning of 1941. In fact, its first edition bears the date of 1940, which is a missed good intention rather than a prevarication. That *Darkness at Noon* beat it into print by a few weeks was an accident, not that the books had the slightest genetic connection. Its author, of whom practically nobody had heard, was "Jan Valtin," the pseudonym of a certain Richard Krebs, of whom absolutely nobody had heard. By the end of the year—of which *Out of the Night* was the best-selling book in America—lots of people would know a good deal about both the book and its author. To read the book was indeed to know the author, at least in theory, for it purported to be an autobiography.

Richard Julius Hermann Krebs was probably born in 1905, the son of a German merchant marine officer. He spent most of his early years in the faraway places of his father's work. He was in China. He attended school, a little, in Buenos Aires. The family was in Genoa when the war broke out in 1914, and had to flee, losing all their property, when Italy declared war on Germany. The war, which was such a disaster for Germany as a whole, was a particular disaster for the family Krebs. The father was or became a political radical and a participant in the famous naval mutiny at Kiel and Wilhelmshaven in 1918, and then disappeared from the scene.

For readers there are perhaps always potential annoyances in authorial pseudonyms. The library patron seeking a book by Mark Twain may find it curious to be required to search under Samuel Clemens. The problem is particularly acute as regards Richard Krebs, alias Jan Valtin. A literary pseudonym is not exactly the same thing as a stage name, and it clearly differs from a false identity. But there was a little of all of these in "Jan Valtin." Krebs had repeatedly lived under false identities during his time in the Comintern. The adoption of false identities was standard operating procedure for undercover agents, even of the most humble sort. Whittaker Chambers had used so many names that he could not be sure that Alger Hiss was lying when Hiss said he had known him only under the name of Crosley, even though neither he (Chambers) nor anybody else except Hiss could remember his having used that name.

But we know Krebs's choice of the literary pseudonym Valtin antedated his arrival in America in 1938, for there are two or three ephemeral pieces published under that name in obscure journals. He took his first day-labor jobs in America under the name Valtin, sometimes—since the name Jan puzzled some Americans—using the Christian name John instead. This was probably not a well-thought-out plan for creating a false identity, and it later caused him serious problems with the Justice Department. "Valtin" also took on the character of a stage name—that is, the name used by a person in a certain specialized capacity. When Krebs thought of himself in the capacity of a writer, he thought "Jan Valtin." With the enormous success of his first book, the pseudonym took on the character of a valuable stage name, as all his business associates realized. People who would pay good money to see a movie with Judy Garland or Cary Grant were less likely to shell it out for Frances Gumm or Archibald Leach. In daily life even his closest friends called him "Richard" or "Jan" indiscriminately; but there is no question that as a writer he was "Jan Valtin." Furthermore, his publisher fully understood the public relations value of pseudomystery, and the manufactured drama of an author so threatening to the forces of evil that his real name must be concealed from them.

It is impossible in this essay to render entirely simple what the author and his friends spent so much effort in making complex, but for purposes of at least partial clarity we shall generally call him by his legal birth name, Krebs, remembering always that the name appears nowhere in the book that alleges to be the story of his life, and that it would have had no particular meaning for hundreds of thousands of his readers.

Young Krebs joined the Communist Party in 1923, the year of the abortive revolution, during which he fought in the streets of Hamburg. He became an agent of the Comintern, operating in several European countries through the Communist-dominated maritime unions and seamen's clubs. He had a brief period of study at the Lenin School in Moscow, a kind of academy for Spies and Saboteurs. He was a Communist courier and, at times, a thug. He was sent to Shanghai, thence to the west coast of America. In 1926 in Los Angeles, under Communist orders, he committed an act of violence, for which he was convicted and sent to San Quentin.

The stay in San Quentin changed his life. He studied writing in extension courses offered by the University of California, and he published some pieces in the prison literary magazine. Released from prison at the end of 1929 and deported, he found himself back in the German seaports. Under the worsening political and economic conditions of that time and place there was no possibility of pursuing a career in writing, but Krebs never abandoned the dream. For the moment he got caught up once again in the intrigues of the professional revolutionist, and particularly with a clandestine group headed by Ernst Wollweber, another ancient mutineer who was now the boss of an espionage ring in Scandinavia. He married a woman who soon joined him in Communism, and they had a son. She is called "Firelei" in the book, to which she contributes its major theme of tragic love.

By now Hitler had come to power, and the German Communist Party was shattered and dispersed. The life of Jan Valtin was not unlike the life of the "Richard" whom Rubashov had so cruelly abused in *Darkness at Noon*. He was captured by the Gestapo and convicted in the trial of the "Red sailors" in Hamburg in 1933. In the Nazi prisons he was subjected to unspeakable tortures. Eventually, with the approval of Party superiors whose communications penetrated into even the darkest cellars, he engineered a ruse. After some years he convincingly pretended to have been converted to National Socialism and won his perilous freedom on the promise of turning double agent.

That Richard Krebs's memory was amazing has some independent verification. But the published autobiography—so lavish in its deployment of names, dates, street addresses, and reconstructed conversations—dissolves into impressionist blurs at certain cardinal moments. Several of these when closely scutinized by his enemies would later cause Krebs serious legal difficulties. Of the narrative soft spots, none is more problematical than the book's ending. Now a pretense double agent, Krebs found himself back in Denmark and under the command of Richard Jensen, described in the book's *dramatis personae* as a "giant Dane, conspirator of the first rank . . . for years the chief agent of the Soviet secret service for all of Scandinavia." The trouble was that Jensen, who thought there was nothing "pretense" about Krebs's apostasy to the Gestapo, put him under house arrest, and prepared to ship him to Leningrad for liquidation. When Krebs made a dramatic escape and flight, Jensen, who according to standard underground routine was holding his passport, had its photograph reproduced on a flyer ("Beware! Gestapo Agent") and sent to the far corners of the Communist maritime network.

Though he had gained a tenuous and temporary safety, he was now a wolf's head for Gestapo and GPU alike.* Such were the circumstances under which "Jan Valtin," now passing as an ordinary seaman, boarded a ship at Antwerp which he left, illegally, at Newport News, Virginia, at the beginning of 1938. It was not his first illegal entry into America. Very curiously, *Out of the Night* leaves unmentioned his escape to America, perhaps because he does not want to draw attention to the fact that he had left behind a wife and infant son, or to explain through what channels he learned, in July 1938, that his wife had been "thrown into the Horror Camp Fuhlsbuettel," or that five months later he learned that she had died

---

* The nomenclature of the evolving Soviet security agencies can be bewildering to a non-specialist. The first Soviet state police agency, headed by the formidable Felix Dzerzhinsky, was called by the partial acronym the *Cheka*. Agents of the state police continued to be called *chekists* long after the Cheka had become the *GPU*, or "State Political Directorate." The GPU was an agency of the *NKVD* (the "People's Commissariat for Internal Affairs"). The abbreviation NKVD itself was widely used as a generic term for the state police. NKVD agents were often called "blue hats," in reference to a feature of their uniform, as well as *chekists*. In this book I sacrifice the pedantry of precise chronology and technical terminology to the usefulness of the common terms GPU and NKVD.

there, perhaps a suicide. "Our son, Jan, became a ward of the Third Reich. I have not heard of him again." Those are the final sentences of the book.

Retrospective evidence independent of the book includes the following. There do exist in *The Daily Worker* and other American Communist publications of the late 1930s and early 1940s various versions of the "Beware!" poster with Valtin's photograph. The poster was one aspect of a vigorous Communist campaign to discredit *Out of the Night*. Moreover, Valtin returned to Germany after the war, found his son Jan, and brought him back to America. After the war, at a time when Valtin's book was still unpublished in any language except English, a leftist Danish politician named Richard Jensen published in Danish a pamphlet entitled *Into the Darkness* which contested Valtin's account of his alleged house arrest and escape from Copenhagen, demonstrating convincingly that the narrative account was geographically impossible. This rare pamphlet is, however, as eloquent in its silences as in its indictments.

According to his own testimony, first in a vastly distributed *Reader's Digest* article called "American Dawn" and then in various chronologies prepared upon the demand or request of the FBI or for various congressional committees, Jan Valtin explained how he immediately headed for New York to become a writer, and catalogued some of the casual jobs (handyman in a Yeshiva, housepainter, etc.) that kept him alive. But even then he held back important details. In 1938 there was living in Manhattan a German-American radical named Robert Bek-Gran, who had impressive revolutionary credentials. In his twenties he had been a part of the brief and tragic Munich soviet of 1919. Having escaped with his life—which was more than many of his comrades had done—he went north to the German port cities. He emigrated to America before the Hamburg Rising of 1923, and became a naturalized citizen. Bek-Gran was the real Red thing, a proletarian revolutionary, or at least *a* real thing, an artisan intellectual, a skilled printer who read more books than he printed. He moved in radical circles and, in 1930, he joined the American Communist Party, where his special portfolio was the Party's German membership. What that increasingly meant in the thirties, of course, was refugees from Hitler. It also meant that his name was known in German Communist circles.

To a young man of twenty, a young man of thirty can seem an ancient of days. Krebs had corresponded once or twice with Bek-Gran from Bremen in 1930, even as he had with his San Quentin writing teacher Arthur

Price and one or two ex-convicts. (Prison rules forbade letters between released and current prisoners, but there were ways to circumvent them.) No letters exist, but Krebs's theme, apparently, was his discouraging attempt to break into print. When Krebs now arrived in New York, very much the worse for wear, he appeared in Robert Bek-Gran's Manhattan printshop. (This was apparently in or around the three-day period between the announcement of the *Anschluss* and the execution of Nikolai Bukharin on March 15, 1938.) Bek-Gran, an honest man, was no longer a Party member. He rebelled before the emerging tyranny of Stalin, and even more before its servile acceptance by American Communists. His politics now were roughly anti-Communist, anti-Fascist, Kautskian-Marxist anarcho-libertarian. These were definitely what one would call "niche" politics. He was deeply involved in the publication of a German-language magazine in New York: *Gegen der Strom*. That meant "Against the Tide," and it was against many tides, beginning with the Party line. The Communists called it "Trotskyite," but it had as little to do with Trotsky as most things to which they applied that adjective. Like most other people, Bek-Gran was mainly concerned with trying to make a living in a major depression. In such spare time as he had, he ran a personal rescue mission for revolutionary waifs and strays lucky enough to get out of Germany alive. Several of these young men had known each other in the German seaports. A group of these he called "my boys"; they called him "Pop."

Krebs was just another of the "boys." Bek-Gran helped him as he had helped others. First he helped him find work. Krebs was undoubtedly struggling, but not in "revolutionary" or "class" terms. His struggle was the more familiar one of the penniless artist in New York: how to find the time and energy and concentration to write after long days of manual labor. Though they shared a radical political background, their relationship was not political. Bek-Gran was a generous soul, and he believed in Krebs's promise as a writer. He nursed him through a serious bout of illness. He tried to put him in touch with sympathetic agents and editors, including Eugene Lyons at the *American Mercury*. The name of Lyons is one of several that will recur in this study with an unwonted sympathy. Normal history is suspect because it is written by the winners. The history of left-wing literature in America is different. It is suspect because it was written by the losers, most of them sore losers at that. Most of the respected histories of the left-wing literature of the thirties are suffused with a nostalgia for a vanished radicalism, and in their pages anti-Communist literary giants such as Max Eastman, Isaac Don Levine, and Eugene Lyons appear mainly as reactionary caricatures.

In their wise comic history of England entitled *1066 and All That*, Yateman and Sellers discuss the conflict between Cavaliers and Roundheads as one in which men "wrong but romantic" faced off against others who were "right but repulsive." Eastman, Levine, and Lyons may have been painfully right about the Soviet Union, but to a certain scholarly sensibility they were no less politically repulsive for their apostasy from socialism and for their "Red-baiting." Surely no man of letters exercised a greater political impact on twentieth-century American political life than Levine. Yet in Daniel Aaron's fine *Writers on the Left* he is mentioned precisely twice, in reference to a public debate betwen him and Aaron's Communist hero Joseph Freeman. Nor does the brief notice even acknowledge that, according to eyewitnesses, Levine mopped the floor with Freeman. At the very least Levine has to have been one of the most successful literary agents, entrepreneurs, and productive busybodies in American history. The impecunious Bek-Gran brought Krebs to Lyons and Levine; the latter would eventually collect a sweet 30 percent of the fat royalties from *Out of the Night*. But on the principle of sweat equity, he had every right to his money.

Through Lyons's agency, Valtin-Krebs actually got a conditional contract for a novel, which he promised to deliver by February 1, 1941. (Little could he have guessed that on that date he would be one of the most famous writers in America.) He was to prepare a sizable sample of the book—a quarter or so. If that proved acceptable to the publisher, he would be paid twenty-five dollars a week for a period of up to eighteen weeks for its completion. It was an adventure novel set on the western seas of South America, written by an admirer of Conrad's *Nostromo*. It was called *Copper from Chuqui*. Krebs got a small grub stake from Bek-Gran and a sympathetic woman named Eleanor Jacob—one of the several people who would later sue him or otherwise claim recompense when he so unexpectedly came into the big money. Now, however, his finances were such that to save money he lived in a tent in Ramapo Valley, New York, while he wrote furiously, turning out more than 100 pages in the month of April 1939. The trouble was that they were not very good pages. Lyons declared the project "unmarketable." That was the end of *Copper from Chuqui*. There is not another reference to it in the whole Valtin archive. The cheap acid paper pages on which it was typed now lie moldering in a library archive in Atlanta.

Lyons, who was among the ablest journalists of his generation, now forcefully gave Valtin-Krebs the sensible advice to be found on the first page of any writer's how-to book: Look in thy heart, and write. The truth was that Krebs didn't know all that much about copper mining in Chile, whereas he knew a very great deal about life in the Comintern, Communist espionage, and the plumbing arrangements in Nazi jails. He should write from his *experience*. Still living in his tent, he wrote his first successful article. It was called "Ploetzensee—Hitler's Slaughterhouse." It was accepted immediately by the editor of *Ken*. *Ken*, then in its second and penultimate year of publication, proved a flash in the pan, but a very bright flash. Hemingway was only one of several big names to illuminate its brief life. Without skipping a beat, Krebs returned to his tent and wrote a second, "Pillar of the Comintern," a short character sketch of Ernst Wollweber, or "Ernst X," as the cautious editor of *Ken* magazine preferred. This was a little riskier. Anybody could bash Hitler with impunity. Bashing a Communist was "Red-baiting." Wollweber cuts a large swath through *Out of the Night*, and he is most definitely a solidly historical personage and a real Communist. We know for a fact that he was the head of the very ambitious Communist espionage efforts in prewar Scandinavia. After the war he appears as one of the top functionaries in the gray and grim Communist government of East Germany, before becoming an "unperson" about 1960. But by then he had already outlived Krebs by a good decade.

This was a coup for Krebs, and buoyed by it he could face another stint of housepainting while he contemplated a second, more substantial piece for Lyons's *American Mercury*. It was called "Communist Agent." Written in July and published in November 1939, it was to prove the engine of one problematical side of Valtin-Krebs's literary fame. People in Washington read the *American Mercury*, especially when Eugene Lyons distributed prepublication copy to interested parties. Benjamin Mandel, the ex-Communist who was the highly competent factotum for the House Committee on Un-American Activities, read it. So did some people in the FBI, whose emissaries came to Krebs in November and offered to put him on the weekly payroll as a special consultant or an informer, depending upon your political point of view. "I declined, stating that I would not work for money, that I had no information to *sell*, but that I would cooperate to the best of my ability whenever I could be of any assistance." But Krebs's literary career as Jan Valtin was beginning to show signs of a possible viability. He began making notes for "ideas" and projects, a dozen or more. He went off on his own to talk to a couple of literary agents.

Though Krebs would later try to blur the fact, the specific origin of the autobiographical project was a conversation he had with Levine in the presence of Rose Wilder Lane—of whom we shall hear a little more later. Levine had even more confidence in Valtin-Krebs's potential as a writer than did Lyons, if only he could steer him away from attempting bad imitations of Conrad or Jack London. Furthermore, instead of writing journalistic "sketches" from his colorful experience, he should write a large and sequential book. One issue, later destined to cause great difficulties, was left unresolved. Would this book be an autobiography characterized by novelistic devices, or a novel characterized by autobiographical convention? Krebs now began in earnest on an obsessive project that also commanded Levine's full attention for both literary and ideological reasons. For several months, from January to June of 1940, Krebs crashed at a modest country place belonging to Bek-Gran in Stamford, Connecticut. Later, Levine put him up in the garage of his own place in Norwalk. The physical production of *Out of the Night* appears to have been among the more strenuous efforts of modern literature. Krebs produced his huge manuscript in about a year; yet large as it was, the final form represented only a fraction of what he had written, the rest having been edited away by Levine in the hundreds of hours of work he lavished on the project.

The book appeared to immediate, explosive praise, followed by reactive controversy. In the contemporary press only one literary phenomenon is invoked to compare with *Out of the Night*, and then to its favor: Margaret Mitchell's *Gone With the Wind*, blockbuster novel of 1936, blockbuster movie of 1939. Many factors contributed to the extraordinary success of *Out of the Night*, including the repellent genius of Henry Koppell, head of Alliance Books. In Germany he had organized an innovative and successful book club scheme, and exploiting the talents of agent cum entrepeneur Isaac Don Levine he went promptly to the Book-of-the-Month Club, whose jury, though supposedly cultural mavens above the fray, were as manipulable as the juries of literary and film prizes today. Levine got the *Reader's Digest* on board; and they had a "digest" ready for their March issue; but Koppell himself seems to have pulled off the coup of arranging an unprecedented two-part teaser (February 27 and March 3, 1941) in *Life*. *Life* was of course a "picture magazine," and it accompanied Valtin's texts with compelling photographs and, in the second installment, an even more compelling, if wholly imaginary, artist's illustration of Gestapo torturers at work on "Valtin."

An Explosive Best-Seller

If *Darkness at Noon* is too good a book to spoil at the mere recitation of its "plot," *Out of the Night* has no plot to spoil. Or, rather, it has the same kind of plot as *Don Quixote* or Ovid's *Metamorphoses*, in which one episode leads to another, which leads to another. It is among the more compelling and exciting adventure stories one will encounter in a lifetime's reading. It is well structured, confidently paced, and for the most part very well written—one might say amazingly well written considering the fact that the author was not a native speaker of English. It offers a thrill a minute, and it is not easy to put down. It teems with colorful characters of the sort often called "larger than life." It is replete with concrete and engaging details of political conspiracy, of life in the merchant navy, of techniques of street fighting, and numerous other arts and crafts probably unfamiliar to most people holding suburban library cards. Among the "Jan Valtin Papers" in Princeton are large files of fan letters from all over America attesting to the book's powerful attraction for general readers. Many of them are detailed and personal, reflecting an intimate connection with elements of the autobiography, and strong sympathy for its author. Many offer food, shelter, or employment. There was something about Valtin's personality, both in the flesh and in the book, that made women think that they could save, redeem, incubate, or resurrect a great soul temporarily subdued by hostile Fortune. Letters from women readers are prominent. At least two of them offer marriage, while a much larger number hint at the benefits of marriage without its contractual restrictions. If there had been rock stars in the 1930s, surely their mailbags would have approximated the Valtin archive.

The book reports more exciting adventure in the life of one thirty-year-old man than might be found in the pooled experiences of several graybeards. Indeed, some were quick to point out that there were too many adventures to credit. There are battles, street brawls, decep-tions, betrayals, and narrow escapes galore. Young Valtin travels to most of the known corners of the earth, usually accompanied by mayhem. And if there is plenty of violence, there is also sex. The sex is of two kinds, both of them mild or attenuated by contemporary standards, but racy enough in their own day. There is the emotionally rich and finally tragic narrative of Valtin's courtship of the young artist Firelei, his recruitment of her to the Communist cause, and their marital life invaded and deformed by the ruthless demands of the Communist Party on the one hand and the concomitant persecutions of the Nazis on the other. Here is the tragic love story of a man who lost everything—down to the lives of his wife and infant child—to fanatical political demand. A second and more pervasive sexual element, which now strikes the reader as nearly quaint, is a general suggestion of lubricity surround-ing many of the female spies, comrades, couriers, and conspirators, not counting the prostitutes, who populate the book. It is from Valtin's day, after all, that a witty definition of a "best-seller" has come down to us: "a book with a shapely wench on the jacket, and no jacket on the shapely wench." Valtin does not in fact use the word "shapely." His absurder term of art is "Junoesque," meaning roughly something between what "stacked" meant yesterday and "hot" means today. Rather amusingly, the Communist literary attack on *Out of the Night* makes much of its alleged "pornography."

The apostles of sexual liberation and free love pronounced themselves scandalized by its recurrent Junoesque episodes. To be fair, the Commu-nists were perhaps more sinned against than sinning in the Silly Sex Sweep-stakes. Their more bigoted enemies ascribed to them levels of satyriasis and nymphomania that, if indulged, would have left them with scant energy for handing out leaflets on the street corner, let alone serious engagement in the "cultural front." One of the more forgettable monuments of Cold War literature was called *Report on the Communist* (1952). It has a whole chapter on sex among the subversives, which includes the astonishing rev-elation that "sex is one of the mainsprings of a Communist's motivations just as it is for everyone else."

But the principal *political* significance of the book, and the element that would make the fate of its author a national *cause célèbre*, was the pre-sentation of international Communism that emerges from the narrative.

Any reader of *Out of the Night* who is even vaguely politically literate must gain at the very least the following impressions:

1. International Communism is a vast criminal conspiracy of fanatical revolutionaries. In fact, Krebs's use of the words "conspiracy" and its derivatives—especially the odd adjective "conspirative"— is one of few indications that though he writes in English, he sometimes thinks in German. Everything about Communism is a "conspiracy"—that is, a plot or cunning revolutionary plan in which generally accepted canons of truth and morality play no part.

2. The Comintern, the ostensible autonomous international expression of the Communist movement, is in fact an organ of Soviet foreign policy directed from Moscow. Comintern agents, who exist undetected by the score if not by the hundreds in all Western democracies, are bent on espionage, sabotage, and the infiltration of labor unions in the most sensitive areas of national economies, such as shipping. Western security services, with the exception of Hitler's, are mere babes-in-the-woods in dealing with this plot.

3. Communist orthodoxy within the movement is rigidly enforced by complex systems of internal spying and informing. Political purgation by means of execution is very common. Every Communist agent will know several colleagues who have been "disappeared" in Moscow, and every agent must fear for his own life.

4. The rise of National Socialism in Germany could have been checked through genuine cooperation between the KPD and other left-wing parties. The conscious Communist policy of hostility to the Socialists—whom they liked to call Social Fascists— enabled Hitler's rise to power.

5. As between the Hitler regime in Germany and the Stalin regime in Soviet Russia, it is not on balance an easy thing to decide which is more brutal, vicious, and dictatorial.

A MOMENT IN HISTORY

Very few historians of the prewar period would today blink an eye at any of these tired propositions, but to most Western intellectuals of 1940 the first four were Red-baiting fictions while the fifth was something like the sin against the Holy Ghost. To understand the drama of Jan Valtin and its place in the creation of American anti-Communism requires the coordination of two chronologies—what might be called the macro-chronology of world events on the one hand, and on the other the micro-chronology of the struggle of Richard Krebs to gain a permanent safe haven in the United States. For like that of so many others, this man's fate became hostage to the caprices of large historical events which it is necessary briefly to call to mind. The nearly universal concern of American opinion makers of the late 1930s, so far as foreign affairs were concerned, was Hitler's Germany. The great enemy was "Fascism." There were three regimes in the "Fascist" camp—Italy, Germany, and Franco's Spain—to which a fourth, Imperial Japan, was often added. The great enemy of Fascism, and many thought the only committed and adequate one, was the Soviet Union. To be anti-Fascist was to be pro-Soviet as the sparks fly upward. The great battleground of the second half of the decade was Spain. There, it was widely believed, enlightened progress, democracy, and socialist hope (the Spanish Republic) squared off against obscurantist reaction, tyranny, and Fascism (Franco's rebels, actively aided by the Germans and the Italians). The Soviet Union heroically aided the Republic while the Western democracies, through their hypocritical policy of "non-intervention," in effect aided the cause of the Fascists.

By 1938, Stalin's purges and/or his double game in Spain had disillusioned a few, like Orwell, Koestler, Ginzburg (Krivitsky), and possibly Krebs himself, but Soviet Communism generally maintained its cachet with Western "progressives" until the announcement of the Hitler-Stalin Pact in August 1939. The pact was a real shaking of the foundations. There were large defections from the American Communist Party, which like Communist parties everywhere had to turn on a dime to accommodate a new "line" that made perfect sense from the *Realpolitik* point of view but violated a mythology of such authority as to have become a virtual axiom of Western politics. Communists now naturally opposed American involvement in the European War, which appeared likely to allow the Soviet Union greatly to expand its territory and influence.

From the beginning of September 1939 to the middle of June 1941—the period of the start of the war in Europe, of Hitler's sensational conquest of France, his frustration in Britain—the Soviet Union was the ally of Nazi Germany, busily gobbling up half of Poland and as much of Finland as Stalin was able to bite off. Western anti-Communists were numerous and vocal, Western Communists beleaguered, defensive, and disingenuous in their rejection of a second imperialist war. All of this changed, again with dramatic suddenness, when Hitler unleashed his invasion of the Soviet Union in June 1941. Now Western Communists rushed to encourage a United Front in defense of democracy, civilization, and the Soviet Union. Roosevelt and Churchill realized that the only force that could defeat Hitler was the Red Army, severely mauled but capable of reinvigoration from behind the Urals with massive investments of American aid accompanied by steady Allied military pressure on either side of the Mediterranean. As our history has repeatedly shown, the coercive powers of perceived military necessity are enormous. Almost overnight American anti-Communism became something rather more than inexpedient or undiplomatic—it became unpatriotic. After *Out of the Night* there would not be another popular "anti-Soviet" trade book published in America until 1945. Only a specialized study could suggest whether this was a result of voluntary restraint or of actual governmental repression. Harper's insisted that Trotsky's biography of Stalin, which they brought out after the war, bear the publication date of 1941. That was when it was ready.

If we fit the micro-chronology of *Out of the Night* into this picture we can see that the book was written in 1940—as France was falling, Britain battling, and Stalin smiling on the sidelines—then published and celebrated in the early months of 1941. This was the perfect, unique window of opportunity for an American anti-Communist blockbuster. But its moment of political shelter was brief. With Hitler's invasion of Russia in June, and the resurfacing of the American Communist Party officials as superpatriot cheerleaders for a United Front, things changed abruptly. And as America prepared for, and then entered the war, they changed definitively.

The political phase of the "Jan Valtin affair" actually began in 1939 when Eugene Lyons published Valtin's article "Communist Agent" in the

American Mercury and Ben Mandel of the Dies Committee read it. But it now became animated on three fronts. (1) The American Communist Party and its vast cavalry of stalking horses set out to debunk the author and its book. (2) Anti-Stalinists in a spectrum running from DeWitt Wallace to Louis Fischer rushed to acclaim, claim, or coopt the book for their own purposes. (3) On the purely commercial side of things, it was obvious that Valtin was a hot property, and there were numerous people whose flaring nostrils picked up the strong scent of money. These certainly included Krebs himself, who, however, now faced the daunting task of following an unfollowable first act, his own.

AN AUTHOR AND HIS FRIENDS

Buoyed by his instant fame and prosperity, Krebs made a number of dramatic personal moves. He married Abigail Harris, the star-struck seventeen-year-old daughter of a family he had come to know through Levine. Young though he was, he was twice her age. This odd marriage, which produced two sons, was not destined to last very long. Next, he bought a house in Danbury, becoming Levine's neighbor rather than his squatter. Seven months later, when the real money started rolling in, he bought and removed to a working farm (Kittemaug Orchards) further east in Montville, but his few months in Danbury were crucial. Seventy-five years ago, New York City was still surrounded by a certain sense of country and real rural life. In those parts of Fairfield County, Connecticut, that are now mainly superhighways, their feeder roads, and large semi-wooded tracts of mushrooming McMansions, there was still a genuine agricultural life, though one that in many instances had already given way to the "country place" of city dwellers. Many people of significance to Jan Valtin and the "Jan Valtin story" lived or at least summered there, and a few of them must now be recalled or introduced.

Krebs's first contact in America, Robert Bek-Gran, though chronically impecunious, had a little country place in which he was able to allow Krebs to recover from a serious bout of pleurisy in 1939. It was at Isaac Don Levine's summer quarters at Norwalk, in the summer of 1940, that most of *Out of the Night* had been created. Krebs had taken a shine to the part of the world in which he had written his book, and when it made him rich, more or less overnight, he himself bought first a little place near Norwalk and then an operating apple farm, Kittemaug Orchards, in New London County. The removal of Krebs and his child bride from the canyons of Manhattan to rural life will require the introduction of three remarkable women.

A somewhat obscure group of Yale alumni, remembered for their contributions to our national literature in the infant days of the republic, are known to literary historians as "the Connecticut Wits." Isaac Don Levine was a member of an informal circle or even colony of intellectuals, writers, artists, publishers, and "interesting people" who made up a kind of depression version of the Connecticut Wits. Three of its more impressive female members would play important roles in the Valtin affair.

The first was Rose Wilder Lane (1886–1968), daughter of Laura Ingalls Wilder, the author of *The Little House on the Prairie*, one of the great books in our literature. Rose Wilder (as I shall call her) had lived the pioneer life, and tried to revive it in her later years. Though she kept the name of a husband to whom she had been briefly married, she was an early model of the independent feminist. She was a friend of John Reed and an early enthusiast of the Bolsheviks, but empirical investigation in Russia soon changed that. She traveled to out-of-the-way places, including Albania, where King Zog proposed marriage to her. She became a crack newspaper woman, a highly competent editor, and a prolific writer of fiction and non-fiction alike. One of her novels, *Let the Hurricane Roar*, should claim a permanent place in American literature. She was a political maverick, tending more and more over the years toward a radical libertarianism. (Perhaps her most famous book was *Give Me Liberty*, 1936.) She was a personal friend of Herbert Hoover and numerous other eminences.

In middle life (she was Krebs's senior by twenty years) she went to ground on a rural property and adopted a lifestyle that was either Thoreauvian or survivalist, depending upon one's perspective. She hated the New Deal, which she regarded as galloping as opposed to creeping socialism, and she condemned the income tax on constitutional grounds. She proposed avoiding tax and Social Security contributions through the somewhat quixotic expedient of radically limiting her income, raising her own food, and generally living the self-sufficient life of her forebears in the Dakota Territory of her birth. This plan shipwrecked when she inherited the quite substantial royalties from the "Little House" series. It hardly need be added that she was a fervent anti-Communist who warmed to the campaign to "save" Jan Valtin. It was in conversation with the post-Protestant Wilder and the philo-Semitic Levine that Krebs had first entertained the idea of *Out of the Night*.

Another resident of those parts was Lillian Symes, also a feminist revolutionary, though of a more traditional left-wing sort. Like Rose Wilder, she was a true American original. Symes was a professional writer, most famously, perhaps, the author of *Rebel America*, a history of radical movements in this country deployed in the confident and lucid prose that also characterizes her frequent contributions to the political press. She became Krebs's ideological emissary for an important section of the non-Communist left. She was a scourge of softheaded "liberals" (like Hemingway, who was at that time a correspondent in Spain) whom she regarded as naive dupes of the Communists. Anyone interested in getting a quick "fix" on Symes about the time of her commerce with Krebs could hardly do better than read an essay she published in *Harper's*, "Communism Twenty Years After," in 1938. "Among the non-Communist radicals of various persuasions, the Party's beating of the war drums along the international front (known as its 'peace policy'), like its wooing of capitalist democracy, is regarded as the rankest opportunism and a betrayal of the mildest form of Marxism."

The blindness of the "liberal" press to the perfidy of Soviet policy in the Spanish Civil War—the issue that turned Orwell, Koestler, and perhaps Krebs himself into fervent anti-Communists—becomes the object of a particular excoriation. As Symes puts it,

> The attitude of Communism's liberal periphery in such matters involves one of the most interesting psychological phenomena of our time. . . . How is it possible for outstanding civil libertarians who wax livid over . . . labor spies, criminal syndicalism laws, book burnings, Reichstag fire trials, concentration camps, and blood purges in certain parts of the world, to wax apologetic or even enthusiastic over Joseph Stalin, the OGPU, book burnings, concentration camps, demonstration trials, blood purges, and the recent elections in Russia? So well-conditioned are the reflexes of that vast periphery through which American Communism operates that the mere asking of this question is sufficient to label one in such circles as a Trotskyist, an agent of Hitler's Gestapo, or a "red-baiter" in the employ of Mr. Hearst—this

in spite of the fact that not even the most persistent baiter could find a hint of red in the Communist Party today.

The strange alliance between the Spartan socialist Symes and the Jewish entrepreneur Levine must have seemed to Party members as unholy as that of "French radicals and German police-spies" with which Marx and Engels had begun the *Communist Manifesto*. They now conspired to aid Krebs.

The third woman, Dorothy Donnell (later Dorothy Donnell Calhoun), was of a different sort, a vernacular New Englander from a comfortable background, well educated, and a highly competent professional administrator in the Justice Department in Washington, D.C. In her younger days she had been an aspiring writer, and in particular she had dreamed of being a screenwriter—a fact of eventual relevance to our story. Determined bibliographical research can still uncover a few of her short stories, not lacking in talent, among the vanished little magazines of the twenties. She was a great admirer of Symes and Wilder, though closer to the former in her own politics, which were mainstream (for Washington) New Deal Democrat.

Her particular job in the Justice Department was the administration of a program for "New Citizens." It involved public relations and brochure writing, among other things. In this capacity she had known and worked with various eminent European refugees, of whom Hitler was guaranteeing a good supply, on their road to naturalization. She was both aware and wary of a tight Communist "fraction" at Justice. It was by happenstance through family associations in the Connecticut Valley that she met Krebs socially at the Levines', even before he had finished *Out of the Night*. Later she would be among the large number of enthusiastic readers of the book, which she thought was both brilliant writing and a much-needed political admonition. Later yet she became a close friend and collaborator of the writer's.

But then his real troubles began. We must take a few moments to follow some of their thematic strands, which of course become tangled, as strands will do. The book was without question a rollicking good yarn. But could it possibly be *true*? Throughout America, a vast game of trivia now began as people in all places mentioned in the book or the *Reader's Digest* article began to nail down their moment of local fame with extratextual details. What was the ship that had brought Jan Valtin to the Tidewater ports in 1938? Answer: the *Ary Lensen*. What was the Bronx "wedding hall" in which Valtin found his first employment in New York? Answer: the *Royal Mansion* at 1315 Boston Road in the Bronx, later to claim a minor place in the history of jazz. What was the hotel in New Hampshire where Valtin had worked as a painter? Answer: the *Spoffard* [actually Spofford] *Lake Hotel*. What color was Valtin's boss when he worked as a housepainter? Answer: *black*. As sales of *Out of the Night* soared, Valtin's name was in every newspaper and magazine, always surrounded by a penumbra of mystery. He was interviewed. He was profiled. He was on the radio. But still no one knew. Who *was* Jan Valtin? Was *Out of the Night* a true account of his life?

A NON-DIGRESSION ON TRUTH AND AUTOBIOGRAPHY

The nature of the "truth" of literary art has been a question vexed since even before Plato. But readers who wanted to know whether or not *Out of the Night* was "true" were asking at a level of common sense rather than from a perspective of philosophical literary theory. It was the crucial question about Valtin-Krebs's book, as well as two others dealt with in this study. It was never directly answered during the period of its author's greatest celebrity. The answer is that it was morally true though often novelistic in detail, but that was not a common view at the time. *Out of the Night* is an autobiography, the life story of the man who wrote the book, real name Richard Krebs, pseudonym Jan Valtin. The particular problem posed by autobiography seems on first glance to be quite clear-cut. Autobiography is, or ought to be, "true" by definition. On the other hand, autobiography is a form of literary art, and all literary art requires artifice. When truth meets artifice, the results can be confusing. There are at least two examples that gained public prominence fairly recently, in 2003. In that year Vivian Gornick gave a talk at Goucher College. Vivian Gornick is a well-known essayist and cultural critic who used to write for *The Village Voice*. (Incidentally, she is also the author of a book about American Communism, though that does not enter the story here.) She is a highly admired feminist whose most famous book is a memoir, *Fierce Attachments* (1987), which consists in part of reported conversations with her mother as the two stroll around Manhattan. The "generational" theme, in its relation to feminism, is an important one in the book, which soon became known as "a modern masterpiece of literary feminism."

In her talk at Goucher Ms. Gornick said, without particular fanfare, that she had made up some of the conversations reported in the book. This rather shocked some people, especially Professor Maureen Corrigan, the book reviewer for the *Fresh Air* program on National Public Radio. Controversy also found its way into print and online journalism. Ms. Corrigan took the view that the genre of autobiography implies a strict contract of veracity between author and reader. To introduce fictional elements into purported autobiography was to abuse the reader in the fashion of a confidence trickster. Ms. Gornick did not much advance the discussion when at one point she said that what she had actually made up was the story that she had made things up. Nonetheless, even amidst the waffle the incident resulted in an interesting discussion of differing modes of truth in literature.

Much bigger than the "Gornick controversy"—just in the proportion that in our country television is bigger than radio and that both are bigger than serious books—was the "Frey controversy." James Frey is a youngish writer and moviemaker of phenomenal popular success. His most famous book and biggest best-seller was his autobiography *A Million Little Pieces*. The success of this book was amplified by Oprah Winfrey, who featured it and its author on her very influential television program. *A Million Little Pieces* is mainly about its author's experiences as a drug addict and alcoholic and his eventual rehabilitation from the curse of substance abuse. With unrelenting self-revelation, Mr. Frey boldly reported numerous anecdotes of his stoned age, reminiscences of the sort that most of us would do our utmost to keep dark. He was a very bad man who said and did very bad things. The general tenor, though not the specific language, was of Methodist conversion.

> From '61 to '67
> I lived in disbelief of heaven
> I drunk, I fought, I poached, I whored,
> I did despite unto the Lord . . .

But if once he was lost, now he was found out; for on the Web site "The Smoking Gun," someone blew the whistle on Mr. Frey's alleged depravity. It was obvious that Frey was a bad guy, all right, but in a manner very different from that depicted in his autobiography. He was a bad man because he had greatly exaggerated his badness, and indeed made some of it up out of whole cloth. The exposed fictions of *A Million Little Pieces* were in part ludicrous and in part mean. Among the former were Frey's alchemical transformation of having been caught by the cops with an open container into a period of protracted incarceration. Among the latter was his tasteless insertion of himself into a tragic automobile accident, over which bereaved parents were still grieving, with which he had not the slightest actual connection.

When accused of not in fact being all that bad, Frey waffled. Oprah Winfrey leaped to his defense, a posture she soon enough repented when further exposures proved that *A Million Little Pieces* was more like a hundred and seventeen big fibs. What happened next was extraordinary. Frey and his publisher were hauled back on *The Oprah Winfrey Show* in metaphoric chains and put through a public shaming reminiscent of the old days of socialist self-criticism. The publishing house, Doubleday, which of course declared itself shocked, invented a somewhat Talmudic protocol by which any aggrieved readers who had bought fiction thinking it was autobiography could get their money back.

But autobiographical fictions have not always proved fully refundable. Among the most famous autobiographies in the Western tradition is the *Confessions* of Saint Augustine, and one of the most famous passages in it is his account of his moment of definitive religious conversion (Book 8). Greatly attracted to a purity of life and understanding, yet also still distracted by the allures of sex and Neo-Platonism—a dilemma most of us can at least half understand—Augustine restlessly and in perturbation of mind walked out into the walled garden of the house he was in, idly carrying with him a copy of the Epistles of Saint Paul he happened to pick up. He sat down beneath a fig tree. From beyond the wall he heard the singsong voices of unseen infants playing a game, otherwise unknown to literary history or archeology, that involved the repeated phrase, *Tolle, lege*—"Pick it up and read it." He then recalled that according to the *Life of Saint Anthony*, a "best-seller" of the day about the great founder of asceticism, Anthony had experienced an instant conversion wrought by his fortuitous audition of a passage from the Gospels. So he picked it up and read it. Opening his little book at random, he let his eyes fall to a passage in the thirteenth chapter of the Epistle to the Romans. Those few verses of text effected his instantaneous and immutable conversion, and they are today attended by millions in all parts of the world as one of the set texts for the "Christian New Year," the first Sunday in Advent.

Augustine was insistent on the obligation of truth telling. He wrote two whole books of considerable philosophical depth about lies and lying. He is here recounting one of the most solemn, sacred, and grace-filled moments of his own existence. Yet there has been sharp controversy among the greatest experts as to whether his story is literally true, or even fairly close to literal truth. Though not among the experts, I side with those who find in his account a constructed exemplary fiction whose elements (fig tree, mouths of babes, Anthony of the Desert, etc.) point figuratively, spiritually, or allegorically to the absolute truth of his religious conversion.

Nor did benign autobiographical fiction die with classical Antiquity. The winner of the 1992 Nobel Peace Prize was Rigoberta Menchú, a Guatemalan woman long active in the social struggles of her native land. She became prominent as the purported author of a purported autobiography (*I, Rigoberta Menchú*, 1983). This book had large sales in many parts of the world. In the United States it became a set text in numerous colleges and universities for various courses in Latin American Studies, Anthropology, Women's Studies, and History. Menchú's life, as related in her book, is very moving—at times tragic, at others inspirational—as she faces the daily indignities and oppressions, large and small, of an unjust social organization and a murderous government.

In 1999, David Stoll, a professional anthropologist with strong interest in Central America, published a deeply researched book called *Rigoberta Menchú and the Story of All Poor Guatemalans*. Stoll had discovered that the life Menchú describes in the book, while indeed typical of many indigenous women in Guatemala, was by no means the "real life" story of Rigoberta Menchú. The actual authorship of the book was not a major issue. We are all familiar with the life stories of interesting but perhaps not particularly literary people "as told to" a professional writer, and this had certainly been of that type. What was at issue was the actual autobiographical truth of the book. Stoll said that many of the most fundamental aspects of the self-presentation were demonstrably false. She had been by no means so poor as she claimed. Her family, actually conspicuous for its comparative prosperity, was by no means so marginalized as she claimed. She claimed to have received no education at all; actually, she had been schooled by nuns. There were fabricated episodes sensational in nature, such as that her little brother had been burned alive by government soldiers while she and other family members were forced to watch.

The ensuing controversy, interestingly, focused more upon Stoll's book than on Menchú's. Menchú did not at first respond to Stoll's specific revelations. In fact, she has never yet responded to them in a detailed fashion. Instead, she attributed to Stoll various foul intentions: the intention to discredit or trivialize the sufferings of the people, the intention to gloss over or even justify the violence of the military. Such was also the tone of much of the vehement criticism heaped upon Stoll by left-wing academic colleagues. His book was from a political or "objective" point of view reactionary. Menchú's book, on the other hand, was clearly progressive, its fundamental spiritual truth far greater than the sum of its individual fictitious parts. Though Augustine's name was not so far as I know mentioned, the implicit concept of allegorical truth was everywhere.

For all their differences, Frey's *A Million Little Pieces* and Menchú's *I, Rigoberta Menchú* are in fact very similar in important ways. Drug addiction and alcoholism are terrible scourges. Dictatorial government and military violence in Latin American countries are terrible scourges. In these two books their respective authors illustrate these evils with respect to their own personal experiences. Furthermore, they use a similar technique, by painting what was already bad as considerably worse even than it was. Like Augustine, they write exemplary fictitious autobiography. How is it to be explained that one author has her Nobel Prize confirmed and the other gets a tongue-lashing before millions of viewers on *The Oprah Winfrey Show*? It is to be explained, as human experience must always be explained, with regard to a large and very complex "context" of place and time, "social factors," "intellectual climate," and other somewhat vague abstractions frequently encountered in history books. The question of the truthfulness of the "autobiography" in *Out of the Night* was to be adjudicated in no other way, which is to say in a political way.

TRUTH AND CONSEQUENCES

According to its severest critics in the American Communist Party, there was no truth in the book at all. It was entirely a fraudulent work of fiction designed with the principal goal of maligning "progressive" politics and

aiding Fascism. Jan Valtin himself did not exist. The probable author of
the book was Isaac Don Levine, a notorious reactionary if not an outright
Fascist. The opposite view was that the book was absolutely true. Every
incident described happened to the author, Jan Valtin (Richard Krebs),
and happened exactly as described. It is possibly ironic that this was the
view that Krebs himself had to adopt. Clearly he had never been entirely
frank even with his intimate friend and collaborator Isaac Don Levine,
who either actually believed or found it commercially helpful not to disbelieve that the book was essentially "straight" autobiography. The publisher
Koppell also at least acted like a true believer. For the fact of the matter was
that while *Out of the Night* might be gripping as a novel, as an autobiography, an "historical document of our times," it was commercial dynamite.
At that moment the die was cast. Levine and Koppell sold the book on
terms that left Krebs no choice, even if he should have wanted to exercise
one.* It was a step that would create big problems for the author. His editor
and his publisher had cultivated the highest aspirations from the beginning, but even they must have been surprised by the trifecta of *Reader's
Digest*, *Life*, and the Book-of-the-Month Club.

An important pillar of Isaac Don Levine's career was his ability to
get "exclusives" with people prominently in the news. A native speaker of
Russian, he often had a comparative advantage in dealing with Russians
abroad. As of 1941 his greatest coup to date was his access to the recently
defunct General Krivitsky, "head of Stalin's Secret Service." He was still
going strong at the time of President John F. Kennedy's assassination, when
he gained unique journalistic access to Marina Oswald, the Russian-born
widow of the assassin. Valtin was potentially his greatest find ever, and he
was determined to present him as the absolutely genuine article. The jury
of the Book-of-the-Month Club, heavily lobbied by left-wing "experts" no
less than by the likes of Koppell and Levine, felt their individual reputations on the line. They required of Koppell, who then required of Krebs,
a detailed memorandum that would provide external textual proof of the
major episodes of the book. It is very difficult to provide external textual evidence of secret espionage operations, but Valtin came up with a
surprisingly impressive document even if some of its citations were rather

---

* Numerous eminent and judicious people expressed full confidence in the literal veracity of the
book. These included (to name a few) Roger Baldwin, head of the American Civil Liberties Union,
Nobel laureate Pearl Buck, Max Eastman, Congressman Jerry Voorhis, and Rose Wilder.

vague, such as "the Hamburg newspapers of the period" or "shipping line records." The lawyers exercised their metaphorical fine-toothed combs, excising from the first edition two or three passages in addition to the 100 pages or so that Levine, at the request of the book club, had cut out simply to make the book slightly less enormous. From that moment on, Krebs was stuck with defending the literal truth of a huge book in which he had in fact taken countless novelistic liberties in recasting his—and other people's—youthful experiences.

In fact there is a kind of "smoking gun" document in the files. Krebs, ever the cheapskate, appears in 1939 to have made a tour of the offices of certain New York literary agents trying to get some free advice. With one of them, a man named Fierst, he had a fairly extensive conversation about narrative point of view in his proposed "novel." Valtin was at that time inclined toward a third-person narrator. Fierst preferred the autobiographical suggestion of the first person. The next thing the agent ever heard about Valtin came with the overnight literary celebrity of his *autobiography*. Fierst, professionally aggrieved, sent Valtin a stiff note.

Fierst never went public, but other embarrassing evidence began to trickle in. Even before the large exodus from Western Communist parties of August 1939 (announcement of the Hitler-Stalin Pact), there had been a steady stream of defectors in the wake of the Spanish Civil War. Ex-Communists, as compared with Communists, were more given to the letter to the editor. The Valtin archive contains many letters of congratulation from such people; but there were other, less welcome communications. The May 20, 1941, issue of *Look* magazine contains a letter, with accompanying photograph, from Morris Appleman (who in *Out of the Night* had made a not insignificant appearance under his Communist name, Mike Pell), an American ex-Communist, ex-colleague of Valtin's from the Hamburg waterfront. The photograph shows the two of them seated with others at a speakers' table at a political meeting. The letter rather genially, though no less effectively, points out the flagrant exaggeration with which *Out of the Night* had presented their joint activities.

There was particular excitement in California, the site of young Valtin's crime and his incarceration. The episode of the crime is one of the most remarkable in the book. According to Valtin, he was summoned by "Getsy," a Russian Comintern boss, to a Los Angeles hotel room. There Getsy ordered Valtin to perform a purge execution, to kill an unidentified man who was a traitor to the cause. He was given no name, no details, only a glimpse of a photograph of "the head and chest of a middle-aged man of heavy Jewish features." After much scrupulous hesitation, and a long and melodramatic conversation about the dialectical necessity of Red Terror, Valtin accepts the assignment: "I found the man whom Getsy's spies had tracked down and assaulted him in broad daylight off a crowded street, knowing beforehand that the assault would end in failure. I struck him once with the butt of a revolver, in a gesture of violence that was more a blundering appeasement of a perverse sense of duty than the expression of an intent to destroy." (p. 179) Captured immediately by vigilant citizens and the police, Valtin was beaten up by his interrogators, then thrown into a hellhole cell ("the filthiest jail of the many I have known") where a brutal racist cop was hard at work on some earlier-day Rodney King. A messenger came from Getsy telling him to suck it up and take the fall; and he was very soon in San Quentin. Here was a narrative equally unflattering in its depiction of Communist crime and of capitalist punishment.

Communist propagandists had excellent sources in the prisons, and excellent access to the mainstream press. The *Sacramento Bee* came out with the first scoop. Prison records showed that "Jan Valtin" could be none other than a German sailor named Richard Krebs, convicted of atrocious assault in Los Angeles and incarcerated in San Quentin between 1926 and 1929. Reporters from competing Los Angeles papers, the semitabloid *Examiner* and the "quality" *Times*, then went to work. The reporter from the *Los Angeles Examiner* was quicker on the draw. In court records he found the name of Krebs's victim: Morris L. Goodstein. In the telephone book he found a Morris L. Goodstein. And in Goodstein's house he found Goodstein himself. Mr. Goodstein, a man in his fifties, was a naturalized American citizen of Polish birth. He was a religious Jew and a registered Republican. He had been a businessman for many years. In recent years he had been a retail haberdasher. He seemed to be an entirely law-abiding citizen, and certainly a law-utilizing one. He had launched no fewer than six lawsuits in the previous decade.

He had never heard of Jan Valtin or *Out of the Night*, but he certainly remembered the day in August 1926 when a strange young man walked into his shop to rob and beat him. For Goodstein was certain that it had been an attempted robbery. The crime took place "in broad daylight off a crowded street" insofar as it happened during daylight hours in the interior of Goodstein's store, which was on Seventh Street. Krebs came in and asked for some shirts and socks. While Goodstein was wrapping them, Krebs attacked him with a pistol used as a club, then fled in order, as Goodstein supposed, to avoid paying for the clothes. The reporter asked that Goodstein allow his photographer to take a picture, then to sign a legal release which he happened to have to hand. Mrs. Goodstein wondered whether there might be a financial dimension to the transaction. A bill of small denomination changed hands, and Goodstein signed.

The following facts emerged in an eventual private investigation. Over at the *Los Angeles Times*, the editor was most unhappy to have been scooped by the *Examiner*, and he sent his ace reporter to catch up with and overtake his competitor's industry. During this man's own visit to the Goodstein household, Mrs. Goodstein took the lead. She raised the question of a payment immediately; and she became irate upon learning the *Times* man's view that yesterday's news is free, like the air we breathe, that her husband had been unwise to sell a fifty-dollar story for five dollars, and unwiser still to have signed the piece of paper. He did toss off at some point that one source of revenue might be Jan Valtin, who now had the resources of a best-selling author. Even as her husband continued to talk to the reporter she went to the telephone, called the office of the *Examiner*, and told them what she thought of having been gypped.

The *Times* ran a long piece designed in such a way as to give the impression that it was not essentially the same story already published by the *Examiner*. It played up the obvious discrepancies between Valtin's version of events and Goodstein's. Goodstein called his lawyer and began discussing his seventh lawsuit: a charge of libel against Richard Krebs, the Alliance Book Corporation, and the *Reader's Digest*. All sums in this story are multiples of five. Goodstein wanted $50,000, though he eventually settled for $500. When Henry Koppell learned of the threatened suit, he immediately wrote a rather stern note to Krebs. He pointed out the clause in their contract that held the author solely responsible for the accuracy of all statements in the book and the publisher fully indemnified; but he generously volunteered to share with Krebs the costs of investigating Goodstein so long as he, Koppell, was in charge of it. The attorney for Alliance Books huddled with Don Levine and expressed the limited satisfaction that at least the stories in the Los Angeles papers had not been picked up by the national press—unless, that is, one considered *The Daily Worker* national.

Benjamin Gitlow, one time head of the American Communist Party, and one of its earlier apostates, included in his book *All of Their Lives* a section entitled "The Campaign Against Jan Valtin," which was actually begun before Jan Valtin had been invented. Krebs had broken with the Party in 1938. We have already encountered his suspicious account of his flight from Europe. He claimed to have escaped from house arrest in Copenhagen, eluding his Comintern jailer, Richard Jensen, who was about to ship him to Moscow for liquidation. According to Richard Jensen, Krebs, having been exposed as a traitor and a Gestapo spy, simply disappeared into the night for his own good. Jensen had Krebs's passport, and he used it to make a kind of "Wanted" poster with Krebs's photograph and the boldface legend "Beware! Gestapo Agent!" He circulated this worldwide through the ubiquitous Communist sections of seamen's clubs. The Comintern authorities rightly suspected that Krebs would head for America, and they made sure that a version of the poster was published, with commentary, in New York in *The Daily Worker*, in February and March 1938. This would put the factual Richard Krebs in New York in something of the position of the fictional Gypo Nolan in the Dublin of Liam O'Flaherty's *The Informer*. Now, in 1941, Krebs was in danger of being "outed" to a much larger public by his own sensational success.

WHAT THE REVIEWERS SAID

Contemporary reviews of *Out of the Night* are useful mainly as an index of the book's impact on general readers. The impact was stunning. Valtin got rave reviews in most of the newspapers and journals. Just as he had ready-made enemies, he had a ready-made claque-in-waiting as well. Freda Utley, a British ex-Communist intellectual who had lost her Russian husband to the purges and barely escaped alive from Moscow herself, praised the book. Pearl Buck, who had been awarded the Nobel Prize for Literature in 1938, gave it a glowing review in the journal *Asia*—a somewhat puzzling venue, perhaps, given the fact that the book's Asian connections are slight. (Mrs. Buck would be a strong political ally of Krebs's in a later hour of need.) Then, too, there was a nuanced but positive notice in *The New Yorker* from Clifton Fadiman, who was in if not of the set of "New York Intellectuals" more famously represented by Lionel Trilling and Sidney

Hook. Fadiman was at that time rising in prominence as the master of ceremonies of the popular radio program *Information Please* and gracefully sloughing off, without any dramatic gestures of political conversion, the hard leftism of the mid-thirties. He was too good a reader not to sniff the aroma of fiction in parts of the book, but he also concluded, soundly, that as a whole the effect was "somehow not phony."

The absurd initial position of *The Daily Worker*—that "Jan Valtin" himself was a fiction—made great advertising copy for the publishers. The teaser brochure put out by the Book-of-the-Month Club, titled "The Truth About Jan Valtin," quoted the Communist press with glee, along with photos of Valtin. The most sustained and vicious attack on the book was the review by Isidor Schneider in the *New Masses* (March 4, 1941). Preaching to the choir is a hallowed tradition among religious groups of all stripes, but his essay "Out of the Sewer" was more like preaching to the organist. By 1941, the "masses" were a small number of radical intellectuals who had managed to swallow, and indeed digest, the Molotov Pact, the Finnish War, and the martyrdom of Poland, not to mention the extraordinary internal political gyrations of the American Communist Party. Though now unfairly forgotten, Isidor Schneider was one of the very few first-rate literary minds to grace American Communism. He was a poet of talent and a smart critic of poems committed to a movement that, as Max Eastman demonstrated, was generally hostile to poetry.

Of course one hopes to learn from a reviewer more than whether that person likes or dislikes the book reviewed. One hopes for an independent expert comment on the subjects treated. There are in the nature of things few public experts on the secret and "conspirative" world the Valtin book described, but two of the reviews offered something along those lines, and though they tended in opposing directions, they may be said to have met in the middle.

In the March 28, 1941, issue of the Roman Catholic journal *Commonweal*, there is a substantial review by the Reverend H. A. Reinhold of Seattle, a priest of German origin who had, fifteen years earlier, been conducting his religious ministry as a seamen's chaplain in Hamburg. He knew the German seaports—the scenes of Valtin's early Communist activities—intimately. He pronounces the depiction of that world in *Out of the Night* not merely truthful and convincing, but astonishingly so. Indeed, he says that Valtin's book allowed him to see, in retrospect, aspects of the political situation in 1930, to which he had been largely blind at the time. "Jan Valtin has opened my eyes and like lightning, illuminating the whole firmament, the patched scenery suddenly grows into an organized whole, and the two competing forces [Communists and Nazis] become rival armies with shock troops, secret services, and general staff and a continuous strategy . . . how naïve were we in our false security, our smug bourgeois and pseudo-Christian confidence that nothing would happen!"

Furthermore, says Reinhold, he has actually conducted research to test Valtin's reliability. From an unnamed German ex-Communist, an "internationally known Marxist theoretician," he has learned the following: "This book is extremely reliable in all things concerning facts and persons. In hundreds of places where I was able to check up, it is absolutely accurate." *Hundreds* of places?

For instance, says his anonymous expert, the depiction of Ernst Wollweber is spot on. "I knew [Wollweber] myself in 1923–24, and I remember him exactly as the Wollweber of Valtin 'in the bud.'" This same authority identifies for special praise a chapter called "Soviet Skipper," in which Valtin narrates, with scant plausibility, how at the age of twenty-seven, and with no previous experience as a ship's officer, he came to have skippered a Russian ship from Bremen to Murmansk. (This was an episode in the book that some later attacks identified as being particularly fantastic.)

Reinhold actually has his own doubts about certain episodes, especially concerning Valtin's alleged hoodwinking of his Nazi captors. "I have no evidence to doubt him. But I am astonished that his shrewd inquisitors would have fallen for such a crude business." "Considering everything," Father Reinhold concluded, "I should say that this book seems to be perhaps 95 per cent correct and 5 per cent 'retouched,' which is a tremendously good record for any autobiographer."

There is a footnote. About six weeks later in the pages of *Commonweal* Father Reinhold's review was answered, after a fashion, by one of the fellow pilgrims of the Catholic left, S. A. Johnson, a friend of Dorothy Day at the *Catholic Worker*. Johnson had no specific expertise, and no specific knowledge, that might debunk Valtin. Yet he smelled a rat, or perhaps a whole colony of rodents. While making it clear that he did not believe very much of what Valtin had to say, his real complaint was not the book's veracity or lack thereof, but its political tendency. It was a reactionary work that—because it dealt so recklessly with suggestions of Communist skulduggery among the maritime labor unions—encouraged resistance to the legitimate aspirations of the American labor movement. That was Dorothy Day's own view, and also the view of *The Daily Worker*.

A second, detailed and impressive review appeared in the special number of *The Modern Quarterly* put together to commemorate its recently deceased founder, V. F. ("George") Calverton. This review is mysterious in several ways. It is not possible to tell exactly when it was written, or by whom. The special number of *The Modern Quarterly* is undated, though one copy I consulted bears a library accession stamp of early May 1941. It is signed "R. M. Firl." All my attempts to identify this person have failed, suggesting that it is a pseudonym. Max Eastman, who had in the old days been a good friend of Calverton and who had published an affectionate memorial essay in the same number, had by that time become friendly with Richard Krebs. Eastman, who clearly thought that *Out of the Night* was a history rather than a novel, wrote to Krebs to express outrage over the review. He put the name "Firl" in quotation marks, indicating that he too considered it a pseudonym, and he attributes the responsibility for publishing it to the ignorance or malice of Nina Melville, Calverton's surviving longtime partner, whom he regarded as a malleable tool of the American Communist Party.

The review itself is substantial (about 1,500 words), well written, and at least apparently balanced in its judgments; and it projects a strong sense of authority. The author either actually is, or convincingly pretends to be, an expert in the history of the German Communist Party. (It is perhaps interesting that this last sentence could apply equally well to Jan Valtin.) Firl's indictment of the book is all the more powerful for its sobriety and rhetorical restraint, so markedly different in its intellectual texture from the crude railing of the Communist press. "The mystery of Valtin and his best-seller *Out of the Night* has not yet been dispelled, since few individuals have the intimate knowledge of personalities and events which Valtin realistically describes in his work on the G.P.U., the Communist International, and the Gestapo. In the interest of historical truth, however, the essential facts about Valtin and his work must be critically examined."

Firl states the problem of *Out of the Night* in the following lucid terms: "If Valtin had written a book of fiction or an exciting story of adventure, it would be of little interest whether he actually experienced the adventures he described. But he and his publisher claim he has written an historical document." Firl clearly believes that a great deal of the book is fiction. Valtin certainly was a Communist agent, but a low-level apparatchik, not one of the conspiratorial leaders. "He belonged to a group of Communist seamen who were delegated by the German Communist Party for messenger work in various ports at home and abroad." He was, in short, a Red flunky.

The book's Achilles heel, if we may indulge Firl in the pathetic fallacy, is its aggrandizement of the modest roles actually played by Valtin into dramatic personal encounters with the likes of Georgi Dmitrov, boss of the Comintern, and Heinrich Himmler, torturer-in-chief of the Gestapo. He attributes this fault to the author's vanity, and to the peculiar tunnel vision imposed upon him by his actual situation. As a very minor grade espionage agent, Valtin "was living as an isolated individual or rather as a member of a little group of isolated individuals." The "narrowness of his work in an isolated group" gave him no access to the larger picture of what was happening in and to the German Party. "With great naïveté Valtin acted as if historical events were decided by an order of a G.P.U. chief. Somebody pushed a button and a revolutionary action was initiated or cancelled—an attitude shared today by the Party's members and fellow-travelers in America."

This is Firl's dismissive conclusion: "Valtin's book would have been a useful and interesting work for the historian and political student if he had given an authentic report of his experiences as a minor tool of the Communist Party and messenger for the underground organization. . . . But Valtin in his book tries to pose in roles he never played."

Of the many early reviews of *Out of the Night*, Firl's essay is probably the most perceptive and astute. But not many people read it, and most of those who did would have been among the far left fringe that made up the dwindling regular readership of *The Modern Quarterly*. Most of them would already be predisposed not to like the book. As for Firl, it is just possible, barely, that he was a Communist plant and that his condescending remark about Party members and fellow travelers was meant to deceive. It is much more likely that he was an astute reader who happened to know a lot about German Communism. In any event, his review disappeared from subsequent discussion.

The "Truth" about Jan Valtin

Between the two of them, Reinhold and Firl pretty much concluded the probable truth. Krebs had been deeply involved in underground Communist work with the Wollweber apparatus, and his book does indeed reveal a specific and convincing knowledge of many aspects of Comintern skulduggery on the German waterfront. Hence its powerful sense of authority and conviction. On the other hand, much of the book is fictional, and many incidents involving the narrator Jan Valtin cannot have been the actual biographical experiences of the author Richard Krebs. In fact much later Krebs did allow, in an interview with the *New York Times*, that his central character was to some degree a composite, in whose experiences the author had amalgamated his own experiences with some reported by friends and colleagues. But that was later, when he was home free.

Between real life and a novel true to real life, however, there is a considerable gap. Krebs and his publisher Koppell insisted on real life. The question of how thoughtfully or advisedly they made such a commitment is now moot. The commitment, once made, obviously could not be altered. At the same time they appreciated the possibility that the controversy about the book's authenticity might stimulate sales. In the *New York Times* of April 4, 1941, there appeared a large advertisement headed "The Truth About Jan Valtin, Author of America's No. 1 Best-Seller." It featured a picture of the book in its latest printing, with a newly designed jacket, and a head shot of Krebs looking pretty grim in his spy-hat and trench coat. "From the day of publication, OUT OF THE NIGHT has been the center of a raging controversy regarding its authenticity," begins the copy. "It was rumored that Valtin did not exist. Later, that he did exist but never wrote the book. Later, that he did write the book but could not possible have lived the fantastic adventures recounted in OUT OF THE NIGHT. Now that America's greatest critics and public figures vehemently proclaim themselves convinced of his book's authenticity, Jan Valtin is being savagely attacked by the sinister forces he exposes with such merciless detail."

Beneath the text are two parallel columns labeled "Hoax?" and "Authentic!"—the "Hoax" column being appropriately on the left. Those casting their votes for Hoax include the voices of *The Daily Worker*, the

New Masses, and *People's World*. Among the authenticators are the afore-mentioned Father Reinhold, the *New York Times* editorial page, and John Dewey, probably the most venerated public intellectual in America. In case the *Times* reader was still hesitating over the difficult choice between column A and column B, there was some final, boldface advice from Mrs. Pearl Buck, Nobel laureate. "Here is all the argument for freedom and democracy. Here is what happens to a human being who gives them up. . . . Its significance is enormous, its meaning at this hour of human history is as wide as the world."

"The Truth About Jan Valtin" was also the title of an unusual ten-page brochure brought out in promotion of the book by the Alliance Book Corporation. This featured some of the same copy as the advertisement, but it had many other features, including letters from readers, letters from people who had known "Valtin" back in the day, in or out of prison, a letter from a teenager in Talladega that concludes: "You may be a German or even a Communist, but here's one American boy that's for you." There are excerpts from reviews, including one by Karl Baarslag, prominent in the American Federation of Labor. "I was howled down by the communist 'faction' in control of the American Radio Telegraphists Association when I charged in 1934 that the Marine Workers Industrial Union of Roy 'Horseface the Bishop' Hudson was a simon-pure communist fake." But Valtin's *Out of the Night* has now vindicated his conclusion. There is a sample of Valtin's San Quentin prose, and there is a brief excerpt from his famous essay "American Dawn."

On the back of the brochure, above the order coupon, are listed four things that the book offers its readers. The third of them is "The first-hand authentic, life-size picture of the dangers, more deadly than 70-ton tanks, now facing the democracies," and, fourth, "An antidote for the enemies of America's tomorrow, who are distorting the truth about today." This is prose that forbids easy parsing. *Who*, exactly, are America's "enemies"? They could be Nazis; they could be Commies. Probably both since Valtin, after all, had had experience of both, and we were amidst the short period of alliance effected by the Hitler-Stalin Pact of 1939. The ecumenical power of Jan Valtin's exposure is underscored by the ecumenical word "totalitarian," then of quite recent invention. His book "explodes the truth about the same ruthless totalitarian efficiency now working day and night to undermine our defenses."

SLEUTHS AT *PM*

There was at this time in New York, in its early months of publication, a left-wing daily tabloid called *PM*, as that was when it appeared on the streets. Its publisher was Ralph Ingersoll, and its news editor was Kenneth Stewart, an ambitious journalist who published the interesting book *The News Is What We Make It*. He was a "soft" fellow traveler, deeply suspicious of Valtin and his book. Among his friends was a "hard" fellow traveler and writer named Wellington Roe. He was the author of unread proletarian novels and an unsuccessful congressional candidate of the American Labor Party—a party whose only successful candidate at the federal level was Vito Marcantonio. At the beginning of March 1941, Roe came to Stewart with a plan to investigate and expose Valtin. Roe already knew, presumably from Communist sources, rather more than most people knew about Valtin. He knew, for example, something about Robert Bek-Gran and the "Hamburg boys." At first the line shared by the *Worker* and the reviewer for *PM*, Selwyn James, was that Jan Valtin was himself a fiction, and that the book was the work of "the clumsy, pulpish hand of Isaac Don Levine." But Stewart and Roe knew that Valtin existed, and that he might even have written a book.

The Book-Club edition of *Out of the Night* was actually a second edition, and at 750 pages, it is about 100 pages shorter than the first. While you or I might think of a few ideas about why one might want to cut down a book of 850 pages intended for the mass market, Roe could think of none except Fascist subterfuge. He and Stewart sat down to the tedious job of collating the texts and of exposing the possible deviationism in their deviations. They talked to anybody they could talk to. Roe had an especially revealing interview with Bek-Gran. Both of them actually talked to Krebs before he had fully grasped their intentions. Later, Krebs became hostile. From him, Koppell and the Alliance lawyers became aware of the project and rattled serving papers at the *PM* lawyers, with considerable success. Stewart decided not to publish an exposé. What he published instead, at Ingersoll's insistence, was the material of a very long (sixteen pages) memorandum to the publisher describing the raw materials that the investigation had dug up.

The net effect was clearly skeptical and suspicious concerning the claims of the book and its promoters, but Stewart and Ingersoll at least affected agnosticism. (Wellington Roe, as we shall see, was not yet ready to abandon the chase.) "The story of Kenneth Stewart's story of 'Out of the Night,'" Ingersoll wrote, "is a story of a journalist in search of the truth." And Stewart added that the truth would be hard to know, since all the principals involved had "either a political or a commercial axe to grind—a sweeping statement which includes the book's enemies, as well as its friends, with total impartiality." Actually, the article did contain the truth, though neither its authors nor its readers were capable of seizing it. *The* crucial truth was that since the time Richard Krebs took his first extension course in San Quentin he had wanted more than anything else, not excluding the world revolution, to be a successful writer of sea stories in the tradition of Joseph Conrad. That was already apparent in a letter he wrote back to his old teacher Arthur Price from Bremen in 1930.

A Campaign of Public Relations

Krebs came to America in a state of total political burnout in order to write adventure novels. He rightly described himself as a "political refugee," meaning that he was fleeing not a particular set of political ideas but the claims of political dogmatism altogether. Few men can have had a more genuine claim to the term. To describe him as a political chameleon would be a bit harsh, but he certainly easily adopted a kind of latitudinarian anti-totalitarianism that could win the friendship of arch anti-Communist Don Levine on the one hand and on the other that of Roger Baldwin, the recovering fellow traveler who was the perennial head of the American Civil Liberties Union.

There were other detractors of *Out of the Night* of a different stamp. In order to understand the political mind of those times, it is necessary to grasp the iconic significance of the Soviet Union in the worldview of "progressives." There were many non-Communist leftists. There were even many anti-Communist, or at least anti-Stalinist, leftists. But the Soviet Union was the one socialist country on earth—the "socialist sixth of the globe," as they liked to call it. Socialism was the baby, the Soviet Union the rather gray and scummy bathwater. The greater the fear of losing the baby, the greater the tolerance of the dirty bathwater. Socialism was being "built" in the Soviet Union. We were witnessing the difficult transition period toward real Communism. This was "the middle of the journey"—to use the phrase chosen by Lionel Trilling for the title of his novel about Gifford Maxim, a character born of the author's acquaintance with the younger Whittaker Chambers. What "Trotskyism" was, in essence, was the heretical attempt to divide baby from bathwater, socialism from Stalin. So there were many attacks on *Out of the Night* that paid no attention to its "truth" or "falsehood," but deplored its "tendency"—a tendency to divert to the secondary, minor, and transient imperfections of a Socialism in progress the scorn and detestation rightly due to the much greater scandals, beyond all hope of reform short of their utter destruction, of Capitalism and Imperialism. How else are we to account for Dorothy Day's holding Valtin virtually or morally responsible for the slaughter of striking coal miners in West Virginia? We shall have occasion in another context to see how widely shared this attitude was among European intellectuals.

Having committed himself and his publisher to the entirely veracious and autobiographical nature of *Out of the Night*, Krebs was now faced with certain insufficiently anticipated implications. If the book was the truth, its author was a thug and a convicted violent felon who had been deported immediately upon his release from San Quentin. How did it come about that he was now once more in the United States? On that topic his book, however truthful, was strangely mute. It is not known exactly what triggered the move made against Krebs as an illegal immigrant, but the move itself was virtually inevitable. The illegal immigrant's hope for a peaceful life is quiet anonymity and a low profile. Valtin had thrust himself forward as a national celebrity. If the Communist camp did not instigate the action of the Justice Department, it certainly warmly seconded the motion. But during the first half of 1941, just as there began a long campaign of Communist origin *against* Valtin-Krebs, there also began a campaign of anti-Communist support in his favor. In some ways the public aspect of the pro-Krebs effort mimicked the conventions of a political campaign. It had three main thrusts. First, Krebs would address his immigration difficulties directly and in writing. Next, Krebs would be personally displayed before, and introduced to, as many people of consequence as it was possible to round up for that purpose. Third, Krebs himself would go on a patriotic lecture tour to as many parts of the country as possible. On all three "fronts" there was success, but on the first there was *wild* success.

Krebs wrote and published in the May 1941 issue of the *Reader's Digest* a kind of *apologia*, a lengthy essay (about 3,500 words) entitled "American Dawn." Before reviewing that remarkable document, however, it is useful to say a few words about the cultural influence of the *Reader's Digest* in the early forties, which was in two words very large. The magazine had 4 million paid subscriptions, and each copy was probably looked at by three or four people. (By the early fifties, in the real Cold War years, the circulation increased fourfold!) It was widely read in the public schools. The magazine did indeed digest or re-edit articles from other journals. (Its enemies charged that these "digested" articles had actually been planted in the first place.) It also commissioned a few original articles. Its articles ranged widely, but there was a definite emphasis on uplift, patriotism, American pluck, and a kind of saccharine ecumenical religion. One of the jokes of my youth was a suggested model title for a *Reader's Digest* article: "I Slept with a Bear for the FBI and Found God." Most writers— including some notorious leftists like Louis Fischer—would practically die to get a commission from the *Reader's Digest*, which paid a fabulous dollar a word.

DeWitt and Lila Wallace were the inventors and sole owners of the *Reader's Digest,* which might reasonably be described as the most successful and profitable periodical publication in history. DeWitt Wallace was its very hands-on chief executive. Like many other fabulously successful and wealthy tycoons, they were not without their arrogances and their eccentricities, and they have received on the whole a bad press. They were people of conservative cultural instinct and great American boosters, but by no means Babbitts. DeWitt Wallace was one of the shrewdest and most competent journalistic entrepreneurs in American history. It is hard to accept, as has been suggested by some recent studies, that he had a malignantly reactionary political agenda for which their magazine was a convenient means of propagation. However, the *Reader's Digest* was for many years the magazine that the American left loved to hate.

As we shall see, the Communists and their friends hated it with a particular fury; but the odium has outlived both the heyday of the magazine and the viability of the Communist Party. As late as 1982, Susan

Sontag caused an uproar among progressives by suggesting that "the émi-grés from the communist countries we didn't listen to, who found it far easier to get published in the *Reader's Digest* than in the *Nation* or the *New Statesman*, were telling the truth." And in fact the anti-Communist martyr and the convert from Communism frequently enough appeared in the magazine's pages, the most famous Red apostates being the likes of Eugene Lyons and Max Eastman, who had a long and happy (and lucra-tive) association with the journal. In one of his autobiographies, East-man remarked that "Writing for the *Reader's Digest*, while not exactly an art, is a highly specialized craft. The magazine is largely concerned with the life of ideas, but as it is addressed to some 50 or 60 million readers—the actual copies printed number over 17 million—the ideas have to be presented with a self-explanatory simplicity. I have learned this craft by thinking of myself as a teacher when writing essays of this kind for the *Reader's Digest*." In June 1941, Eastman burnt the last bridge to his left-wing past with an article entitled "Socialism Doesn't Jibe with Human Nature." Thus wrote the old editor of the old *Masses*, to the cha-grin of the new editor of the *New Masses*. In the meantime, the *Reader's Digest* had preempted the masses.

It is at this point that a certain Sender Garlin makes his first, though surely not his last appearance in this book. Sender Garlin was a long-time literary apparatchik of the American Communist Party. He ended his days at a great age only quite recently as an elder statesman of the progressive community in Boulder, Colorado. He had a long association with *The Daily Worker*, for which he was for a time their man in Moscow. Later he had a literary column in that paper called "The Constant Reader" in which he took note of books to be praised or blamed. In 1943—after the United States was joined in military alliance with its fellow demo-crats in the USSR—he brought out a dime pamphlet of some thirty pages under the title *The Truth About Reader's Digest*, a riposte, one presumes, to *The Truth About Jan Valtin*. It is a brief catalogue of criminals who have been endorsed by the *Reader's Digest*. Certainly Valtin features largely in it, where he is presented as a Gestapo agent as well as a literary hoaxer. William Gropper, the genius artist of *The Daily Worker*, graces the pam-phlet with three remarkable caricatures of famous Fascists whose careers have been enhanced by their glorification in the *Reader's Digest*: Francisco Franco, Charles Lindbergh, and Jan Valtin. It is perhaps the brisk market for Gropper that has made the pamphlet something of a bibliographical rarity today.

So it was in the forum most despised by the Communists that Valtin would plead his case. Krebs was already friendly with two men—Eugene Lyons and Max Eastman—who were close to Wallace. Together with the publisher Koppell, they had arranged for the publication of excerpts from *Out of the Night* in the *Digest* in February and March 1941. Later on, Krebs himself became friendly with Wallace. (There is a letter from Wallace to Abigail Krebs thanking her for the gift of Garlin's pamphlet, which he had heard of but not yet seen.)

"American Dawn" appeared in the May issue. A prefatory note explained that many readers wrote to Krebs, including several who had directly known of or participated in events described in the book. "Many others wrote to ask Mr. Valtin (or to use his real name, Richard J. Krebs) such questions as these: 'What was your purpose in laying before the Americans the terrible exposures in this book? Where do you yourself, a former communist agent, now stand in regard to Communism and Fascism? What does America mean to you?' To answer these sincere and important questions Mr. Valtin has written the following article."

Having myself read through large files of letters written by his book's readers without finding any of these questions asked, even once, I must suggest that this is a soft pitch tossed in Valtin's direction by the editors of the *Reader's Digest*. Valtin certainly knocked it out of the park. Practically overnight "American Dawn" was declared a classic of contemporary prose. It seems that everybody was reading it, citing it, taking it as a text for sermons or for tenth-grade English classes. It was treated as a newly discovered sacred text of the American Civil Religion of Liberty, Decency, Opportunity, and Fair Play. In addition to the 4 million copies circulating among paid subscribers, DeWitt Wallace had arranged for a free distribution of at least 750,000 offprints of the article on its own.

Valtin reviewed some of the biography related in *Out of the Night*, but this time penitently. Of the crime that sent him to San Quentin he wrote: "It was inevitable that, sooner or later, I should come into serious conflict with the law of the country whose hospitality I abused." But for him an American prison offered opportunities unavailable to him as a free man in Old Europe: "As a convicted criminal in America, I might have a university education—an education that in Europe is the hall-mark of the upper classes!" In another place: "the prison food I ate was better than the food I had had on European ships during my years at sea." And in yet another: "I saw, at last, that a convict in America enjoys incomparably more intellectual and spiritual freedom than a 'free' man under totalitarian rule."

This is what a large section of the American public wanted to hear, and what practically nobody was unwilling to hear. Valtin was engaging with one of the classic themes of our history and our literature—American exceptionalism as portrayed in *The American, A Yank at Oxford, An American in Paris,* and now *A Lumpenhund in San Quentin.* In very general terms he continued his autobiography where he had left it off. This was his *American* autobiography, and given the seriousness of the stakes and the close scrutiny to which he knew it would be subjected, it is probably a reliable source for tracing the genesis and composition of *Out of the Night.* All the great American themes are in this essay, or at least the self-flattering ones—dream the impossible dream, the sky's the limit, opportunity is everywhere.

What is the purpose of his book? "It has no hidden political purpose. It has a threefold human purpose. I wrote it to raise an insurmountable wall between a monstrously mistaken past and my firm determination now to live a normal and constructive life. I wrote it as a monument to the betrayed courage and devotion of Firelei." Everyone in America was supposed to know that Firelei was the name of his martyred wife. "And I wrote it to show free men and free women that the salvation of mankind cannot be the work of tyranny disguised as the way to freedom. . . ."

And what are your current politics? "I have ceased to believe in any 'political program.' But I have a conviction that human beings can struggle successfully for a form of life that is decent and just and fair, within the framework of democracy as it has developed in the United States." And unobtrusively, without fanfare but also without any possibility that it will be overlooked, he enumerates "the right of the individual to free enterprise" as one of the great political blessings of the land he would make his home . . . *if only.*

"Now that *Out of the Night* has found its way into thousands of homes, the cry has been raised: 'Jan Valtin is an alien! He entered illegally and must be deported!' True, I have come to America without observing the formalities of lawful entry. But I came the way millions had come to these shores before me—in search of freedom and opportunity. I came to America to elude the assassins of Hitler and Stalin, to begin a new life, to prove to myself and to other men that I am not unfit to lend a hand in constructive endeavor." Whatever slight chance of actual deportation to Germany Krebs faced was probably dissolved completely the moment that the copies went into the post.

In the waning days of that same month of May he gave a more practical demonstration of his conversion to the new American spirit somewhat abstractly outlined in his essay. He spent two days testifying before Martin Dies and his colleagues on the House Committee on Un-American Activities (HUAC). He followed that up with a day split between the State Department, where he was able to identify "many" photographs shown to him of "persons suspected of subversive activities and passport frauds," and a "gathering of Congressmen" organized by Jerry Voorhis, Democrat of California, and Noah Mason, Republican of Illinois, to hear his advice concerning "totalitarian technique and how to fight it." His unwavering strategy was now clear. He was not an "anti-Communist." He was an "anti-totalitarian." Thus he reports that "I also was approached by two representatives of Henry Ford, the industrialist, with an offer of a series of nationwide broadcasts against Communism. I made the condition that I would broadcast against Communism only if I were given one anti-Nazi broadcast, financed by Ford, for each anti-Communist broadcast." (The plan was never realized.)

Just as a certain number of the members of the American Communist Party were physically unattractive, cranky, socially inept, needy neurotics, so a certain number of the small battalion of ex-Communists gathered around the Dies Committee were physically unattractive, cranky, socially inept, needy neurotics. They suffered further the daily humiliations of all turncoats who depend for their daily bread on being turncoats. In a perceptive essay, Arthur Koestler listed prominently among the factors perpetuating the intellectual blindness of Communist true believers their fear of embarrassment "by undesirable allies, by approval from the reactionary camp, their triumphant I-always-told-you-so." To deplore the shifting policy of the Comintern did not necessarily mean that one agreed with the rants of Texas Baptists about godless Communism. Krebs always felt superior to most other committee witnesses, though he did become friendly with one or two.

San Quentin prisoners no doubt read *Out of the Night* with a particular interest, but it penetrated other prisons as well. In the state penitentiary in Raleigh, North Carolina, Fred Beal read and savored the book. Fred Beal was a rare specimen within the American Communist Party, for he was a genuine Yankee proletarian Communist from the textile mills of Massachusetts. In 1929 he was one of the leaders of the infamous textile strike in Gastonia, North Carolina, in which an officer of the law had been shot and killed. For this crime, of which he was certainly innocent, he was convicted and sentenced to a long prison term. This infamous injustice was to the liberal mind as flagrant as the earlier convictions of Tom Mooney and Warren Billings, Sacco and Vanzetti.

Together with several other railroaded strikers and organizers, Beal jumped bail and, aided by New York Communists, fled to the Soviet Union. This tragic group found little but misery and disillusionment in the socialist fatherland, where their propaganda value was soon exhausted. Beal worked for a while in the famous tractor works in Kharkov, and he actually saw firsthand the ravages of the famine in the Ukraine. He experienced the stultifying regimentation, the material want, and the psychological terror of daily Soviet life. He eventually concluded that life in a North Carolina prison pounding boulders was to be preferred to life in the Soviet Union building socialism. Miraculously, he got out of the country and back to America, where in 1937 he published a remarkable book, *Proletarian Journey*, in which he told his story. This was, and is, a fine book; but it was not widely read. Beal was denounced and indeed sabotaged by the American Communists, who successfully blocked other segments of the labor movement from helping with his court appeal. He surrendered to North Carolina authorities and began a prison term most of the country considered a disgrace. Brought from prison to Washington before the Dies Committee, Beal testified that Communist strategy in Gastonia had never been to win the strike but to increase the misery of the millworkers to raise their class-consciousness.

Toward Beal—a true as opposed to a rhetorical "comrade" in shared experience—Krebs directed a rare act of uncomplicated charity. He sent him two dollars, a sum less risible then than now, in the hopes that he might be able to buy a few snacks and toilet articles. He also sent him a book with the following note: "This is the best thing that has ever been published about the situation in Russia." The book was *Darkness at Noon*. The two men received their separate pardons about the same time in 1941. Beal deserved his.

A second phase of the campaign, designed to win over influential liberal thought, was led by Roger Baldwin, one of the founders of the American

Civil Liberties Union (ACLU) and its longtime executive director. Baldwin probably came into contact with Krebs through Max Eastman, whose sister Crystal had been prominent in the pacifist milieu in which the ACLU had been born, but he developed an independent friendship with the German writer. In interjecting himself so energetically into the Valtin affair, Baldwin was animated by a possibly overcompensatory anti-Communism. He had visited Russia in pre-Stalin days and allowed himself to be taken in in a rather naive fashion. Like many other early "pilgrims," his later disenchantment was painful and dramatic. Amid much ethical hand-wringing he had felt obliged to rid the ACLU board of its Communists, a group that had included the famous Elizabeth Gurley Flynn. By the time of the Cold War the pacifist had become a metaphorical warrior, publishing in 1953 one of the more scathing denunciations of the Soviet Union, *A New Slavery*. He was convinced of the truth of *Out of the Night*, and recognized its potential for demystifying Stalinism for the kind of liberals who made up his organization. He doubtless saw something of his own younger self in Jan Valtin.

Baldwin was an excellent politician, and he had considerable influence among the liberal lawyers of New York, Philadelphia, and Washington, who in turn often had the ear of the U.S. Attorney General, Robert Jackson. From the start, he understood that Krebs's aim must be nothing less than citizenship by naturalization. He eventually allowed Krebs to realize that aim, but for the moment he intended to move sensibly in a gradual fashion. First would come a public relations blitz, then a campaign for a gubernatorial pardon in California.

Baldwin seems to have been a man of luminous character and very wide acquaintance. He was ideally placed to introduce Krebs to influential business leaders, journalists, writers, politicians, and society matrons. He organized numerous luncheons specifically for this purpose. It was at such a luncheon that Krebs had met Markoosha Fischer—who then felt compelled to write him with the probably superfluous news that his friends Lyons and Levine were not good socialists—and at another sat next to Norman Cousins, with results, as we shall see, probably fatal to the literary aspiration of another literary felon. Considering that he was a waterfront goon, an ex-con, an autodidact, and a non-native speaker of the English language, Krebs handled himself with amazing aplomb in social situations that must have been for him novel and potentially intimidating. It is impossible to survey the Valtin archive without running up against evidence of the man's serious imperfections; but no more is it possible to escape the conclusion that many admirable and remarkable people thought him a remarkable and admirable person.

Krebs was doing well for himself by doing good for his cause. He got a fat check for "American Dawn," and he now took to the lecture circuit in earnest. Abandoning Abigail, his child bride, to protracted solitude back at the apple farm, he traveled all over America, wherever his agent could book him for $100 or $125. There were many speakers' bureaus and lecturers' agencies, and Krebs, a hot property, had signed up with one of the best. Despite the comparative fortune he had made from his book, he continued to worry about money, of which he kept niggling records. His lecture tours gave cover for his stalled writing. There is also at least the hint that his travels protected him from the emotional intimacy of marriage for which he yearned but was apparently ill suited. At least this is what Abigail Krebs had come to conclude when, some years later, she divorced him, citing "emotional cruelty." She wrote of the agonizing loneliness of the country-side in which she had been abandoned. He went to civic clubs, churches, synagogues, and college campuses. His themes were carefully chosen and concentrated primarily on recent European political history and the Nazi menace, but he also spoke of generic "dictatorship" and "dictators" in a way that left little doubt of his opinion of Joseph Stalin. He talked about spies and saboteurs (something like a national obsession in the early for-ties), their aims and their techniques. He talked about the uniqueness of "American freedom." He had a plan to "stir up revolt in Europe" against Hitler (also the subject of one of his published articles).

He did not lecture directly out of his book, but always, everywhere, in question-and-answer periods, he was brought back to its more sensational and sentimental episodes. It was a bad night's work that did not end with his autographing a dozen or more copies of his book. If there was anyone in America who had not read the book, or who failed to associate it mentally with "fundamental American values," it was not for want of Krebs's trying. He ostentatiously invested in War Bonds, and publicly encouraged others to do so. His lecture tours might be described as old-fashioned Communist agitprop modified for his personal need to avoid prosecution. Wherever he went through Middle America (though the term did not yet exist), he encouraged good folks to write to the Attorney General on his behalf. Fran-cis Biddle became Attorney General in August 1941, and his office had for weeks been receiving spontaneous demonstrations that "the workers," most of whom appeared to live within a ten-mile radius of lower Manhattan, were outraged by Jan Valtin's dangerous presence on American soil. Now he got mailbags full of warm endorsements of Valtin's character from the Methodist mothers of Missouri. In a few places where they were strong enough, such as Chicago, Communists actually picketed the lectures and barracked the speaker; but they were spitting against the wind.

The old idea of the Chautauqua, or traveling college, was not yet dead, and there were occasions on which he met fellow lecturers in a variety of different fields. One of these with whom he struck up a continuing correspondence was the movie actress Elissa Landi, a polyglot Austrian aristocrat who, after a brief but quite successful career in Hollywood, became an English-language novelist and poet. I have neither searched for nor found definite evidence of any real irregularities in the newly married Krebs's dealings with his numerous women friends, but something in the tone of Landi's communication with him might lead one to wonder.

To the category of "lectures" must be assigned a strange incident that caused a certain stir in the national press. Toward the end of March or the beginning of April 1941, Valtin made a "surprise" (i.e., unannounced) speech over radio station WOL. No transcript or recording of it survives, but we can tell from comment in the press that it must have previewed the themes of "American Dawn." The speech was sponsored by the "New Citizens" program under the direction of Dorothy Donnell. This meant that at a time when the Department of Justice was holding an unserved warrant for Richard Krebs's detention as an illegal alien, he was participating actively in a program of the Department of Justice for duly naturalized "New Citizens." The comrades were not alone in thinking that this was a somewhat peculiar arrangement.

JAN VALTIN GETS A LITERARY SECRETARY

Valtin's account of his three years in San Quentin is very brief, but it is consistent, within a reasonable latitude, with what later investigation confirms or suggests. "San Quentin gave me far more than it could take away. It had developed in me a passionate reverence for the universe of letters. . . . I became a contributor to the prison magazine, the *Bulletin*. . . ."

(pp. 179–80) He mentions studying journalism in an extension course offered by the University of California. He worked hard at his literary English. He taught German and studied Spanish and French. The records confirm that he took no fewer than seventeen different extension courses during his comparatively brief stay. We have no independent confirmation of certain other claims: that he maintained surreptitious contact with the Comintern, that he established a secret cache of revolutionary literature and founded "Marxist schooling circles and an atheist league." He was only twenty-one years old, and it is a little hard to see him in the numerous leadership roles he assigns himself.

In his book he mentions no one from the prison universe by name. Since the work is thick with the specifics of names, dates, places, and addresses, this is an unwonted vagueness. But very shortly after the book appeared, numerous friends and acquaintances from the Big House rushed to communicate with him. The very first was a colleague of Arthur Price, the San Francisco journalist who had been his writing instructor. Price was away on vacation when the anticipatory Book Club brochure was distributed. The colleague who was briefly taking Price's place saw it and asked him: "Isn't this Valtin the German fellow that took your course?" When Price looked at the book, he immediately recognized many pages he had seen before.

Among the first of many fellow ex-cons to be in touch was one who was to play a brief but significant role in the deployment of the "Valtin case." Gilman P. D. G. ("Pat") Rankin was the black sheep of a family, though now in reduced circumstances, of the kind that gives its children many Christian names. He was a man considerably Krebs's senior, a veteran of the Great War, and a newspaperman of large experience. He claimed to be "mostly innocent" of the serious financial irregularities of which he was convicted; and once paroled he had in fact won, after a hard struggle, a commutation of his sentence. In 1928 he had been the editor of the *San Quentin Bulletin* and had known Krebs well. Rankin was paroled from prison a year or so after Krebs had left. The economic opportunities of the early 1930s were not softened by the stigma of criminal conviction. His wife divorced him, and in 1941 he was living in genteel poverty with his widowed mother in her modest house. His son, Gil Junior, was an apprentice radio announcer on KFWB. It was in an attempt to save the son the humiliation of identification with a known felon that the father adopted the name "Pat" (from Pater).

It is of some interest that Pat Gil Rankin barely alludes to Krebs's political ideas, whereas he grovels rather embarrassingly before his maritime prowess. Krebs is "the Skipper," and the use of this nickname by other contemporaries from San Quentin strongly suggests that Krebs acquired it there. Valtin speaks of studying "Astronomy" and "Map-Making" and "Bowditch's *Epitome of Navigation*." Rankin actually says that he studied navigation under Valtin. In any event, throughout the course of his continued commerce with Valtin, Rankin rather tediously begins or concludes his communications with flourishes of a nautical lingo apparently picked up from Popeye the Sailor Man.

The "unprecedented" two-part installment of *Out of the Night* had appeared in *Life* magazine on February 27 and March 3, 1941. This was shortly after the suspicious death of General Kritivtsky, and within months of Trotsky's assassination, and the commentary to the *Life* pieces capitalized on the drama of an author whose work had been so like an invitation to assassination by either the German or the Soviet secret police as to drive him into hiding. Rankin wanted to communicate with his old friend, but didn't quite know how to do so. So on March 6, 1941, he wrote to the "Secretary" at Alliance Books enclosing an unsealed note for Valtin. Identifying himself as "Ex-Editor, S.Q. Bulletin," he wrote thus: "I am identifying myself above in specific manner as the first editor to pass upon the published MSS of the author of OUT OF THE NIGHT in order that you will not hesitate to forward to the calliope-voiced, stopple-eared, son-of-a-sea-cook the note I am enclosing herewith for him." Of course he read all of *Out of the Night* as soon as he could get his hands on a copy, after which he wrote again to Krebs in a letter that makes a possibly revealing observation. He thought that he recognized a number of incidents in the book from stories he had earlier heard from the author's own lips. "My impression is that some less competent collaborator has messed around with your MSS and injected an unnecessary element of romanticism at some spots." In fact, the "romanticism"—Valtin's relationship with Firelei—had come into his life only after he had left San Quentin.

Pat Rankin had once been Jan Valtin's editor; he began to dream of being his editor once again. He was currently underemployed. He offered, for a fee of $100 per month and expenses, to work for Krebs. To explain how a rising literary star would take on as his right-hand man an incompetent and burnt-out embezzler is no easy task. People suddenly translated

from penurious obscurity to affluent celebrity react along a spectrum ranging from going for the gold Cadillac to sticking with the old pickup. Krebs
was definitely of the latter sort. His asceticism was a deeply ingrained
revolutionary habit. For scholars of our credit card generation, of course,
the depression mentality ubiquitous in the primary materials from prewar
America often seems unfamiliar, alien; even so, the Valtin archive is full of
evidence of a parsimony edging over into meanness. Fiscal frugality went
hand-in-hand with Krebs's nearly praeternatural capacity for work. His
obvious unchanging ambition was to be a commercially successful writer.
As for the domestic context of that writer's life, one deduces that he was
seized of two slightly incompatible visions: that of the gentleman-farmer
and that of the gentleman-sailor. He was able to be both, sequentially, and
after a fashion. The money from *Out of the Night* bought a working apple
orchard in Connecticut. Later he traded that (failing) investment for a
watery place on the eastern shore of Maryland where he had boats and ran
a desultory water taxi business.

Krebs liked to do things—and unfortunately also people—on the
cheap. He was stingy with his wife and shockingly stingy with certain
friends in need, like Bek-Gran and Ben Mandel, without whose earlier aid
he would, if alive and undeported, still have been painting houses in the
Bronx. The exploitation of people, the supposed central sin of capitalism,
was a fundamental principle of dialectical materialism as it had operated in
Krebs's entire political life. Pat Rankin was eminently exploitable, cheap,
and he was in California, where a job needed doing. For unless Krebs's
powers to deceive far exceed mine to detect—a possibility by no means to
be dismissed—he was flabbergasted by Morris Goodstein's suit and what it
implied. Had he attacked the *wrong man* by accident? Had he intentionally
been set up by "Getsy" to remove him by "dry" liquidation? The annals of
Comintern villainy provide numerous analogues in either genre.

One alarming possibility at least should be mentioned, the so-called
worst case scenario. It is that young Krebs was indeed simply an armed
robber who got caught and that the older and more cunning Krebs was an
inventive liar who went through the motions of investigating Goodstein in
order to protect the fiction of the non-fiction of *Out of the Night*. It seems
inexplicable, however, that he would have jeopardized his project so recklessly by presenting as fact a fabrication so easily discoverable.

For the Communist debunkers of Valtin's book, Morris Goodstein appeared to be a priceless asset, and for a brief period he became the Republican darling of *The Daily Worker*. No whisper of any Getsy ("Russian agent in charge of G.P.U. operations on the Pacific Coast of the United States a decade ago," according to Valtin) exists outside the pages of *Out of the Night*. This is hardly a devastating fact in itself, since an important characteristic of secret agents, perhaps, is secrecy; but it did little to stifle the charges of fraud. Furthermore, Sender Garlin came up with other disturbing facts. Krebs, who according to the book simply took the fall and copped a guilty plea as ordered, had actually consulted with a competent public defender. Though Krebs had said little in court, what he did say was unfortunate. He explained his assault only by saying that "The Jew made me mad." A stenographic note recorded a judge's opinion that during the proceedings the defendant at times appeared to be not entirely mentally competent. Thus was born Krebs the anti-Semitic mental defective of later Communist journalism. Krebs now hired Rankin to investigate Morris Goodstein in the hopes of determining that, in 1926, he had been indeed a member of a Communist *apparat*.

Krebs's publisher Koppell, who was nearly as tightfisted as Krebs, agreed to this arrangement. Goodstein was certainly a threat to Valtin's credibility, but Koppell's lawyer had convinced him that the grounds for a successful lawsuit against Alliance were lacking. He predicted, accurately, that Goodstein would settle "for a fishcake." Koppell was willing to agree to any plan that did not cost more than $500—that amount to include both the "investigation" and the settlement. In other words the "investigator" was to buy Goodstein off as cheaply as possible, and keep whatever change there was. Whatever else it was or was not, however, the indiscreet passage in *Out of the Night* pretty clearly was not an intentional libel intended to defame Goodstein. The retired haberdasher went away with his $500 "fishcake," and as an issue relevant to the truth claims of *Out of the Night*, the matter dropped from the sight of nearly everyone but Sender Garlin. That is all one would ever have heard of Rankin, were it not for another of Isaac Don Levine's bright ideas.

Jan Valtin's spectacular rise to celebrity brought with it many problems for Krebs, personal, legal, and professional. The first professional problem was what might be called the paradox of the red-hot property. What was he to do next, and how could it possibly meet expectations so high? Levine had various ideas. Alliance the publishers jumped at the idea of an *Unpolitical*

Journey and announced it as forthcoming. This was to have been a feel-good history of the "Americanization" of a European refugee. So far as I know it was never anything more than a title. But another, more productive idea soon emerged. Krebs had actually learned his craft as a prisoner in San Quentin, where he had worked with the admirable Arthur Price in university extension courses by correspondence and where, in the prisoners' literary magazine, the *San Quentin Bulletin*, he had published his first pieces.

Most of Krebs's prison pieces were not exactly stories. They were brief "character sketches" or "scenes" that responded to specific writing assignments in the courses he had taken. But they unquestionably displayed talent and an opportunity for a kind of literary embryology. From what acorns did such mighty oaks as *Out of the Night* grow? Besides, the prison house had its offbeat allure. American literary history has seen episodes of "chain-gang chic," the most famous of recent examples being Norman Mailer's discovery and promotion of Jack Henry Abbott, the sociopathic sociologist who wrote from and *In the Belly of the Beast*. But whereas Abbott rather spoiled things with a recidivist murder, Valtin was hawking War Bonds and publishing essays in praise of free enterprise in the *Reader's Digest*.

This book of short sketches would be called *Bend in the River* (the title of one of the better pieces). It was in the course of Levine's negotiation of a very favorable second contract for it that it was decided the new book needed prefatory material that would establish the prison background. Who might write such a preface? Who better than his old friends Arthur Price and Gilman P. D. G. Rankin? After all, what Rankin claimed was true: he had indeed been Valtin's first editor. In these circumstances Krebs brought him to the apple orchard in Norwalk as his "secretary," where he would work for room, board, and "expenses." He moved into one of the decayed buildings at Kittemaug Orchards. This was probably for a time a relationship satisfactory to both. Krebs had in effect the services of a valet, and Rankin felt that he had been seated at the right hand of greatness with his own big chance to break into the literary big time.

Rankin's literary aspirations, incidentally, had a fine pedigree. San Quentin Penitentiary, during the years he was there, would appear to have housed about as much literary talent as any given summer session of the Bread Loaf Writers' Conference. The place was practically crawling with aspiring and published authors. The star alumnus in terms of celebrity was Robert Tasker, who became a successful screenwriter in Hollywood; but there were several others. The most colorful, perhaps, was the Canadian Herbert Emerson Wilson. Wilson was the younger brother of a once famous cult leader named "Brother XII." He himself had been a Baptist preacher until, around 1916, he gave up saving souls for cracking safes, at which art he excelled. Eventually he published several books, including a monument to his craft—*I Stole $16,000,000* (and those were *prewar* dollars, as they used to say)—and successfully sold the rights to Hollywood. Among Wilson's papers at the University of British Columbia is an unpublished essay, "Prison Literati," in which he extols the literary prowess of at least a dozen of his contemporaries, not including Tasker and Krebs, of whom he was apparently unaware.

Arthur Price wrote a warm, generous, even moving prefatory letter for the book. Rankin's much longer preface, which must have tested Levine's editorial patience to an extreme, is serviceable, though threatening on every page to collapse in sycophancy and overwriting. But the real problem with *Bend in the River*, which from the commercial point of view was something between a flop and a mere severe disappointment, was that Valtin's own pieces were not all that good. They were, after all, flimsy juvenilia produced as writing exercises for a college extension course. Readers wanted another blockbuster. It required a trained literary embryologist to find the Jan Valtin of *Out of the Night* in what was simply quite good work for English 101A. And unlike most other "prison writing," there was very little prison in them.

Rankin had had some experience in newspaper work, but he was of course also a crook. To the low criminal cunning presumably natural to Pat Gil Rankin, he had added the studiedly colorful rhetoric of a reader of Damon Runyon. His bumptiousness and self-importance led to delusions of grandeur and to more trouble for Krebs.

While *Bend in the River* was in press, Krebs's great champion Roger Baldwin was organizing a series of lunches and dinners at which he could introduce the writer to influential people. At one such lunch Krebs met Louis Fischer, who had not yet published his *mea culpa* in *The God That Failed*. About two weeks later (March 10, 1942), Markoosha Fischer, who also had not yet published her own apostatizing memoir, *My Lives in Russia*, wrote Krebs a gushing fan letter in German. She said that *Out of the Night* was the most meaningful book she had ever read, but she still had an agenda. She thought she could detect beneath the book's surface the spirit of "a true revolutionary who has remained true to his ideals." This was the letter, already mentioned, in which she alerted him to the fact that his friends Lyons and Levine were not approved of by upstanding leftists (*anstaendige linkstehende Leute*).

Louis Fischer—who remained a loyal Stalinist much longer than was good for the health of his reputation—had disliked Lyons intensely since the days when they were both American correspondents in Russia. In his autobiography he goes out of his way to depict Lyons as a bourgeois sybarite more interested in buying up the antique furniture of the ruined Tsarist "former people" than in getting to know anything about Soviet life. In fact, Lyons's books about Russia were far more honest and probing than anything Fischer had achieved. In the *Saturday Review of Literature* of March 7, 1942, Burnet Hershey, president of the Overseas Press Club, published an article called "They Pointed the Way" in praise of various writers, mainly foreign correspondents, who had given early warnings of the dangers of totalitarianism. There he said in passing that "Jan Valtin's books are generally conceded to have been blue-penciled either by Eugene Lyons or Isaac Don Levine," two of the most conspicuous way-pointers.

When enumerating his skills as a possible employee, Rankin had written to Valtin: "Any move I make will be wholly in the clear, must be wholly legitimate and ethical, and can be depended upon to be diplomatic and discreet." Circumstance now offered him an opportunity to show what he meant by diplomacy and discretion. Rankin happened upon this snippet, and apparently thinking that Hershey was a sub-editor of the *Saturday Review*, wrote to him at the magazine a letter in which ignorance vied with impudence and effrontery with buffoonery: "Dear Scribe Hershey: Being a roughneck newspaper-man and hack writer, I don't indulge in much highbrow informative reading. . . ." He had, however, read the stuff about the blue-penciling. "My main job just now is that of secretary to Jan Valtin, whom I have known since 1928. If you'll read his (not yet distributed) 'Bend in the River,' you'll find me amply identified. I am his friend first; and his secretary when shaved and sober. If there's anyone more familiar with his affairs today than I am, I miss my first two guesses . . . it is an entirely mistaken belief that anyone blue-penciled 'Out of the Night.' . . . And the only blue-penciling that was done in 'Bend in the River' manuscript or proof-sheets was done by me. . . ." None of this was to disparage either Lyons or Levine, "unquestionably competent men," but the record needed to be set straight.

After a considerable delay, someone at the *Saturday Review*, probably Cousins himself, turned over this remarkable letter to Isaac Don Levine. Levine's reaction was a controlled explosion in the form of a letter to Rankin (June 30, 1942) recorded for posterity in Levine's archives at Emory University. From the perspective of one who knows something about poor Rankin, Levine's righteous indignation is likely to sound like cruelty. He did not know Rankin, of course, or even of Rankin's existence, and thus cannot have known that he was breaking a butterfly upon the wheel.

There are two most palpable hits, one at the beginning, the other at the end of the letter. Levine begins thus: "I want to tell you that . . . Mr. Norman Cousins [editor of the *Saturday Review of Literature*] sat next to Richard at a dinner given by Roger Baldwin recently. When Mr. Cousins asked Valtin about his secretary, a certain Pat Gil Rankin, in connection with the letter of March 23 he had received from you, Valtin told him he had no secretary and knew of no such person! This—on the authority of Mr. Cousins, an unimpeachable source as far as I am concerned."

This hardly shows Richard Krebs in a good light, but it must have been devastating to Rankin. To be informed of one's nonexistence in the eyes of one's hero is a hard thing, but there was worse to come. The publication of his twenty-page introduction to *Bend in the River*, still in press, was to be the highlight of his small, sad life. He could not know, as Krebs obviously had never told him, that Levine himself was the one who had come up with the idea of including him at all. There was a good deal else he didn't know. "To complete the record, since you mentioned 'Bend in the River,' it will interest you to know that I am the editor, both by contract with the publisher and in reality, of that volume; that I edited with my own hand your manuscript; that I have in a fat envelope all the scraps which I cut with my own scissors out of the potpourri which eventually emerged as 'Bend in the River.' . . ."

Levine's final menace must have been almost superfluous. "I am writing to you first . . . and have not even broached the matter as yet to Valtin, who incidentally dropped in here yesterday when I was away. I hope you don't mind my enclosing an airmail envelope for a quick answer."

Answer was there none, and Pat Gil Rankin recedes into the background of our history. This episode shows Rankin to be a fool, but it hardly shows Krebs in a good light either. He clearly had never told Rankin the truth about the composition of *Out of the Night*, and that suggests that he had in effect and perhaps in fact lied about it to his own aggrandizement. His history is strangely littered with unacknowledged benefactors. At least he didn't fire Rankin forthwith. Rankin is last heard of in November 1942, being let go for "financial reasons." His exit is graceless. "Maybe you'll have some suggestions" about other possible employment, he wrote to Krebs, "but please eliminate those that have to do with Koppell or any Jew outfit. The Hebes are too smart for me, and I'm just smart enough to figure out that the only way I can keep 'em from beating me is not to do business with 'em."

In other ways, however, Levine's letter offers invaluable testimony concerning some of the otherwise obscure circumstances around the making of *Out of the Night*. Summarized below are a few of the most salient facts.

- Eugene Lyons had "drafted the first of a series of articles for Valtin" which, however, he was unable to peddle to any magazine. He then introduced Valtin to Levine.
- It was Levine who proposed that Valtin attempt a book like *Out of the Night*, and he made the suggestion in the presence of Rose Wilder Lane.
- Valtin wrote most of the book while living in Levine's small country place in Danbury through the summer of 1940. He wrote, and Levine edited, at breakneck pace. "I edited—at the rate of about 16 hours a day for about ten weeks—his torrential output."
- It was Mrs. Levine who came up with the title *Out of the Night*.
- The writing was all done by Valtin and by him alone.
- Part of Levine's Herculean task was to cut down to something approaching manageable size what Valtin had written, which he did first in the galley proofs for the first edition, then making a second more modest pruning to meet the wishes of the Book-of-the-Month Club.
- Levine acted, by contractual arrangement, not as Valtin's *agent* but as his *editor*. It was only after the completion of *Out of the*

Night that Levine contracted to be Valtin's agent, though Krebs apparently now pays no attention to the legal contract "and has been dealing with publishers, magazine editors, lecture managers, etc., all by himself."

A Brush with the Law

There is no doubt that the American Communist Party launched a coordinated campaign of defamation against Valtin-Krebs and clamored for his deportation. In his recantation of 1948, *All of Their Lives*, Benjamin Gitlow, onetime leader of the Party, included a section entitled "The Campaign Against Jan Valtin." (Gitlow had befriended "Valtin" early, before he gained fame. But he dropped him over something Krebs had said or done.) Certainly Krebs himself often publicly stated that "the Communists" were the source of all his problems. That may have been a comforting thought, but it was objectively absurd.

Krebs might now as Jan Valtin be a literary celebrity and a contemporary equivalent of the Man in the Iron Mask, but he had certain problems that, considered from the conventional and legal points of view, as they very soon were considered, were grave. He was an illegal alien who had been convicted of a violent felony, had served serious prison time and been deported from the United States. Now he had entered the country illegally a second time, making him a recidivist, and beginning in December 1941, he would be an *enemy* alien to boot. He had written a best-selling book, which he insisted was as true as the Gospel of Luke, that detailed a life of fraud, deception, and subterfuge in the service of the Communist Party, the final act of which was pretending to be a Nazi Party agent. There was significant pressure from Communist front groups, fellow travelers, and irate superpatriots like Westbrook Pegler to have him deported again. This was an experience that definitively moved Krebs from ex-Communism to anti-Communism.

He seems only partially to have anticipated this curious dilemma of his own making. In early March 1942, the papers were full of speculation about the likelihood that the Justice Department would move against him. Krebs realized then, if not before, that he was in serious peril, and he secured the services of an excellent immigration lawyer, Morris Ernst.

Toward the end of the month he was summoned to Ellis Island, where he was arrested on suspicion of immigration violations. The bond was set very high: $5,000, a sum that suggested either that he was a desperate criminal or a high risk for unlawful flight. He and his lawyer paid the bail immediately, making sure that the assembled press reported that the money was being put up in the form of previously purchased "Victory" bonds. Ernst made a statement to the effect that the arrest was simply a matter of tired routine, an inconvenience to be endured on the short and certain road to complete vindication. That is the sort of whistling in the dark that one expects from one's lawyer.

On March 24, *Time* magazine summarized the situation quite accurately, but hardly without a point of view. "Valtin-Krebs was living last week in New York with his girl-wife, 17-year-old Abigail Harris. Around the former German terrorist and Red agent swirled a storm of conjecture and argument: was his autobiography true or a hoax? Valtin-Krebs & friends said it was true; no respectable evidence has yet been produced to show that it was anything else. And if it was true, under present alien laws, he was liable to deportation back to Germany whence he had fled." For the next several weeks editorial pages across the country debated Valtin-Krebs's appropriate fate, rather in the manner of a fraternity rush. The title of an editorial in *Look* magazine in May was typical: "Should Valtin Get the Boot?" (The answer was a tolerant "No.")

As his friend Ben Mandel told him in so many words, Krebs had not a legal leg to stand on. The only court in which he stood a chance was the court of public opinion. He had some powerful friends in the literary world, but probably many more enemies. He set out to exploit the former and neutralize the latter. The coalition of his friends was no stranger than that of his enemies. He had built a community of sympathy that bridged liberals and conservatives. Through Lyons and Levine he met various influential members of the burgeoning ex-left like Max Eastman and of the current but anti-Communist left like Roger Baldwin of the ACLU. Friends on the right were easy to find. DeWitt Wallace came on board early. The *Reader's Digest* article "American Dawn" was reproduced in a quarter of a million offprints for free distribution through schools and civic clubs. Its flattering theme: the therapeutic power of American freedom to redress the political pathologies of Europe. True to Krebs's Marxist education, he set out tirelessly to appeal to the "masses." He seems to have answered every fan letter he received with a specific and often detailed personal reply. He autographed hundreds of books.

Atrocious assault and attempted murder usually have consequences beyond the literary. Quite apart from the fact that Richard Krebs was the most literarily successful illegal enemy alien in America, he was a violent criminal and felon convicted in the state of California. His only hope of evading deportation was to erase the felony conviction, and the only way of doing that was securing a pardon from Governor Culbert Olson of California. The grounds of his appeal were unlikely to make any lawyer's heart sing: he had had a hard life, and written a book that made a lot of money and angered a lot of leftists. But he pulled it off, with lots of help from his friends. Some sense of the difficulties Krebs faced must have been apparent when he assessed the character of the two men in whose hands his fate lay: the governor of California, and the Attorney General of the United States. To win the ear of the former he must first placate the latter, for a pardon would be virtually out of the question if the federal government first moved to deport him.

Culbert Olson, the governor of California, was an American original, a roustabout turned lawyer, a Utah Mormon turned atheist, an old Bryant Democrat turned semi-Socialist. He was a friend of "Fighting Bob" LaFollette and Upton Sinclair, and a protégé of Franklin Roosevelt. He was decidedly friendly to organized labor, especially when compared with his predecessor Mirriam, the "butcher" of the Longshoremen's Strike of 1934. Among his first gubernatorial acts was the issuing of a pardon to Tom Mooney, probably the most famous labor martyr in any American prison. (Not much later he also pardoned Mooney's co-defendant, Warren Billings.) He was probably the most left-wing governor in America, and one of the least likely to sympathize with "Red-baiters."

California was but the western front of a bicoastal campaign for Valtin-Krebs's exoneration. Toward that end, a gubernatorial pardon was a necessary but insufficient preliminary. The eastern front was in Washington, D.C., where the Attorney General, beginning in 1941, was Francis Biddle. Biddle was a patrician lawyer and jurist, in his generation *the* Biddle of the Philadelphia Biddles, so to speak. He was of a type always rare, and today nonexistent, in American public life—aristocratic, well educated, and highly literate. His wife was a poet; he himself was a beautiful writer, a novelist and a biographer of ability. Like Alger Hiss, he had clerked for

Oliver Wendell Holmes, and venerated the man. His legal career went from distinction to distinction. He was one of the judges at Nuremberg. His political leanings were, by American standards, distinctly left, those of an "advanced" liberal. When he left public service, he was for a while the chairman of the Americans for Democratic Action, a group which many Republicans of the day found distinguishable from the Socialist Workers Party only with the aid of powerful optical instruments. This was the man who would have to decide whether the government would or would not move to deport Jan Valtin.

Olson and Biddle, who differed so markedly in background and style, were from another point of view the most natural of political allies. One article of marked congruence was their shared phobia of "enemy aliens." The policy of the internment of the ethnic Japanese residents of California, an episode that has been an indelible stain on the legacy of a great president and indeed the history of our nation, was largely the work of two men who were among the great "liberals" of their time. That sobering fact can perhaps remind us that life, unlike history, is prospective, not retrospective. The American prospect at the end of 1941 was that the United States faced probable invasion and that California would be a blood-soaked battleground.

The famous Executive Order 9066 mandating the internment camps was signed only on February 19, 1942. But on the very day of the declaration of war against Japan, Biddle had already directed the FBI to start arresting "enemy aliens," which soon would include Germans. There was a great fear of espionage, a greater fear yet of sabotage. Once again, historical retrospection may render such fears exaggerated if not absurd. They did not seem so then. And here, clearly, the greater fear was of the Germans. "Japs" were physically conspicuous, but "Nazis" might be indistinguishable from that sizable portion of the native-born population of German extraction.

These worst fears were ratified when in June 1942 eight German agents were successfully landed by U-boat—four on Long Island and four near Jacksonville, Florida. These men, all of whom could pass for Americans, had been heavily bankrolled, and well trained and equipped for serious sabotage. They were very briefly at large, and did manage to get off the beaches and into the country, but they achieved nothing in terms of their mission. Their leader, George John Dasch, very soon got cold feet and turned himself in to the FBI. Before the month was out, they had all been captured and brought to Washington for a military trial. The episode lay buried and forgotten in the history books until it was disinterred by legal officers in the Bush administration in their search for possible precedents for the category of irregular al-Qaeda "enemy combatants." In the summer of 1942 it seemed to confirm the propaganda-fed fear that saboteurs were all about us. Francis Biddle conducted the prosecution himself, gaining six convictions and six death sentences, four of which were immediately carried out.

Now Richard Krebs, alias Jan Valtin, was a German saboteur. He had written a whole book about being a saboteur. Since 1938, the International Communist Party had been distributing public notices arraigning him as a Nazi agent. They repeated that claim now. And as for the Valtin book, it too was a work of sabotage, the literary version of throwing glass shards into the gearbox of Allied unity and harmony.

MEANWHILE, A NEAR MISS IN HOLLYWOOD

Some books are practically made for the silver screen, and most people who read it thought that *Out of the Night* was one of them. Adventure, danger, suspense, violence, tear-jerking tragic romance, steamy sex—all of this and more was wrapped up in an eventually patriotic and morally uplifting true story for our times. Certainly, Krebs himself had all along been thinking about Hollywood, and this is why even before the book's publication, he had talked the eager Dorothy Donnell, the aspirant screenwriter, into working with him on a screenplay. At the time of publication, Levine was Valtin's editor, but not yet his agent. Krebs was actually under legal obligations to Koppell at Alliance, but he simply brushed them aside as he entertained thoughts of turning *Out of the Night* into a movie. As always he wanted to maximize his money. He already lamented having signed the 30 percent agreement with Levine. He wanted to handle Hollywood on his own, but he was determined not simply to sell the rights to the book. He was sure he could make more money if he produced a finished screenplay.

He and Dorothy Donnell fell into the plan to work on the project together. Donnell would do most of the work, and simply for the love of the project, in her free time. Krebs would in the meantime move on rapidly with a "next project." He thought that arrangement, which he did not share with Koppell or Levine, was one made in heaven. At a rate that nearly equaled his own, Donnell produced a remarkably competent screenplay, and got it into the hands of agents in Hollywood. She had worked quickly, but not quickly enough.

The screenplay was finished shortly before or shortly after Hitler launched Operation Barbarossa on June 10. Red Beard put an end to Red-baiting for a season. *Out of the Night* was untouchable. There is no doubt that in the Cold War period some left-wing Hollywood writers were victims of political persecution; but the anti-Communists had no monopoly on the appetite for censorship. The talented Communist screenwriter Dalton Trumbo, whose name was prominent on the infamous Black List of writers to be shunned on political grounds, became a legendary emblem of the Free Speech Movement in Berkeley. We may forget that Dalton Trumbo was a blacklister before he was blacklisted. We have a postwar letter of his in which he boasts that, thanks to Communist influence, Hollywood has produced nothing "so untrue or so reactionary as *The Yogi and the Commissar, Out of the Night, Report on the Russians, There Shall Be No Night*, or *Adventures of a Young Man*. Nor," Trumbo continued with sarcasm, "does Hollywood's forthcoming schedule include such tempting items as James T. Farrell *Bernard Clare*, Victor A. Kravchenko *I Chose Freedom*, or the so-called biography of Stalin by Leon Trotsky." That list could serve as a bibliography of the American Communist Party's most hated books of the 1940s. Such "Russian" films as Hollywood would produce during the war—*Mission to Moscow* and *The North Star*—bid fair to give mawkish propaganda a bad name.

The fact of such informal censorship is confirmed in a letter from Albert Lewin, of Loew-Lewin, Inc., one of the most famous producers of the period. Somewhat tardily, Krebs tried to engage the aid of Levine in promoting the stalled screenplay. Don Levine, who had friends and contacts everywhere, was well connected in Hollywood. "Allie" Lewin was an old friend of his. Levine had suggested that a personal appearance of his own in Hollywood might help matters. Lewin demurred. "Although 'Out of the Night' would not be an easy book to make into a picture," he wrote on June 25, "I thought it would surely have sold long before this because of the enormous popularity of the book. I have made some enquiries and have been told that there was considerable interest among some producers, but that Washington indicated its disapproval out of a desire not to offend Russia. Evidently the attack on Russia will make it still more unlikely that anyone would want to make an anti-Communist picture now."

Donnell took the setback with a degree of philosophical resignation nearly incredible, saying that she had learned a great deal from it. And she sympathized with Krebs. "What a pity," she wrote at the beginning of July, "that you have been so harassed and nagged by worries about your status that you haven't another book to follow up on your first great one immediately." There might be some consolation in the interest being shown by Day Tuttle, a New York theatrical producer, who wanted to adapt the book for Broadway. But that idea simmered languidly on a back burner for years without ever coming close to a boil. Meanwhile, Ben Mandel of HUAC was trying to sell the writer one of *his* ideas. Valtin's next project "should be a message to warn America in the present emergency. For example, why not an eloquent description of some city in Germany prior to the Communist or Fascist putsch, depicting the people calmly living on a volcano, as they are doing here."

Some revisionist historians of American Communism have shown that Communism, or at least some Communists, were much more culturally and socially "mainstream" than we might ever imagine looking back from beyond McCarthy. At least in New York there were some professions—secondary and college education, the social services, writing and journalism, publishing, the retail book trade among them—in which open membership in the Party was by no means entirely remarkable. Government service was something else again. The number of covert Communists and hard fellow travelers who had entered "Washington" in New Deal agencies, which became so controverted a question at the time of the postwar troubles with Senator McCarthy and President Truman's loyalty oath policy, is uncertain. What is more certain is that there were quite a few able and intelligent non-Communists working in government who believed that there were lots of them.

In Washington, in her day job, Donnell became aware of two disturbing facts. The first was that there was within the Justice Department a pressure group of Communist inspiration seriously lobbying for Richard Krebs's deportation. The second was that the writer Wellington Roe, the "hard" fellow traveler who had worked on the aborted "exposé" of Valtin for *PM*, had been stalking the halls of the Justice Department trying to make appointments to talk to people about his current research into "deportation cases." Alarmed, Donnell turned to a friend of hers, Chester Williams, an expert in public relations and a member of the small army of publicists and propagandists associated with the large bureaucratic expansion of the New Deal. Williams was a principled anti-Fascist and anti-Communist, and he took a helpful interest in Valtin-Krebs's situation. He rightly recognized that Valtin, whose political formation was entirely European, had a tin ear for the American political scene. He offered the writer useful advice concerning the methods and content of self-presentation most likely to be helpful to him.

In 1941, Williams held the title of "Director of Adult Civic Education" in the Office of Education (not yet a cabinet department). This highly competent man was an expert on propaganda and public relations, and he later set up "war awareness" centers in all of the states. He published several books and many pamphlets, and he collaborated with Walt Disney on a comic book, *Victory March*, now a sought-after rarity. On April 8, 1941, Krebs wrote to Williams asking his advice as to how he might best win American public opinion for his cause. Williams, who had already apparently written an effective letter on his behalf to Attorney General Jackson, answered at great length on April 13.

His principal advice was that Valtin should now concentrate "on special articles for mass distribution magazines," postponing work on another book. He is clearly referring to such articles as "Communist Agent" or "American Dawn." He needed to convince Americans of his usefulness, his sincerity, and his "ultra-humility." He was quite blunt. *Out of the Night* "gave many people the impression that it was a damned exciting yarn by a very imaginative writer. Thousands upon thousands do not take it as serious exposition of realities . . . the fact is that your book is unbelievable to the majority of Americans." While "the frequent interludes about sex conquests have great appeal," he must remember that most Americans were actually Puritans, who "feel pleasantly shocked on the one hand and antagonistic toward the author on the other hand."

Williams comes close to stating explicitly a truth that, so far as I can tell after reading through the man's entire literary remains, Krebs himself never grasped. It is that Jan Valtin, the hero of *Out of the Night*, is a selfish, sinister, and cynical character whom it is not very easy to like. "Your stuff must be more believable—achieved through disciplined *understatement*— more respectful of the moral code—achieved by playing down the sex interest, being ultra-humble, etc. . . ." Americans did not want to hear about the Communist conspiracy. "The fact that this conspiracy is a brutal fact, is beside the point . . . if you feel that you could write a brief pamphlet on the communist and nazi methods of appealing to youth in this country, I would be interested in it."

Of many other interesting observations, one is notable: "I understand that you have a Hollywood offer." That was not true; Donnell had received strong expressions of interest but no definite offer. "Steer clear of Hollywood for the present! You ought to avoid creating the impression that you are in any sense a publicity seeker—out to exploit your experience by any bizarre method at hand. Hollywood, as you may know, is full of fellow-travellers. They could do you a lot of damage with the public."

The Communists wanted Jan Valtin deported for two reasons: to eliminate a uniquely effective source of anti-Communist propaganda; and to dramatize their claim that the man was a fraud and his book a grotesque hoax. His defenders wanted to block the deportation for precisely the opposite reasons. They applauded his power as an anti-Communist witness, and they had an interest—financial, ideological, or both—in preserving the autobiographical authority of *Out of the Night*.

On the Waterfront: Harry Bridges

Richard Krebs was not the only Communist expert in waterfront and maritime unions. On the west coast there was Harry Bridges, Australian by birth, among the two or three most famous labor radicals in America. He had been one of the leading figures in the big and bloody waterfront strike of 1934, and he headed the International Longshoremen's and Warehousemen's Union (ILWU) for decades. In 1941, the Roosevelt government, Francis Biddle Attorney General, was making a second unsuccessful attempt to deport Bridges. In general the New Deal had been friendly to labor unions, but following the Hitler-Stalin Pact, Bridges, a covert Party member, was leading the ILWU in the party line summarized by the slogan "The Yanks Ain't Coming"—that is, an isolationist policy that threatened Roosevelt's Lend-Lease policies. The Communist position, of course, was that they refused to aid Britain in a war against Stalin's ally, Adolf Hitler.

It was inevitable that Bridges and Valtin would meet in the minds of newspaper columnists and political commentators. Harry Bridges wielded enormous economic power and represented a significant threat to civil order. Jan Valtin wielded no economic power but represented a significant propaganda threat to the Communist Party. It was rather difficult to explain why one man should be deported for lying about his membership in the Party while another man, a convicted felon at that, should be adulated for having spent a lifetime lying about his membership in the Party. Some of Krebs's friends thought Biddle had made an actual deal: he would soften the blow of Bridges's deportation by deporting Krebs. I have not found evidence of that; but Francis Biddle certainly set out to project an image of fair-minded firmness.

On the weekend of September 27–28, 1941, Jan Valtin gave one of his standard famous-author patriot talks. The audience was the New York State Librarians Convention, meeting in Schenectady. One local press report was glowing, describing the performance as "inspiring." Out on the west coast, however, the State Advisory Pardon Board was only half inspired. It met on Tuesday, September 30, to consider a regular agenda of business, plus one or two special items, including a petition on behalf of Richard Julius Hermann Krebs that he be recommended for a gubernatorial pardon. The four voting members in attendance divided evenly over the issue, with two in favor and two against. According to the board's rules, that meant that the request had been denied.

A friendly newspaper account reported this in a rather odd fashion. "Author Jan Valtin, who sharply criticized Nazi activities in his book 'Out of the Night,' lost an appeal for a pardon to escape deportation to Germany. The writer could, however, still win a pardon when the matter comes before Gov. Culbert L. Olson." It is not exactly a lie that *Out of the Night* "sharply criticized Nazi activities," but it is enough of a partial truth to hold the line until a really good lie might be found. The article reflects the patriotic reluctance shown in nearly all quarters of the American press to criticize the government of the Soviet Union or its mode of government. That had manifested itself immediately upon Hitler's invasion of Russia the previous June. After Pearl Harbor and America's entry into the war in which America and Russia were "democratic allies," it became virtually absolute.

The question of a pardon for Krebs was precisely the kind of decision any sensible politician might hope to evade. There were powerful partisans on either side of the issue. Whatever he did would win Governor Olson enemies without at the same time securing much useful support. Olson had already in effect agreed to the pardon, but he very much hoped to be able to present his action as his desire to carry out the will of the people. The deadlock at the State Advisory Pardon Board was not helpful to his cause.

But the fix was in, and with a little help from the anti-Communist conspirators in the Justice Department, Krebs was still able to win. Donnell and her friends had for months been searching for the right "in" with Olson. They needed an emissary with impeccable left-leaning New Deal credentials, an alert anti-Communist but not a "Red-baiter," and a man with personal ties to Olson.

The pro-Valtin forces had been using Congressman Jerry Voorhis, a popular liberal Democrat who represented a district in Southern California, as their point man. Voorhis certainly knew his way around Washington, and he had some influence with Biddle. But the real problem with regard both to Biddle and especially to Olson was how to capture their attention. America was still in a Depression, the ramifications of which presented most public officials with a full-time job, and overwhelmed private sorrows such as Valtin's. Help offered by Voorhis might have been a palpable blow against the Communists, who attacked him in their press. That did not protect him from being fatally smeared as "soft on Communism" a few years later in the elections of 1946, when he was defeated by a Republican upstart named Richard Milhous Nixon.

The man who closed the deal on the coast was Jonathan Garst. Garst was one of the great men from Coon Rapids, Iowa, the other being his brother Roswell, who became an agricultural seed tycoon. (Later, Nikita Khrushchev toured their old family homestead, now a world-famous model farm, during his visit to America.) Both Garsts were thick with Henry Wallace, whose different roles through the years included those of secretary of agriculture, vice president, and presidential candidate of the Progressive Party in the 1948 election. Both brothers were at the very forefront of progressive thought about agricultural production and food distribution; it was, indeed, their agricultural expertise that was the basis of their shared anti-Communism. They understood very well, as a surprisingly large number of other intelligent Americans did not, the practical meaning of the disaster called "the collectivization of agriculture" in the Soviet Union. Jonathan knew in 1940 that the Plains States could and one day would be shipping vast amounts of grain to Russia.

Jonathan Garst was at this time running a New Deal agency in California. He and Culbert Olson were both from western, rural backgrounds, and both were self-made men. They saw eye-to-eye on practically everything. Garst was actively pro-labor, but also a staunch opponent of Harry Bridges. He must have been aware of, and perhaps even credited the "scenario" in which Krebs's fate was balanced against that of Bridges. In any event he agreed to "handle" the Krebs matter with the governor, and he came to Olson with a sound political solution, which was to do to the California Advisory Pardon Board what Franklin Roosevelt had tried but failed to do to the U.S. Supreme Court: "pack" it with reliable votes. After all, only one vote was needed. Olson made a judicious appointment of a fifth member of the Pardon Board. The board itself could not reconsider so soon a case so recently before it, but it was certainly able to give advice to the governor when asked for it. In the week leading up to Pearl Harbor, Governor Olson, acting on his own initiative but in accordance with the preponderance of the advice of his Pardon Board, granted an unconditional pardon to Richard Krebs.

Naturally, the news was overwhelmed by the Japanese attack and lost in its reverberations. On Monday, December 8, Krebs telegraphed various military offices expressing his desire to be allowed to join one of the branches of America's fighting forces. For the time being, however, the government would think his form of service should be on the patriotic lecture circuit and in the celebrity-led campaign to sell War Bonds.

The Com-Rats Strike Again

Richard Krebs's legal pardon, with its implicit recognition of a tremendous grassroots support for the man throughout the country, meant that he was in theory eligible for naturalization. The fact that the United States was now at war with Germany rendered functionally absurd any suggestion that he might be deported to that country or, indeed, to anywhere else. He seemed to be home free. But the "Com-Rats," as he had taken to calling them, had a card up their sleeve, and in the first summer of the war they played it.

There was in a concentration camp in California—where the preferred term was "detention center"—an enemy alien by the name of Erich Krewet.

Krewet was a German merchant seaman, a Communist and Comintern agent, and an old and unfriendly rival of Richard Krebs. One of his Party names, the one he had been using on the coast, was Rix. He was five years older than Krebs, whose career as a waterfront thug he had watched since its inception. Quite apart from the old hostilities, Krewet, like every other Communist mariner in the world, had seen the posters naming Krebs as a Gestapo agent. He had also an intimate knowledge of the Valtin-Krebs "case" as it had been displayed in the American press.

The ability of incarcerated Communists to carry out operations from their prison cells was nothing short of phenomenal. It is a theme in many prison memoirs, including incidentally *Out of the Night* itself. According to Jorge Semprún, who was there, the Communist inmates practically ran Büchenwald. Gaming the system of a low-security "detention center" was child's play for Erich Krewet. In March 1942, Krebs under the name of Jan Valtin wrote an article entitled "No Revolt in Europe—Unless we Promote It." This was to be published by Lyons in the *American Mercury* and then "selected" by the *Reader's Digest* editors for reprinting. The burden of the article was that the Western powers, using the techniques developed by the Bolsheviks, could and should stir up a revolt in Nazi-occupied Europe. There was nothing particularly anti-Communist about this essay except, perhaps, in its warm endorsement of tried-and-true Communist methods of sabotage and subversion.

Krewet made of this essay an occasion of the Red counterattack. He wrote a very artful letter addressed to Krebs but sent to the *Reader's Digest* ostensibly for publication. Krewet knew that the *Reader's Digest* did not publish such letters, and he probably didn't care whether they even forwarded it to Krebs. (They did.) His real intended audience was the Enemy Alien Control Unit in Washington. He wrote such a letter as he could be sure would be reported to that vigilant body by the military censors at his California camp. He insulted Krebs roundly for having literally sold out his old comrades to the Nazis, taking generous pay for his cooperation with the Gestapo. For once, Krebs's conspiratorial radar failed him. He threw the letter away in disgust without thinking through its implications.

Krewet had written the letter at the end of July 1942, but bureaucratic inefficiencies kept it from being evaluated by the sleuths until *after* Krebs had received his pardon in California. Had the Enemy Alien Control Unit intervened earlier, it would almost certainly have blocked Olson's move, and effected a very different end to our story. Even when at the end of November Krebs was ordered to Hartford, Connecticut, for an immigration hearing, he did not seem to have grasped the situation. *PM* was also puzzled. Why were the immigration people acting at this late date? At the hearing, Krebs was blindsided when the government produced Krewet, who accused him of crimes so ecumenical that his prosecutors were offered a large menu of options, including revolutionary terrorism, Fascist subterfuge, and simple common or garden variety fraud.

After a few days in which the Immigration Appeals Board in Hartford deliberated and consulted with the Attorney General's Office, G-men arrested Krebs at his Connecticut lair and carted him off once again to Ellis Island. Once again the national press warmed to the bonanza. The title that appeared over several of their stories was perhaps inevitable: "Into the Night." *Time* magazine's coverage confirms the general contours of Whittaker Chambers's account of the backstage war at that magazine between him and the fellow travelers. He had given Krebs a rave review. All the news coverage, on the other hand, was not merely negative but nasty. *Time*'s story began with a lengthy list of aliases used by Krebs over the years, the last of which was Jan Valtin. The clear implication was that Valtin and his book were simply the latest manifestation of a lifelong pattern of deceit. It quoted the harsh words of the Immigration Appeals Board in Hartford: "His life has been so marked by violence, intrigue, and treachery that it would be difficult, if not wholly unwarranted to conclude that his present reliability and good character have been established. . . . It appears that he has been completely untrustworthy and immoral."

Yet Krebs's situation appeared worse than it actually was. If there had been no real danger of deportation the previous spring, when America was still technically neutral, there was none at all now that the United States was at war with the Nazi regime. The decision was that Krebs would be returned to Germany "after the war." Furthermore, Attorney General Biddle knew something of which the Immigration Appeals Board was ignorant. Erich Krewet, whose telling denunciations had been so influential with the board in Hartford, was not merely a Communist agitator but a close colleague and personal friend of Harry Bridges, public enemy number one in Biddle's internal rogues' gallery. Furthermore, the whole Valtin story was a big one among the professionals in the maritime unions, and Bridges himself had been damning Jan Valtin as a "Gestapo agent" and provocateur ever since the book appeared. Biddle might fail to deport Bridges, but he was damned if he was going to let the Communists have the supplementary satisfaction of Valtin's deportation. (There were, of course, excellent grounds for Krebs's deportation and only most feeble ones for Bridges; but that was neither here nor there.)

There was an outcry from the patriots. The Attorney General's Office began a leisurely review of the board's findings and reassessed them in the light of Krebs's numerous patriotic contributions in the form of his public lectures and his hawking of War Bonds. After three months, in March 1943, he was released from Ellis Island to allow him to volunteer for military service. This was all carefully arranged. He would serve with the Army, but in the Pacific theater. The pen being mightier than the sword, his work would be that of a writer/historian. The scenario was orchestrated to create a helpful paper trail of Krebs's patriotism and, if possible, his heroism. He began working on a novel, *Japs Die Hard*, but did not get far with it. The actual monument to his military service is a book called *Children of Yesterday: The 24th Infantry Division in World War II* (1946), now a sought-after item in its original edition among collectors of military history. It is written in a hard-boiled Hemingwayesque style much in vogue at the time. In theory, Krebs was still in jeopardy from the Immigration Appeals Board's old findings of 1942, but Roger Baldwin was able to use his congressional connections to give the case a definitive resolution. On January 24, 1947, enabled by a special member's bill brought forward by Representative Jerry Voorhis of California, Richard Julius Hermann Krebs became a citizen of the United States by naturalization.

WRAPPING THE TRUTH IN DARKNESS

Out of the Night is a strange colloid suspension, in which little blobs of fact are captured in a viscous medium of fiction, or perhaps vice versa. In any event, the book needed either more fact or more fiction. Aside from his wife's name and his own, Krebs seems rarely to have used pseudonyms within the body of his book. Given his subject matter this was extraordinary and, to me, unaccountable. He had a phenomenal memory. The man could remember with accuracy the street addresses of decade-old conspiracies, but he would then place within those offices, bordellos, or habitations activities of a highly imaginative sort. Perhaps he believed that after the carnage wrought by Hitler none of his old co-conspirators could possibly still be alive. If so, his judgment blundered. No fewer than three real people, identified by their real names in the book, later emerged to voice protest.

Monsieur Cance, the local GPU boss in Le Havre with whom Valtin comes into contact immediately upon being debouched from the ship on which he had been deported from Galveston, sued his French publishers, but this little story belongs to the Kravchenko affair of the next essay. Richard Jensen ("giant Dane, conspirator of the first rank") is a major and malign character in the book. When Valtin was captured and imprisoned by the Copenhagen comrades, with the certain intention of liquidating him, it was Jensen who was in charge. Jensen eventually (1946) wrote a whole little book (subtitled *Jan Valtin, Gestapo Agent No. 41*) in which he dismissed *Out of the Night* as utter fiction. But this was after the war, when the Cold War was already heading for a whole different level of confrontation.

One living ghost, whom we briefly encountered earlier, might have rattled his chains a bit louder to good effect. One of the characters mentioned in the book is an American Communist named Morris Appleman (Party name Mike Pell), a fellow maritime saboteur. In May 1941, in response to *Look* magazine's query as to whether "Valtin should get the boot," Mr. Appleman, now of Brooklyn, sent the editor of *Look* a letter and a photograph. The photo showed Appleman, Valtin, and a few other Party activists seated at a speakers' table while Albert Walter (head of the Maritime division of the Comintern and another "real life" character in the book) addressed a meeting. According to Appleman, the meeting took place in Hamburg in 1932, and its subject was the case of the "Scottsboro Boys"—a famous episode in the sordid history of American racism and injustice, and a worldwide boon to Communist propaganda. Appleman was not particularly indignant, but he suggested readers be wary. "As an adventure story 'Out of the Night' is a thriller; as an autobiography it must be taken with a grain of salt; as a historical document it must be ruled out."

Ernst von Waldenfels, the German journalist who has made the most, indeed the only serious researches into Krebs's life, frankly calls *Out of the Night* an "autobiographical novel."* He was able to establish beyond doubt

---

* Ernst von Waldenfels, *Der Spion, der aus Deutschland kam: Das geheime Leben des Seemanns Richard Krebs* (Berlin, 2002).

a number of concrete facts that, once known, alter forever one's reading of the book. Its sentimental heart is the tragic figure of Firelei, Valtin's wife and Communist co-conspirator. Her real maiden name was Hermine Stöver. She was not a Fleming but, like Krebs himself, a North German. She was from a bourgeois family. She was indeed an artist, or at least had an interest in design and painting. She did indeed join the Communist Party, and like many Communists she was for a time in a Nazi jail; but she left both the Party and the jail well before Krebs left for America.

According to Waldenfels, Firelei (Hermine Krebs) died of a blood disease in a hospital near Hamburg on November 15, 1938. The six-year-old son Jan was not "a ward of the Nazi state." He was living with his maternal grandparents. A man who has ruined his wife's life through a fanatical political commitment and then abandoned her in consequence of its further demands, who knows her to have died of natural causes in a hospital but who tells us in his autobiography that she died in prison, and possibly by her own hand, that man is likely to inspire the amateur psychoanalyst in all of us.

There is, however, no need simply to speculate about his feelings of guilt. Waldenfels publishes a letter that Krebs wrote to one of his mother's relatives just after he had heard the news of Hermine's death. This was in December 1938, when he was working as a painter for "a Mrs. Fromkin" in Far Rockaway. "After she left prison in 1936, she succumbed to various illnesses. A gift from Adolf Hitler to one of the loveliest daughters of the land. Nervous collapse. Heart problems, a general depression. . . . On the day that Hitler came to power my Mother died. My friends died beneath the swastika, many by suicide, others tortured to death. The rest were buried alive. My brother was burned alive by Göring's orders. And now this. I find it grotesque that I am still alive."

This is the *cri de coeur* of an anguished and grieving man who despises his own existence. Yet even in a humble private communication the mode is not simple prose but poetic embellishement. Like the Cumaean Sibyl, he "wraps the truth with darkness." Dr. Johnson famously said of Milton's *Lycidas* that "where there is leisure for fiction, there is little grief." Yet there are griefs so large, perhaps, as to be approachable only through fiction. In 1941, at the time of the *PM* attack, an irreverent "interview" with Valtin by *The New Yorker*'s "Talk of the Town" man appeared: "He was a tremendous, ham-handed, gap-toothed, likable fellow, with a certain rugged

geniality. . . . 'While I was writing the book, I worked at the Delmonico
Hotel as an interior decorator, fixing curtains and stuff. Then I went down
to Far Rockaway, painting bungalows for a bitch at twenty-five dollars a
month, ten hours a day, seven days a week. She asked me to work Christmas Day and I quit.'" That was precisely the time Krebs was learning of
his wife's death. By now all sentiment has been replaced by the bravado of
the best-selling mystery man.

But Krebs had been mixing his own life with fiction for quite some time.
Waldenfels suggests, almost certainly correctly, that the very names "Firelei"
and "Valtin" were lifted from a novel published by Vicki Baum in 1928, also
made into a film, in which the central characters were called Firilei and Valentin. The Austrian novelist Vicki Baum is sometimes credited with invent-
ing the very model of the "best-selling novelist" that later became a nearly
universal aspiration among writers. Greta Garbo's most famous line—*I want
to be alone*—was spoken in the voice of one of Baum's characters.

When Father Reinhold said in his review of *Out of the Night* that the
book was 95 percent fact and perhaps 5 percent fiction, he was making at
the very least a serious error of mathematics. For he also said that he found
incredible certain aspects of the account of Valtin's capture, torture, and
incarceration, and of the stratagem by which Valtin convinced his captors
of his conversion to National Socialism and his willingness to work for
them as a double agent. Altogether those episodes take up about 200 pages,
roughly a quarter of the book. Not merely do they strain the credulity.
They also contain a large proportion of the relatively small amount of the
book's bad writing. "Aside from her finery, she was still the pink-fleshed,
large-breasted, capable traitress of 1933." That is a description of Her-
tha Jens—identified in the *dramatis personae* as "assistant and mistress to
Inspector Paul Kraus of the Gestapo, a statuesque peasant girl who before
Hitler's rise to power had been confidential secretary to communist leaders
in Hamburg"—who usually sits in semiprovocative pose during Valtin's
numerous flagellations.

This part of the book is in the old and literal sense of the word fantastic, but it was in 1940 quite beyond any cultural surveillance. The Nazis
were so very beastly in fact that there was no beastliness that could not be
ascribed to them with impunity in fiction. There were strict cultural limits
to Red-baiting, but none at all to Nazi-bashing. The tradition going back
to the first war, with its propaganda posters of spike-helmeted Huns with

bloody chops, and its stories of Belgian babies tossed into the air to be caught on bayonets, had been revived. Largely under Communist tutelage, the most extravagant anti-Nazi rhetoric had been "mainstreamed" among Western liberals during the period of the anti-Fascist coalition and the Spanish Civil War.

Yet it is precisely in the period of Krebs's life dealt with in this section —1935, 1936, early 1937—that the mysteries of his actual biography, probably now beyond any documentary resolution, played out. The conclusions I have come to have no special authority, but they make plausible sense amid intentionally confusing evidence. It seems obvious that he cooperated with the Nazis and became a "double agent." That is perhaps too grand a term for the modest level of his actual services to either side, but it must serve. His collusion with the regime must have been protracted, and it must have been discovered by his former colleagues. The dramatic scenes of his captivity and escape from Jensen in Copenhagen are obvious fabrications. It seems likely, too, that he abandoned his wife and child under circumstances far less heroic than those suggested in *Out of the Night*. Whatever the actual circumstances were, the desperation of his situation was no doubt real. Finally, by the time he arrived in America in 1938, he was essentially out of politics altogether and sought only that writer's life of which he had dreamed ever since his first publications in the *San Quentin Bulletin*, and toward which he had already made futile gestures amid the social chaos of Germany in the early thirties. That is to impugn the sincerity neither of his anti-Communism nor his anti-Nazism, but his ambition was to write great sea stories, not to advance a political debate. His actual problems in America were not different in kind from those of any other illegal immigrant seeking to stay in the country; they were of course magnified by specific political circumstance and by the astonishing fame of a novel presented, without sufficient forethought, as autobiography.

Krebs brushed up against the truth, probably inadvertently, in a letter to Levine sent late in his stay on Ellis Island (March 15, 1943). He had made up a chronology of his activities and whereabouts during the previous five years. "Occasion may arise to answer the Communist-spawned lie that 'Valtin was a Nazi agent within the past five years.' *Out of the Night* is the answer to all that went before." It is a very curious thing to deny that one has been a Nazi agent *within the past five years*.

The "truth about Jan Valtin" will always demand the oblique glance, the likely guess. When Levine assessed the size of the book and its panoramic scope, he made a useful suggestion. Would it not be a good idea to put at the back, by way of a "reader's guide," a list of the thirty or forty most important recurring characters? This Valtin did, and it is indeed helpful to a first-time reader. He calls it a "Who's Who." I deduce, however, that the author worked rather quickly at this, and that the little descriptions he gave sometimes reveal what he actually *thought* about his characters rather than what he had *said* about them in the text. In a few instances there are inconsistencies, which may also be clues.

For instance, one of the few Communist operatives who get a pretty good press in the book is Albert Walter, the head of the Maritime section of the Comintern, and Valtin's immediate boss. This man, a fellow sailor and an acquaintance of Lenin's, seems to have been something of a father figure to Krebs. He actually liked the man. Valtin writes in the "Who's Who": "Deeply attached to his aged mother, Walter—to save her life—turned traitor to the Soviet cause when he was seized by the Nazis." Might not a good man, for a good cause, be forgiven such coerced treason?

More revealing, perhaps, is an inconsistency concerning Firelei herself. In the final paragraph of the book, Valtin says that "in December, 1938, I received a message which told me that Firelei had died in prison. Did she, herself, put an end to her life? Was she murdered in cold blood?" But in the "Who's Who" he wrote simply that "the Nazi secret police took her life to avenge the author's escape." That is, in perhaps the most possibly acceptable way he could find, Krebs admits that he was the *cause* of his wife's death.

There was undoubtedly sufficient evidence concerning Krebs available in his FBI file and elsewhere to have sunk him. But here it was greatly to his advantage that the bloodhounds pursuing him came out of Communist kennels. With enemies like that, he didn't need friends, though of course he had plenty of them. J. Edgar Hoover knew a lot of the truth, but as usual his chief concern was the public image of his own agency. What most infuriated him about Valtin-Krebs was not his politics, whatever they might be, but that in some of his magazine articles and very often in his public lectures he was peddling the view that sabotage (presumably *Nazi* sabotage) was a huge and pressing danger in the United States of America.

Hoover thought this the most irresponsible kind of fearmongering, and quite possibly a suggestion that the FBI was not doing its job. Furthermore, by the time whistle-blowers appeared on the scene, their whistling was drowned out in a cacophony of postwar alarums. When Richard Jensen published his exposé in 1946, even among the relatively few people who read Danish circumstances hardly encouraged any widespread interest in political archeology. Besides, there were plenty of skeletons in Jensen's own closet. In the flattened coastal cities of the western zone of Germany, where there were certainly knowledgeable witnesses, most people had other things on their minds, too. A German translation of *Out of the Night*, entitled *Diary of Hell*, appeared only in 1957. By then, Krebs was long dead and the Cold War at an advanced stage.

What kind of person was Richard Krebs? Hardly less mysterious than Jan Valtin. Knowledgeable people of ability and moral weight—Roger Baldwin, Dorothy Donnell, Max Eastman, Don Levine, Rose Wilder, and many others—obviously had real feelings of affectionate friendship for the man. Of course they also had, in varying degrees, coincidents of political agenda or even of financial interest; but there must have been sentient warmth there that cannot be felt through the documents.

In his active semipublic life, he had encounters with hundreds of people. His attitude toward them seems often to have been instrumental and utilitarian. He often needed help, lots of it, and he was not shy about approaching those who might provide it. His papers do reveal some evidences of generosity, as when he sent two dollars to the incarcerated Fred Beal. Unfortunately, there seems to be more evidence of his lack of it. Perhaps we are all more scrupulous in our behavior toward those whose help we seek than toward those who seek ours. His treatment of his first American wife, Abigail Harris, was appalling, and the history of their marriage suggests on his part an incapacity for easy intimacy. A raging "workaholism," fueled by a reservoir of energy that amazed most people who came into contact with him, was its unsatisfactory surrogate.

Krebs's treatment of Rankin, which seemed to begin in generosity, ended in the despicable. Two of the people to whom he owed the most were Robert Bek-Gran and Ben Mandel. Both of these men were, like Krebs, ex-Communists of precarious social station. Bek-Gran had taken him in when he had nothing and provided him with the means that allowed him to make a start on his writing. Mandel had given him comfort, support both moral and financial, and effected invaluable introductions in New York and Washington. When Bek-Gran himself needed help later on, one of the "waterfront boys" practically had to beg Krebs for a small subvention.

When the blockbuster article "American Dawn" appeared, Mandel wrote Krebs a note of congratulations, but with qualifications. The article, he said, caused him "some personal disappointment." He thought that Krebs could have been more generous in his acknowledgment of help. Only three personal names appear in the article: Arthur Price, his old writing teacher; Isaac Don Levine; and Rose Wilder Lane. He virtually had to mention them. His writing career would never have begun without Arthur Price. *Out of the Night* began in a conversation with Don Levine and Rose Wilder. "Now, it seems to me," wrote Mandel, "that you could easily have mentioned my name in the article along with Don and Rose Wilder Lane—without any sacrifice to yourself and in simple justice to one who stood by you when the going was tough—so tough perhaps that it might have meant your failure to complete your book."

Krebs was a survivor, and in him an avidly pursued self-interest was very often on the surface. The terminology of post-traumatic stress disorder had not yet been coined in 1950. When a strange fellow named Howard Unruh shot thirteen people to death in the streets of Camden, New Jersey, one autumn day in 1949, the term of art settled upon by the newspapers was "crazed veteran." One truth about Krebs-Valtin—a truth applicable as well to other authors in this book—was that he was a damaged man. A scholar of post-Communism in Eastern Europe has written that "Just as a war, long after it is finished, leaves behind it the scars of its ravages in the souls of the survivors, those of victims and killers alike, totalitarian power leaves in the soul the scars of its terrors and its violence."

YESTERDAY'S NEWS

The rest of the story of Richard Krebs's life has its own fascinations, but it has little relevance for his anti-Communist manifesto. After the war, Krebs removed from rural Connecticut to Betterton on the waters of the eastern shore of Maryland. There he set himself up in a kind of water taxi business, which never amounted to much, and he engaged in local life as a kind of rustic celebrity. Abigail left and divorced him. After some time, he remarried. His third wife was an unassuming and pleasant woman, without literary or political connections of any kind, the daughter of a local hardware dealer. He struggled to continue writing, but had little success. He did publish two postwar novels. The first, *Castle in the Sand* (1947), exploits the Chesapeake setting in which he spent his last years. It had some small success in the Australian market—more than it had in America.

As soon as he could, Krebs had reclaimed his son Jan from his in-laws, and he made an extensive trip to postwar Germany, of which there are many interesting reminiscences in the Valtin archive. (For example, there are numerous clippings about German ex-Communists, with whom he had actually been acquainted, such as Margarete Buber-Neumann. He clipped the article about the Kravchenko affair from *Stern* magazine.) He was very interested in the problem of the DPs (displaced persons) in Germany, and he took that as the subject of a second novel, *Wintertime*, which appeared in 1950, just before his death. These are both books of a mediocre quality, as he was well aware. His papers are full of sad testimonies to his realization—and that of the literary professionals with whom he was dealing—that he was failing. The postwar years had a dark side, but on the whole the national mood was one of prosperity, progress, and a return to cultural "wholesomeness." These were new topics, new themes for which Krebs was ill equipped. He tried to live a "normal" life as president of the PTA or mentor of the Cub Scouts, but it was rather a facade.

In a newspaper interview shortly after the publication of *Out of the Night*, Valtin-Krebs had waxed ebullient: "All this that has happened is hard to believe—it is impossibly implausible. Here am I, who, in 1938, was hunted, friendless, a slave working twenty hours a day for thirty dollars a month and living on scraps. I write a book. A book club takes it; thousands of copies are sold. I have just married a beautiful young American girl. I live in a comfortable country place. And I have so many plans!" Now his beautiful young wife was gone, and he had no plan that seemed to work. He was in therapy, and seriously considering suicide.

On New Year's Day, 1951, Richard Krebs died of a suddenly appearing and rapidly progressing pneumonia. Around the fringes of the burgeoning literature of Cold War espionage there have appeared a few suggestions that this was an "unnatural" natural death, but such tardy retribution would have been pointless. He was a forgotten man. At his funeral service in the old Episcopal church next to his property, a few of his former friends gathered: Isaac Don Levine, Roger Baldwin, Ben Mandel from the HUAC among them. The *New York Times* ran an obituary of respectable length— but of the genre "Whatever Happened to . . . ?" What had happened to Richard Krebs alias Jan Valtin was that, in the old Marxist terminology that once ruled his life, he had completed his "historical role." He had written one great book that helped to change the times before the times moved on without him. Though his moment yet recedes at rapid pace, it is perhaps not too late still to rescue both author and book from another well-known Marxist fate: the dustbin of history.

For many years Victor Kravchenko refused to allow his photograph to be published as, following the advice of the FBI, he led a peripatetic and often clandestine existence. He nonetheless had an "author's portrait" prepared for the promotion of his second book, *I Chose Justice*. He was a handsome fellow whom many women found attractive.

Well dressed and groomed, the charismatic Kravchenko makes a typically vigorous intervention in the Paris courtroom in which his civil action against *Les Lettres françaises* was being heard. The protracted trial regularly drew standing-room-only crowds of spectators. Though Kravchenko won only the symbolic judgment of a single franc, the propaganda damage he inflicted on the French Communist Party was enormous.

I CHOSE FREEDOM

The First Defector

VERY SOON AFTER THE ATTACK on Pearl Harbor, the United States found itself in a state of war with two militarily mighty adversaries, Japan and Germany. Germany, while not exactly an afterthought, was not in the forefront of most Americans' minds. It was Japan that had destroyed our proud fleet, and it was against Japan that we prepared for immediate offensive action. Europe, with the exception of the British Isles and a few neutral nations, was in the hands of the Nazis. German armies had seized most of European Russia. They had destroyed or imprisoned Russian soldiers literally by the millions. Only the Red Army, grievously damaged but seemingly inexhaustible in its reserves of troops, challenged Hitler's forces on the ground.

For nearly two years the principal American contribution to the European War came not from American armies but from American factories. Roosevelt's Lend-Lease legislation allowed a supply of war materiel to Russia that must still today seem staggering to us in its quantity and effectiveness. Without this American aid, the Red Army almost certainly would have been defeated. Without the Red Army, Hitler almost certainly would have become the master of all Europe.

This temporary congruence of interests was called an alliance, but it was a strange one. *The Strange Alliance*, indeed, is the title of a book published in 1947 by John Deane, who as a U.S. Army officer had spent part of the war in Russia attempting to execute Russo-American military cooperation. One special project was the attempt to negotiate a system whereby long-range American bombers could land at special bases in Russia for refueling—a system that would allow them to strike deep within the German-occupied territories in places the Russians themselves could not touch. Deane found that so far as the Russians were concerned, the give-and-take of alliance was characterized by a great deal of take and very little give. His Russian colleagues were suspicious, ungrateful, secretive, xenophobic, unfriendly, and nearly paralyzed by the inability to make even the necessary little decisions of quotidian business without first consulting with an apparently endless chain of central command.

If the American presence in wartime Russia was modest and equivocal, the Russian presence in wartime America was large and confident. The volumes of Lend-Lease shipments were so large that the Russians required for their administration what was essentially a corporate headquarters on Sixteenth Street in Washington. A large staff of military and industrial experts, technicians, accountants, purchasing agents, transportation consultants, engineers, translators, chauffeurs, police agents, and secretaries worked there. One of the executives was a Ukrainian named Victor Andreyevich Kravchenko, a man in his late thirties, an engineer by training, an executive by experience, a captain in the Red Army by rank, and a metallurgist by specialist expertise. One final category must be mentioned: he became the first Soviet duly certified "defector."

Kravchenko arrived in North America in the summer of 1943, already planning his escape. His work—supervising and expediting the shipment of industrial products within his spheres of expertise—was taxing, and it took him to several centers of American heavy industry. He developed a minimal ability to function in English and to use the transportation system. On April 1, 1944, a Friday and the end of a work week, he slipped away from Washington to New York. To the extent he could, he had made careful preparations to leave his work in transparent order, for he planned never to return to it. On Monday, April 4, as his Soviet colleagues were beginning to wonder about his whereabouts, Kravchenko was making a dramatic statement at a carefully prepared press conference at the *New York Times*. Two years later he would publish an autobiography, *I Chose Freedom*, destined to play a crucial role in the formation of Western public opinion as the Cold War intensified.

Kravchenko's press conference was a masterpiece that resulted in a second masterpiece, the account of it in the *New York Times*. It must certainly have been worked out thoroughly in advance with his advisers, and in particular with his Russian-American intermediary at the newspaper. The front-page article, which bore no byline, began thus: "Accusing the Soviet Government of a 'double-faced' foreign policy with respect to its professed desire for collaboration with the United States and Great Britain and denouncing the Stalin regime for failure to grant political and civil liberties to the Russian people, Victor A. Kravchenko, an official of the Soviet Purchasing Commission in Washington, announced his resignation yesterday and placed himself 'under the protection of American public opinion.'"

After a lengthy paragraph describing Kravchenko's extensive governmental experience, the following was added: "Mr. Kravchenko declined for patriotic reasons to discuss matters bearing on the military conduct of the war by Soviet Russia or to reveal any details bearing upon economic questions, particularly as they affect the functioning of lend-lease as handled by the Soviet Purchasing Commission and in Russia."

We can admire the very careful construction of this statement. It does not speak of "defection," "flight," "escape," or "asylum." The word used is the comparatively undramatic "resignation." Kravchenko does not appeal to the American *government*, but to American *public opinion*. Finally, he stresses his Russian patriotism. While he certainly impugns the sincerity of the Soviet Union's friendship for its "allies," he is scrupulous in deflecting attention away from issues of military collaboration or of the probity of the Lend-Lease operations—a potentially embarrassing issue from the American side.

Insofar as he was able to do so, he effectively blunted any possible charges of personal turpitude, treachery, want of patriotism, or the sowing of discord. The buttering up of the American administration becomes almost oppressive in Kravchenko's lengthy written statement—well over 1,000 words—which made up the bulk of the story. His experience in the United States had "served to crystalize in my mind views and sentiments I had long felt in Russia." The Russian people, wrote Kravchenko, yearned for certain freedoms—the very "four freedoms" of FDR. In case readers didn't get it, Kravchenko added, shamelessly, that "The Russian people have earned a new deal. . . ." The statement also contained a lengthy critique of Soviet foreign policy, which, in its characterization of Soviet aims in Eastern Europe, turned out to be much more accurate than the supposed protocols of the Yalta Accord.

In his memoir, Victor Kravchenko reports that the moment he received his posting to the United States he started thinking seriously about flight. The matter was decided, at least in his mind, by the time he reached American soil. Such a "plan" as he had included not merely "defection" but striking a palpable blow against the regime he hated. This means that he was contemplating some important publication long before it had become a functional possibility. Still, it is one thing to dream of a move so daring and so dangerous, quite another to effect it. He had no experience even of foreign travel. His only languages were Russian and Ukrainian. He might *choose* freedom, but how, concretely, was he to *gain* freedom? His book opens, in authorized epic fashion, *in medias res*. Its opening scene introduces Kravchenko in a taxicab on his way to Washington's Union Station, there to board a train for New York and his own modest rendezvous with history. The question is: How did he come to be in the taxicab?

Later, during the protracted period that *I Chose Freedom* was in the process of publication, Kravchenko dropped into the offices of his publishers, Scribner's, two or three times a week, where he was a great favorite with the secretaries on account of his friendliness and expansive courtesies. It appears that during his posting to the Washington office of the Russian Purchasing Commission he had displayed a similar open-hearted friendliness to the staff. He had come to America with the firm intention never to leave, but he had as yet no definite plan. A casual, friendly contact with a member of the clerical staff of the Purchasing Commission would prove to be his first step to freedom.

The entire Lend-Lease operation had, for the Russians, a double purpose: the acquisition of as much materiel as possible; and military and industrial espionage. Kravchenko later testified that his bosses jokingly called their espionage gleanings "super Lend-Lease." It is probable that dozens, and perhaps scores, of Soviet agents entered the country under the cloak of "Lend-Lease business." Harry Hopkins, whom Roosevelt had appointed as the program's tsar, was tireless in its administration and interpreted its enabling law very "liberally," to use his own word. What that meant was that he didn't pay all that much attention to the law, and the Soviets got millions of dollars worth of goods that Congress had explicitly omitted from the legislation. This history later became a liability for the Democrats in the domestic politics of the McCarthy era. The American entry point for wartime flights to and from Russia was Great Falls, Montana. A U.S. Army officer stationed there, Major George Racey Jordan, looked on in dismay as large numbers of undocumented Russians, given all the courtesies afforded to diplomats, flew out of Great Falls carrying uninspected "black suitcases." Jordan suspected that these suitcases contained

the booty of massive industrial espionage. He began keeping his own informal records of Lend-Lease transactions. After the war a book based upon
his diaries was widely distributed by the right-wing John Birch Society.
Kravchenko himself made a telling analogy: he likened the lavish exports
to Russia to the scrap metal eagerly sold by Americans to the Japanese in
the 1930s. That bread cast upon the waters had returned in the unpleasant
form of the poet's "nipponized bit of the old Sixth Avenue El."

As Kravchenko later testified to a congressional committee, the Washington office was actually under the control of a covert NKVD team.
All the executives of the commission were Communist Party members,
though most, including Kravchenko, were under instructions to conceal
that fact. The most important business was conducted in closed meetings
attended only by Party members. In the typical pattern of domestic Soviet
industries, there were secret police spies everywhere; but though their
ubiquity could be taken for granted, their specific identities remained
unknown.

This was a most powerful technique of social control in the Soviet
Union, but it worked somewhat less well in America. There were practical limits to the powers of the NKVD to operate in Washington, especially for the relatively small number of Russian-speaking U.S. civilian
employees required of an enterprise so large. There was no group more
suspect to the NKVD, nor more assiduously penetrated by their spies,
than the Russian diaspora in Europe. Their control of the American
scene was much less secure, and their possibilities for invigilation outside
of the Sixteenth Street office quite meager. It was apparently through
friendly, innocent chat with one of the American clerical employees that
Kravchvenko came into the chain of acquaintanceship eventually linking him with the New York "Mensheviks," and in particular with David
Dallin. The key intermediary was a Soviet woman working at the Purchasing Commission. This woman was named Sara-Sonja Judey (née
Veksler); and twenty years earlier in Berlin she had known Lilia (Lola)
Dallin, David's wife.

Dallin (1889–1962) was one of a triumvirate of the leadership of the
old Menshevik Party, which had first been exiled to Paris and then, in 1940,
moved to the United States. Along with Boris Nikolaevsky (1887–1966),
sometimes called "the father of Kremlinology," Dallin made knowledgeable and authoritative contributions to the more scholarly kind of Cold

War literature. His most famous, or at least his most controversial, book was *Forced Labor in Soviet Russia* (1947).

Dallin, who lived in New York, came into discreet contact with Kravchenko. Kravchenko had had sufficient experience with the NKVD to be wary, but even so he was taking a great risk. One of Dallin's "friends" at the time was Mark Zborowski, the anthropologist-spy, not yet exposed as a Stalinist agent, who had actually taken up residence in the same apartment building with Dallin. When he wasn't writing about Polish shtetls from the anthropological perspective, Zborowski was an expert Trotskyite-watcher for the NKVD. Eventually Trotskyites grew so thin on the ground in Paris that he became for a time head of the operation he was supposed to be infiltrating. According to John Earl Haynes and Harvey Klehr, Kravchenko and Zborowski actually crossed paths at the apartment building in March 1944—but without Zborowski's knowing who he was.* Thus the security apparatus that did not diagnose Kravchenko's infidelity during the process of his vetting in Moscow nearly discovered him by accident through Stalin's continuing obsession with Trotskyism. Indeed, Kravchenko was very lucky, but also smart and prudent.

We must remember that these "Mensheviks" were, and considered themselves to be, genuine revolutionaries. Most of them no longer shared the fantasy of the old Trotsky clique that they might one day mount to power, but there was about them a memorial aroma of conspiracy. Dallin and his wife were perhaps what Lenin and Krupskaya might have been had they remained in Zurich in 1940. Most of us have friends, acquaintances, colleagues, and "contacts." They were among the groups to whom the historians assign a "circle."

The Ukrainian engineer was mightily impressed with the older man. Here was an old revolutionary, like his own father a pre-Stalinian socialist. Here was a man with a vast knowledge of Russian history, passionately pursued. Here was a Russian patriot who made the clearest distinction between the "Russian people," whom he loved, and the "Stalin clique," whom he hated. Above all, here was a man who demonstrated both in word and deed that it was possible to flee Babylon and fight against it. What Kravchenko did not at first know was that Dallin was not so pure

---

* Haynes and Klehr are prominent scholars of American Communism. Among their books is *Venona: Decoding Soviet Espionage in America* (New Haven, 1999).

in his prelapsarian radicalism as to eschew intimate relations with the FBI
and with such specimens of American left-wing demonology as Max Eastman, Isaac Don Levine, and Eugene Lyons.

Defection was no simple or easy act. To sever forever the political commitments and habits of a lifetime, to abandon vulnerable family members, a spouse, children, parents, to leap into the darkness of a profound
cultural alterity, these are not things easily undertaken. Later on in the
postwar period, in what might be called the Golden Age of Defection, we
find famous defectors of a certain cultural sophistication and experience,
people who had done some traveling and had at least the rudiments of
a cosmopolitan outlook—dancers, athletes, chess players, and diplomats.
Kravchenko was a purely parochial, dyed-in-the-wool cradle Communist.
He had been nowhere, had no foreign contacts, spoke and read no languages other than Ukrainian and Russian.

Nor was defection all that easy as a practical matter. In 1991, the
Milwaukee police found a young lad, Konerak Sinthasomphone, naked
and injured in the street. He was fleeing from his captor and tormentor,
one Jeffrey Dahmer. But Dahmer himself appeared on the scene and persuaded the police to discount the boy's wild protests. In fact, the police
gave the boy back into the control of Dahmer, who took him home and
dismembered him, retaining his skull as a keepsake. Very similar was the
fate, *mutatis mutandis*, of many thousands of Russian nationals who had
the good fortune, early in the war, to be overrun by the Wehrmacht and
sent back to Germany as indentured laborers. After the briefest moment of
postwar liberty they were forcibly transferred by their British and American liberators to the commissars, who shot a few before sending the rest on
to the Gulag under conditions of transport worthy of the imagination of
Dante Alighieri. As it is, we must rely on the remarkable memoir of Nina
Markovna.

Some historians date the actual beginning of the Cold War from
the defection of Igor Gouzenko, whose evidence led to the unmasking
of the "atom spies" Alan Nunn May and then, by domino effect, Klaus
Fuchs, Harry Gold, David Greenglass, Julius and Ethel Rosenberg, and
others. The history of Gouzenko's defection begins in macabre comedy.
Gouzenko was a code expert working in the Soviet Embassy in Canada in
1945. He was a technician and a family man, not a political ideologue, and
his courageous and consequential defection was essentially based in the

motives that had inspired immigration to North America for more than a hundred years. He disclosed to the Canadians, and hence to the Western Allies, evidence of large-scale Soviet espionage directed against them, and especially against their joint program of nuclear research.

The goons from the NKVD were only part of his problem. Having arrived at his existential decision, poor Gouzenko, wife and infant child in tow, wandered around official Ottawa trying to get somebody to take him seriously. He went first to the press, an institution whose vigor and independence had amazed his Russian consciousness. He had, after all, the story of the year if not the decade. But it was near closing time at the *Ottawa Journal*, and the Slavic Deep Throat found only a bemused brush-off. At a government office he was told, in effect, to come back on Monday during normal working hours, when he might fill out the appropriate form. The commitment to counterrevolutionary vigilance was so weak in the Dominion that Gouzenko would have been a dead man, and that very soon, had it not been for the kindness and mental acuity of a neighbor.

Later in the Cold War, defection would develop its protocols of decorum, but Kravchenko was a real pioneer. His was not the flight of an Orlov or a Krivitsky—men whose lugubrious gestures remind one of Michael Corleone trying to go straight. He had been principally the victim, rather than the perpetrator, of Soviet crime, and if he could not be encouraged by models of previous success, he at least could not be discouraged by models of previous disaster. He was, after all, a Soviet executive. He knew he needed a *plan*.

KRAVCHENKO AND THE FBI

To Gary Kern, a professional scholar who recently published an exhaustive book on the Kravchenko case, goes the considerable credit of wresting the FBI files from an unnecessary and certainly unhelpful secrecy.* The bureau's files concerning Kravchenko are bulky, and, as available under the Freedom of Information Act, they are riddled with the annoying censors' deletions that make of them something of a giant Sudoku grid. But

---

* Kern's book is *The Kravchenko Case: One Man's War on Stalin* (New York, 2007).

Kern has analyzed them thoroughly. Our purposes are adequately served perhaps by the long summary memorandum prepared for J. Edgar Hoover by Hoover's right-hand man, D. M. Ladd, completed on April 11, 1944, a week after the dramatic press conference with the *New York Times*.

Although the FBI had been long aware of Kravchenko's activities, contacts, and intentions, they were blindsided by two aspects of the defection. The first was the length, eloquence, and political potency of Kravchenko's published statement. Though inexperienced and indeed naive in many of his assumptions, Kravchenko had a sensitive regard for the delicacy of the international situation. (He also had a much more accurate view of Stalin's intentions than the president of the United States or his secretary of state, but that is another matter.) The United States and the Soviet Union were military allies locked in a desperate struggle with their common and detested Nazi foe. Kravchenko regarded himself, with good reason, as a Russian patriot. He wanted to do nothing to harm Allied unity or to comfort the German enemy, and he was genuinely mortified when Goebbels immediately picked up the *New York Times* story for purposes of his own propaganda. Under these circumstances, Kravchenko had planned to limit himself to a very modest and general "statement of resignation" of no more than 100 words. He conveyed this intention to his FBI contacts.

When he got to New York on the Friday, however, he was induced to change his mind. There appear to have been two principal factors. In the first place his friend Joseph Shaplen at the *New York Times* echoed the advice he had already received from his prospective literary agent and confidant Eugene Lyons. Both men thought that Kravchenko's proposed minimal statement would hardly be newsworthy, and that certainly it would not be effective in laying the foundation for the prospective book that by now was looming as large in their imaginations as in his own. This was of course also the view of another adviser, the ubiquitous Isaac Don Levine. But Kravchenko had long thought of his "resignation" as an offensive rather than a defensive act. He wanted, in good Marxist fashion, to "strike a hard blow." Like so many other "anti-Soviet" writers, he felt obliged to exploit his rare, indeed nearly miraculous opportunity to address a Western audience and to speak for millions of the mute oppressed. (Jerzy Gliksman actually entitled his book *Tell the West*; one of Solzhenitsyn's titles is *Warning to the West*; and as early as 1930, a book by Vladimir Tchernavin was entitled *I Speak for the Silent*.) So, he spent much of the weekend writing his new, extended, and powerful statement for the press. Various counselors almost certainly helped him, but the voice was the authentic voice of Victor Kravchenko.

The second way in which the FBI was surprised was related to the first. Kravchenko became a very big story—page one, not page seventeen. The FBI, alert to the same political sensitivities that constrained the defector himself, had been most restrained—nearly reluctant—in their three earlier interviews with Kravchenko. There were no interrogations, not even much shadowboxing, merely vague and inconclusive soundings that left Kravchenko, who had had years of experience with the NKVD, understandably dubious concerning FBI competence, let alone their interest in or ability to protect him. (Indeed, given the fact that the Soviet Purchasing Commission was crawling with dozens or scores of spies, the FBI's complaisance with regard to the whole Lend-Lease operation throughout the war might be judged heroic.) Now that he had "resigned" from any connection with the Soviet government—had in effect thrown himself as a stateless refugee upon the indulgence of American public opinion—the FBI had spent three days in slightly more vigorous but still pretty perfunctory debriefing sessions. "The questioning of Kravchenko has to date barely touched the surface of his fund of knowledge regarding Soviet activity both in this country and abroad," noted Ladd.

The bureau reasonably feared that it had been drawn into a major international incident of great potential danger. Hoover had been suspicious of Kravchenko from the start, fearing that he was the agent of a plot to embarrass him and the bureau. Kravchenko's news conference effected less change in the director's attitude than one might have expected. Both in his newspaper statement, and then more fully in his FBI interviews, Kravchenko had placed his actions squarely within the highly sensitive context of international relations. Fortunately the Russians, while not doing much to alleviate Hoover's suspicions, relieved him of his worries about an "incident." According to them, nothing had happened, or very little. At first they said nothing. They then said that Kravchenko was a nobody—not an engineer, not an "expert," not an executive, just a filing clerk. The fantastic lies constituting his press conference were a desperate attempt to disguise an ignoble act of poltroonery. He was scheduled to return to Russia and active military service, the cowardly fear of which had inspired his libels and his treasons.

The draft dodger cum traitor "scenario" was the one also adopted postwar by most Western Communists and fellow travelers, and it grieved poor Kravchenko sorely. He had held the rank of captain in the Red Army. Despite the fact that his expertise was desperately needed in the industrial sector, his enemies in the NKVD, having failed to eliminate him in the usual manner, had managed to have him sent to the front, where he had fought stoutly, but inconveniently avoided being killed. (His beloved brother, Constantine, had already given his life for the Fatherland.) When Stalin ordered all engineers and other vital industrial experts from the front to the factories, he had been among those plucked back. Still it was a near miracle, perhaps attributable to the disturbance of communication in war-ravaged Russia, that he had passed the NKVD vetting for a posting to Washington, D.C.

Matters had proceeded roughly in the following manner. When Kravchenko met him, Dallin the Menshevik was just putting the finishing touches on a book called *The Real Soviet Russia*, in which he dealt in a matter-of-fact fashion with such questions as the rise of the bureaucratic class, the system of slave labor camps, and the malign motives of Soviet foreign policy. The book was, among other things, a stinging rebuke to the liberal fashioners of the "Stalingrad syndrome" as defined by Koestler. In his preface, Dallin had written that although international relations perhaps had to be conducted on the basis of "conventional truths and conventional lies," the obligation of the scholar was to truth. He intended to give the news about Russia, even if it ran counter to the "healthy optimism" so many American opinion makers sought to embrace. "From the optimistic to the ridiculous is only a short step. Otherwise, what is the use of a free press and of free science?" Indeed we have already seen, in the history of Jan Valtin's *Out of the Night*, the powerful taboo against speaking ill of the Soviets instituted, with the suddenness of *Blitzkrieg* itself, on the day that Hitler unleashed Barbarossa. Dallin's book was published by Yale; it is unlikely that a commercial publisher would have taken it on in 1944.

Kravchenko wrote of himself (p. 308): "We Russians are gregarious folk, warm and talkative and quick to kindle in friendship. We wear our hearts on our sleeves. I am no exception in this respect." He kindled with friendly warmth toward David Dallin, who openly encouraged Kravchenko's hopes of escape. His example *as a writer* was a further inspiration.

For his part, Dallin genuinely liked Kravchenko and understood, as very few of the American friends Kravchenko eventually made ever could, both the physical dangers and the larger psychological difficulties that accompanied such an action. But of course Dallin himself, as a vulnerable alien living in America on sufferance, was taking a huge risk in getting involved. In researching this book, I slowly came to an awareness of the effectiveness with which experience of the Soviet police state destroyed those instincts of human trust I once thought natural. But Dallin met Kravchenko's courage with courage of his own. He also understood and appreciated the nature of Kravchenko's career attainments and difficulties. Dallin was gathering materials for his next book, on forced labor. Here was a highly ranked manager, fresh from the Soviet Union, who was a fountain of information concerning many aspects of Soviet industrial production, factory life, and labor economics. Dallin had independently concluded that the brunt of the war industries was being carried by slaves. Kravchenko said that it was, in so many words. Dallin wanted to see his book in print.

Dallin got Kravchenko's permission to mention, in one of his chats with his FBI friends, that he knew a Russian, anonymous, who might want to seek asylum. The FBI staff was noncommittal but not discouraging. Kravchenko had some meetings with FBI agents to discuss hypotheticals. Hoover, personally involved as ever, was deeply suspicious. He feared an NKVD plant and a conspiracy the aim of which was not espionage but the embarrassment of his agency. On the darkling plain of spy-versus-spy, it is armies of paranoids that clash by night. He was also reluctant to stir up a hornets' nest in Washington, where the question of appropriate levels of Lend-Lease to Russia was still being raised by conservatives for whom it had become their last means of expressing what was in fact an opposition to the entire program.

As in any negotiation, the side that knows what it wants has a distinct advantage. Kravchenko knew what he wanted, and so he "won." He wanted physical security, such cooperation in establishing a disguised identity as might be required, and financial security for about eighteen months, a period long enough for him to complete his book and—as his awestruck assessment of American industrial might encouraged him to hope—for the war to be over. What the FBI *should* have wanted—and what he surely would have been willing to give them—was such information as he might have about Soviet espionage efforts within the Purchasing Commission and about illegalities and profiteering on the part of the American contractors supplying the Russians. We know from the Iraq War, as from every war, that for certain commercial interests it is an ill wind that blows no one any good. Yet what Hoover appeared most eagerly to want to know was whether Kravchenko was out to harm the FBI.

One historian, who is wont to fault the FBI on every possible occasion, finds Hoover's behavior in the Kravchenko affair contemptible. Such an imputation is unjust. By no means did Hoover use the affair to press an "anti-Communist" agenda. Others were certainly interested in that angle: David Dallin, for instance, or William C. Bullitt, the former American ambassador to the Soviet Union, who became involved. Just as he fretted about being embarrassed himself, Hoover was scrupulous to avoid any possible embarrassment to either the executive or judicial branches. He went through channels, all the way to the president. So, instead of exploiting Kravchenko to the full, Hoover investigated him.

Kravchenko got much less ambiguous support from the "literary" people, five of whom were particularly important. The role of Eugene Lyons was so large as to require more extensive description presently. Kravchenko also was helped considerably by both Isaac Don Levine and Max Eastman. Levine knew everything there was to know about Slavic, and Eastman about Anglo, anti-Sovietism. Eastman had long since finished "drifting" away from socialism. He was at the helm of a literary speedboat. Among the three of them, they were able to arrange for Kravchenko loans and advances against future writing, including a particularly sweet deal with a $15,000 advance from *Cosmopolitan* magazine for a series of articles. (The salary of a beginning college professor in 1944 was about $4,000 per annum.)

There were two other important players, one of whom has already been mentioned. On the title page of Dallin's *The Real Soviet Russia* is the legend "translated by Joseph Shaplen." Shaplen, fully fluent in Russian and English, was the reporter for the *New York Times* who had arranged Kravchenko's effective press conference with that paper. He may also have written the article resulting from it. The other man was Charles Malamuth, a leading expert on Russia and the translator of several works of Russian literature. He was the translator and editor—for the author was murdered before he could complete his work—of Trotsky's biography of

Stalin. That poignant work bears the publication date of 1941, followed by a second date of 1946, the year it actually appeared. Harper's printed a small note, a little gem of circumlocution, explaining the circumstances. The real circumstances were that the Roosevelt administration had placed an effective ban on "anti-Soviet" books the day after Pearl Harbor, though a few managed to sneak through. Malamuth was then a professor at Cornell, and his house was one of many places where Kravchenko hunkered down over the next months.

Of his book, Kravchenko wrote in his postscript that "I . . . worked on it month after month under harrowing conditions of persecution and threats against my life. I was obliged to wander from city to city, continually changing hotels and private residences, living under assumed names and assumed nationalities, finding safe 'hide-outs' in the homes of Americans or my own country-men." There is no evidence that he was actually pursued by Communist agents, but the FBI had advised the "moving target" strategy. And despite what he says, one has the feeling he came to enjoy the drama of the false identities. Besides, the FBI was keeping a close watch on him. Hoover bugged the Soviet Purchasing Commission and put wiretaps on Kravchenko's phone at the Park Crescent Hotel in New York, and, whenever he could, on the phones of his hosts—Professor Malamuth's phone in Ithaca, among them. Aware of Sara-Sonja Judey's contacts with Kravchenko, he tapped the Judeys' phone.

What he found out from his bugs was that either Kravchenko was playing it absolutely straight, or the bureau was faced with a huge, devilish conspiracy perpetrated by actors of Academy Award standards. M. V. Serov, the covert Party chief at the Russian Purchasing Commission, was in a state of shock. No doubt only part of this related to his amazement at Kravchenko's deed. He was in deep difficulty, having just received that sort of urgent invitation to return for consultations in Moscow that all Soviet officials dreaded. Kravchenko's eavesdropped friends were excited, and his eavesdropped enemies distressed, about what might be forthcoming in the book. The debunking campaign was being planned well before there was any actual book to debunk. Meanwhile, the peripatetic Kravchenko addressed himself to his daunting task.

Kravchenko Becomes a Writer

The manner in which *I Chose Freedom* was written was complex but not particularly mysterious. There was nothing literary and Soviet in New York that did not involve the intermediation of one or more of a small group of Russian-speaking experts. The three most important were Isaac Don Levine, Gene Lyons, and Max Eastman; but David Dallin and Boris Nikolaevsky (the "Old Bolshevik") were also active. Kravchenko was in cahoots with all of them. The Kravchenko "case" was in the headlines for weeks and months in the spring and summer of 1944, and everybody in the publishing world anticipated a book. According to his own testimony Kravchenko began writing almost immediately, and his early arrangement with Eugene Lyons was inevitable. Lyons, at this point only Kravchenko's literary agent, approached Max Perkins at Scribner's and told him the terms on which he could have Kravchenko's book. Perkins was interested in seeing the manuscript, which at that point did not exist. Kravchenko knew a great deal more about steel tubing than he did about literary composition. Nevertheless, both from evangelical and apologetic motives he threw himself immediately into writing down the life experiences that culminated in his defection. As writing so often is, his experience must have been a strange mixture of exhilaration and agony. He had a great deal to say, but little idea as to how to say it. Perhaps he got through it by imagining that he was producing one of those autobiographical "reports" that were the favorite genre of the NKVD, only on a vast scale.

By the summer of 1945, with the war against Germany ended and that against Japan ending, Kravchenko had a very large number of words on paper. He was not quite up to Jan Valtin's rate of production, but he approached it. Lyons took one look at his protoplasmic results and, without mentioning his subcontractual arrangement to Perkins, quickly passed them on to a competent bilingual native speaker. This woman, whose name was Miriam Levine (no relation to Isaac Don), had done commissioned translations from the Russian on a piecework basis before. To Perkins she later described the manuscript as "an unruly mass of closely written papers . . . about the most illiterate, illegible, and unimaginative piece of writing I had ever come across." She nevertheless grasped the "political dynamite" of the contents and the fact that Kravchenko was an industrial engineer, not a writer. So she translated his bundles of ink-splotched foolscap, metaphorically holding her literary nose the while. A nearly completed translation—meaning a repellent hodgepodge of disorganized materials written now in the English language—came to the board at Scribner's. This was as highly competent, experienced, and judicious a group as could be found in America. They reached easy agreement on two points. The first was that the material was genuine, novel, uniquely authoritative, and of great historical and cultural import. The second was that Kravchenko could not write his way out of a wet paper bag, so the manuscript would need a collaborative revision of a drastic and most unusual kind.

The job inevitably went to Eugene Lyons. This may have been Lyons's idea or hope from the beginning, though invisibility and anonymity did not come easily to him. He certainly made a good deal of money out of the arrangement (40 percent of the royalties). From his point of view, at least, he earned every penny. Kravchenko had little understanding of the literary problems, and he suspected the motives behind the necessarily radical recasting of the material. Lyons did a first cut in Russian, until he had a narrative with logical sequence and shape. Then he put it into fluent literary English. Then every English sentence had to be orally translated back into Russian and approved by Kravchenko, to whom Lyons's *American Mercury* style often sounded strange or puzzling. Translation is not a mathematical science by which fixed verbal equivalents are transposed according to inflexible principle. Lyons was after cultural as well as linguistic translation. He wanted a text that *flowed.*

Kravchenko kept making new revisions. Though perhaps neither he nor Lyons realized it, they were in effect using the intensive methods developed by the early Jesuits to teach Latin to youngsters. Not surprisingly Kravchenko improved his (book) English rapidly, and this led him to want to reconsider passages whose English he had already previous approved. Lyons started to despair of ever arriving at a finished copy. He began to refer to Kravchenko as "the 'author,'" with sinister quotation marks. He found Kravchenko "a most difficult guy," even beyond the linguistic problems. Their personal relationship cooled, though both remained professionally correct. Kravchenko eventually made his view of things quite clear when he told Scribner's that he would never again collaborate with Lyons.

But they kept at it, with Kravchenko believing and insisting that every word in the book was in fact his own. Even when they got to the stage of printed galleys, Kravchenko was still demanding major surgery. Some years later Charles Scribner, in reviewing the history of the book's publication for Kravchenko's French agent, wrote that "Mr. Kravchenko's editing of the galley proofs and the ensuing alterations were far in excess of what we usually permit and we received from him a sum of money in payment for this." In other words, Kravchenko was willing to *pay* to make sure the book said exactly what he wanted it to say.

So, was *I Chose Freedom* written by Victor Kravchenko? That question was repeatedly put to Max Perkins, and he always answered it not with a yes or a no but with a brief but scrupulous description of the process just outlined. For him it was "not at all what is known as a ghost-written book." At a fairly early stage of things, Lyons had written a progress report to Perkins. "We are inclined to include my name in the authorship: 'as told to Eugene Lyons' or 'in collaboration with' or some other formula. The writing has turned out to be so 'literary' or at least professional that it might be best to tell the whole story of the collaboration out loud."

There is quite a lot implied in that statement. Notice, first, the plural "We." It suggests that the honeymoon period was not quite over. But there is also an implication that the idea of a stated collaboration is a new one, brought about by the evolution of the project. The manuscript now begins to look like the work of a professional writer—rather than the memoirs of an engineer—and that should be explained. But even had Kravchenko himself continued to agree to have Lyons's name on the title page, it is most doubtful that Scribner's would have agreed. Lyons was simply too controversial and too easily dismissed on grounds of bias. He was a man, after all, who had entitled the leading chapter of *The Red Decade*, his most widely read book, "In Defense of Red-Baiting." The people at Scribner's were not afraid of controversy, and expected even more opposition to *I Chose Freedom* than they actually got; but they would not intentionally expose a soft flank. Charles Scribner's peer at Random House, Bennett Cerf, whose "leftism" receded in the fifties and has now been largely forgotten, once published a letter in which he compared Lyons, politically, with Senator Theodore Bilbo and Gerald L. K. Smith, two of the most repugnant racist demagogues ever produced in America.

There is a great deal more of Kravchenko in *I Chose Freedom* than there is of any recent American president in his State of the Union address. But as anyone who has tried to teach writing knows, the common belief that "ideas" or "materials" can easily be isolated from the language in which they are expressed is a mistaken belief. So there is also a good deal of Eugene Lyons in the book. In other words, it was a "translation" in a medieval rather than a modern sense, like Chaucer's translation of Boccaccio in *Troilus and Criseyde*.

Kravchenko's book begins *in medias res*, with its protagonist in a Washington taxicab headed for Union Station and the "freedom" of his title. That literary device was one of hundreds supplied by Lyons. It is an effectively breathless beginning that would be lost were there any conventional Introduction or frontmatter. There is, however, a very brief Postscript, signed in the form of a letter or legal document with a large and typographically gauche line-etching facsimile of the author's signature. It is a combative political statement that explains why the book was written, but says little about the how of it. "Naturally, I wrote this book in my native tongue, Russian, so that it had to be translated, the English text edited from an American vantage point before publication in English. . . . I personally checked and edited the final version."

That is the truth, but so far from being the whole truth that it infuriated Miriam Levine when she picked up the finished product. She found not so much as a thank you to a typist, let alone any kind of acknowledgment of the work she knew Lyons must have shouldered. She wrote to Maxwell Perkins, who up until that time knew only that "a friend" had produced the original English version, "simply to get the business off my chest and to register with you my annoyance with Kravchenko's cavalier attitude and actions." She pointed out that, however powerful the contents of the book might be, "if they had been presented to the reading public in their original form—no one would ever have read beyond page one."

Victor Kravchenko was conspicuous for what the old Communists called "culture"—meaning a certain fundamental civility comprising personal hygiene, tidiness of dress, table manners, and certain forms of courtesy. He was a great favorite with the office staff at Scribner's, and particularly with a Miss Wyckoff, a secretary who handled his mail for him. With her, he was lavish of gratitude and compliment. But it apparently never occurred to him to give over a few lines of his book to acknowledge the people who had made it possible. This "cavalier" attitude reflected not a character flaw but a cultural misprision. Like many people who have suffered injustice and oppression, he was deeply angry. I have found no one who worked closely with Kravchenko who really liked him without major reservation. For his part, he was offended by the vast American ignorance of Russia, and by the assumption, apparently frequently encountered, that the alternative to being a soulless Communist bureaucrat was a soulless Rotarian. He regarded himself as a Russian patriot, and struggled to maintain some arena of personal and political independence. Some readers found him insufficiently grateful to America as a whole. He never would have written anything approaching the tenor of Valtin's "American Dawn."

A Romantic Interlude

Kravchenko had a flair with women. He had been divorced from one Russian wife and perhaps abandoned a second when he came to America. His book touches upon more than one extracurricular affair. This account must now follow Victor Kravchenko, briefly, into one of those digressions that might be described as stranger than non-fiction. In one of her autobiographies, Brooke Astor tells how she met her first husband, John Dryden Kuser, as a blind date at a party at the Ivy Club in Princeton in 1918. This appalling specimen of the American ruling class was the grandson of John F. Dryden, the founder of the Prudential Life Insurance Corporation and for a time a U.S. senator (R-NJ), and the son of Colonel Anthony Rudolph Kuser, a notable conservationist, one of whose private game reserves is now by his gift the exquisite High Point State Park in the extreme northwest corner of the Garden State.

The virtues of the elders seem to have expired in Dryden Kuser (1897–1964), as he was known, whom Brooke Astor married when she was only seventeen. He never amounted to much, though he did become an elected member of the New Jersey state legislature. According to Brooke Astor he was also a wife abuser, a drunk, and a womanizer who, after ten years of unhappy marriage, sent her away to get a divorce. They had one child, Anthony (Tony), who has of late been in the news amid unpleasant rumors of mistreatment of his mother, now recently deceased. In an interview with the *New York Times* some years ago, Mrs. Astor said that she "learned about terrible manners" from the Kuser family. "They didn't know how to treat people."

Needless to say, there was a great deal of money in the Kuser family. After describing the sybaritic life of the circles in which the Kusers moved, Brooke Astor remarked: "It was enough to make you a Communist." Then, again, *au contraire*, as W. C. Fields used to say.

Dryden Kuser had one sibling, a younger sister named Cynthia. Her rebellion against the oppressive greatness of her sires was much more colorful—and certainly more fun—than was Dryden's. Cynthia Kuser was beautiful and she was brilliant. She had had every advantage of education and foreign travel, and she was a remarkable linguist. She had independent political views—indeed, independent views of every kind. Furthermore, both of her parents had been dead since the early 1930s. She shared with her dreadful brother a vast fortune. She was the kind of sex goddess men dream of, but who show up mainly in James Bond novels.

In November 1946, at a publisher's party, Victor Kravchenko met Cynthia Kuser. She was actually married at the time to a man named Theodore Herbst, but neither then nor at any time in the future did that make much difference. There was chemistry. They left the party together, and Kravchenko walked her through falling snow a short way to the Scribner's bookshop window, in which stacks of copies of *I Chose Freedom*, still in their pristine jackets, glistered in the streetlights. The Communist and the capitalist heiress exchanged admiring glances. They then took refuge from the storm in a hotel, very much in the spirit and in the end with very similar results as in the fourth book of the *Æneid* when Dido and Æneas take refuge from the rainstorm in a cave.

There is a great deal more to the story, which can be found in Gary Kern's biography of Kravchenko. Though they never married, Cynthia and Victor entered into a long-term, melodramatically secretive relationship, which produced two sons who were raised by a nanny in bizarre seclusion in the Arizona hinterland and who, for many years, did not know who their father was. The relevance of Cynthia Kuser to the narrative of this book is primarily linguistic. She had spent a good deal of time in France and spoke French very well. Victor Kravchenko might soon have excellent use for a French-speaking confidante.

I Chose Freedom

What was in *I Chose Freedom*, this substantial book of nearly 500 pages? Of autobiography, the book's mode, there is more than one subgenre. There is autobiography meant to convey the uniqueness of a particular personality. Such is Rousseau's *Confessions*. There is autobiography presented as moral model or exemplification. Such is Augustine's *Confessions*. There is autobiography that serves to explain and justify a controversial or dramatic public career. Such is Newman's *Apologia*. And there is autobiography that is a window on time and place. Kravchenko's book combines the features of the latter two. He sets out to explain why and how he "chose freedom." "To explain it," he writes, "I must rehearse my whole life and the life of Russia as it touched mine."

His life was, in effect, the very paradigm of twentieth-century Russian history. He was born in 1905, the year of the stillborn revolution, in which his father, a railway worker, had participated. His earliest memories were of his father's absence in a political exile from which on occasion he escaped for brief periods. One of the first impressions one gains from reading the histories of the period is of the comparative amateurism and halfheartedness of Tsarist repression when compared with later "Bolshevik firmness." Kravchenko's father, who was still living at the time of his defection, was a lifelong inspiration to him.

He experienced all the typical personal and social difficulties of the chaos of the collapse of the old regime in the midst of a horrible world war that was immediately followed by years of a barbarous civil war attended by chaos and famine. "The dead, millions of them, were buried and by a kind of unspoken agreement no one referred to the catastrophe." Life began anew in the summer of 1922. Lenin had suffered his first stroke but was still living, and the country was alive with purpose. The young Kravchenko volunteered for work in the Donetz Basin. He joined the Komsomol, the Communist Youth Brigade. He became a true believer. In 1929, he applied for and was accepted to membership in the Communist Party.

Kravchenko witnessed at firsthand the terrible suffering in the Ukraine during the first Five Year Plan. At the age of twenty-five, in 1930, he went to Kharkov to study engineering. He was aware of the terrible conditions in the Ukrainian villages, and, as a Party member, he was seconded to participate in the forced collectivization of agriculture which in 1932 involved the state-sponsored famine, known in Ukrainian as the *Holomodor*, in which many millions starved to death. Like Lev Kopelev and other former true believers who have written of their firsthand experience in these events, Kravchenko somehow managed at the time to rationalize the horror as historical necessity. One chapter is particularly terrible, even though it is practically free of gross violence and mass murder. Eugene Lyons, the master of the lurid styling of *American Mercury* and the *Reader's Digest*, had called it "Eliena's Secret." (Other of his titles include "Horror in the Village," "Harvest in Hell," and "My First Purge.") Eliena was a beautiful married woman with whom Kravchenko fell in love during his time at Kharkov. Her secret was that she had bargained with the secret police to free her husband from a concentration camp. Her part of the bargain was to work for the NKVD as a glamorous come-on with foreign engineers and industrial consultants for purposes of surveillance and industrial espionage. One of the most disturbing revelations of the book is the fashion in which the Soviet system poisoned even the most intimate and tender of human relationships—the same theme that Koestler handled in his fictional treatment of Arlova.

Kravchenko was an expert in metallurgy, with a particular specialty in steel pipes and tubing. He was in charge of a rolling mill at Nikopol. This was a major appointment, and as an executive he enjoyed personal privileges grotesquely discordant with the lives of his wretched workers. On the other hand he lived a joyless life of unending pressured labor and anxiety. He noted, from the professional point of view, the actual effects of Stakhanovism, the constant pressure to meet "norms," the ceaseless scapegoating and endless searches for wreckers and saboteurs.*

One of Kravchenko's great themes is the Purge, or rather purges,

---

* Stakhanovism takes its name from an actual coal miner, Alexei Stakhanov. In 1935 his mining team was said to have achieved, through a combination of innovative efficiencies and increased personal effort, a huge increment in the average hourly rate of coal extraction. Stakhanov was declared a Soviet "hero of labor," and a wave of supposedly voluntary competitive industrial athleticism (Stakhanovism) swept through all levels of the Five Year Plan. Stakhanovism was vigorously encouraged by Soviet propaganda as a patriotic duty. Its Western critics saw in it simply a version of the much execrated production-line "speedup" of capitalist industry. Kravchenko was of the opinion that it actually impeded rather than promoted sound industrial production.

plural. He survived the immediate aftermath of the Kirov assassination with a near miss; but everywhere around him friends and acquaintances were going under. That they were invariably innocent of the preposterous charges brought against them could not absolve them of their real fault: being compromised in a political system gone quite mad. He gives vivid firsthand accounts of the banal and horrible proceedings of the rigged meetings of the Purge commissions, the Party caucuses, and the factory workers. Kravchenko's own ordeal came in what he calls the "Super-Purge" of 1936. In the context of wide reading in the "Gulag library," Kravchenko's experiences were actual relatively mild ones; but in their protracted delineation they seem truly ghastly.

Part of the power of *I Chose Freedom* is its utter believability. Kravchenko was an important executive in what can be regarded as a huge industrial enterprise—the heavy industries of the Five Year Plans—but he did not move in exalted circles. It is not entirely easy to credit Jan Valtin's intimations of intimacy with Georgi Dimitrov or Willi Münzenberg, or his account of a personal interrogation by Heinrich Himmler. Kravchenko knew only one great man, Sergo Ordzhonikidze, member of the Politburo and Commissar for Heavy Industries, and for a long time one of the closest of Stalin's personal friends. Nothing could be more natural than that one of the country's experts on pipe-rolling should come to Ordzhonikidze's attention. The commissar appears to have appreciated Kravchenko's abilities, and in a few instances he was able to help him cut through red tape.

This was perhaps enough to make him be regarded as Kravchenko's "protector" in the eyes of the NKVD, and it may have been one of the things that got Ordzhonikidze himself in trouble. He died suddenly in 1937. It was passed off as a natural death, though in fact it was probably a suicide and possibly a murder. "The very next day I received a called from Gershgorn." This Gershgorn, a sinister officer of the NKVD, was Kravchenko's own personal Inspector Javert. Gershgorn persecuted him remorselessly. The standard technique was to telephone him during the day and order him to report for an interrogation session at midnight—this following a strenuous day's work and as a prelude to another. Through the small hours Gershgorn would browbeat—and occasionally simply beat—him, in the attempt to get incriminating evidence about others already caught in the mesh, or the admission of some peccadilloes of Kravchenko's own that might then become the stuff of a serious prosecution.

Kravchenko barely avoided the Gulag, but he had ample evidence of its existence and its nature. Having survived investigation by the skin of his teeth, he was reassigned to Taganrog in the Rostov region in the Urals. Kravchenko's job was to take over the pipe-rolling division of a huge steel manufactury—once a showpiece of the Five Year Plan, now in chaos as a result of the purging of its brilliant manager and other key staff. As any map of the Gulag will show, Rostov was surrounded by camps, and only a blind man could have been unaware of them. In a lengthy chapter entitled "Labor: Free and Slave" he outlined his understanding of the major role played by forced labor in the process of industrialization.

Particularly powerful are Kravchenko's chapters about Russia at war. Kravchenko lost his elder brother to death in battle. He himself served as a Red Army officer. It is obvious that many thoughtful Russian Communists had the deepest reservations about Stalin's pact with Hitler. It is obvious as well that many were entirely aware of the mind-boggling incompetence with which the German invasion was met at such vast expense in life and materiel. But of course they kept a terrified silence. They tried to find within the horror of the war itself some promise of a postwar liberalization and reform—hopes dashed by the reassertion of the bleakest tyranny as soon as the tide of battle turned.

His special metallurgical expertise made Kravchenko more valuable to the Lend-Lease operations than as cannon fodder on the front. Thus it was that after a meticulous political debriefing, during which Kravchenko successfully convinced the NKVD that he bore no ill will from his previous experiences with their enterprise, he was chosen to go to Washington, D.C. That very moment, he tells us, he decided to choose freedom.

As is frequently true in literary study, the qualities of Kravchenko's book appear most clearly in the profile of a comparative context. An obvious parallel presents itself, that of the book written by Igor Gouzenko, the cipher clerk in the Soviet Embassy in Ottawa, whose defection in September 1945 exposed the ring of "atom spies" and, according to one scholar, "started" the Cold War. Gouzenko says explicitly that he was inspired by Kravchenko. The title of his own book (*This Was My Choice*, 1948) obviously echoes Kravchenko's title. Gouzenko was a much better writer than Kravchenko. He went on to write a serious novel, *The Fall of a Titan*, that invites a comparison, not entirely ridiculous, with Pasternak's *Doctor Zhivago*. There is a great deal more real drama in Gouzenko's escape than there was in Kravchenko's. Gouzenko's masters pursued him hotly; Kravchenko's were taken completely by surprise. And of course the result of Gouzenko's action—the exposure of a spy ring—had huge international political impact.

Yet *I Chose Freedom* is a superior book to *This Was My Choice*. This is not because it pioneered a popular Cold War genre. The critical advantages of priority and novelty may be considerable, but they are not conclusive. What is conclusive is the extraordinary content of Victor Kravchenko's *life* as revealed in his book. Kravchenko was seventeen years older than Gouzenko. He had vivid memories of the Revolution and the civil war. He had grown to maturity before Stalin came into his full power. Kravchenko had had intimate experience of the workings of Soviet heavy industry. He was a witness to the horrors of agricultural collectivization. Dozens, and perhaps hundreds of his friends, colleagues, and associates had been through the purgatory of "purgation." Although he himself barely escaped the Gulag, it had been a close thing, and he had intimate and painful experience of police persecution. He was, moreover, of a gloomily reflective cast of mind. He had meditated, fruitfully, on his experiences. He undoubtedly has what could be called an "anti-Soviet" view. But the tremendous condemnation of Russian Communism in *I Chose Freedom* grows organically from the man's history long before it is shaped by a philosophy.

AMERICA READS KRAVCHENKO

In 1946, very few Americans knew anything about actual Soviet life, except that they probably would not like it. Kravchenko's book taught them why their instinct was right. It dealt with the brutality of daily industrial life, and its disastrous inefficiencies and mendacities. It dealt with political oppression. It dealt with material want to the point of starvation. It touched upon the slave labor system. It brilliantly captured an atmosphere of nearly universal social fear. All these topics, however, arose organically from the life story of a man who very successfully presented himself as a microcosm of a vast enslaved population of decent, ordinary people whose unsatisfied wants and unmet needs were the wants and needs of decent, ordinary people everywhere. In Kravchenko's book there is the clearest possible dichotomy between the suffering millions and the small clique of Communist tyrants who torture them. Only in the very final chapters— Kravchenko's account of his experiences in North America—do we find the kind of propagandistic comparisons between two "systems" that were the staple of a certain mode of anti-Communist literature. One suspects that in the pillorying of Henry Wallace, for instance, or the review of the movie *The North Star*, we may see something of the agenda as well as the prose of Eugene Lyons. But the overwhelming impression left by the book is of its authenticity.

According to Jan Valtin, one of the fields identified as promising for Communist penetration on the "cultural front" was the book world—publishing houses, bookstores, and libraries. Whether there was any special truth in that claim, some of the correspondence in the Scribner files about *I Chose Freedom* is at least amusing in this regard. A private reader, one John Myers, wrote to Perkins to express his "hopes that in particular the stupid editors of the *New Republic*, the *Nation*, and *PM*—(whose support of the USSR is sickening) will see it and be forced to take cognizance of what goes on under Stalin as reported by a man who is *not* a reactionary." The book had no such effect on the editors of those particular journals. An undated note, signed only "A Yankee," addresses the conspiracy in the bookshops. "I recently bought a copy of 'I Chose Freedom' at the Doubleday, Doran bookshop at Grand Central Station, South arcade. The clerk immediately tried to sell me a book by a pro-communist explaining that I ought to buy two controversial books while I was at it. I told him that the book I wanted was factual, whereon he tried to say that things in Russia had changed since the author had left."

The word "controversial" appears to have been selected as the proper adjective at central headquarters. Mrs. Grace W. Baker, the librarian of the Brooklyn Museum, wrote indignantly to Scribner's to protest the receipt of a *gift* of Kravchenko's book. A specialized library devoted to fine porcelains and so on clearly had no use for "such titles." Furthermore, "I would like to add that I personally object to the wide distribution of controversial literature at a time when the world is seeking peace."

A librarian who objected to the distribution of books is not the strangest political phenomenon of that age; but *I Chose Freedom* appeared as a threat to world peace chiefly to such peacemongers as on occasion filled the Madison Square Garden for peace rallies sponsored by the Russian-American Friendship Committee. The "warmongering" aspect of Kravchenko's book had been established early in a review written by a journalist named Raymond Arthur Davies (no relation of Ambassador Davies) for the June 1946 issue of *Soviet Russia Today*. This propaganda organ, secretly subsidized by the Soviets, was published by Communists for fellow travelers, under the editorship of Jessica Smith, the wife of John Abt, perennial chief counsel for the American Communist Party. The Abt-Smiths probably held the endurance record for harrassment by HUAC. Davies's review was republished in a large run of tearsheet offprints. These were then distributed at the numerous "peace rallies" and "peace lectures" given throughout the country, but especially on the east coast and in the Chicago area, by pro-Communist "peace experts." One such lecture was given at various Massachusetts venues by Erica Mann, whose impeccable anti-Fascist credentials derived both from her role as the daughter of Thomas Mann and her connections with the prewar German Communist Party. Davies's review had a lurid title: "he chose freedom . . . to advocate war against his country," and it included the memorable judgment that "Isaac Don Lyons Kravchenko has done his usual kind of job."

In fact there was nothing "usual" about *I Chose Freedom*. It was an eyewitness account of important events spanning the whole history of Bolshevik power, made by a Russian Communist of consequence, experience, and authority. There was nothing like it in the anti-Soviet literature, and with those for whom the mere mention of the names of Lyons or Levine was not a sufficient judgment of condemnation, it was likely to cause problems for the Communists. They would have to deflect Kravchenko's consequence, deny his experience, and refute his authority. The book's potential was fully appreciated both by Communists and anti-Communists. The preparations for the destruction of his character began long before he had completed the book. Evidence suggests that members of the old Comintern staff—the Comintern itself having been on paper abolished by Stalin in 1943 as a gesture to Roosevelt and Churchill—worked on a response. Much of the Davies review from *Soviet Russia Today* appeared in a circular letter sent to all members of the British Parliament, each of whom had earlier received from anonymous friends a copy of Kravchenko's book. Communism was marginal both in America and in Britain, where very little could be done to blunt the book's effect on public opinion. But the Communist strategy adopted was in a sense a rehearsal of the pattern to be followed some years later in France, the much more important arena of the book's influence.

On the whole, however, the public "critical reception" of *I Chose Freedom* in America was almost uniformly positive. Readers were hungry for real news about the Soviet Union, and this book was full of it. Its sales were excellent, and Scribner's soon made a deal to have it brought out in a mass market edition from the Garden City reprint house. The work thus followed the trajectory of *Out of the Night*. But this was no longer 1940. The shrill vituperation of the marginalized Communist and fellow-traveling press probably did it more good than harm. I have found only one negative review by a competent authority in the popular press—that of Walter Kerr (a fellow traveler) in the *New York Herald Tribune*. According to a casual aside by Kravchenko, it was not unknown for a man to drop dead of starvation in the streets of Moscow in 1942. Kerr had been there then and found the suggestion preposterous. (When the European editions of the book appeared, numerous "displaced" Slavs wrote in confirming Kravchenko on this and other disputed points.)

The Soviets expressed, mainly through their Western surrogates but also in *Pravda*, their disdainful indignation at Kravchenko's monstrous fiction. On the other hand, the NKVD got busy in an entirely factual way. One of the interesting and engaging features of Kravchenko's narrative was the revelation that even in the grinding police state of the USSR there were still people who, in the intimacy of friendship, would and did on occasion talk truthfully and express a loathing for their masters. Kravchenko made a point of trying to disguise the identities of any such people mentioned, but he did a rather poor job. Soviet experts have estimated that as many as twenty such people were identified and arrested by the secret police. Their fates are unknown, but probably also unpleasant. This may constitute an indictment of the author's carelessness, but it also suggests the truthfulness of the narrative from which detectives were able to draw their evidence.

A number of intellectuals deplored the book as an incitement to war. This was of course the Party line, but it was a possible reading. Kravchenko had stated quite clearly what a lot of people already believed: that the Soviet Union had begun preparing for war against America even while it was still fighting the Germans. The "peace offensive" carried on by the Soviets with increasing fervor in the years just before the Korean War, and taken up nearly as loudly by their European and American friends, made no mention of one factor that has been ignored also by some more recent historians of the Cold War. That is, that to maintain that coexistence was possible was a capital political heresy. On February 5, 1946, Joseph Stalin had made a very important speech. It was in fact the only speech of his election campaign, and although the result of the voting was hardly determined by it, the solemn circumstances did add maximal gravity to his utterance. It carried, from the political point of view, the weight of a declaration *ex cathedra*. He said that war was both inevitable and proximate. The strong implication was that the war would begin, soon, with an attack by the Americans on the Soviet Union.

His judgment was not subjunctive or contingent. War was not dependent upon whether the West did or did not do this or that. War was written in the Revelation to Karl Marx. The Marxist theory as developed by the Russians held that the "system" of capitalism necessarily produced alternating periods of boom and bust, with the busts of incremental severity. The reaction of capitalism to economic depression was political repression and centralized Fascism at home and abroad external aggression, imperialism, and war. The two world wars of the twentieth century were to be explained in these terms, which also infallibly predicted the third. Under these circumstances, the only policy for the Soviet Union could be to put itself on a war footing immediately.

The Communists charged that Kravchenko had, from the very outset, been a tool of the American intelligence agencies. As a matter of fact, at the time of Kravchenko's defection the American intelligence agencies were, like the American president, still torpid in their appreciation of any malignity of Soviet motive. A Soviet defector at that time was not a triumph but a potential embarrassment. The vital thing for U.S. policy was to keep the Red Army on its remorseless offensive against the Germans. A *Realpolitik* so *Real* as to cooperate with the monstrous cover-up of the Katyn massacre was hardly likely to make much fuss about a single "minor clerk," as Kravchenko was called by the Communists. To accede to his request for asylum was honorable, but the authorities made as little fuss about the matter as possible. The publicity stunt of going to the *Times* was not their idea but Kravchenko's—probably with the advice and help of

David Dallin and other of the "Mensheviks" with whom he was in contact in Washington. He thought, not entirely unreasonably, that the publicity could be a life preserver. It would be very difficult for the American authorities to hand him back to the Russians once his story was in the public domain. The later history of Soviet defection, attempted and achieved, vindicated Kravchenko's strategy. This is not to say that the episode was free of all political opportunism and manipulation. David Dallin, who was hard at work on his book on Soviet slave labor, was not alone in recognizing the potential authority of Kravchenko's witness. Eugene Lyons and his friends, who specialized in debunking Soviet and Communist claims, also applauded Kravchenko's project and wanted to see it come to fruition. But essentially Kravchenko was on his own as he set out to make a reclusive life in America and to write his book.

By the time he had finished it, a very great deal had changed. The war was over and with it such febrile "friendship" as had grown up between the United States and the Soviet Union. There are as many theories of the "beginning" of the Cold War as there are historians to find them, but one recent book plausibly locates it in the aforementioned "Gouzenko affair" in Canada, when in September 1945 another "minor clerk," though this one in intelligence communications, defected with a satchelful of documents that exposed a vast Soviet espionage conspiracy at work in several Western nations. When Gouzenko's actions, which according to his own testimony were in part inspired by newspaper accounts of Kravchenko, led to the discovery of the "atom spies," the diplomatic climate changed definitively.

Kravchenko's book appeared in the spring of 1946 in the period between George Kennan's composition of the "Long Telegram" and its expanded publication in the famous "X" article in *Foreign Affairs*. The plenary enslavement of Eastern Europe, the Berlin Air lift, Korea, the refuge given to Cardinal Mindszenty, most of what we think of when we think of the Cold War, still lay in the future.* Hence Kravchenko

---

* Joseph Cardinal Mindszenty (Jósef Pehm, 1892–1975) was the deeply conservative Primate of the Roman Catholic Church in Hungary. A determined anti-Communist, he was persecuted by the postwar Communist regime and after a show trial sentenced to life imprisonment in 1949. Briefly released at the time of the Hungarian Revolution of 1956, he took refuge in the U.S. Embassy in Budapest at the time of the Soviet invasion. He lived in the embassy for fifteen years before finally being expelled from Hungary. The protracted and widely bruited episode of Cardinal Mindszenty's asylum provided a propaganda bonanza for anti-Communists.

appeared on the American scene at a crucial time. The Cold War had its international fronts, but also its domestic one. The nearly universal shift in American public opinion concerning our "great democratic Russian ally" left what remained of the American Communist Party, like all national Communist parties of that time a wholly owned subsidiary of Joseph Stalin, permanently abandoned. It was in this climate that McCarthyism would eventually emerge, though it is too often forgotten that McCarthyism was one excess that answered another, namely, the incomprehensible naïveté of several American administrations with regard to Soviet motives and capacities. That naïveté is, indeed, one of Kravchenko's themes.

THE FRENCH CONNECTION

Kravchenko's significance for the American political scene was by no means insignificant, yet it was probably greater abroad. A famous historian has written that the most significant event in eighteenth-century English history happened in France. A similar claim might be hazarded for the history of American anti-Communism. *I Chose Freedom* was a major success in the United States, though not the runaway sensation that *Out of the Night* had been in 1941. It was in France that the book's success was truly phenomenal. Although the French book market was only a quarter the size of America's, the French translation (*J'ai choisi la liberté*) sold about in the same numbers as did the original English-language edition. In 1947, the political situation in France was delicate, and in order to understand Kravchenko's significance, it is necessary to make a brief review of the fortunes of French Communism at the end of the war, touched upon more thoroughly in treating of *Darkness at Noon*. The Party boasted considerable strength and enjoyed a wide popularity, even affection. It claimed to have lost 75,000 members to Nazi firing squads, and while that figure was of course exaggerated, the Party did have some claim to have been the "heart of the Resistance." The Communists certainly had some organized armed forces.

We know now that French Communist leaders had entertained the hope that in the collapse of the German occupation and the heat of German retreat they might transition the country into a "popular democracy."

This hope had never been very realistic. It was much easier to establish popular democracies in places liberated by the Red Army. When Stalin with surprising warmth welcomed the advent of a coalition headed by General de Gaulle, the Party leaders abandoned all immediate revolutionary ambitions. Their next hope was to "bore from within." If they could enfeeble and isolate the very strong executive, and gain acceptance of the idea of a General Assembly vested with plenary powers, there was a good chance they could, like Hitler, gain dictatorial power through popular elections. But it very soon became clear that an all-powerful legislature was not to be. The situation was somewhat paradoxical. The Communists were growing in numbers and in parliamentary clout even as the prospect of the full power they sought became ever more elusive.

A crisis arose in May 1947 over a strike at the nationalized Renault works. The Socialist Paul Ramadier had become premier at the beginning of the year, with several Communists in his cabinet, including the party leader, Maurice Thorez, as vice president. The government, with the Communists concurring, had adopted stringent wage guidelines, which the strikers' demands would violate. After a certain amount of graceless vacillation, the Communists decided to back the strikers, *but not to leave the government*. Ramadier forced and won a vote of confidence, and then fired the Communist ministers, who even then were still refusing to resign. His decisiveness was much admired by the American press. And when he soon thereafter took France into the Marshall Plan, an action abhorrent to Moscow, the essential isolation of the French Communist Party was complete. This was a crisis but also a useful clarification, as it obviated the need to pay obeisance to the legal fiction that the French Communists were part of a harmonious coalition of "progressives" in the spirit of the Popular Front.

Like Krebs before him, indeed like many recovering Marxists landed on American soil, Victor Kravchenko took to the unplanned economy with gusto. He was first amazed, then delighted by the apparently boundless opportunities for individual initiative leading to possible remuneration. His contract with Scribner's actually gave the publisher the option of negotiating foreign rights to the material. But this was a fine point that Kravchenko had overlooked, and the Scribner files preserve many patient attempts made by various members of the firm to explain the situation to the author. Kravchenko insisted, however, in cutting his own deals. It is a testimony to a probably vanished commercial gentlemanliness that Charles Scribner eventually simply conceded the point on the grounds that the author had misunderstood the contract.

Even in France there were still more than a few "literary" people who were not Communists or fellow travelers. One such was a young, entrepreneurial journalist of aristocratic name and mien, Jean de Kerdéland. Such modest fame as he commands in this country today is due to his *History of the Wines of France*. Jean de Kerdéland was very well educated, and fluent in the English language, from which he sometimes made professional translations for the press. In November 1946 he chanced to meet a businessman recently returned from the United States, whose conversation turned to the enormous financial success of *I Chose Freedom*, of which he happened to have a copy to give to Jean de Kerdéland. He told him the book had sold 2 million copies—misinformation rectifiable by the adjustment of a decimal point here or there.

M. de Kerdéland was greatly impressed by Kravchenko's memoir, in which he saw a political tendency consonant with his own views as well as a potential best-seller in French translation. He tried to reach Kravchenko, but Kravchenko was in those days not easily found. He received mail through Scribner's, where he frequently dropped in, but he by no means answered all of it. He lived a discreet if not secretive life. He often traveled incognito, under the code name of "Peter Martin." When Jean de Kerdéland failed to receive replies to his letters, he determined to go to America and find him. Once in America, he presented himself at Scribner's, but also under a prudential and polynational pseudonym—Alex Martin! Through Scribner's, Kravchenko agreed to a cloak-and-dagger meeting at a New Jersey bar, and there the two false Martins met, got on famously, and clinched a deal.

De Kerdéland made the mistake of advertising the forthcoming translation, which he had himself undertaken, so that his long months of arduous work were seasoned by various petty harassments and even death threats from the French Comrades. He and Kravchenko's French literary agent placed the book with Editions Self, a small house that had recently published de Kerdéland's *De Nostradamus à Cagliostro*. None of the parties involved had reason to repent of the arrangement. All told, the edition approached half a million copies.

ORIGINS OF AN *AFFAIRE*

L'affaire Kravchenko was four years in the making. Kravchenko had defected in the spring of 1944. Scribner's had published *I Chose Freedom* in the spring of 1946. The French translation *J'ai choisi la liberté*, Self-published, appeared in the spring of 1947. A year of attacks in the left-wing press led Kravchenko to file his lawsuit against *Les Lettres françaises* in the spring of 1948. He had first been attacked in the liberal daily *Le Monde*, whose reviewer expressed his disdain for "the race of apostates and renegades." This was not unlike the treatment he had received from an American fellow traveler in the *New York Herald Tribune*. Much more ferocious was the attack from the Communist press. On November 13, 1947, *Les Lettres françaises* launched the attack that would become the "Kravchenko affair."

Kravchenko had an abundance of French enemies, and he chose his battleground with care. If the French Communists were the "men of the *Résistance*," *Les Lettres françaises* was the "journal of the *Résistants*." It had been founded during the time of the German occupation by Jacques Decour and Jean Paulhan. It was then an underground publication, which became legal only with the liberation of 1944. Paulhan, who died in 1968, was one of the "saints" of the non-Communist French left. Decour was a Communist executed by the Nazis in the spring of 1942. Their originating collaborators included François Mauriac and Louis Aragon, among the most famous of Catholic and Communist writers respectively. No more superior credentials could be imagined in French intellectual life.

Before the end of the war Claude Morgan had entered the picture. He was among the more prominent Communists in French publishing, and he directed the journal in the immediate postwar period. He was destined to play a major role as one of the defendants in the lawsuit Kravchenko would eventually initiate. Though *Les Lettres françaises* never became an official organ of the French Communist Party, its more ecumenical origins had been forgotten by 1945, and it was generally and plausibly regarded as the voice of "literary" Communism in France.

At this point, if not before, American officials became quite interested in Kravchenko's propaganda value. It is not true that the State Department or American intelligence dreamed up the plan to sue *Les Lettres françaises* in a French court. That was Kravchenko's own initiative—undertaken, incidentally, at considerable personal financial expense—to his everlasting credit. What is true is that American officials aided and abetted, discreetly but effectively. They collaborated with anti-Communist elements in the French government. They facilitated Kravchenko's travel. They expedited his communications while in France through embassy mail. On the other hand, they were very concerned that no "American fingerprints" be detectable in the trial. For this reason, they refused Kravchenko's request for an official governmental statement detailing the circumstances of his defection. This would have been very useful to him. At the time of his defection his courage had been matched only by the scrupulosity of his Russian patriotism, and now he was being accused of cowardice and treason. But American officials remained, officially, aloof.

In taking elaborate care to leave no fingerprints, they left a number of large, muddy boot tracks instead. The first crisis came over getting Kravchenko to Paris, where the Communists were already arranging various spontaneous demonstrations of public outrage. French officials were edgy and suggested that it would be best for him to travel incognito. The Americans cooperated in constructing a false identity, and "Paul Kedrin," duly credentialed, was put onto an Air France flight to Paris. But if you are going to do false identities, you need to be really good at it, as the Comintern experts in Copenhagen had been in Krebs's day. In a country where more than a quarter of all votes go to the Communists, it is not surprising that there were some Communists in and around Air France. The Communists knew all about "Paul Kedrin" before he even got on the plane. They also knew that there necessarily had been collusion between the American and French authorities. Now they were able to say, as they did repeatedly at the lawsuit trial, that Kravchenko was himself a CIA agent.

The French police could and did protect Kravchenko's person, but they could not shield him from an atmosphere of poisonous hostility. The French left-wing press, and not only the Communists, kept up a barrage of vitriolic invective. They could no longer say he didn't exist—that had been the first claim, as we remember it also was the first claim against Jan

Valtin—but they could and did label him a coward, a traitor, a Gestapo agent, and a pathetic tool of American imperialism. The lawyer Izard and others had already decided how the trial would be presented: "Kravchenko *versus* Moscow!" The Communists tried to circumvent this with a mass rally, advertised on huge posters all over the city, devoted to the theme of "Kravchenko *versus* France!"

Of course Kravchenko had powerful and able French allies as well. As violent as pugilism can be, it at least obviates some of the uncertainties of shadowboxing. The "clarification" of the position of the French Communist Party, taken together with the situation in the peoples' republics of Eastern Europe, threw into sharp relief the barriers between the Communists and the parties whose primary loyalties were to France, and legitimated their greater or lesser explicit anti-Communism. This period saw the definitive check of Communist political ambitions in France. The Communists were banished from government, not to return until the time of Mitterrand—and then under debilitating constraints. Though it was not yet clear to the observers of the day, the same period saw the definitive check of Soviet ambitions in Western Europe altogether. On the very day that the Kravchenko verdict was pronounced—April 4, 1949—a French delegation was in Washington for the formal signing of the security treaty that put the "T" in NATO.

French anti-Communists correctly diagnosed the golden opportunity offered by the trial of *Les Lettres françaises*. They further anticipated, as the Americans probably did not, the ferocity of the attack that would be leveled against Kravchenko. They prepared for it in several ways but, as we shall see, their most effective move was to secure on Kravchenko's behalf the services of a legal genius and a moral giant, Georges Izard.

THE *PROCÈS KRAVCHENKO*

The *procès Kravchenko* was of that recurrent genre of legal spectacle, of which there are seldom fewer than two per decade, called "the Trial of the Century." The international press reported it widely. At its conclusion, and even before judgment had been determined ten days later, there appeared in Paris a volume, of 700 pages, publishing the stenographic record. Indeed, this had been planned and commissioned by Kravchenko's own lawyer, Georges Izard. A few months later, in somewhat shortened form, it appeared in an English translation under Izard's spiritually accurate title of *Kravchenko versus Moscow*. There have been at least two French books written about the trial. Gary Kern reports on it in detail. The nature of the testimony is not in doubt; but even at the time observers were aware that what they were watching was ten parts political theater to one part civil action, and its analysis today demands the skills of a drama critic no less than those of a legal expert.

There is by now more testimony on record *about* the trial than there was in the trial itself. Most of the principals involved later wrote about it, some of them at length. Kravchenko himself wrote a whole book about it (*I Chose Justice*, an obvious title for a sequel). André Wurmser and Claude Morgan, the defendants, both eventually wrote about it, with varying degrees of ex-Communist penitence. Their ferocious lead lawyer, Joë Nordmann, wrote about it with hardly any penitence at all. Izard's biographer wrote about it. The various perspectives revealed in these memoirs are only slightly more convergent than those of *Rashomon*, but as we have good transcriptions of the testimony it is possible to proceed with some confidence.

The trial was closely followed in many capitals through the international press. Back in New York the people at Scribner's, who of course were nearly as aggrieved as was Kravchenko himself at the accusation of fraud, watched with some apprehension. They had come to have a certain affection for the man, though they were also keenly aware of those aspects of his personality that might spell disaster in the courtroom.

There is one, if only one, contemporaneous account that does justice to the drama. Among the journalists present in the Salle de Justice was Nina Berberova, already a *grande dame* of the literary world of the Russian emigration and, later, my colleague on the Princeton faculty. She was covering the trial for a recently established émigré journal, *Russian Thought*. Why such a journal had only recently been established in Paris, the capital of the White Russian diaspora since the early twenties, where according to perdurable legend half the taxi drivers were Tsarist noblemen, is itself of relevance to our theme. So great was the intellectually coercive power of French Communism in the immediate postwar period that no such publication could obtain the necessary bureaucratic license to publish so long as Communist ministers served in the coalition government. The foundation of a journal devoted to Russian thoughts other than those authorized by the Soviet Embassy became possible in 1947, however, when the Communists were in effect expelled from the government.

Russian Thought gathered Berberova's articles and published them in a little book on newsprint. (The scarcity of stocks of decent paper is one of the recurring leitmotifs of the intellectual history of the period.) The author's passing remark in her autobiography that the last copies must have long ago crumbled into dust encouraged admirers to seek out an uncrumbled exemplar or two, and the book has now been republished in several European languages. One of Berberova's great advantages was her polyglot command of the many tongues in which the trial was conducted. The official language was of course French, a language of which Kravchenko had very poor command, though he could shout loudly and somewhat unintelligibly in it. Most of his witnesses testified in Russian, and a few in Ukrainian. Kravchenko himself made often vehement interventions in Russian, and sometimes in Ukrainian, with occasional asides in English. Margarete Buber-Neumann offered her extraordinary testimony in German. Most of the spectators were in the situation of first-time viewers of an unfamiliar opera. The general drift of the plot was clear from the program notes, but the immediate verbal drama was often obscure pending the official translation. Among the commentators at our disposal, Berberova was unique in her capacity to grasp the immediate drama of every moment.

The principal *dramatis personae*, apart from the plaintiff Kravchenko, were the two defendants and the two principal lawyers for the plaintiff and the defendants. There were technically three personal defendants: André Wurmser, the editor of *Les Lettres françaises*; Claude Morgan, one of its frequent contributors; and Sim Thomas, the author of the alleged libel, "How Kravchenko Was Fabricated." His lack of appearance somewhat simplified matters in terms of hearing his testimony. Wurmser and Morgan were two hard-core, hard-line Communists, who regularly referred to themselves as "we, the men of the Resistance." One of the two founding editors of *Les Lettres françaises*, Jacques Decour, who had been shot by the Nazis, accompanied them as a spectral presence, frequently invoked.

Maître Nordmann

Far more important than the defendants, from the point of view of the trial's fortunes, was their principal lawyer, Joë Nordmann, a man of great ability and energy. Joë Nordmann was a bourgeois Alsatian Jew, born in Mulhouse in 1910, when it was German territory, and raised there during the 1920s, when it was French. History, geography, and personal inclination alike attuned him to the Germany of his youth, the Germany of the inevitable Communist revolution. In 1930, his parents presented him with a graduation present of a trip to London. He persuaded them to allow him to go to Moscow instead. He was in Red Square for the May Day celebrations of 1930, and what he saw changed his life forever. Like so many others he was appalled when the bright left-wing hopes for Germany were crushed in the rise of Fascism. He joined the French Communist Party in the year of Hitler's ascent to power, 1933, and spiritually he never left. While still in his twenties Nordmann had gained a reputation as an able, forceful, and "engaged" lawyer, particularly in Communist causes. He had the opportunity to experience firsthand the anti-Semitism so widespread in the French legal profession of that day. He agonized over Spain and nearly joined one of the International Brigades. A friend convinced him that his talents would best be employed doing legal work for the Republican cause.

To one who has read so many apologetic confessions of French ex-Communist intellectuals, Nordmann's constancy in the Communist cause will seem refreshing and perhaps even admirable. Claude Morgan would live to say that, had he only known then what he knew *then*, he would apologize to Victor Kravchenko on bended knee. Pierre Daix actually did so, metaphorically speaking. He had calumniated Kravchenko outrageously, but lived to repent and to write a preface for a new French edition of Kravchenko's book. André Wurmser, looking back at his acceptance of the Communist mythology then in vogue, called himself a *pauvre cuillon*. This is a phrase best left untranslated, but it is rather stronger than "blithering idiot." Nordmann goes no farther than to say he suffered from "blindness" with regard to the Soviet Union. About everything else he was right, for he was "on the side of peace."

Willi Münzenberg introduced into popular usage the term "innocent" (as a noun) to denote someone who from noble motive promoted some aspect of the Communist agenda without ever realizing its true purpose or implications. There were literally thousands of such people in the front organizations of the West. In fact, Münzenberg often called the fronts "innocents' clubs." Another term, this one of disputed origin, was less complimentary: "useful idiot." This is a little strong in English, where "idiot" suggests actual mental defect or pathology. In the European languages, the word is still closer to its Latin origin in *idiota*—a radically ignorant or unlearned person, someone who is "out of it" in terms of what was actually happening in the arrangement of worldly affairs. In such a sense did Saint Francis call himself *idiota*. That sense, too, is what Dostoyevsky had in mind with Prince Myshkin. Useful idiocy often had little connection with intellectual capacity or achievement. Frédéric Joliot-Curie, a Nobel laureate in Physics, was among the most useful idiots in French Communism in the 1940s and 1950s. It becomes clear from reading Nordmann's autobiography, published half a century after the Kravchenko affair had run its course, that he was of their number: an idiot of elevated intelligence, to be sure, and of impressive professional skill, an idiot animated by the most sincere and high-minded principle, but still an idiot. He expressed aggrieved surprise that anyone could accuse him of Stalinism.

"*Moi, stalinien?*"—that's an actual sentence from his book. He was not a Stalinist, he tells us. He was a Socialist. Stalin was the charismatic leader of the world's leading Socialist country. He admits to a "mental obturation, the reflection of a spiritual state which marked the postwar period." Like so many others, he was guilty not of lying but of blindness.

All the defendants, indeed all the Communists in France, presented themselves as heroes of the Resistance. They called themselves the party of the 75,000 *fusillés*—people executed by Nazi firing squads. There was some truth in the sentiment, though not much in the arithmetic. But Nordmann really was a hero of the Resistance. The great prestige he brought to the Kravchenko affair had been constructed during the German occupation and the Vichy regime. Nordmann rationalized the Hitler-Stalin Pact, according to the now familiar argument that sees Stalin as a victim of Anglo-French pusillanimity at Munich. He tried, as did many others, to escape to French North Africa to join the military struggle, but he was stopped in Spain, interned briefly, and sent back. Having returned to France, he was the principal organizer of the National Front of Lawyers, a kind of legal fifth column operating both in the territories of the Vichy regime and in occupied France itself, with the goal of defeating or moderating, at least to the degree possible, the intended effects of Fascist policy. Comparatively young as he still was, he brought to the Kravchenko trial a prestige unrivaled among the very large number of left-wing lawyers in France.

Nordmann says that he defended his clients in full good faith, vigorously, possibly with excess, but with sincerity. In fact, his conduct was deeply dishonest in ways he apparently could not admit even in old age. Why "dishonest"? The most splenetic attack on Kravchenko that had appeared in *Les Lettres françaises* had been signed by "Sim Thomas." At no point in the trial was there a discussion of Mr. Thomas's strange first name, which was presumably a Gallic mistake for one of two possible American-sounding names, "Sid" or "Sam." The lack of discussion probably reflects the fact that every person in the courtroom knew that "Sim Thomas" had not written the article. But Nordmann knew rather more than most. In every Western country in which the Communist Party operated legally, there were among the journalists one or two who might be described as literary hit men. Character assassination was by no means their only line of work, but they were very good at it when needed. We have already encountered three such Americans: Sender Garlin of *The Daily Worker*; Isidor Schneider of the *New Masses*; and the freelance Wellington Roe. The author of "How *I Chose Freedom* Was Fabricated" was a French journalist, otherwise somewhat obscure, named André Ullmann. Nordmann, along with his clients André Wurmser and Claude Morgan, knew this.

The issue here is not of course anonymity or pseudonymity *per se*. George Kennan published his famous essay "The Sources of Soviet Conflict" (1947) in *Foreign Affairs* under the signature of "X." Quite apart from the fact that everyone in the know knew that "X" was George Kennan, the essay obviously stood or fell on its own merits and not on the prestige or authority of "X." It was quite different with "Sim Thomas." He claims to have been intimate with the American intelligence officers who had concocted this book to which Kravchenko brought nothing but his name. It was on the basis of his privileged knowledge than he asserts that Kravchenko is a mentally unstable alcoholic and a moral degenerate. This is not an argument presented pseudonymously. It is a literary fraud and a bald-faced lie. It is doubtless the duty of a defense lawyer to defend his clients. It is not his duty to embrace their falsehoods, or to continue in the courtroom the character assassination of their false writings.

Nordmann had been involved in an earlier episode in the battle of the books, this one concerning *Out of the Night*, which appeared in a French edition only after the war, in 1947. Its appearance was guaranteed by some prepublication publicity of a sensational nature. Immediately after the war, in 1945, two French newspapers had published some excerpts—the same excerpts apparently that had been selected for the *Reader's Digest* in 1941— of local French interest.

Richard Krebs was released from San Quentin at the beginning of December 1929 under an order of deportation. He sailed from Galveston three days later, disembarking at the first port of call, Le Havre, horny, hungry, and lonely. "Beyond a breakfast and a chance to dry my clothes there were three things I wanted most. I wanted to hear the word 'Comrade.' I wanted a woman. I wanted to feast my eyes and brain on something that was impersonal and beautiful at once." (p. 181) Within a short time all his needs had been met at 58, rue Montmirail, the home of the head of the Comintern *apparat* in Le Havre, "a French schoolteacher named Cance." Cance's second in command was his voluptuous wife, a former dancer. Krebs became their houseguest while his *bona fides* was being checked out by wire with Communist headquarters in Berlin. One evening Cance hosted a bibulous party, at which the shapely Mme Cance danced in "a flowing garment of raw silk, held together by a golden chain around her waist," while her husband fiddled. They later acted out a pantomime entitled *The Death March of the Paris Commune*. A little later the Cances telephoned a friend, Comrade Suzanne, and summoned her to hurry over to assuage Comrade Krebs's urgent needs. "Is she a prostitute?" asked Krebs. "*Mais non*," replied M. Cance, aggrieved, "*elle est une activiste!*" As for Comrade Cance, "he was still at his secret post as late as 1937, at the time of the abduction of the White Russian leader, General de Miller, all traces of whom were lost at Le Havre, where a Soviet steamer left on the morning after the abduction."

Such soft-core pornography was still pretty racy stuff in 1941, and it enraged puritanical Communists like Isidor Schneider, author of the review "Out of the Sewer" in the *New Masses*. Perhaps this also accounts for its inclusion in the *Reader's Digest* selection. Precisely on which side of the murky line between truth and fiction in Valtin's book this story falls, I cannot say. There is in the Valtin archive a document, compiled by Krebs, purporting to be a list of rules for Comintern "illegals." One of the rules is that agents should have sexual relations only with prostitutes or female comrades.

The trouble was that in 1947 Le Havre's representative in the National Assembly was a Communist Party deputy by the name of Eugène Cance, whose residence happened to be at 58, rue Montmirail. This man was a red, white, and blue patriot and yet another hero of the Resistance. He would twice be elected mayor of Le Havre, and although ten years older than Krebs, would outlive him by more than thirty. M. Cance died only in 1982. Cance's house, according to *Out of the Night*, commanded a view of "the wide sweep of the harbor with its cleverly camouflaged shore batteries and fortifications." Joë Nordmann, retained as a lawyer in Cance's suit against the French publisher, pointed out with scorn that there are *no* fortifications at Le Havre. Hence the whole book was a pack of lies, and slanderous lies to boot.

Nordmann had apparently not inquired as to how Jan Valtin might come to know Cance's name, his profession, his musical instrument of choice, or his address. The story of the Le Havre idyll is one of several naive slips in *Out of the Night* which his publisher's lawyers could not be expected to catch. Krebs's experience had not prepared him for the fact that a few of his Comintern acquaintances from the 1930s might still be around alive, unpurged and politically impenitent. In fact, there were several who had come in out of the cold to the warmth of political respectability. In 1947 Ernst Wollweber, having not yet achieved "unperson" status, was a thriving senior henchman of Erich Honecker in East Germany. We have already seen the reappearances of Richard Jensen as a labor leader in Denmark, and of Morris Appleman (alias Mike Pell) as a contributor to the letters page of *Look* magazine. And there was Eugène Cance, representative of the good people of Le Havre.

Nordmann won this suit easily, but the terms of victory were strangely modest. The plaintiff asked only for a cessation of all publicity about the matter. The French publishing house of Werfel waited a discreet period while they again went over the book with their now vigilant lawyers at their sides, then published it with all references to M. Cance removed and no reference to him or to his late legal unpleasantness mentioned in their publicity. Nordmann took from this experience the conviction of "a vast anti-Communist conspiracy which would come to know, in McCarthyism, a major increment." That conviction of an American conspiracy he brought to the Kravchenko trial.

Maître Izard

Kravchenko's principal lawyer, and therefore Nordmann's principal adversary, was *Maître* Georges Izard. Izard was born in 1903 at Abeilhan in the South of France, where his father was a teacher and administrator in the school system. When he was still very young, his family moved to Béziers. Throughout his life he spoke with the residue of a southern accent that could amuse the Parisian sophisticates among whom he spent so much of his professional and social life.

In 1921 he went up to the capital to college, where among his classmates were numerous eminences, including Jean-Paul Sartre, the future cardinal philosopher, and Jean Daniélou, a future philosophical cardinal. One learns with a shock that there were other circles besides that of Ernest Hemingway and Gertrude Stein. Izard had been raised a "cultural" Catholic. He now reencountered his own religion as a dynamic intellectual—and social—force. He actually studied with Etienne Gilson, then just beginning his career at the Sorbonne. He joined a Catholic youth group made up primarily of socialist activists. His intimate friends included Jean Daniélou and Emmanuel Mounier, near geniuses the both. The friendship with Daniélou changed his life in more ways than one, for he married Jean Daniélou's sister, Catherine. By worldly standards this would have been a "good" marriage for the son of a provincial school official. The Daniélous were people in "society." Mounier, who became the editor of *Esprit*, was a lay ascetic committed to his version of Franciscan poverty. He was that kind of anti-Communist for whom the second greatest of all sins is anti-Communism. Jean Daniélou was a professional celibate. Izard was neither; he was an engaged Catholic layman immersed in a world he was not entirely of. The group's single greatest source of inspiration was undoubtedly Charles Péguy—proletarian, mystic, socialist, nationalist, bookseller, journalist, dynamo of literary energy and production, a Christian so radical in his Catholicism as to decline to practice it, killed at the Marne in 1914.

To Péguy, Izard devoted his first book (*La Pensée de Charles Péguy*) in 1931—a collaborative work shared with Emmanuel Mounier and Marcel Péguy, Charles's son—even as he was starting his career not in the academy or in letters but in the law, and beginning to raise a young family. One of Péguy's conversions—he had several, or perhaps an unfinished conversion in several stages—had been occasioned by the Dreyfus affair, in which he confronted head-on a reactionary and anti-Semitic strain in French Catholicism that would survive in its virulent form in Vichy. Like other Dreyfusards, Péguy regarded the injustice committed against Alfred Dreyfus as a stain on the French national honor, but he went further, and put the matter in explicitly theological terms. France groaned beneath the oppression of a kind of social primal lapse. So long as the injustice remained uncorrected, the nation of France would be "in a state of moral sin."

It was at the period of his university days that Georges Izard became committed to the two cognate causes that would guide his life: liberty and justice. These are grand words, and there are few indeed who would not claim to pursue the ideas standing behind them. For Izard, both concepts while *laïc*—that is, grounded in the civil constitution of the state—were derived from basic Christian doctrine. Meaningful moral action depended upon the radical freedom of the human will. Liberty was necessarily the condition that enabled the maximal individual exercise of that freedom. The field of play was therefore the arena of the individual—the "grammatical fiction" of the Communists in *Darkness at Noon*. Izard's concept of justice was illuminated by the *sol justitiae*, the "sun of righteousness," the Christ of the Incarnation. Justice could be founded only in truth.

In 1930, while the young Nordmann was thrilling to the future revealed in the marching phalanxes on Red Square, Izard, too, was making his own commitment. That was the year that he and several of his friends founded *Esprit*. *Esprit* is often described as a "journal of radical Catholic thought." That is not untrue, yet it is so far from being the whole truth as to be misleading. The history of interwar Europe is sometimes presented as a stark contest between revolution and reaction, with the Spanish Civil War its purest expression. This is consistent with the taste for dynamically interacting polarities that is central to Marxism and many other modes of modern thought. There are other ways of viewing the matter. In an essay of permanent value ("Tradition and the Individual Talent"), T. S. Eliot argued that the very essence of artistic tradition required the continual modification of individual innovation and interpretation. With regard to literature, the specific subject of Eliot's essay, the idea was at least as old as Horace's *Ars poetica*. Pope expressed it in a famous couplet:

> *True wit is nature to advantage dress'd,*
> *What oft was thought, but ne'er so well express'd.*

The founders of and contributors to *Esprit* were deeply traditional in their commitment to a Christian humanism, though many of their more conventional fellow Catholics could hardly know it, so innovative and so demanding was their expression of it.

Izard called himself a born "political animal," and his politics were always "left." He refused, he said, to cede Catholicism to "reaction." The 1930s were, of course, the heyday of the Popular Front and his earliest political successes were as a "frontist." He later became a member of the Socialist Party. He was one of the signers of the manifesto, which appeared in *Esprit* in November 1947 immediately following the implementation of the Marshall Plan, that maintained that only a Socialist Europe, united and independent of either of the competing superpowers, could avoid the apocalyptic war that was otherwise inevitable. Its publication was virtually simultaneous with the appearance of "How *I Chose Freedom* Was Fabricated" in *Les Lettres françaises*—and the vast dissemination (about 100,000 copies) of the essay by the Communists in pamphlet form. Kravchenko's book itself had appeared in an initial printing of 30,000 in May.

Such leftist credentials were insufficient to shield Izard from vicious personal assault in the Communist press during the trial. His status as a comfortable bourgeois did not go unmentioned, but it was subordinated to his professional turpitudes. He had done work for various American corporations—"notably Coca-Cola," said Nordmann. At that primitive stage in the history of globalization, McDonald's had yet to establish its first franchise, so that working for Coca-Cola was probably the greatest of known thought crimes.

Saint Augustine had written that most of the Platonists of his day had been able to accept Christianity at the small cost of making some minor changes in their vocabulary. The French Catholic left of the 1930s seems once to have entertained a hope for a similar kind of undefined spiritual absorption of the Communists. Yet there were real differences between them, which no verbal legerdemain or even the most malleable lexicon could resolve. Thus it was that in the courtroom of the Salle de Justice more than a single allegory was being acted out. The Soviet Union was indeed the unindicted defendant in the shadows. At the time of its founding, the young editors of *Esprit* had joked that the Communists might choose to counter it with a journal called *Matière*. Now the two lawyers faced each other across the vast chasm betwixt dialectical materialism and Christian humanism, between the *zéro* and the *infini*. Izard clearly saw the struggle in the same terms as Whittaker Chambers: was God to rule, or man alone?

ODD BULL, ODDER CHINA SHOP

Kravchenko's deportment at the trial has been criticized, and perhaps not unjustly. Yet it must be remembered that his life experience had done little to tutor him in the majesty of the Law. Soviet justice was characterized by a sodden core of essential criminality surrounded by a bright penumbra of punctilious and inessential legalities. Thus the police could and did regularly extort a false confession from a man by torture, but it was absolutely necessary to have the signature on the confession in the proper form. Police agents could search your dwelling place with a vigor that left it looking like the aftermath of a tornado, but they were required to effect their depredations in the presence of two witnesses randomly dragooned from the neighborhood. Kravchenko had been beaten up by officers of the law, but he had never seen or even heard of a trial in which the outcome was honestly in doubt, to be decided, for good or ill, on the basis of sincerely evaluated evidence. Such horrors of the *ancien régime* as the trial in *The Brothers Karamazov* had been swept away by "revolutionary justice."

Proceedings were scheduled to begin at half past one on January 24, 1949; and even before they began, the Communists suffered their first setback. The capacity audience was very large, and while it did contain a sizable Red claque, they were outnumbered by Kravchenko's sometimes obstreperous supporters. He was one of the last to arrive in the courtroom, and as he entered, spontaneous applause broke out in the public seating. Kravchenko smiled broadly, like a champion, and caught the crowd's energy. Over the months of the unexpectedly long trial his popularity appeared to grow. He often held court to his admirers during the breaks, signing copies of his book thrust at him by autograph seekers. He would converse with them in bad and voluble English, and sometimes in his embryonic French. (The trial lasted so long that he made considerable progress in this language by the time it ended.)

To understand the importance of the action brought by Kravchenko it is necessary to encounter the invincible ignorance on the part of a large section of the Western intelligentsia with regard to the state of civil liberties in Stalin's Russia. The theory of Soviet Marxism demanded the most draconian abolition of the most fundamental of human rights: economic freedom. It insisted that all individual aspirations of entrepreneurship and all local concerns for self-betterment or family prosperity were simply "bourgeois" markers socially constructed by the junked capitalist system. It was perfectly correct to destroy people with bourgeois attitudes and to create people with proletarian attitudes. The phrases "class war" and "building socialism" were not mere metaphors. Both the destruction and the construction were vehement and coercive.

Under these circumstances Western leftists, had they had the inclination to criticize the Soviet Union, could have had plenty of grounds for doing so. But in general all the minor tyrannies of which they disapproved—suppression of the freedoms of speech, of the press, of assembly, of religious practice, and so on—could be forgiven or at least tolerated on account of the huge economic tyranny of which they approved. Thus Harold Laski, for instance, was well aware of the absence of most civil rights, the want of habeas corpus, the system of administrative justice, and other essential features of the Soviet system. He wrote about them, but he was able to regard them as venial and transient flaws that did nothing to vitiate the desirability of the "workers' state."

The concentration camps were of a different order. This was not because of any dissonance between the idea of penal coercion and historical Bolshevik practice, but because of the unique role of the concentration camp in the moral iconography of Nazism. The concentration camp was the institution of Nazi iniquity *par excellence*. During the period of Hitler's consolidation of power in the mid-thirties, many of the political prisoners in the camps were German Communists. Hence they were central to the Party's international martyrology. As the instruments of the Holocaust, the extermination camps in Poland were the stage sets of crimes so heinous as to challenge the credulity of history. They had been a principal focus of the Nuremberg Trials, among the final projects of the alliance among the Soviets and the Western democracies. Concentration camps were a Nazi thing. They were *the* Nazi thing.

It was both inevitable and surprising that forced labor would be the issue on which Western public opinion toward the Soviet Union finally took its definitive negative turn. It was inevitable, first, because of the sheer grandeur of the hypocrisy. Though history shows our capacity to accommodate even the most obvious ironies, the realization that the workers' paradise was a nation of slaves and that the foundation of Russia's much vaunted "rapid industrialization" was not noble self-sacrifice but a brutal and criminal coercion, once it became general, had a dramatic effect. The surprising factor was the timing. The general situation had been known in America in the 1920s, when there had been a brief threat of sanctions against "slave" imports. There had been unimpeachable eyewitness accounts of the brutalities in the camps at least from the 1930s. On the day the Roosevelt administration formally recognized the Soviet regime in 1933, more than a year before the assassination of Kirov unleashed the serious Terror, there were already thousands in the camps.

Next, there was among leftists the nearly universal belief—one of the crueler triumphs of faith over science—that the Nazi and the Soviet regimes were polar opposites. The unifying idea of the Popular Front and of the International Brigades of the Spanish Civil War was that of "anti-Fascism." In this regard, the Soviet Union was seen as the vanguard of the international anti-Fascist forces. It was this delusion, whose ideological progeny are still active today, that made the Hitler-Stalin Pact of 1939 such a bitter pill for so many. In 1940, in his *Soviet Russia and the Crisis of Socialism*, Max Eastman included a chapter entitled "Stalin Beats Hitler Forty Ways." The number was not metaphorical; he actually made a list of forty ways in which the Soviets outdid their Nazi competitors in "Fascist" iniquity.

No one refuted Eastman's forty theses—they just ignored them. The first mystery about the "secret" of the camps is why there could have been a mystery in the first place. The origins of the Gulag antedate even the Bolshevik *coup d'état* of 1917. They are implicit in the Marxist doctrine of class war, and explicit in the earliest writings of Lenin. Beginning no later than the end of the civil war, well before Stalin's advent to power, the first of the eyewitness accounts reached the West. These continued in increasing volume and detail throughout the early thirties. The later thirties—the classic Age of Purgation—see a veritable river of testimonies that in the wake of the liberation of the Poles in 1942 became a veritable Niagara. All of this, however, was treated by French intellectuals with the dismissive nonchalance that might greet the occasional rumblings and minor eructations of a volcanic mountain beneath which lay a city of ancient foundation. A few earth scientists noted the phenomena. A few within that few issued futile protests or unattended warnings. Only in 1973, with the first published volume of Solzhenitsyn's *Gulag Archipelago*, did French intellectuals as a whole notice that the mountain was on fire. That was more than two full decades after the end of the Kravchenko action.

A French Civil Action

The conduct of a French civil action is very different from the conduct of a similar action in Britain or America. It is at once more pompous and more informal. Even so, this *procès* must have approached the limit of even Gallic permissiveness. The judge has such broad powers as an umpire that much depends upon his temperament. There is a difference between impartiality and indifference. Judge Durkheim was so careful to be scrupulously fair that he seemed at times to be indifferent to the nearly chaotic eruptions, interruptions, and shouting matches that were daily fare. So, from a journalistic point of view, what was already a very hot property because of its matter became all the more newsworthy through its manner of proceeding.

The action began with Judge Durkheim reading off the roll of participants and scheduled witnesses, though even as he did so Kravchenko seemed to be bursting to leap up and read a prepared statement. He several times needed to be shushed. Durkheim began reading various incriminated passages from the poison pen of Sim Thomas. Kravchenko was a drunk, a coward, a braggart, a lecher, an embezzler, and a liar. Those were his venial sins. What made matters serious was that he was a deserter and a warmonger. He had been putty in the hands of the FBI, who had so much on him that he was forced to follow their instructions and write an anti-Soviet book. At this task he failed, as he had at all his professional duties in Russia. Under these circumstances, American agents had to write the book themselves. All this was translated in bits and pieces. Kravchenko made no effort to disguise an incremental displeasure. Next, Durkheim read out a contemptuous essay by Claude Morgan, whose argument was simplicity itself. Only the foulest villain could work in the service of the despotism described in the book. Hence: "There are no two ways about it. Either Kravchenko is a liar or he is contemptible."

Through all this Kravchenko's body language was apparently that of a bucking bronco temporarily held in the restraining chute of a rodeo arena. When offered the opportunity, he leaped to his feet and began a carefully prepared and impassioned statement. A metaphorical tremor of apprehension rattled the front bench of the defense. The first victims of propaganda are sometimes the propagandists themselves. Nordmann and his colleagues seem honestly to have been expecting a shifty blackguard or a stumblebum. Instead, Kravchenko was large and commanding, approaching nattiness in a tasteful suit, vigorous, coherent, voluble, and self-confident to the point of insult. So far as anyone could tell from the reaction of the Russian speakers in the public seats, he was also spellbinding. He immediately faced, head-on, the most serious charge against him—that he had deserted his country in time of war—and counterattacked. How did his behavior differ from that of Maurice Thorez, leader of the French Communist Party, and until quite lately the vice president of France? To avoid conscription Thorez had in time of war fled to Germany, then allied with the Soviet Union, and thence to Moscow. He had been tried and convicted *in absentia. Maître* Nordmann rose in indignation. It was entirely impermissible that a foreigner should come into a French courtroom to cast aspersions upon a distinguished French statesman. A skirmish of "moral equivalences" then began.

"Kravchenko's another Doriot, the enemy of his country. . . . Every anti-communist is an anti-français." Jacques Doriot, the Judas Iscariot of French Communism, had upon his expulsion from a high position in the Party become an open Fascist. Wurmser's strategy was to wrap himself and his journal in the tricolor. According to the familiar script, the soul of French patriotism was the Resistance, and the soul of the Resistance was the French Communist Party. But in the France of the immediate postwar period the skeletons were far too numerous to be confined to even a capacious closet. One of the liveliest sets of bones was the record of the French Communist Party *before* the occupation, during the period of the

Nazi-Soviet Pact and the fall of France in the summer of 1940. Kravchenko pointed out that while he was fighting on the front, Maurice Thorez, the top French Communist, was sitting things out in Moscow. For the purely pragmatic reasons of his "unity" policy, de Gaulle had chosen to pardon him after the war.

For Kravchenko, the trial offered the opportunity for a direct assault on Soviet Stalinism, whose somewhat unlikely surrogates were two odious French journalists and an imaginary American agent of the OSS. For many of Kravchenko's numerous supporters, as typified by his brilliant left-wing lead attorney Georges Izard, the nearer enemy was Francophone Communism. Kravchenko made no attempt to disguise his motives. Nordmann asked him why, if he wanted to insult Communists, he didn't insult *American* Communists. Why did he choose France for his odious performance? The answer was very direct. The American Communist Party was paltry in its numbers and most feeble in its power. The French Communist Party on the other hand was large and potent—and it was wholly in the pocket of the Soviet tyranny. To deal it a blow might amount to something. In his autobiography, Nordmann says that this exchange confirmed his worst suspicions. Kravchenko was indeed an American agent.

This conclusion makes sense only within the context of French Communist belief in the postwar period. The Soviet Union was the house of peace. America was the house of war. It was the duty of all patriots to advance the cause of peace. To be anti-Communist was to be anti-*français*—"un-French." There was in the French Parliament no "Committee on Un-French Activities," but if there had been one, its victims would have been businessmen and clerics suspected of anti-Communism. Anti-anti-Communism was the nearly universal reflex of the left. Just as Kravchenko insisted upon the distinction between Russia as a governmental tyranny and the Russian people, the *Esprit* group tried to maintain a rigorous distinction between Communism as Platonic form and Communism as Soviet institution. For this reason they were appalled by the very idea of anti-Communism. "Anti-Communism," wrote Mounier in 1946, "is the necessary and sufficient crystallizing force for the resurgence of Fascism." It is difficult to account for this fantastic idea. The Soviets, discarding the promises of Yalta without so much as a meaningful feint at deception, were imposing brutal puppet states throughout Eastern Europe. The Iberian dictatorships were puny and isolated. Leftists or liberals were in the ascendant in every other nation in Europe. Yet the fear was a resurgence of "Fascism."

The defendants' best argument against Kravchenko was not without some force. It was in effect this: to speak out against the Soviet regime in the American press, while Russia was still locked in agonizing and uncertain conflict with Germany and while France was still under German occupation, threatened Allied unity. It was an act of treason against Russia and, perhaps by extension, against France. In the view of several of the defense witnesses, Kravchenko's press conference of April 3, 1944, could have delayed the D-Day planning, or scuttled planning for a second front altogether. That may seem fantastic, but the belief of many Communists that the puppeteers of Wall Street would be quite content to sit back and watch the Browns and the Reds battle each other into extinction was not entirely a paranoid delusion. It had been a commonly held Western "scenario" before the promulgation of the Molotov-Ribbentrop Pact, and according to a view still held by some historians a scenario that made the pact plausible if not inevitable. After June 1941 it became a part of the intellectual repertory of a different strain of American isolationism. Even among prominent political thinkers there were indeed those who held such a view, among them Freda Utley, the Anglo-American ex-Communist whose ex-ness had been considerably hastened by her Russian husband's disappearance in a purge.

Kravchenko was sensitive to this argument. He had recognized its potential dangers, and anticipated it thoughtfully. He presented himself now, as always, as a Russian patriot, and I have found no reason to doubt his *bona fides*. Stalin he regarded as a usurping tyrant, and the Soviet regime as a monstrous apparatus of coercion, cruelty, and injustice, not to be confused with Russia and the "Russian people." He had been careful and deliberate, he explained, to say nothing about the economic or military situation in his homeland until the war was over. He could not be responsible for Goebbels's having used his defection in his propaganda pieces. So also had he used Molotov's warm words of congratulations to Hitler upon his triumph in Paris in June of 1940!

The conventions of the French court made the trial far more than a duel of lawyers. There was a ceaseless babble of argument, invective, and interruption. One of the more amusing stage directions in Renaissance drama, rivaling Shakespeare's "Exit, pursued by a bear," is "Offers to stab him." There are photographs taken at the trial for which either of these would not be inappropriate captions. More than once Kravchenko seemed ready to hurl himself physically at the defendants' bench. More than once the defendants' witness General Rudenko seemed ready to descend from the stand and attack Kravchenko. Moscow had sent to Paris various people who, it was hoped, could help the defense in discrediting Kravchenko. Among them was General Leonid Rudenko, brother of the more famous General Roman Rudenko, who had been the lead Soviet prosecutor at Nuremberg. Leonid Rudenko had known and worked with Kravchenko years before in Russia. He was unprepared for a situation in which he could be subjected to sarcastic questioning from the plaintiff and his lawyers, and his frequent bursts of temper were a source of amusement to Kravchenko's supporters. Often the black-robed solemnity of the courtroom gave way to the boisterousness of the athletic stadium. There was frequent bickering about the translation, with occasional spontaneous interventions from White Russians in the hall. Not to be outdone, the defendants Morgan and Wurmser themselves took vigorous part in the questioning.

Adopting something of the pregnant nonchalance of a French Perry Mason, Wurmser put the following question to Kravchenko: "How does *A Doll's House* end?" He posed the question, naturally, in French. The judge looked perplexed. The Russian translator looked perplexed. *Maître* Izard looked perplexed. Wurmser himself affected surprise that the translator found difficulty in a question so simple. Thus prodded, the translator now put the question to Kravchenko. The exact Russian used has not been recorded, but according to knowledgeable witnesses, it might best be represented in English with "How does the house of a manikin die?"

Kravchenko had no idea at all of what this question was about, and he waxed indignant. Wurmser expected Kravchenko to be without a clue and found in his ignorance the indisputable proof of fraud. It was a moment, not unique in this trial, lost in translation. On page 70 of *I Chose Freedom*, there is an allusion to Ibsen's play, *A Doll's House*. While he was a student in Kharkov, Kravchenko chanced to meet a beautiful married woman, Julia, the wife of an important Ukrainian Communist official, "R." Although she lived in a private house in a kind of "bourgeois" comfort known only to the *crème* of the Communist *crème*, her marriage was not a happy one, and she did not love her husband. Kravchenko was greatly attracted to her, but also aware of the potential disaster resident in her husband's prominence and power. The two entered into a semi-affair. Acting as a sort of go-between, Mary, a female friend of Kravchenko's, who was also a friend of Julia's, reported to him the unhappiness of Julia's marital situation. "I know it sounds like something out of Ibsen's *Doll's House*, but Julia feels herself caught and imprisoned. She says being the wife of R— is like being the wife of a grand duke and she thinks it makes a mockery of the sufferings of the Russian people."

In *I Chose Justice*, when describing his experiences at the Paris trial, Kravchenko explains this linguistic moment in detail. *A Doll's House* is a great play, but a somewhat cryptic title. The play's central character, Nora Helmer, is of course the "doll," and the house is the confinement of her cramped marriage to Torvald Helmer. The image of the "doll" becomes prominent only at the very end. It is for this reason that when translated into German, and thence into Russian, the play was titled simply *Nora*. That is the title under which it entered the Russian repertory in pre-revolutionary St. Petersburg. Titles are quite frequently altered in foreign translation. Koestler's *Darkness at Noon* gained its huge French fame as *Le Zéro et l'infini*. *Out of the Night* was published in France as *Sans patrie ni frontières*. Ibsen's early translators often took other liberties with his text in order to make it more accessible to their audiences, such as altering the unfamiliar Norwegian names of some of the characters (including the major character Torvald here) along more familiar Franco-German lines. The play did make a lasting impression in Russian intellectual circles, however, and later on the Russian word *kukol'nyi* (dollhouse) was recorded in a Russian-German dictionary as meaning in a metaphoric sense "an inadequate marriage." But neither Wurmser nor Kravchenko could have enjoyed my advantage of consulting the learned monograph by Nils Åke Nilsson, *Ibsen in Russland* (1956), in which such fine points are discussed.

There is not the slightest reason why an educated Russian woman of the 1930s could not invoke the title of an Ibsen play frequently cited in socialist literature as an unmasking of the sterilities of Western bourgeois life. Kravchenko himself was no professor of literature, but he read widely. There are quite a few unforced literary references in his books. Some of them may have been suggested by Eugene Lyons, but he had enthusiasms of his own. In the Scribner archive is evidence of the fact that Kravchenko personally, out of his own pocket, paid for an English translation of Alexei Maksimov's novel *An Uncertain Heart*, which Scribner's then published, more or less to keep him happy, knowing it would command only modest sales.

THE CAMPS

At this late date, after Nikita Khrushchev's denunciation of Stalin, after Solzhenitsyn, after Chernobyl, after the collapse of the Soviet Union, it is no easy thing to reconstruct the mental world of the early Cold War. Yet it is necessary to try to do so if we are at all to understand the behavior of the antagonists, and especially of the Communist lawyers and witnesses. Most of them were not insincere. Instead, they were infected with a theory. Capitalism and Communism were universally regarded as two parallel social and economic systems locked in a dynamic adversarial struggle, but there are marked limits to the usefulness of this assumption. There is no Capitalist Party of France, or of Britain, or of the United States, no Capitalist International with an office on Wall Street or in the City of London. Very few capitalists have read so much as a word of Adam Smith, Hayek, or Milton Friedman. In fact, quite a few have never heard of them. Corporations and enterprises may have articulate structural hierarchies and group "philosophies," but capitalism itself has neither a central headquarters nor theoretical texts commanding wide obeisance.

It is very different with Communism. The very essence of the classical Communism of the twentieth century was faithful submission to a political center and intellectual assent to certain canonical writings of Marx and Lenin, and later Stalin, Chairman Mao, and a few others. The findings of medievalists who have investigated the nature of "textual communities" in the monasteries and among heretical or reforming groups are probably relevant to an understanding of the majority of French intellectuals in 1950. "From the eleventh century such groups began to play the role of laboratories of social organization," writes Brian Stock, "attempting both to improve their own communities and to offer a model of betterment to society at large."

The Communist Party was one vast textual community and laboratory of social organization so certain of the benefits of its "model of betterment to society at large" as to attempt, from highest moral principle, to

impose it by persuasion, fraud, assassination, revolution, or Soviet invasion. This Marxist textual community was not only persuaded that it had
a program for the betterment of society; it was persuaded that it had the
only such program. Seldom has a commitment to abstract theory so thoroughly subordinated the evaluation of empirical evidence. By the end of
the war even the most sensible and anti-Soviet leftists like George Orwell
were convinced of capitalism's utter bankruptcy. Capitalism was not "in
decline" or entering yet another "final crisis"—it was stone-cold dead.
"At least one thing is certain," wrote Orwell in 1940 in his essay "Inside
the Whale," "laissez-faire capitalism is finished." In the second half of
the twentieth century capitalist production and wealth creation probably
exceeded that of all previous historical periods combined, developing, as it
did so, in ways unimagined in the time-warped economics of Karl Marx.
Soviet Communism died before several of the principal participants in
the Kravchenko trial did. Not the blackest reactionary in Paris could
have dreamed up that scenario in 1949. No small part of the revolution
involved the "camps."

The English word "camp" (as in "concentration camp") had by now
become one of the most terrible words in the French language too. The
defendants' lawyers exerted their utmost ingenuity to banish them from
the Soviet Union. Camps have barbed-wire fences. Certainly the horrible
fenceless compounds in which so many wretches lived and died in the taiga
really could not be called "camps." Well, said one witness, the place was so
remote and hostile that to walk away from it was suicide, not escape. Well,
said another, the guards had an "imaginary fence," and they shot anybody
who reached it. Ah, said Heiszmann, Nordmann's assistant, these were not
camps. These were "industrial zones." But since this business of the camps
was soon to have a whole trial of its own, we may for the moment pass on.

The essential question in this trial was simple: was *I Chose Freedom*
a truthful and reliable book? To affirm that it was true was to indict the
Soviet regime of crimes, cruelties, brutalities, incompetences, and hypoc-
risies so numerous and profound as to be, quite literally, beyond the powers of the French Communists even to entertain in the most hypothetical
fashion. These included, in addition to the daily torments of Stalinist
life, the Gulag system, a vast genocidal famine engineered to force agricultural collectivization, and the Great Purge. The Purge of course had
also been the central matter of Koestler's book, though there presented

in representative miniature. Kravchenko wrote of it as a huge national catastrophe sweeping like a poisonous wind across every inch of the vast Russian soil.

Nordmann and his colleagues could not prove that Kravchenko did not exist. Their cruder attempts at character assassination were refuted by the empirical competence of the plaintiff in the courtroom. Their claim that though he existed and was superficially functional he never wrote the book was eventually countered by his production of the monstrous manuscript itself, or at least some version, state, part, or parcel, of the repellent sheets of crabbed handwriting that had so alarmed the translator Miriam Levine in New York. This left them with the option of trying to demonstrate that what he said about himself was untrue, and that what he said about Stalin's Russia was both untrue and motivated by the agenda of warmongering American imperialists.

Nordmann was in frequent contact with the Soviet Embassy, whose staff were sufficiently alarmed to help him in two concrete ways. First of all they were able to supply him with documents, some of which at least were actual unforged originals, from Kravchenko's various dossiers in the USSR. Second, they would bring witnesses from Russia to testify to Kravchenko's personal turpitude and to refute the book's slanderous lies and misrepresentations concerning the Soviet State. These witnesses would be in addition to those eminent French intellectuals and other Western fellow travelers and useful idiots already organized by the defense.

This last group included two British eminences: the left-wing Labor MP Konni Zilliacus, a cosmopolitan Yalie who spoke French and Stalinese virtually without an accent, and the "Red Dean" of Canterbury, the Most Reverend Hewlett Johnson, who reported the assurance of the Russian primate himself of Premier Stalin's friendliness toward the practice of religion. They were joined by the oily American propagandist Alfred Kahn, one of the Communist slimers of Jan Valtin. The French intellectuals included many Communist celebrities: the novelist Vercors, author of *Le Silence de la mer*; the physicist Joliot-Curie; Jean Baby the theoretician; Roger Garaudy, who by the 1980s would abandon Communism to become a Muslim and a Holocaust denier; and several others.

In her autobiography, Nina Berberova recalled her astonishment as she watched Nordmann's procession of eminent witnesses. "To see with my own eyes how a former minister, or a world-known scientist, a Nobel Prize laureate, or a Sorbonne professor with the Legion of Honour in his lapel button hole, or a famous writer would take the oath and under oath affirm that there never had been and were not any concentration camps in the U.S.S.R., was one of the strongest impressions of my entire life." Her surprise was possibly unconsidered, or perhaps only rhetorical. A solemn and self-righteous prevarication was, after all, simply a rhetorical and bloodless manifestation of such "Bolshevik firmness" as in the hovels of Ukrainian villages and the interrogation rooms of the Lubyanka took more violent and sanguinary form. Kopelev, in identifying Bolshevism as the most destructive social malady of the twentieth century, defined also its typifying characteristic: "the lie."

Perhaps the cruelest stratagem of the defense was to bring from Russia and put on the stand Kravchenko's ex-wife, Zanaida Gorlova. She testified that her hateful ex-husband, of whom she was thanks to the nonexistent God now happily free, was a drunkard, a pathological liar, and a wife beater. No act of dishonor or cowardice lay outside his normal routine. Kravchenko had written that Gorlova's father was among the "disappeared" purgees. This fact was certainly true, as other witnesses later confirmed; but Gorlova was forced to testify that her father was alive and well and enjoying a peaceful Soviet senility. This couple had been most unhappily married. The circumstances of their reencounter did little to relieve the odium between them. Izard wrote dryly that the episode suggested a "marital non-reconciliation meeting." Had he married again? No, shouted a wit from the audience, "he chose freedom!" Otherwise the encounter was not very funny. The plaintiff behaved disgracefully, contradicting in bellicose and threatening terms that he was bellicose or threatening. Many years later, after Kravchenko was dead, his Russian son Constantine confirmed that his mother's perjury had been cruelly coerced, a fact hardly in need of confirmation to anyone who had been in the courtroom. The episode left an unpleasant aroma. It did little to suggest that Kravchenko was a genial or amiable person. Yet even more did it dramatize a point made in so many Soviet memoirs: the poisonous results of the state's sovereignty over the intimate lives of men and women. Readers of Koestler—meaning pretty nearly everyone in the room—had to remember poor Arlova, so similar to Gorlova in name and fate.

The argument of Kravchenko's book is an argument from *experience*. The Communists countered it with their argument from *authority*. If a famous novelist, a famous politician, a famous physicist said something alleged of the Soviet regime was not so, then it was not so. The cache of Soviet documents presented a real threat. Kravchenko claimed to have been in the Komsomol, the Communist Youth Brigade. He claimed to have studied at the university in Kharkov. Nordmann produced an ancient questionnaire, undoubtedly filled out in Kravchenko's own hand, where that information was lacking precisely at those points where it would be expected if not required. But Izard and Kravchenko, almost certainly with the help of the American, British, French authorities in occupied Germany, had developed their own terrible weapon.

In the wake of Barbarossa, the Germans had sent back to their homeland many thousands of conscripted East Europeans to work in industry and agriculture. Their history is the stuff of tragedy on a vast scale. Of many books that record it, *Nina's Journey*, the autobiography of a Ukrainian-American woman named Nina Markovna, is among the most moving. Then, under the circumstances of the sometimes chaotic German retreat in the winter of 1944–45, many others were displaced westward. By the time the advancing American forces met the advancing Red Army, there were literally hundreds of thousands of them within the frontiers of the old Reich.

These were the DPs, or "displaced persons." Stalin, whose personal ineptitude was in large measure responsible for the grim disasters of the early German advance, chose to blame the victims. He made the following famous remark: "There are no Russian prisoners of war; there are only Russian traitors." He was as good as his fantastic word. Those Russian POWs lucky or hardy enough to still be alive and ambulatory after their ordeal in Nazi camps were sent as soon as possible to the Siberian Gulag by their liberating comrades. A similar fate, preordained by the protocols of the Yalta agreement, awaited many of the slave laborers in the British Zone of occupation. Still, even after a massive cleansing of "traitors," there were some scores of thousands of Poles, Russians, Ukrainians, Letts, Czechs, Romanians, Bulgarians, and other assorted refugees left in the DP camps. On the whole this population would do anything, often down to and including suicide, rather than return eastward.

Izard was pretty sure of the grounds of their reluctance, and (mainly financed by Kravchenko personally) he had circularized the DP camps, the church relief agencies, and likely political groups to discover whether there might be any people who had firsthand knowledge of the labor camps in Russia, of the administrative justice of the NKVD, or other matters raised by Kravchenko's book. This proved a brilliant commercial as well as legal maneuver, since it augmented the already enormous success of *I Chose Freedom*. Candidates came out of the barbed wire by the score. Especially numerous were the Poles, large numbers of whom had been kidnapped and imprisoned by the Russians in 1940, then released to fight the Germans in 1942, and who now stayed on in the West rather than return to their Russian-controlled homeland. But there were also many, many Russians whose ferocious anti-Communism, first born of fear, was now animated by indignant hope.

Izard and his team were able to pick and choose with the discrimination of a choreographer at a Broadway audition call. Among those he chose were some who had known Kravchenko well during various episodes related in his book. Others knew Gorlova well. The threatening blank space on the questionnaire lost its power to intimidate when the lawyers actually found one of Kravchenko's former Kharkov professors. So, as one after another French intellectual took the oath and swore there was no slave labor in Russia, and one after another Russian slave laborer testified as to the minutiae of Gulag life—and death—the surreal dialogue continued.

MARGARETE BUBER-NEUMANN

In retrospect, most observers agreed that Kravchenko's most effective and poignant witness was Margarete Buber-Neumann, who was at that time forty-seven years old, a writer and living in Stockholm. Her book—*Under Two Dictators* in its English translation—is among the dozen or so most impressive Gulag memoirs. At that time, it had just been published. Margarete Buber was a highly cultivated middle-class German, who married Rafael Buber, the Communist son of the celebrated Jewish theologian Martin Buber, and with him had two children. She had been in the German Communist Youth movement, and joined the KPD in 1926, at the age of twenty-five. She brought to the revolutionary party intelligence, ability, and a commitment bordering on fanaticism. Her marriage to Buber ended in divorce in 1929. Among others whose attention she attracted was Heinz Neumann (1902–1937), one of the top lieutenants (and rivals) of the inarticulate Ernst Thaelmann, the official proletarian head of the KPD. Buber and Neumann entered a "Communist" or common-law marriage. He had a way with women. "To many young female communists he was still the romantic knight of revolutionary adventure," wrote Jan Valtin, who had worked with him. "Among Party belles the phrase, 'I have slept with Heinz Neumann' sounded like the proud equivalent of 'I have received the Order of the Red Banner.'"

As the husband's eminence was to prove the wife's doom, it is necessary to say a word or two about Heinz Neumann. He was a very important figure, who commands four columns in the recent and indispensable biographical dictionary of German Communists. The scion of a rich Berlin commercial family, his attempt to redeem his unfortunate class origin took the form of compensatory violence. He was an enthusiastic Stalinist and, for a time, a personal favorite of Stalin's. Neumann was the chief organizer of the bloody Cantonese pseudorevolution of 1927. Its only effect was the large-scale (meaning thousands, not hundreds) slaughter of Chinese coolies. According to Franz Borkenau, the historian of the Comintern, the whole episode was probably engineered for the sole purpose of giving Stalin a "revolutionary event" to display at the Fifteenth Party Congress, at which Trotsky's disgrace was sealed, and that of Kamenev and Zinoviev initiated. "Heinz Neumann, about whose character no single man in the Comintern had the slightest doubt, was deliberately chosen because his dash, his careerism, and his absolute lack of scruples, made him the right person for the task." His enemies and rivals, growing in number, thereafter called him the "Executioner of Canton." Among the most disturbing pages of *Out of the Night* are the accounts of the street fighting between Communists and Nazis in Hamburg in 1932. Valtin reports Neumann's bloodthirsty command: *Ich will Leichen sehen*—"I want to see bodies!"

Such was Margarete's unlawfully wedded spouse. According to her testimony, her husband was already falling from grace without realizing it. He was determined to fight Hitler, while Stalin had decided to tolerate him. By 1935, the Neumanns were living in Moscow, but most uncomfortably, as they were both under oppressive political suspicion. Her Jewish ex-husband and her children had fled to comparative safety in Palestine. In April 1937, Heinz Neumann was arrested by the NKVD and, apparently, shot a few months later. Margarete never saw or heard from him again. The widow told to a spellbound courtroom the usual tale of the grieving families of the "disappeared"—the trudging from prison to prison in search of information, the rude insults of police bureaucrats, the endless waiting at jail gates and office guichets, the final, terrible silence.

After various other brutalities, including the refusal of an exit permit, she herself was arrested in June 1938. Following a typical regime of protracted interrogations hardly distinguishable from torture sessions, she was sentenced by troika to five years at labor in Karaganda, in the high-rent district of Siberia. When she dared to ask to have her case reviewed, she was transferred to a special punishment camp. She testified to many of the horrors so common in the Gulag literature: the cruelties, the inadequate housing, the brutal cold, the forced prostitution, the killing labor, the endless, searing hunger. "The inmates of these punitive camps had to work from dawn till sunset. They worked in the fields and received the worst possible food. The system in Soviet concentration camps is to exert pressure on the prisoners by making their food dependent on the amount of work effected. That is why inmates of the punitive camps get the worst food of any."

But in 1940 she was without explanation taken back to the Butyrki prison in Moscow, given an excellent meal, and handed a note that said: "Your sentence of five years hard labor has been commuted to immediate expulsion from Soviet territory." Only when she was put into a prison train heading westward did she realize the significance of her liberation. She was among a carload of German Communists being returned to Germany in the cooperative spirit of the Hitler-Stalin accord. At Brest-Litovsk, blue-capped officers of the NKVD turned her over to gray-clad German officers whose caps bore the death's-head insignia of the S.S. Now began a new series of interrogations, horrible in their similarity to those she had undergone in 1938. Five months later she was incarcerated at Ravensbrück, where she met and befriended Milena Jesenzka, Franz Kafka's old girlfriend, to whom she devoted her most successful book.

In ancient mythology the blind seer Tiresias, who had the unique experience of having been both a man and a woman at different stages of his life, was able to answer Zeus' question: who has the greater pleasure, the man or the woman? Frau Buber-Neumann, whose experience was not quite unique but certainly most unusual, was able to answer a question of like construction: whose concentration camps are more horrible, Stalin's or Hitler's? She answered less directly than Tiresias, but it was clear that in her experience at least, Stalin had the edge in barbarity.

This testimony was devastating, since to raise any parallel between the Nazi and the Soviet regimes—as obvious as it might be to anyone equipped with eyes—was anathema to the Communists. But to raise it and then decide the case, on balance, in favor of Hitler—*insupportable*! From the defense lawyers came the arch remark that Frau Buber-Neumann was guilty of ingratitude to the Soviets, whose army had, after all, liberated Ravensbrück! Years later Nordmann offered a semi-apology for the browbeating of this witness, and, by implication, several other witnesses. He thought he could discount their testimony because they were either kulaks or Trotskyites. The implication, of course, was that slave labor camps were perfectly appropriate for kulaks and Trotskyites.

DAVID ROUSSET, THE FRENCH KRAVCHENKO

Kravchenko won his suit against *Les Lettres françaises*. The court perhaps did its best to minimize the meaning of his victory by awarding him the insulting token damages of a single franc. Morgan and Wurmser spoke of their "moral vindication," but that was for most sensible people as convincing as their solemn protestations that only in the Soviet Union had penology arrived at a level of humane perfection worthy of civilization. The truth is that Kravchenko had struck a devastating blow against the pretensions of Western Communist propagandists. He had done so on his own initiative, expending many of his own resources, and calling upon his own indomitable courage. His was a major Cold War victory. Rarely has a single individual achieved so large a premeditated goal. The full impact of what Kravchenko had done would not be admitted in France, however, until his deed had been reduplicated by a Frenchman. That is exactly what happened in the copycat civil action brought by the French journalist David Rousset against *Les Lettres françaises* in November 1950.

French anti-Americanism is no new phenomenon. It probably reached its acme under the second Bush administration, but things were not a great deal different in Truman's day. Although the Kravchenko affair had a dramatic impact on French public opinion, its "Americanness" remained something of an advantage for the Communists. One of Wurmser's more poetic flights was his contemptuous charge that Kravchenko was "a poor marionette whose strings are 'MADE IN THE USA.'" For us this is merely a wistful reminder of a time when manufactured goods so labeled were found in markets throughout the world; but for Wurmser it was a palpable hit. To the degree that the results of the trial could be associated with American manipulation, to that same degree could they be wished away as Cold War propaganda rather than legal findings. The Rousset affair allowed no such mental circumventions or evasions, for it seemed an all-French production. I say "seemed," because such evidence as I have found suggests that there was more direct and concrete American and British collaboration with Rousset than with Kravchenko. The Kravchenko case immediately eventuated in two books: Izard's annotated transcripts called *Kravchenko versus Moscow* and Kravchenko's own *I Chose Justice*, neither of which had particularly robust sales in France.

But the book that came out of the Rousset affair was a best-seller. It was called *Pour la vérité sur les camps* (*The Truth About the Camps*), and it recorded a good deal of the choicer testimony from the witness stand. Rousset was not an American, not a CIA agent, not a capitalist running dog. He was a far left journalist who bore in his body the most precious political stigmata of his own suffering in a Nazi concentration camp. It is true that to the Communists he was a "Trotskyite," a deviationist from the Party line; but that theological distinction meant little outside the Communist Party.

David Rousset was a man of considerable cultural and political prestige for the French non-Communist left. Raised like Gide in an atmosphere of severe Protestant rectitude, he had already before the war earned a considerable reputation as a journalist, and the reputation was of the sort to excite the enmity of the Gestapo. He was a self-described "socialist," and a signer of the manifesto already referred to which held that only socialism could save Europe. He was that kind of socialist, of course, whom the Communists in Germany had called "Social Fascists" and whom the Communists in Russia had shot. For the Communist he might be a "Trotskyite," but there was no way they could paint him as a second Kravchenko, that is, as either a "traitor" or an American lickspittle. Not merely was he an alumnus of a Nazi concentration camp—a credential which in those circles perhaps alone rivaled the prestige of a career in the Resistance—he was perhaps France's greatest authority on the Nazi camps, the author of the remarkable *Universe concentrationnaire* (1946), translated into English as *The Other Kingdom* (1947), a book that for its time makes him a peer of

Primo Levi and Elie Wiesel. His project raised in the most explicit way the forbidden subject of a moral equivalence between the Nazi and the Soviet regimes. His initiative was immediately seconded by *Le Monde*, by François Mauriac's *Combat*, and numerous other authoritative voices of French liberalism.

Rousset's first move followed Kravchenko's strategy. He took out a two-page advertisement in *Le Figaro littéraire* for November 12, 1949. It was an appeal addressed to all former political prisoners who, like himself, had been confined in Nazi concentration camps. It asked their support in establishing an international commission to look into the question of forced labor camps in the Soviet Union, rumors of which had become increasingly current in Western Europe "for the last five years"—that is, the time since several hundreds of thousands of Poles had out of military necessity been liberated from the Gulag in order to fight Germans. Rousset himself was not agnostic on the matter. He stated quite baldly that the Gulag system existed not as an aberration but as an integral part of the Soviet economic system. The commission should be comprised exclusively of former prisoners, whose unique experiences gave them unequaled expertise and protected them against being hoodwinked. It would be open to former prisoners of all political stripes, including Communists. Rousset well knew that at least one of the official French associations of former prisoners was a Communist front. He was forewarned and therefore forearmed for the abuse now heaped upon him.

There was an imprudence born of desperation in the Communist counterattack launched in *Les Lettres françaises* a few days later. There had been nothing in Rousset's advertisement that explicitly involved the journal or the Kravchenko trial, but history could not be evaded. *Les Lettres françaises* published a very strident front-page essay that attempted in its spirit to invoke the righteous indignation of Zola's classic intervention in the Dreyfus affair: "Pierre Daix, prisoner number 59,801 at Mauthausen, responds to David Rousset." Pierre Daix was among the highly disciplined French Communist internees who in effect ran Mauthausen from the inside. In the postwar world, his contributions to French cultural life were impressive. As an art critic, and in particular as an expert on Picasso, his work still commands respect. In 1949 he was among the hardest of hard-liners. His certificate of suffering might be a match for Rousset's.

Like literally dozens of other French Communists prominent in the

Cold War, Daix documented his eventual defection from Moscow in an autobiography. Its aims are as face-saving as most but its content somewhat less self-serving than many. His account of the Rousset affair denies knavery at the expense of confessing folly. He wrote his essay without commission in spontaneous indignation, and, at that time, he believed that what he wrote was true. It was, he says, the celebrated Communist poet Louis Aragon who arranged its publication in *Les Lettres françaises*. Its principal libels taken up in the civil action were two: (1) that Rousset falsely maintained that Soviet citizens could be condemned to forced labor by administrative organs; and (2) that the alleged eyewitness accounts of Soviet concentration camps were nothing more nor less than recycled Nazi propaganda. These were propositions impossible to defend. The first was refuted by the clear text of the Soviet criminal code in its officially published form; the second was an invitation to revisit precisely that body of evidence that had already in the Kravchenko action done irreparable harm to the Communists' pretensions to moral nobility.

In this "second Kravchenko" trial, even more clearly than in the first, the real defendant was the Soviet system. The silent acknowledgment of this fact led to a slightly different Communist strategy, signaled in the first instance among comments from the fellow travelers. If Rousset's commission of inquiry were to be established at all, it should be established in an even-handed manner. It was grossly unfair that the Soviet Union be the only subject of inquiry. Certainly, Spain and Greece (at that time the most conspicuous "Fascist" states) should be included. Indeed, so should France itself. The argument of "selective morality," when raised by men of the moral stature of an Albert Camus or a Bertrand Russell, could have considerable force, as several Cold War episodes show. But the implied concession that everybody does it lacks the purity of the claim that we don't do it. To advance it was already a surrender, as well as an invitation to examine Soviet penology from a dangerously comparative point of view. Indignation at the discovery that there were undoubtedly unpleasant prisons in Greece in which Communists suffered abominably, for instance, might be softened by the concomitant discovery that there were more people in the Russian Gulag than lived in all of Greece, period. It could lead one to contemplate the differences as well as the similarities among "concentration camps." That was the term rightly used in the left-wing vocabulary of the late thirties to denote the squalid tent cities temporarily established along the French Mediterranean in which thousands of undocumented refugees from Franco's victory for a time languished in demoralized inactivity relieved only by endless games of *boules* and checkers—the habitat of Koestler's *Scum of the Earth*. What, then, would one call the crude barracks hastily erected in the sub-Arctic, where the wretched inhabitants died in their hundreds from ailments more dangerous than boredom?

Buried among the Cold War debates within the chambers of the United Nations in the autumn of 1949 is the stillborn attempt to establish a commission on forced labor. The laconic report of the Economic and Social Council reads thus: "An effective resolution on action to be taken against the use of forced labor was delayed because of the inability of the Council members to agree on how a commission of inquiry should be set up and what exactly was the definition of the term 'forced labor.'" Of course any such agreement would have foundered on the question of invigilation. The Soviet representative, the unmemorable Mr. Arutiunian, declined to invite "American spies" to wander about Vorkuta or Kolyma, especially since "the corrective labor laws of the Soviet Union were the most humane in the world and provided not only for the punishment but reeducation of the individual with a view to his participation in the continuation of socialism in his country."

This effort, however, was destined to bear fruit in another orchard. Gerald Corley Smith, a British diplomat whose name will be forever honored in connection with the ecological protection of the Galápagos, had at that time the unenviable task of leading the charge of his parliamentary Light Brigade against the stone wall over which Arutiunian scowled. Corley Smith had managed to arm himself with a copy of the Soviet law code concerning "corrective labor" *in Russian*—a fact of some significance, since Arutiunian had claimed to find no fewer than forty-three mistranslations in Corley Smith's verbal brief. The eighth article of this code says in the clearest language that the people sent to "corrective labor" camps include both those found guilty by a court and those condemned "by the decree of an administrative organ," the official euphemism for the secret police "troikas" that sent folks northward and eastward quite literally by the hundreds of thousands. This useful document now came into the hands of David Rousset.

Rousset's lawyers were two close friends of his political persuasion, Gérard Rosenthal and Théo Bernard. Their collaboration guaranteed that this second trial would be more carefully prepared, more coherent, in short more polished than had been the Kravchenko trial. What they lost in unpredictable courtroom drama by having a restrained Frenchman rather than a volatile Ukrainian as a client they made up for in the increase in control and focused high seriousness. Both the Communists and Rousset had learned lessons from the earlier trial. The Communists sought to limit the grounds of debate and demonstration. Rousset and his team set out to summon an absolutely all-star roster of witnesses. Margarete Buber-Neumann's testimony had had a double effectiveness. Brilliant in the courtroom, it had also stimulated large sales of her book *Under Two Dictators*. Rousset summoned her for a second innings, and he lined up several other authors of what was by now the rapidly burgeoning genre of "Gulag studies." Four whole years had passed since the publication of *I Chose Freedom*. Victor Kravchenko had proved to be a pioneer in a flourishing genre. It was in this connection that the lawyer Vienney, the understudy to Joë Nordmann, who was also back for a return match, made the remark I cited in my Introduction: "But all your witnesses have a book."

There was no longer much room to hide. Some incorrigibles, it is true, simply dismissed Rousset's evidence as fraud and fabrication. A common claim among this group was that all the horror stories ascribed to the Russian scene had been lifted bodily from the testimony in the Nuremberg Trials actually relating to Nazi atrocities. Quite apart from being fantastic, this desperate ploy was also dangerous as it suggested to the mind, as Buber-Neumann had, a displeasing congruence among totalitarian regimes.

But the "intellectuals" as a whole were forced to more subtle and convoluted casuistry. A British historian, Ian Burchall, has recently published a book about Jean-Paul Sartre as an anti-Stalinist; for "there can be no doubt whatsoever that he publicly condemned the camps." Yes, said Jean-Paul Sartre, there are concentration camps in Russia. And yes, again, people can be sent to them without judicial process. On the whole, however, it was best not to talk about them, lest the conversation comfort or embolden anti-Communist "dogs." These were truths, but secret or Gnostic truths, to be shared only among the initiates of his political journal. It is unthinkable that the man who would not shake the anti-Communist hand of Arthur Koestler would have said them in an open courtroom. If he never actually said, "*Il ne faut pas désespérer Billancourt*," that sentiment was attributed to him with a justifiable rhetorical license. It is a witticism that encapsulated an attitude of "worse the evil you do not know than the evil you know."

The medieval philosopher Averroës posited a theory of the "double truth." A thing could be true according to reason, but false according to theology, or the other way around. On the question of "revolutionary" Terror, Sartre and Merleau-Ponty, like Gramsci before and Marcuse after them, continued in their socialist Averroism. Their minds were capacious and supple enough to hold on to a "double truth" that may intrigue some college professors but was likely to sound like mere sophistry to the more conventional moralists who define public opinion. Kravchenko knew nothing of medieval philosophy, but he entitled one of his chapters "The Two Truths."

The official defendants this time were Claude Morgan (whose real name was Claude Lecomte) and Pierre Daix, the Emile Zola wannabe. The lawyers were the familiar Joë Nordmann, and his bulldoglike assistant, Paul Vienney, the sort of fellow you wouldn't want to meet even in the best lit of alleys. Nordmann began by claiming that the court lacked jurisdiction to hear the case, since it was not a bona fide French legal action but a propagandistic attempt to embarrass the Soviet Union and "the Soviet penal system, which is the most progressive and advanced in the world." Hoots of laughter from the public benches suggested an alternative assessment of Soviet penology.

This principal judge, M. Colomiès, was no Durkheim. He threatened to silence the defendants if they insisted on speaking irrelevance or nonsense. Vienney wanted to talk about Stalingrad. Nordmann wanted to talk about the atomic bomb and American aggression in Korea, about America's plan to declare war on Russia. The presiding judge said, No, the subject of discussion will be the charge of libel raised by David Rousset. "I want to say simply one word," said Joë Nordmann in twenty-seven words: "we would be happy to know which are the foreign embassies that are determining the decisions of a French court!" At this point, according to the record, there were "animated protestations in the hall."

The Communists had failed utterly on their three substantive points, such as they were. There *was* a *prima facie* case. The court *was* competent to hear it. There *was* ample precedent for the calling of witnesses to the truth or falsity of alleged libels. It was this third finding that Nordmann most feared, and his fear of it accounts for the maladroit maneuvers that angered the judge and increased the contempt of many observers. There is

actually a photographic record of the moment at which Vienney is prais-
ing the Soviet penal system, chubby David Rousset laughing out loud in
amused amazement. The photograph accompanies an article by Mauriac in
Le Figaro, "David Rousset Has Already Won." He writes: "We don't need
any other proof beyond the maladroit attempt of the Stalinists to keep the
witnesses from appearing. You see, M. Wurmser, he should have killed
them all. Your masters are still too humane, for a few victims escaped."

This bitter remark merits a small meditation. The reference in "he
should have killed them all" is of course to Stalin. The chances of surviving a protracted term at forced labor under Article 58 were not good. The
chances of successful escape from the Soviet Union to the free West were
practically nonexistent. Yet so vast was the Gulag population that even tiny
mathematical probabilities yield what are in objective terms large numbers.
If only one tenth of 1 percent survived and escaped, there were perhaps
twenty thousand potential witnesses who might respond to an appeal such as
Rousset's. If only 1 percent of that group were psychologically sound, coherent, educated, literate, and "motivated"—such people as write memoirs, for
example—he still would have had a couple of hundred to choose from.

Of those choice prospects who did present themselves, Rousset's lawyers brought sixteen to depose before the court. Though it was not quite
true, as Vienney had remarked, that they *all* had books, most of them did.
And in that terrible library was revealed the ineluctable confirmation of the
representative truth of Victor Kravchenko's memoir.

Elinor Lipper was a starry-eyed young Swiss Communist who fled the
degeneracy of bourgeois life to take up residence in Moscow in 1937. This
was just in time to get caught up in the Purge, which she managed to do
within six months of her arrival. It would be eleven years before she got
out alive—possibly a record of endurance for a Western slave laborer. Her
book, published in Switzerland in 1950, had the title of a Victorian trav-
elogue: *Eleven Years in Soviet Prisons and Concentration Camps*. Most of
her time was spent in one of the deadliest regions of the archipelago, the
frozen gold fields of Kolyma, reachable only after a ghastly "middle passage" across the Sea of Okhotsk to Magadan. (This was the topography of
Eugenia Ginzburg's better known memoir, *Journey into the Whirlwind*.)
The nearly surreal calm of Lipper's book, its want of "rhetoric" or forceful
indignation, makes it at times sound almost like a scientific report rather
than an indictment of high crimes against humanity.

It even has some amusing passages, one of which has topical American interest as it concerns Owen Lattimore. Professor Lattimore was a rebarbative China expert on the faculty of Johns Hopkins University. He was a fellow traveler and perhaps a Soviet agent. He became one of the more celebrated victims of Joseph McCarthy, who gave him single-handed credit for the "loss" of China to the Communists. In 1944, in the company of Vice President Henry Wallace, Lattimore found himself on a goodwill and fact-finding mission to our great democratic allies in Magadan, where the pair of innocents abroad were entertained by the local prison camp commandant. Lattimore later published an article entitled "New Road to Asia" in the *National Geographic* that is classic "progressive" propaganda: "Magadan is also part of the domain of a remarkable concern, the Dalstroi (Far Northern Construction Company), which can be roughly compared to a combination Hudson's Bay Company and TVA."

It all depends how "rough" one chooses to be in one's comparisons. Dalstroi was the administrative body that ran the vast slave labor empire in all of Kolyma. Through similar rough-and-ready conversion the Birkenau-Auschwitz conglomerate can be compared to a combination of the Cudahy Meat Packing and Waste Management corporations. Ms. Lipper, who was in the largest of the women's camps at the time of Wallace's visit, allows herself some rather heavy sarcasm over this visit and over the supplementary enthusiastic remarks concerning the Siberian scene offered by both Wallace and Lattimore. These had included praise for the humane and progressive attitudes toward penology to be found in the Soviet Union and appreciation for the high quality of some needlework in the local shop. Elinor Lipper was aware that the needlework was the slave product of brutalized Orthodox nuns, and the "local shop" a Potemkin front hastily organized for the distinguished American visitors. When taxed on the subject, Lattimore grumpily said that he considered it impolite to scrutinize one's host. As for Ms. Lipper, whose highly detailed account he seemed reluctant to credit, he remarked gracelessly: "Well, it looks as though she got out, didn't she?"

Jules Margolin, a Jew from Pinsk, was a Zionist who had the luck to be on a visit from Palestine to relatives in Poland when the Red Army gobbled up its half in 1939. Five years in the Gulag cured him of his youthful socialism. He wrote his brilliant book immediately upon his release in 1945, but could publish it neither in America, where anti-Soviet books

were still unwelcome, nor in Israel, where his insufficiently heroic attitude toward Zionism offended some important people. Nina Berberova
and Mina Journot translated it into French for Calmann-Lévy, the publishers of Koestler, where it appeared in 1949 under the title *La Condition
inhumaine*. The title of course made ironic allusion to the famous novel
of André Malraux, *La Condition humaine* (*Man's Fate*, 1933), which presented a heroic vision of the Chinese Communist Revolution that Owen
Lattimore could, and did, warmly approve. A decade before Solzhenitsyn
began writing *The Gulag Archipelago* and two decades before he published
it, Margolin wrote of his long exile in "the country of Ze-Ka, the only
country in the world where there is no debate about the USSR, no illusion,
no mistake." The Ze-Ka, more familiarly known simply as "zeks," took
their name from the long Russian phrase *Zaklioutchony-kontrevelutioner*,
"counterrevolutionary prisoners."

Alex Weissberg was a German physicist, a Communist, and a friend of
Arthur Koestler, upon whom he prevailed to write the Introduction to the
English-language version of his memoirs. This appeared during the course
of the Rousset action. Neither its British nor its American title (*Conspiracy
of Silence* and *The Accused*, respectively) is particularly well chosen. The
conspiracy of silence is the taboo that surrounded discussion of the Gulag;
the "accused" is of course the first-person narrator, who like Kravchenko
spent a very long time being hounded by the NKVD prosecuting investigators. In fact the book is reminiscent of Kravchenko's in many ways,
as is unsurprising from authors with such similar technical backgrounds.
While it clearly underwent a careful copyediting, its structural infelicities
and repetitions attest to the fact that, like Kravchenko, Weissberg was not
a professional writer.

What he was was a first-class academic physicist. Kravchenko's book
documents the grievous harm done to Soviet industrial production by the
purges and incessant police interference that caused frequent abrupt personnel changes and created an atmosphere, endemic to Soviet socialism,
in which managers feared innovation, shunned initiative, and delayed even
trivial decisions by passing them up a nearly endless chain of command
to the creators of the "planned economy" in Moscow. Weissberg was a
research physicist, his specialty being low-temperature physics, a field in
which Soviet science excelled. His story illustrates the extent to which a
political paranoia could cripple even the most vital scientific research.

It is nearly meaningless to say that he was innocent of the charges brought against him, since virtually all the prisoners were innocent; but Weissberg was among that group, actually quite numerous, who long continued to believe that with the exception of their own aberrant cases, the rigors of the police system were necessary and just.

In late 1938, several members of the Politburo, including Stanislas Kossior, one of the principal executors of the Ukrainian genocide and an official "hero" of the Soviet Union, were purged. This circumstance led someone to opine to Weissberg that "Fascism has begun in the Soviet Union." Weissberg, reacting in anger, called the man an idiot. There was only one thing remarkable about this exchange: its setting. Two men who had never seen each other, and never would see each other, were tapping out the "conversation" in so-called Prisoners' Morse Code on the aging water pipes of Kholodnaya Gora prison. At that point, Weissberg had for more than two years been hounded, imprisoned, abused, and tortured by the state police, who had successfully forced him to absurd confessions of crimes against the state. He had by then come to view Stalin's regime as wholly wicked and illegitimate. But he could not bear the thought that the country had deviated so far from "socialism" that it might be "Fascist." "My indignation was real. Despite my experiences in prison I was still capable of honest anger at any suggestion of a parallel between the Soviet Union and Fascist countries." Among the recurrent types encountered in the prison books is the unrepentant Stalinist who believes that he alone has been arrested because of some inexplicable bureaucratic error, soon to be rectified, and accidentally thrown into a cell crowded with dozens of real assassins, traitors, spies, saboteurs, and wreckers. If such men as these struggled to keep faith with the Big Lie, we can hardly be surprised by the mental aberrations of French journalists or lecturers in the universities.

Among the two or three most useful idiots in France was Frédéric Joliot-Curie, the Nobel laureate in Physics. He was one of the prize properties of the postwar French Communist Party, for he would swear on his scientific authority to such useful facts as the Americans' use of germ warfare against the Koreans. At the time that Weissberg's trouble began, Joliot-Curie was not yet a member of the Communist Party but Koestler still was, and still susceptible to the "mistake" theory. Koestler set out to try to help his friend Weissberg by gathering testimonials from eminent physicists as to Weissberg's excellent reputation for academic research and moral probity. Though Joliot-Curie did not know Weissberg personally, he knew of Arthur Koestler, and he was happy enough to sign the letter. It did no good, and everyone forgot about it—except for Weissberg's wife, who put it away in a file.

From the moment Weissberg came forward to take the oath, Nordmann, the youthful Germanophile, joined by Vienney and the defendant Morgan, protested the monstrous affront of a wretch so miserable as to speak the language of Karl Marx daring to criticize the Soviet Union. After the familiar shouting match, the warning to Morgan, the brief recess, the court reconvened to hear the reading of the long forgotten letter, once addressed to the Procurator-General of the Union of Soviet Socialist Republics, now addressed to a French courtroom, attesting to Weissberg's scientific eminence, his moral probity, his socialist purity. It was signed by a group of self-identified "friends of the Soviet Union," prominent among whom were Irenée and Frédéric Joliot-Curie. This *coup de théâtre* left Morgan fulminating. That was on the fifth day, midway through the trial, and it was all uphill for the comrades after that.

Jerzy Gliksman was another Polish Jew. His murdered brother had been one of the leaders of the Jewish Socialist *Bund*. Gliksman called his book *Tell the West*—a title that makes explicit one of the principal aims of many Gulag memoirists. It was horrible enough that the Gulag existed. It was more than the soul could bear that its existence should be denied by Western intellectuals. Most of the worst stories are in one way or another Polish stories. Josef (Joseph) Czapski was a cosmopolitan and aristocratic Pole who spent much of his early life in France. He had been born in Prague in 1896 and studied in St. Petersburg. In Paris he followed painting, and with some success. You will find his works in a few European and American museums and in the pages of the auction catalogues. He was the author of a monograph on Cézanne. Though an expatriate, he was also a patriot. In 1939 he was an officer in the Polish army, and he suffered the fate of so many other Poles, civilian and military alike, who had retreated into eastern Poland in recoil from the Nazi advance: he was interned by the Soviets. A fortuitous circumstance saved him from being murdered along with thousands of his fellow officers in 1940. Later in the war he fought gallantly with the reconstituted Polish army at Monte Cassino, where by the cruel ironies of warfare Polish soldiers, almost all of them Roman Catholics, participated in the destruction of one of the most holy monastic sites in Christendom.

When Hitler invaded Russia and nearly captured its two principal cities, Stalin, desperate, entered into an agreement with General Sikorski, head of the Polish government-in-exile in London. Stalin would liberate the Poles in Soviet captivity in order that they might join a Polish army being organized under General Anders in Persia. This was the amnesty that liberated Gliksman and many thousands of others who were destined to become a hard core of anti-Soviet witness and propaganda in the West. As the army began to form, a mystery immediately presented itself. Where was the officer corps—roughly thirty thousand strong—that was last seen in several Russian internment camps in 1940? Stalin himself had promised, on no less than five occasions, that *all* Polish military personnel incarcerated in the camps would be released. Where were all the officers of the Army of Poland?

The answer to that question, as yet known only to the Politburo, a few of the higher officers in the NKVD, and the executioners themselves, was that they had all been murdered, most of them in the Katyn Forest of extreme western Russia in May 1940. Anders made urgent inquiries of the Soviet authorities, who tried various prevarications, most of which boiled down essentially to the suggestion that they must be somewhere in the "East." Joseph Czapski was the Polish officer appointed by Anders to go to look for them. His travels from one unhelpful and sullen NKVD office to another must have been the most macabre wild-goose chase ever recorded, and it *was* recorded, in Czapski's brilliant book *The Inhuman Land*. It was in an allusion to this memoir that Vienney had offered his sarcasm about the high percentage of authorship among Rousset's witnesses.

The invading Germans overran Katyn in the late summer of 1941, but the NKVD had done a fair job of hiding the graves. They would discover the horrible truth only by accident. Early in 1943, a scavenging wolf dug up some human remains. With the spring thaw the Germans began to expose the graves, stupefied by the scope of what they were discovering. For Goebbels, it was a propaganda bonanza beyond the powers of even his vivid imagination. For Stalin, it was a problem to be faced resolutely with a Big Lie. The Germans had of course committed this atrocity themselves! Such skepticism as was manifested by the London Poles, who asked for an independent neutral inquiry by the Red Cross, was made the cause for the indignant Soviet Union to break diplomatic relations. Every bit of forensic evidence confirmed every bit of the known history of the Soviet takeover in eastern Poland, but Churchill and Roosevelt at least paid lip service to the official Soviet line. Long before the first report of the gruesome discovery, Czapski had deduced the truth. In the Cold War period the Katyn massacre, though denied by Communists in all lands, became a most powerful item of anti-Soviet propaganda and a permanent difficulty for successive Polish Communist governments. The Russians finally admitted the truth in 1990. At the time of the Rousset trial in 1950 they were only at the end of the first decade of a five-decade lie.

Czapski had been in the internment camp at the Starobelsk Monastery, from which he had been transferred before the slaughter. It was not a pleasant place, but it was not one of the labor camps of Vorkuta or the Kolyma. He later stated that he was one of only eighty-four of the thousands of officers interned there who got out alive. Czapski had not in fact been in the Gulag, but he was one of the few living Westerners who had ever been in what might be called Gulag Headquarters at Orenburg, south and east beyond Kuibyshev.

Czapski began his testimony with a straightforward, forceful defense of Rousset. He obviously had intended only a very brief statement confirming that what Rousset had said concerning the Soviet Union in his newspaper "appeal" was true, and (here was a dig at Pierre Daix) that anyone at all knowledgeable about the Soviet scene knew the elementary facts about condemnation by NKVD troika. He also said quite explicitly that he was acting in the spirit of the title of Gliksman's book: *Tell the West.* Only as a kind of afterthought did he start to tell about his search for the Katyn victims. All three of the defense principals—Daix, Morgan, and Nordmann—behaved abominably in this episode. In the most insulting language Nordmann accused Czapski of rehashing old Nazi propaganda, of serving the Nazi *Propagandastaffel.* The meaning of this remark was that Czapski was taking the same line the Nazis had taken in attributing the atrocity to the NKVD. It was "a provocation invented by Goebbels . . . in the spring of the year 1943." Czapski replied that on the contrary, he had come to the conclusion quite independently, and had reported his opinion to General Anders back in January 1942.

Pouncing on this as though it were a fatal weakness, the defendant Daix challenged Czapski to explain himself. Czapski answered quite calmly what he had reported to Anders: that he knew for a fact that the Polish officers had been slaughtered by the Russians in May and June of 1940. The animated outrage from the defense bench may have been strategic, but it was more probably spontaneous. In any event, there were disruptive howls of uproar. The behavior on the defense bench became so outrageous that Judge Colomiès, after issuing two warnings, and once again expelling Claude Morgan from the room, called another "cooling-off" recess. When things calmed down and the hearing began again, the judge, apparently considering Czapski's testimony complete, did not recall him to the stand. Thus it was that the West's only expert on the Katyn massacre gave no evidence about it beyond his summary findings. That was probably a missed opportunity. The Rousset trial had such an impact that it is conceivable that Czapski's fuller story, known only to readers of *The Inhuman Land*, might have accelerated the snail's pace at which Western historians of a certain political drift came to write about this monstrous crime.

"El Campesino" was the nom de guerre of Valentin González, one of the three Communist general officers in the Spanish Civil War. The name means "the Peasant," and he was indeed a poor worker from Estremadura, one of the poorest parts of Spain, and exactly the kind of authentic proletarian beloved of Communist propagandists. While there can be no doubt of his abilities or his courage, "El Campesino"—as opposed, perhaps, to General González—had been in large measure a propaganda invention of the left-wing press. He was the male counterpart to Dolores Ibárruri, "La Pasionaria," with whom he was destined later to have difficulties in Moscow. The newspapers had made of him a kind of Sergeant York of the Jarama front. The lawyer Rosenthal, who probably had the best sense of drama on the plaintiff's team, introduced him with the muffled drums of portentousness. He was about to present a witness who would not testify in the fashion of earlier witnesses—not in the fashion of the "Jewish philosopher Margolin" or the "Polish sociologist" Gliksman or the "fragile" Elinor Lipper. These people had testified with a calm composure that contrasted with the content of their testimony. El Campesino would testify with . . . and here Rosenthal paused, as though searching for the *mot juste*, which, while he paused, was supplied by a shout from the audience: *avec haine*! Rosenthal confirmed this, yes, "possibly with *hate*."

One tires of using the phrase "tragic fate" of this or that group of disillusioned Communists. There were tragic fates enow. Even so, the history of the Spanish Communist refugees in Russia has its particular poignancy. At the time of Franco's rebellion, the Spanish Communist Party was tiny. It grew dramatically, of course, but the Spanish Communists were native converts who lacked the two decades of acculturation and bureaucratization of "real" Communists—that is, Soviet ones. Following their defeat, six thousand of them removed to Russia, where most of them had grave difficulties, often of a fatal kind. A small clique of hard-core Stalinists, including the "Pasionaria," seemed to thrive on naked totalitarianism, but according to El Campesino, by the time he got away in 1948, there were barely 1,200 left, including the new generation of offspring.

At this point M. Claude Morgan shouted: "Liar!" El Campesino continued. Morgan interrupted again: "The trial of the Soviet Union conducted by a Spanish Kravchenko! . . . Here's a parade of a whole gang of bandits, of traitors, who have come to conduct a trial of a great allied nation. . . ." Indeed, it did seem that suddenly, in its tone, the proceedings had reverted to the style of the Kravchenko trial. But this time there was a judge of sterner stuff. He called a brief recess. When Morgan continued to fulminate, Judge Colomiès threw him out of the courtroom. Things were not going well for the Comrades.

El Campesino's story is among the most horrendous in the Gulag literature. He arrived in Moscow a supposed hero of the Communist military. Almost immediately his mild independence of mind got him in trouble. It was more hateful to Stalin's Spanish toadies—with "La Pasionaria" at their head—than to the NKVD itself. The war was on, but he was refused permission either to fight in the Red Army or to leave for one of the Western armies. Though technically free, he was put to forced labor building the Moscow subway. With two young compatriots he effected a nearly impossible escape, on foot, to Persia. But he was recaptured in Tehran, where the NKVD operated with impunity. He was returned to Russia. He went through all the usual tortures of NKVD administrative justice, though to a degree unusual in its severity and grotesquerie. He was sent to Vorkuta— along with Kolyma, the worst of the Siberian camp complexes. There he nearly worked himself to death as a Stakhanovite in the coal mines. A second, nearly successful escape attempt led to a nearly terminal reincarceration in central Asia. In the great Ashkhabad earthquake of 1948, he was by providence or cosmic caprice one of the few survivors in a camp where the entire records department, together with its personnel, was wiped out.

He was able to gain release, and on a third attempt to get to the West via Persia he succeeded.

El Campesino was a rough soldier, and he described brutality brutally. In most of the camps a small minority of hard-core criminals—murderers, rapists, armed robbers, united in their depravity and their bond of thieves' honor—exercised an internal reign of terror over the much larger population of "politicals." They sometimes shared with the guards, who themselves were often recruited criminals, the *de facto* right to rape any woman zek of their temporary fancy. Anticipating Solzhenitsyn, El Campesino had undertaken large oral research among the ever-changing populations in his various jails and camps, and had created a map of the prison world within a prison world that was the Soviet Gulag regime. His testimony was horrible, and it concerned very recent events. He had hardly been in freedom for a year when he answered Rousset's invitation.

Once again, prerequisite to understanding the impact of this testimony is an appreciation of the place of the Spanish Civil War in the political consciousness of midcentury Europe. That war had been a contest between good and evil in their purest and most unambiguous forms. The cause of the Spanish Republic was one that united the entire left, and against which only Fascists could contend. According to Communist mythology, the Soviet Union had been the unflagging friend of the Republic, and the Party the military heart of the struggle. Several books, most famously Orwell's *Homage to Catalonia*, had already exposed some of the Communist iniquities in Spain. But here was the most famous Communist general of the war overtly asserting that the Communists had done their best to shatter the alliance of the Popular Front, that it "had established a reign of crime and terror in the Republican zone, both at the front and behind it," that the Party had proved itself incompetent to arm or feed the Spanish population or conduct its war. El Campesino said from the witness chair that Soviet Communism was merely "fascism with a red flag." He said he would prefer ten years of incarceration in France to five years of freedom in Moscow. All this came from the mouth of a man every socialist, indeed every liberal, had regarded as one of the heroes of our age.

From its distant observation post the Soviet Foreign Ministry rushed to the aid of *Les Lettres françaises* by sending a telegram addressed to the judge and defense attorneys offering its own assessment of the character of El Campesino. Though not quite so long as Kennan's famous Long

Telegram, this one was sufficiently long—printing out at about five feet—to express the Soviet opinion in some detail. El Campesino was both a political and a moral monster. He was a disciple of Hitler and a Falangist. Numerous depositions from laborers who had worked under his foreman's lash on the Moscow subway dig attested to his cruelty and brutality. He beat his wife, and stole his little girl's clothes. His personal life was one of "orgies and endless scandal." This sizzling scroll, which had the tenor of the Book of Jeremiah and was nearly as long, was a source of merriment in the non-Communist press.

Margarete Buber-Neumann had been so effective at the Kravchenko trial that Rousset was eager to get her to return. She did so with something akin to pleasure. Once again, and this time with a focused precision, she categorized in moral equivalency the Hitler and Stalinist regimes. This was what El Campesino had just done, and this time the Communists were unable to produce colleagues and contempories to refute her. Nearly the entire community of German émigrés in Moscow had been killed or had died in Russian or German camps. Still, as recently as 1947, a number of eminent American academics had signed a public statement attacking "the fantastic lie that the U.S.S.R. and the totalitarian states are basically alike."

The seventh day of the trial began with Nordmann's calling as a witness Jean Laffitte. This Laffitte was a Communist Party apparatchik who headed a front called the *Combattants de la paix*—"warriors for peace," so to speak. He was principally a character witness on behalf of the writer Pierre Daix, and he was able to give an impressive account of Daix's history as a patriot, a resistant, and prisoner in a German concentration camp. None of this was new, and none of it was relevant to the actual issue—that is, whether Daix's article constituted a libel. Théo Bernard was handling the questions for the plaintiff with this witness. He started down a hypothetical line. He understood that Laffitte did not believe that there were concentration camps in the Soviet Union. But *if there were* such camps, then would he agree that they should be condemned?

LAFFITTE: That is to put the problem back to front . . .
BERNARD: But it's the question I am asking you.
LAFFITTE: Personally, I repeat to you, that from what I have seen and what I know I am entirely convinced that such camps do

not exist, and that all that stuff is nothing but a tissue of lies. I believe that is clear.

BERNARD: It's very clear, but you haven't answered my question. I well understand that you do not believe in them. But I don't think you have been, for example, to Kolyma. If in Kolyma there exist camps such as those that have been described to us—which I don't know either—if that were true, would you agree to condemn them?

LAFFITTE: If you were to ask me, "If your mother were a murderer, would you condemn her?," I would answer you: "Sir, my mother is my mother, and will not be a murderer!"

This response pretty well brought the house down. Pomposity is never a good rhetorical strategy. Pomposity instantly deflated by spontaneous laughter is a rhetorical disaster. For years following, the phrase "the mother of Jean Laffitte" or simply "Laffitte's Mommy" was in current use among liberal wits as a reference to Communism, the French Communist Party, or, occasionally, Stalin himself.

The decision was for the plaintiff. And as the plaintiff was not a Soviet turncoat living in America, but a native-born Frenchman and a hero of the non-Communist left, this time the damages were significant. Judge Colombiès awarded 100,000 francs to David Rousset personally and ordered the defendants, upon pain of further significant fines, to publish an explicit apology prominently in the pages of *Les Lettres françaises*.

I CHOSE JUSTICE

Victor Kravchenko walked out of the Salle de Justice the winner of a symbolic civil action against an impecunious literary publication, an international celebrity, and the basest villain in the history of Soviet Communism since the recently hanged General Vlasov and before the soon-to-be demonized Marshal Tito.

It is improbable that Russian agents would have made an attempt on Kravchenko's life. The fallout of Gouzenko's revelations severely disrupted the whole Soviet espionage apparatus throughout North America, and a very great deal had changed since the days of Krivitsky, when a

Russian agent could virtually taunt him on American soil. An assassination attempt, successful or not, would have been pointless if not counter-indicated, and of course extremely risky. Kravchenko was no Trotsky, the center of a movement or cause, real or imagined. Such exemplarism as might reside in his punishment was slight, its propaganda risks enormous. But neither Kravchenko nor the FBI knew that or could be certain of it, and at the very least Kravchenko needed protection against the harassment of the domestic comrades who, though rapidly declining in numbers, still did exist.

The commercial success of *I Chose Freedom* was deeply gratifying to author and publisher alike. Even before he had finished writing it, Kravchenko was trying, with the active encouragement of Max Eastman, to sell Scribner's on a rather vague plan for a book about Stalinist tyranny. He now proposed a different and more logical sequel, a book about his Parisian adventures in vindicating his autobiography. This book, obviously, would be called *I Chose Justice*. Max Perkins, alas, was now dead, but others at Scribner's were welcoming to the idea. One problem presented itself: who would be the Eugene Lyons of *I Chose Justice*? For Kravchenko had already made it clear that that person could not be Eugene Lyons himself. As for Lyons, he refused to be fired. In his mind it was he who had fired Kravchenko. The question was never formally raised. As the scene of the new book would be Paris, it was desirable to find for Kravchenko a literary tutor with some French experience.

There was among the Scribner's authorial alumni a man named Waverly Root, who had recently published a remarkable, enormous, and now unjustly neglected history of World War II called *The Secret History of the War*. Root was an old newspaperman who had spent much of his youth in Paris as the correspondent for major American newspapers. Much later he wrote a charming memoir about life in Paris in the 1920s in which he claimed the distinction of being the only person in the city who never met Hemingway. He published books on Wagner and on gastronomy, if one is allowed the semantic distinction. The sales of the triple-decker *Secret History of the War* hardly repaid the enormous labor that must have gone into its writing, however, and Root was now living in modest circumstances among dairy cows and pullets deep in the country in Vermont.

He could use the money, and he told Scribner's that he would be willing to consider the job provided that Kravchenko was willing to fork out $100 up front to pay for his travel to New York for a consultation. It was not easy for him to get away. He had to arrange for someone to feed the chickens. The $100 was not an advance or a loan, but a business expense and, perhaps, a test of Kravchenko's seriousness. If he was expecting Kravchenko to balk, as his letter seems to suggest, he was in for a surprise. Kravchenko responded with alacrity, and an initial meeting was sufficiently promising for the men to enter into an agreement.

Kravchenko was prepared to be generous, but on a piecework basis. He probably hoped (unrealistically) that the new book might equal *I Chose Freedom* in success, and he was not willing again to sign away in advance a percentage of the royalties. It is unlikely that Root ever learned of Lyons's sweet deal, and in his current circumstances a few thousand dollars, though it would feed a lot of chickens, was not chicken feed. Root's task was, of course, considerably easier than Lyons's. The subject matter was finite and contained—a dramatic episode in a man's life rather than the life itself. Kravchenko had by now a considerably improved command of English. He had also learned something about writing, though not enough to relieve Root of the difficult task of imposing a coherent narrative upon the materials that Kravchenko brought to him in seemingly random order. The resulting book, though useful commentary on Kravchenko's character and motives, achieved nothing like the success of its predecessor. Kravchenko subsequently wrote an article or two, but he was not destined to be a professional writer.

KRAVCHENKO'S END

The ripples from Kravchenko's book gradually subsided in volume and force; and when the water was again still for a moment, the man quickly faded from the American public consciousness. Living as he did a withdrawn and disguised life, with a furtive intermittent and weird family life, he never really put down roots in the United States. As the Cold War rapidly intensified, he became more and more Yesterday's Man. The year 1948 came and went with its own major events: the Hiss case; the fizzle of the presidential candidacy of Henry Wallace and his supporters in an imagined popular front; the heretical independence of Marshal Tito of Yugoslavia. Senator McCarthy came and went. Joseph Stalin died. There was the Korean War, the workers' revolt in East Germany, the abortive Hungarian Revolution. The number of Soviet defectors grew to platoon size, and only the most recent defector was in the news. Soon World War II seemed a long time ago.

Kravchenko did not seek publicity, but he did seek existential meaning. He had been an engineer and a metallurgist, so that the last venture of his life, while amazing, is not without its logic. He invested heavily in mining operations in South America. The investment began with the commitment of his money, but it did not end there. He became involved in the execution of the actual mining operations. He had to some degree in his youth mastered the semicriminality of socialist industry. The semicriminality of industrial life in Peru, where bribes and kickbacks might appear as lines in operating budgets, defeated him. Kravchenko got in way over his head.

To the headaches of business ruin were added dramatic health problems. He had never done much to maintain his body, but he had done much to degrade it. In particular, he was a chronic heavy smoker. Already by the time he was fifty he was beginning to suffer from emphysema; by the time he was sixty, his lungs were as ruined as his business prospects. He was greatly distressed by the world situation, and in particular by the American prosecution of the war in Vietnam. He continued to fear the world triumph of Bolshevism. From our retrospective viewpoint today, that worry will seem unfounded. From the prospective viewpoint of the early 1960s, it was considerably more plausible.

In *I Chose Freedom*, Kravchenko several times mentions feelings of despair that led him to ponder his own self-destruction. Now he was a prematurely old man, terminally ill, financially ruined. His life was a tangle of masquerades, secrets, and pseudonyms. He had no religious faith and practically no family intimacy. On February 25, 1966, Victor Kravchenko, alone in his apartment, killed himself by a gunshot to the head.

Of the several stock photos widely circulated during the Hiss affair, this portrait of Whittaker Chambers was popular with his supporters and detractors alike. The double-chinned, jowly face with its glance askance invited two adjectives that became canonical in journalistic accounts of Chambers: "pudgy" and "shifty-eyed."

 FINAL ★★

U. S. Weather Forecast
SUNNY—MILDER
(Details on Page 2)
Week's Weather Chart
on Page 58

Sunday ⚛ Mirror

 FINAL ★★

Vol. 19. No. 4.   NEW YORK 17, N. Y., SUNDAY, JANUARY 22, 1950   C 112 PAGES   Including 20-Page Magazine, 16-Page Comic Section and a 16-Page Metropolitan Section.

HISS GUILTY!

Faces 10 Yrs., $4,000 Fine on Perjury Counts

The actual issue in the two trials of Alger Hiss—a charge of perjury—was from the start overwhelmed by a larger cultural allegory. The trials were followed avidly by partisan audiences who often saw in them, depending upon their political view, either the tip of a vast iceberg of Communist conspiracy among New Deal elites, or the reckless and demagogic persecution of a simon-pure liberal. The New York *Sunday Mirror* of January 22, 1950, suggested its point of view with its largest type font.

WITNESS

Perhaps the greatest American masterpiece of literary anti-Communism is Whittaker Chambers's *Witness*, which appeared in 1952. The book's power derives from many internal energies, but its impact on American public opinion can be accounted for chiefly by two facts. By the time the book appeared, the Cold War had emerged in a settled shape. Most people had long since made up their minds about the Soviet Union, and needed now to make up their minds not about Soviet perfidy but about which Americans had aided that perfidy, and how. Koestler, Valtin, and Kravchenko wrote from a European point of view about European matters. Chambers wrote not just against Communism generally but against American Communists. Furthermore, his book was from even before the moment of its publication widely regarded as a continuation of the controversial role he had played in the Hiss affair. Two audiences awaited *Witness*: a large public scandalized by Alger Hiss's treason; and a small army of elite reviewers who either actually believed in Hiss's innocence, or could regard such technical guilt as he might bear as venial when compared with the mortal sin of the means of his exposure.

Whittaker Chambers came to public prominence through the agency of Richard Nixon, and their names will be linked through history. Nixon said of his friend Chambers that "he was probably the greatest writer of this century." Another president, Ronald Reagan, at the ceremony at which he awarded Chambers a posthumous presidential Medal of Freedom, said: "As long as humanity speaks of virtue and dreams of freedom, the life and writings of Whittaker Chambers will ennoble and inspire." It is unlikely that the reputation of any writer could survive such a critical assault. Chambers has paid the price. His remarkable book *Witness*, which by any just canon of literary history should claim its place within the great tradition of American autobiography, now lives in ignominy in mainly unvisited bibliographies of undergraduate courses on the Cold War.

In fact, it would be wrong to limit the field of comparison to American letters. Chambers might seem provincial when compared with a Koestler or a Krebs, but he was a genuine internationalist who worked for an international criminal conspiracy. Many people who worked with him in his conspiratorial work, including for a time Alger Hiss, thought he was a European. At least four classics of European autobiography have left formal traces on his own book: the two very different *Confessions* of Augustine and of Rousseau; Goethe's *Wahrheit und Dichtung*; and Newman's *Apologia pro vita sua*. Simply from the artistic point of view, *Witness* is worthy to be mentioned in their company.

The sophistication of the enterprise begins with his title. The word "witness" is a double entendre, a word with a double valence, one positive, one negative. In the "Letter to My Children" with which the book begins, Chambers attempts to answer their supposed question, "What was my father?" His answer: "I was a witness. I do not mean a witness for the Government or against Alger Hiss and the others. . . . A man is not primarily a witness *against* something. That is only incidental to the fact that he is a witness *for* something. A witness, in the sense that I am using the word, is a man whose life and faith are so completely one that when the challenge comes to step out and testify for his faith, he does so, disregarding all risks, accepting all consequences." (p. 5) This almost certainly is an homage to the most famous of all one-word autobiographies, the *Confessions* of Saint Augustine, with its very conscious exploitation of two senses of Latin *confiteor*—to confess a sin, to confess the greatness of God. There are dozens of such literary finesses in Chambers's book.

Sam Tanenhaus, whose excellent biography of Chambers (1997) is alone among a growing library of "Hiss-Chambers books" to pay serious attention to Chambers's qualities as a writer of literary prose, briefly noted also some literary complexities of the passage with which the book proper opens (the "Letter to My Children" is a sort of General Prologue). "In 1937, I began, like Lazarus, the impossible return. I began to break away from Communism and climb from deep within the underground where for six years I had been buried, back into the world of free men. . . . [A] title of an Ibsen play I have never read [*When We Dead Awaken*] somehow caught and summed up for me the feelings that I could not find any other words to express—fears, uncertainties, self-doubts, cowardices, flinchings of the will—natural to any man who undertakes to reverse in mid-course the journey of his life. At the same time I felt a surging release and a sense of freedom, like a man who bursts at last gasp out of a drowning sea." (p. 25)

Chambers is like Lazarus called forth from his tomb by Jesus (John 11:43); he is also like Jonah cast forth from the sea. The specific pattern of imagery, however, suggests that he "is" Jonah in the sense that Jesus used the "sign of Jonah" (Matthew 12:39–40), where Jonah in the belly of the fish is like Jesus himself, buried in "the heart of the earth"—in the "underground," indeed—before his Resurrection. Jonah was cast into the sea in order to save his shipmates; hence the "sign of Jonah" invokes the very ideas of propitiation, penance, expiation, and renewal that are the religious center of *Witness*. Jesus uses that expiatory "burial" in the sea as an emblem of his own death and Resurrection.

The middle term that links and clarifies two biblical images is Dante's *Divine Comedy*, that most famous of all stories of a "man who undertakes to reverse in mid-course the journey of his life." From the beginning of the *Commedia*, Chambers takes not merely the image of the fearful narrator: fearful both in the dreadfulness of a moral situation and in the magnitude of the work of narration to be achieved—*che nel pensier rinova la paura*, the mere thinking about it renews his fear. He takes also the narrator's situation. For the first months of 1937, Whittaker Chambers, born in 1901, was thirty-five years old, as was Dante when, at least for purposes of exemplary fiction, he wrote the first line of the *Divine Comedy*: *Nel mezzo del camin di nostra vita* (in the middle of the road of our life).* There is almost certainly a further, more local association. The publication of Lionel Trilling's novel *The Middle of the Journey* was one of the major intellectual events of 1947. Its subject is the dilemma of the political progressive with regard to the claims of Communism. The book's central character, Gifford Maxim, is a tormented apostate from the American Communist Party. Years later, after Chambers was dead, Trilling wrote in a preface to a re-edition of the novel that Gifford Maxim was based on Whittaker Chambers, an acquaintance

---

* This midpoint is of course biblical: "The days of our years are threescore years and ten . . ." (Psalms 90:10). Dante was born in 1265. The fictive date of the action of his poem is 1300. Hence the poet-pilgrim, thirty-five years old, would literally as well as allegorically be "in the middle of the journey of our life."

of the author's since college days, thus announcing to the world what many people in New York intellectual circles had known all along. Certainly Chambers knew, and for him the phrase "middle of the journey" would necessarily have a political as well as a moral valence.

So we have here writing that makes serious demands upon a reader. Yet one will search in vain in the contemporary reviews of *Witness* for an adequate acknowledgment of the depth of Chambers's own literary learning. His autobiography, whatever else it may be, is the very emblem of a liberally educated mind. He repeatedly engages the classical literary tradition in an easy, unforced manner so very different from the Bartlett-ransacking of political speechwriters with which we have become familiar. His conscious "intertexuality"—or artistic use of literary allusion, as we used to call it—would merit an extended essay, and deserves at least cursory notice here.

The general epigraph for his whole book he takes from the opening scene of *Hamlet*, and it signals an intention no less clearly than did Koestler's epigraphs from Machiavelli and from Dostoyevsky:

> *If thou art privy to thy country's fate,*
> *Which, happily, foreknowing may avoid,*
> *O speak!*

The obvious relevance of these lines is to Chambers's chosen role of whistle-blower. He writes to alert his fellow citizens of an intended fate to which he is privy. To those who know its etymology, as Chambers obviously did, "privy" conveys the idea of a secret knowledge known to few. But the obvious is only the beginning of the passage's appositeness. The speaker here is Horatio, the "thou" addressed by the ghost of Hamlet's murdered father. The vision of this apparition has terrified the night watch, who have invited the skeptical Horatio to be a witness. When the ghost appears, Marcellus says to Horatio: "Thou art a scholar; speak to it, Horatio"—an odd remark, requiring some consideration of Renaissance attitudes to the authority of ghosts. It is also useful to remember when revisiting, as we later must, Chambers's remarkable essay called "Ghosts on the Roof." What Shakespeare's ghost has to reveal is nothing less than the rottenness in the state. Chambers suggests that he was both the ghost and the witness to the ghost, the revealer of the foulest political treachery imaginable, the one who is both its victim and its avenger. And at the end of the tragedy—a word Chambers repeatedly uses—he is left like Horatio, to absent himself from felicity awhile, and in this harsh world draw his breath in pain, to tell the story.

The body of Chambers's text is tautly laced with significant poetic allusions. He frequently pays silent homage to classic texts, English and Continental, especially German. Following his departure from Columbia, Chambers and friends traveled to Germany in 1923. He mastered its language to a sufficient degree to earn a meager living later as a translator for the English-language press. (*Bambi* was his one great best-seller.) He could and did read Marx in German, a feat few American radicals could claim. German was the shared language of the international Communist movement, and his speaking proficiency was undoubtedly one of the talents that made him attractive to Comintern recruiters. Some important episodes of *Witness* report conversations held in German, including his late night seminar with Walter Krivitsky. Germany in the early 1920s was the expected arena of Communist revolution, and 1923 is often identified as the culminating year of a premature revolutionary process that had begun in 1917. Chambers would have returned from Europe only a month before the doomed—or perhaps betrayed—Communist uprising in Hamburg in late October 1923 so vividly described by Jan Valtin in his early chapter "Scapegoats on the Barricades."

Although Victor Navasky and others have made heavy weather of the different dates Chambers gave for his break with the Communist Party, his own narrative makes clear that the "break" was not a single definitive event but a continuing process—as it was also with Krebs, Kravchenko, Koestler, and probably every other Communist who became an ex-Communist—one punctuation point of which took place when "in 1935 or 1936 I chanced to read in the press a little item of some nine or ten lines": the report of the execution of a Red Army general, Dmitri Schmidt, of whom he had never before heard. To Chambers this meant Purge, and Purge meant that "the Communist Party of the Soviet Union had begun to condition itself for the final revolutionary struggle with the rest of the world" and "was literally sweating blood." (p. 76)

For many Americans the most famous association of Whittaker Chambers, and perhaps indeed the only one they know of, is his role as an accuser of Alger Hiss. We shall soon review the fundamental facts of the "Hiss affair," but for the moment let us follow the rhythm of *Witness* and accept its authorial point of view. By the late thirties Chambers, who had been an underground Soviet espionage agent for several years, began, as he says, to "reverse course." He repented of his spying and began a gradual process of breaking with Communism altogether. At a late stage of this "break," Chambers tells us, he made unannounced visits, over a period of time, to four of his alleged criminal co-conspirators—Harry Dexter White, Julian Wadleigh, Abraham George Silverman, and Alger Hiss—with the aim of persuading them, or frightening them, into breaking with the Party or at least giving up their espionage. The last visit was to Alger Hiss, his only reported close friend among the four, just before Christmas 1938.

The visit was a disaster from the point of view of its stated aim. The only thing that got broken was the friendship between the two men. "I had never liked Harry White. I had no particular feeling, one way or the other, about Wadleigh. Silverman was merely a curious co-worker. But Alger Hiss and his wife I had come to regard as friends as close as a man ever makes in his life. By *unnumbered little acts of kindness and affection*, by the *pleasure* [italics added], freely expressed, which they took simply in being together with my wife and me, they had given us every reason to believe that their feeling for us was of the same kind as our feeling for them." (p. 70) I join Chambers's critics in suspecting this passage of exaggeration—or of blindness. The Hisses and the Chamberses knew each other far too well for Alger Hiss to prevail in his bold perjuries; but if these were indeed "friends as close as a man ever makes in his life," that life must have been a lonely one. And in fact it is obvious that Chambers is here appropriating language from Wordsworth in his "Tintern Abbey," where the poet tells us that

> *oft in lonely rooms, and 'mid the din*
> *Of towns and cities, I have owed to them*
> *In hours of weariness . . .*
> *feelings, too,*
> *Of* unremembered pleasure: *such, perhaps,*
> *As have no slight or trivial influence*
> *On that best portion of a good man's life,*
> *His little, nameless, unremembered, acts*
> *Of kindness and of love.*

Chambers then—perhaps not by way of quotation so much as by an association of ideas in a highly literary mind—picks up Wordsworth's "lonely rooms . . . towns and cities" in his gloomy account of the immediate postlude of the break. "What lonely trips men make. That night ride from Washington back to Baltimore was one of the loneliest I shall ever make." (p. 73)

At his final dinner with the Hisses, Chambers tells us, they were joined by Priscilla Hiss's young son, Timothy Hobson. "Timmie was delighted to see me." Speaking of unremembered acts, at a recent scholarly conference concerning Alger Hiss, Dr. Timothy Hobson, then twelve and now 82 years of age, affirmed with no ambiguity that neither on that night nor on any other of his life had he ever laid eyes on Whittaker Chambers. Chambers left Alger Hiss, having failed to dent his Communist commitment, with the self-pitying remark that he expected a "bleak" Christmas. "But Christmas, 1938, was not bleak," he writes. That was because he found a new comfort in his family life, and a nascent sense of joy in the Christmas "story," which "for the first time in our lives, I tried to tell my children."

> *Noël! Noël*
> *Christ is born in Bethlehem.* (p. 75)

This garbled snatch of a carol looks quite odd on Chambers's page, but it plays off, with perfect thematic decorum, against one of his favorite German texts. The first earthly scene of Goethe's *Faust*, in which the great scholar bitterly acknowledges the uselessness of his life's quest, is called simply "Night." It is a long nocturnal soliloquy interrupted by the appearance of a spirit or apparition (as at the beginning of *Hamlet*) and a visitation from the cynical Wagner. At its end Faust has finally determined upon self-murder. Indeed the cup of poison is at his lips when he hears a choir of angels singing an Easter hymn:

> *"Now is Christ arisen . . ."*
> *I hear the message clearly indeed, but I lack only faith . . .*
> *and still this hymn, known to me from childhood,*
> *again now calls me back to life!*

It is hardly possible to read what I will call the first "movement" of *Witness* without realizing that it is introducing a large *religious* drama of which the principal themes are conversion, penitence, and resurrection. That these themes have so seldom been discussed in the "scholarship" is perhaps to be explained by the fact that the book's first readers were predisposed by historical circumstance to seek to the exclusion of all else a secondary *political* drama.

A BRIEF HISTORY OF A CRISIS

Whittaker Chambers (1901–1962) was an American journalist. From 1924 to 1937 or 1938 he was a member of the American Communist Party. He worked for a time on the principal Communist journals in New York before being recruited, around 1932, to go "underground" as a secret agent and liaison between a supervisor in a Soviet intelligence agency and a group of American Communists who were using their positions as government officials in Washington to purloin confidential materials to which they had or could gain access. It is in the nature of covert operations to be covert, and we know very little more about him during those years than he chooses to reveal in his autobiography, which we may suspect of selectivity. He left the Communist Party in either 1937 or 1938. By 1939 he was becoming fairly prominent in the public sphere as a journalist, and in that year he made his first attempt, somewhat oblique but externally documented, to warn government officials about the dangers of Communist infiltration in Washington. Beginning in that same year the world war began, a war that monopolized the nation's whole attention and energies between 1941 and 1945. He first testified against Alger Hiss in 1948. He published *Witness* in 1952.

That is the sketchiest of chronologies. To understand the emergence of the American anti-Communist consensus, it is necessary to review what happened in the decade between 1938 and 1948, the decade of World War II and the birth of the Cold War. In the Western democracies, the enormous effort of World War II had raised great hopes among political liberals. The war had defeated Fascism, which had so long been regarded as the world's primary political ill that few people appeared to be able to imagine any other. Domestic reforms long delayed by economic slump and the desperate struggle against Fascism might now be achieved. In Western Europe, socialist and statist political programs were broadly popular. European intellectuals could imagine no future that was not a socialist future. In Britain, a Labour Party victory ejected Churchill and started creating a "welfare state"—a phrase that began as a catchy contrast to "warfare state," warfare by nearly universal consensus being the fruit of "capitalism" and "imperialism." Though their hope was actually illusory, in France the Communists seemed to have a reasonable chance of coming to power by electoral means. The situation in the United States was of course very different for, among other reasons, accidental constitutional and calendrical factors. Still, many hopeful souls looked for the "completion" of the New Deal.

Franklin Roosevelt had been elected for a fourth term in November 1944. By that time it was clear that the war was won, certainly the war in Europe. Even so the president, already dying, was dead before Berlin fell, and Harry Truman became the longest serving lame duck in our history. To the "what ifs" of that history we might add, What if there had been a general election in America in November 1945? But the next general election was in 1948, after a period of three years that were definitive in forming the American anti-Communist consensus.

The year 1948, the year of the Hiss-Chambers drama, was itself a kind of perpetual "Kronstadt" for most Americans, with two major symbolic events preceding the confrontation of the two men in August. On March 10, Jan Masaryk, the Czech foreign minister, either jumped or was thrown to his death in Prague, giving symbolic confirmation to the completion of a Communist coup in Czechoslovakia. Masaryk was America's favorite foreign diplomat, certainly liberal America's favorite. He was American-educated and American-espoused. He was the son of the great martyr of the nation destroyed by those European policies of appeasement that the Allied war had so expensively redeemed. According to him, the "iron curtain" was a phantasm of Winston Churchill's imperialist brain. It was perfectly possible for democratic Czechoslovakia to have friendly relations with the Soviet Union, whose intentions were benign and whose actions honorable when placed in the necessary historical perspective. And then he was dead, splattered on a pavement.

A couple of months later the Soviets, in violation of the most explicit agreements of the conquering Allies, closed off Western access to Berlin.

The American response was the great Berlin Airlift, the success of which was perhaps even more extraordinary in psychological than in materials terms. Most Americans failed to see how the Soviet vetoing of Czechoslovakia's participation in the Marshall Plan or the starvation of the children of Berlin were the actual contributions to world peace so belligerently proclaimed by Gromyko and Vyshinsky in the assembly rooms of the United Nations. As for the United Nations Organization itself, it appeared politically impotent, an arena for the increasingly outrageous oratorical misbehavior of Communists. It was in this context that on August 25 Whittaker Chambers confronted and accused of Communism the man whose greatest civic achievement had been to transport the UN Charter to American soil.

In November 1948, in perhaps the greatest upset in American presidential history, Harry Truman defeated the Republican Thomas Dewey. Far from being a victory for the "left," however, this election actually witnessed the American left's definitive humiliation. For while the two major political parties began their decades-long contest to see who could appear more anti-Communist than the other, the American "left" demonstrated that it was either unwilling or unable to repudiate an American Communist Party abjectly servile to Moscow, minute in its membership but mighty in its mischievousness. Whether Henry Wallace was or was not a "fellow traveler" depends upon one's linguistic metabolism. He was the former vice president of the United States, with the emphasis on former. Roosevelt had dumped him for Truman in 1944. He next became secretary of commerce, from which post Truman later had fired him, noisily, for his pro-Soviet views. In 1948, he became the presidential candidate of the Progressive and American Labor parties.

Wallace was vociferously supported by the American Communist Party, whose infiltration of his campaign and influence on his rhetoric were successful far beyond what its tiny numbers might suggest. He received over a million votes, but still finished in fourth place, trailing even the racist Dixiecrat candidate, Strom Thurmond. Nearly half his votes came from the five boroughs of New York City, and even then did not reach 10 percent of the entire New York vote. (The state went for the Republican Dewey, its governor.) That was the end of the American "left" as a potential electoral force.

This was the historical moment at which Chambers was exposing

Communist spies hidden within the interstices of government agencies. Depending on how one looked at things, Chambers emerged from the episode as one of the most famous or notorious of living Americans. *Witness* thus differed from the other masterworks of anti-Communism in the history of its reception. *Out of the Night* and *I Chose Freedom* burst upon a reading public who had never before heard of their authors. *Darkness at Noon* lay quietly germinating in the political soil of postwar France. But practically everybody in America had followed the "Case," and practically everybody in America knew that Whittaker Chambers and Alger Hiss were writing books about it.

A very great deal has been written about the "Hiss case" or the "Chambers-Hiss affair," and what was already complex has at times been mystified beyond all hope of penetration. Yet its elements are straightforward and easily grasped. Whittaker Chambers was a Russian spy, one of an organized group of American Communists who specialized in stealing, copying, and forwarding to Soviet intelligence agents sensitive documents from various bureaus of the American government. Technically, Chambers was a "courier." His job was to transmit to his superior in Russian intelligence, Colonel Bykov, the illegal gleanings of his fellow Communist conspirators.

The Washington spies, according to Chambers, included Alger Hiss (1904–1996), a lawyer, a New Dealer, and a distinguished civil servant. Chambers underwent a gradual disenchantment with Communism accompanied by a gradual religious conversion. In 1939 he went to work for *Time* magazine, in which organization he eventually rose to the highly remunerated level of senior editor. In that same year, his disgust at the announcement of the Hitler-Stalin Pact led him to go in secrecy to the security authorities to report the presence of Communists in various government agencies. Neither then, nor following interviews with FBI agents in subsequent years, did anyone take action on the basis of his revelations.

In the changed political climate after the war there was a sharp rise in hostility toward the Soviet Union and, in consequence, to Communists and Communism generally. Alger Hiss had risen to a certain prominence. He had been one of the few American diplomats at the Yalta Conference. He had played a leading role in the foundation of the United Nations Organization. The House Committee on Un-American Activities, which had changed its focus from pursuing American Fascists to pursuing American

Communists, was active. A confessed ex-Communist spy named Elizabeth Bentley gave lurid revelations concerning an American spy ring. Whittaker Chambers at long last was called before the committee. He named names, including, conspicuously, the name of Alger Hiss.

Called before the committee in his turn, Alger Hiss denied the allegations. He at first claimed not even to know Whittaker Chambers, then, after a dramatic confrontation with his accuser, said he had known him, slightly, under an alias of George Crosley. He challenged Chambers to make the accusation in an unprotected place. Chambers did so, on national radio, triggering a libel suit. It was for a time touch and go as to which man would be believed and which indicted for perjury. On the whole sentiment was against Chambers, but he and Richard Nixon reversed matters with the dramatic revelation of documents incriminating to Hiss that Chambers had secreted at the house of a relative in New York in 1939. In a wonderful *coup de théâtre* abetted by Nixon and other members of the investigating committee, Chambers had now, after nearly a decade, gone back to New York, fetched the purloined documents, and stored some of them (small canisters of microfilm) in a hollowed-out pumpkin on his Maryland farm. These were the eventually world-famous, if slightly misnamed, Pumpkin Papers. Chambers alleged that the purpose of his bizarre mode of document storage was security, but many of his critics judged it to be the crude melodrama of a publicity stunt.

Hiss continued to proclaim his innocence, vehemently, but his answers to important questions were seriously unsatisfactory. He was indicted for perjury and tried in federal court. A first trial ended in a hung jury, with a third of the jurors not certain of guilt beyond a reasonable doubt. At a second trial Hiss was convicted and sentenced to federal prison. The trials, which were characterized by episodes of high drama, were avidly followed throughout the country. Most of the direct evidence consisted of Chambers's unsupported verbal charges, and Hiss's lawyers attacked him with vigor. But there were also several pieces of physical evidence. One particularly crucial item was an old Woodstock typewriter that had belonged to Priscilla Hiss. Some of the copies of stolen documents had been typed on this machine.

Hiss outlived Chambers by more than thirty years, and during that time he continued to maintain that he had been innocent. He and legal friends drafted elaborate legal briefs in an attempt to have the matter reopened, but no court found sufficient merit in them to act. Although the circle of people debating the Hiss case has diminished greatly over the decades, the whole matter remains to some extent a matter of heated controversy even today—as we shall see.

While Alger Hiss did his time in Lewisburg Penitentiary, Chambers retired to his Maryland farm to write a book that was part *apologia pro vita sua*, part religious meditation, part political history, and part courtroom thriller. It took him much longer to write than he had planned, and it turned out much longer than he had at first intended.

Chambers knew he had a winner when the *Saturday Evening Post* paid $75,000 for serial rights to the book, of which they eventually published ten installments reaching 50,000 words. When the first "teaser" installment of *Witness* was published at the beginning of February 1952, newsstand sales were more than 100,000 above the weekly average. Normal circulation for the magazine was in excess of 3 million. Then the publishers, too, knew they had a winner. *Time* magazine found it significant that for the first time in its history, the *Post* eschewed a pictorial cover in favor of a purely typographic display proclaiming *Witness* one of the great books of the century.

Sam Tanenhaus draws attention to the possibly symbolic fact that Chambers's words bumped into the next week Norman Rockwell's rendition of three despondent cheerleaders whose team has just lost a close basketball game. It was as though Chambers's words now joined Rockwell's pictures in American popular iconography. In another place Tanenhaus notes the irony of the later exaltation of Whittaker Chambers as an "all American" hero for having written a book so deeply indebted to European literary models. Yet to the extent that "ordinary Americans" read books at all, a very large numbers of ordinary Americans read all or parts of *Witness*. The larger number who read only the *Saturday Evening Post*'s selections would of course have a very clear sense of the religious themes of the book, which stand out more articulately when unaccompanied by so much legal transcription.

Thus, a former government official was convicted of perjury partly on the basis of the testimony of an ex-Communist journalist. That was the "Hiss affair," or might have been if it could have avoided the instant allegorization that its principals, its seconds, and most of its national observers discovered therein. Of course, some of the allegories discovered beneath the historical sense claim our attention. The first was based in the superficial dramatic contrast presented by two men who actually had a great deal in common. Alger Hiss was trim, handsome, well dressed, well groomed, a kind of model of understated good taste and professional efficiency. Whittaker Chambers was fat and sloppy. If there were clothes that fit or suited him, he had yet to discover them. Hiss had good teeth—the dental allegory loomed large—whereas Chambers's decayed mouth was held together only by metal lavishly but tardily applied. Hiss had impeccable academic credentials—Johns Hopkins, Harvard Law. Chambers was a Columbia drop-out, an intellectual drifter, an autodidact. Hiss's professional career began brilliantly when he clerked for Oliver Wendell Holmes, perhaps still the most famous jurist in American history, and continued on track through private law practice to distinguished government service. Wherever he went, he formed a circle of admiring professional colleagues. Chambers had few social skills and fewer friends with whom he might practice them. He had considerable writing skill, but no real writing career. For several years in his and the century's thirties, years during which he might have been "establishing himself," he had lived a semiclandestine life under a series of assumed names. By 1948, he had indeed achieved professional success as a senior writer for a mass market newsmagazine where, however, he was a controversial and polarizing colleague thought by many to be arrogant, cranky, reclusive, and dictatorial.

The theatrical casting, as Arthur Koestler pointed out, was all wrong. History had violated the fundamental principle of the white hat and the black hat with a recklessness that would never pass a Hollywood screening room. When the beauty contest became a writing contest, Chambers would win hands-down, but only after a certain battering. By the completion of the second trial, ending in Hiss's conviction, most of America was convinced that Hiss was a liar and a spy. Yet among an influential segment of the liberal establishment, including the press, whatever Hiss might have done (even assuming that he might in fact have "done" something, which many still denied) paled in comparison with the poltroonery of the "moral leper" and "informer," Whittaker Chambers. The great newspapers have files of periodically updated obituaries of famous people just awaiting their deaths. Now they were ready with reviews of Chambers's book, some of which, at least, differed in their intention from obituaries but slightly, awaiting only the addition of some superficial mention of the book's contents. This is to say that *Witness* entered a world in which opinion was already hopelessly divided, and in which most minds were already firmly made up.

WITNESS AND ITS EARLY REVIEWERS

In the historical circumstances it was perhaps inevitable that so many of the book's first reviewers thought it was a story about the "Case," whereas in actuality the "Case" merely exemplifies a larger argument. "I think Hiss is innocent . . . ," began Charles Wright, in one of the *contra* essays in the *pro* and *contra* debate sponsored by the *Saturday Review* in May 1952. "Mr. Chambers is the author of one of the longest works of fiction of the year." Fiction was also the principal charge in Merle Miller's hatchet job for *The New Republic.* He was the only critic known to me who proclaimed the book to be poorly written, though that was the least of its sins. Certainly Merle Miller was a qualified expert on the question of biographical fiction, since his own biography of Harry Truman appears to have invented most of the president's more memorable apothegms. He found a grotesque disparity between Chambers's apocalyptic view of Communism and the "tiny" size of the spy ring revealed within the government. Although Miller identified no specific fictional element in the book, he convincingly identified many unconvincing passages. The question of autobiographical truth that bedevils a reading of Valtin's *Out of the Night* is troubling, though in a different way, in *Witness* as well. It is a question that deserves a subtler adjudication than it has received. It is doubtful that *Witness* is less truthful than Rousseau's *Confessions.* Generally speaking, in literary history an author's claim to be ruthless in self-delineation has been the prelude to considerable artifice. To forbid the autobiographer the right of presenting himself in the most positive light would perhaps doom to extinction a most valuable literary genre.

There were at least two reviews from the in-group of the "New York Intellectuals," and they were very different in spirit. In *The Nation*, a journal just then beginning a half century of increasingly quixotic defense of Alger Hiss's innocence, Irving Howe published a scathing review entitled "God, Man, and Stalin." It dismissed without actually engaging the religious theme, which it thus reduced to near travesty: "If Chambers is right in believing the major bulwark against Stalin to be faith in God, then it is time for men of conviction and courage to take to the hills." It might have been pointed out to Mr. Howe, who continued to live in Manhattan, that Chambers, rusticated on a Maryland farm, had long since done that. *The Nation* returned for a second crack at Chambers in the autumn with an essay by John Strachey. Its essence was repeated in Strachey's book *The Strangled Cry*, the chief idea of which has already been adduced in relation to his attack on Koestler. For Strachey, Chambers—even more conspicuously than Koestler—represented the turn away from rationality.

The best review of the book from among the old circle of political radicals—by no means meaning the most favorable or approving review, merely the deepest and fairest—was by Sidney Hook in the *New York Times Book Review*. Hook was formidable within the group of New York Intellectuals for at least three reasons. He was in the first place a professional philosopher who brought an intimidating rigor to political argument in which passion was often the surrogate for persuasiveness. He was also a real Marxist—meaning that he actually had read and thought about the original Marxist sources, developed his own understanding of them, written about them. Finally, he was not merely an absolutely simon-pure anti-Communist intellectual; he was an anti-Communist activist, and one of the leaders of the Congress for Intellectual Freedom. (The annoyance that Hook could inspire in his fellow intellectuals is suggested by a comment tossed off by François Furet in his *Passing of an Illusion*. Furet, who "without apology" spent several years in the French Communist Party during the period of its most slavish Stalinist indenture, criticizes Hook for his "self-righteousness" in priding himself on having avoided doing so.)

Hook's long review of *Witness* for the *New York Times Book Review* was entitled "The Faiths of Whittaker Chambers." Hook was a philosophical agnostic who thought that the God hypothesis was unlikely to be true. He was also a recovered Marxist who fully grasped the cryptoreligious character of 1930s Communism, the opiate of the intellectuals. He thus anticipated the attitudes captured later in the title of an influential book by Jean-François Revel—*Without Marx or Jesus*. Hook took Chambers's religious conversion seriously, but exposed what he thought was Chambers's own shallowness of thought concerning the relationship of Communism and Christianity. Hook, who had been both witness to and victim of the left-wing "groupthink" in New York intellectual circles in the 1930s and

1940s, made two points that would never be entirely forgiven by his fellow New York Intellectuals. First, he asserted that the epic scope of Chambers's book, and its grounding on every page in concrete detail, situation, geography, and personality, practically guaranteed the essential truth of the book's presentation of the Hiss affair. That is, he insisted that the book began with a strong advantage of historical plausibility. More grievous still, perhaps, he identified and affirmed Chambers's courageous and practical intentions. "May [*Witness*] inspire others who until now have feared the wolf-pack of the anti-anti-Communists to come forward to testify to the truth. . . ."

That is a remarkable phrase, "the wolf-pack of the anti-anti-Communists." The idea of such a "wolf-pack" was offensive to many in the 1950s, and its reality has been greatly obscured in the rich historiography of McCarthyism. But the excesses of anti-Communism of the 1950s, while unforgivable, are not entirely inexplicable. There was a widespread belief among leftists that all anti-Communism was illegitimate, because attacks on Stalinism must have either the intended goal or the unintended result of discrediting all progressive thought, socialism, "the workers," or some other target whose privilege was deemed absolute. This point of view, common enough in New York, reigned supreme in Paris. It was repeatedly made explicit in testimony in the Kravchenko lawsuit. Jean-Paul Sartre gave it classic formulation: "Every anti-Communist is a dog." It is hardly surprising that the tone of *Witness* sometimes suggests that of a man pursued through a dark bayou by yapping bloodhounds.

Some of the bloodhounds had actually started sniffing around some years earlier. "Shortly before I began to testify in the Hiss Case," Chambers wrote, "*Time*, in an unusual gesture, reprinted [Chambers's essay] *The Ghosts on the Roof*, to show how uncannily right it had been about foreign affairs at a time when so many had been wrong." This is a boast almost too insufferable to be redeemed even by its essential truth, and it exemplifies perhaps the charge of smarmy smugness or outrageous self-righteousness brought against Chambers by his critics. His remarkable essay was a "fairy tale" in which the ghosts of the murdered Romanovs joined Clio, the Muse of History, atop the roof of the Livadia Palace in Yalta where Stalin was meeting with Churchill and Roosevelt. Clio was trying to get a peep, through a fissure in the war-damaged roof, of the proceedings of the Yalta Conference. With this extraordinary conceit Chambers had tried to dramatize the draconian news blackout, so frustrating to all Western journalists, surrounding the conference to which Alger Hiss had accompanied the dying president. But the real meat of the essay was in the postmodern conversation among Clio and the murdered Tsar and Tsarina, in which two themes were prominent: the continuity in Russian imperial and expansionist policies under the tsars and under Stalin; and Stalin's extraordinary skill in bamboozling Roosevelt into the belief that postwar arrangements in Eastern Europe would actually be ordered on a "democratic" basis.

To anticipate the Cold War reality of late 1948 at the beginning of 1945 perhaps did not require actual clairvoyance, but it did require the courage to offend a prevailing liberal optimism concerning Soviet intentions that approached the status of dogma in right-thinking circles. So great had been the success of what Chambers called the mentality of the Popular Front that to criticize the Soviets fell somewhere between bad manners and potential treason. Very few were the voices like that of Archbishop Curley, who would say in so many words: "We of the United States are fighting side by side with Stalin, the greatest murderer of men the world has ever known . . . the man who murdered the old Bolsheviki, the slayer of millions of his own people, the man who in sheer savagery grinned while 3,000,000 people were dying in the Ukraine for lack of food which he had taken from their mouths." That *Time* would republish "The Ghosts on the Roof" confirms Chambers's claim that he had reversed the magazine's line on Soviet Russia, even as the weasly editorial note that introduced the piece showed that his superiors appreciated the risk they were running. When in *Witness* Chambers rehearses the publication history of his old essay, he summons forth by bibliographical aside another Yalta ghost: Alger Hiss. Chambers would have known the secret significance of its republication.

CHAMBERS AND NIXON

The "political" reading of *Witness* given to it by most of its contemporaries was almost inevitable, and it has set the tone for much recent historical discussion of the Hiss case. Much of this has centered on the relationship, personal and thematic, between Whittaker Chambers and Richard Nixon. For just as Chambers left the field for the obscurity of a self-regulated exile, Richard Nixon went on to become president of the United States, and perhaps the most disgraced politician in American history. Chambers and Nixon became real friends. In *Witness*, Chambers is lavish in his praise of Nixon, and the sentiments are reciprocated in Nixon's own book, *Six Crises* (1962), in which he fully acknowledges the importance of the Hiss case to his life and career. It is useful to bear in mind that at that time nobody, perhaps least of all Nixon himself, could have predicted his extraordinary political resurrection. He had been defeated by Kennedy in 1960. He was defeated in the California gubernatorial race of 1962. That should have spelled the end. By the time he was elected president in 1968, Chambers had been dead for several years, and the political landscape had changed dramatically. It is important not to give Chambers too much credit for the creation of Richard Nixon; but in the light of some recent historical writing it may be even more important not to give Nixon too much credit in creating Whittaker Chambers.

Nixon was a skillful politician. He came by his anti-Communism honestly—meaning by temperamental leaning and intellectual conviction —but he also found it highly congenial and politically effective. Neither Jerry Voorhis, the popular incumbent whom Nixon defeated for a House seat in an upset in 1946, nor Helen Gahagan Douglas, whom he trounced in the 1950 Senate race, was by the wildest stretch of the imagination a Communist. Nixon of course never said they were Communists. The genius of his method was to suggest that they were not sufficiently *not* Communists.

The nature of his smear campaign against Voorhis was highly conventional, a version of the eternal battle of the spunky, righteous, and scrappy local boy against the comfortable Washington insider who has lost touch with real America. Voorhis, used to winning and expecting to win, ran a gentlemanly campaign vulnerable to underdog tactics, especially when the underdog was a pit bull. Even so, Nixon barely won.

Things were very different in the Senate campaign of 1950. The campaign against Douglas—the "Pink Lady"—was far dirtier, and its easy success demonstrates the large increment in popular American anti-Communism in the first five years immediately following the war, a very great deal of which was directly related to the Hiss case. Now to be "pink"—or in Douglas's case "pink down to her underwear"—one didn't have to *do* anything. One simply had to be insufficiently vocal in the denunciation of Communism. Perhaps the most politically costly witticism in American history was Harry Truman's description of the Alger

Hiss affair as a "red herring." Tricky Dick's best trick by far was to hold all Democrats accountable for this rhetorically potent moment of presidential opacity.

In assessing the popular impact of *Witness*, it is necessary to appreciate the political revolution of the year in which it appeared: 1952. The Democrats had been in uninterrupted power for twenty years. Much of the New Deal had been implemented in more or less lasting form. Yet so unpopular had Harry Truman become that he actually lost the New Hampshire primary to the crusading reformer Estes Kefauver, and then withdrew from the field. Adlai Stevenson—selected in the good, old-fashioned way by the machine bosses—was everywhere routed by Eisenhower except in Dixiecrat states, in Kentucky, and in West Virginia.

The degree to which popular anti-Communism played a role in the general election is suggested by the extraordinary performance of Joseph McCarthy in the year 1952. McCarthy's infamous Wheeling speech dated from early 1950. He had by no means as yet finished wreaking havoc, but he was far from being unopposed in the Congress, especially in the Senate that would eventually censure him. He had long since showed his ugly side—if indeed he had a fair one—and he was already under strong attack from liberals and some moderates. Even Dwight Eisenhower had seemed to offer an oblique condemnation of his tactics. McCarthy represented a state, Wisconsin, famous in the history of American liberalism as the home of "Fighting Bob" LaFollette. It was a state with considerable demographic and ethnic variety, and with a strong presence of organized labor.

In the senatorial primary of 1952, Joseph McCarthy faced an able, highly respected, and well-financed Republican rival who made an explicit issue of his (McCarthy's) reckless anti-Communism. And since anyone could vote in the primary, he also faced the opposition of as many Democrats as the CIO and others could turn out against him. Nor did they fail by not trying. In that primary election Joe McCarthy received more than 100,000 votes in excess of the *total combined* vote of all other primary candidates, Democrat and Republican alike. After that, his reelection in the November election, even against a strong and principled Democratic opponent, was a foregone conclusion.

Political scientists and journalists descended on Milwaukee and Madison in the wake of the senator's primary victory. They found that the explanation of his overwhelming victory was no secret. Many people who voted for him didn't much like him personally. Quite a few were uncomfortable with, or even appalled at, his tactics. But there was a very widespread perception that McCarthy was the "only one" or "one of few" who were doing anything about the "problem" of American Communism that loomed so large in the minds of the American electorate. There was, and is, one problem with calling McCarthy's enterprise a "witch-hunt," as was frequently done by Democrats, and has been memorialized permanently in Arthur Miller's great play *The Crucible* (1953). The problem is this: there never were any witches, but there were some Communists. Faced with believing with Truman that there were *no* Communists in government and believing with McCarthy that he had a list of 205 (or maybe 57) of them in the State Department alone, most Americans were inclined to split the difference. After all, everybody knew about *one* Communist: Alger Hiss.

Of course McCarthy was not the "only one who was doing something about Communism." There was also Richard Nixon, who in the year 1952 became vice president of the United States. History has anthologized the more maudlin and outrageously self-promoting passages in Nixon's famous "Checkers Speech," in which he advanced on television his public defense of a slush fund which by its exposure was threatening his place as Eisenhower's running mate on the Republican ticket in 1952. Schoolchildren now knew about the little dog Checkers, and perhaps even about Pat Nixon's cloth coat. But if the speech had been mere mawkish self-pity or comedy, it would not have worked. A very large audience of "ordinary Americans" listened to what he said:

> Take Communism. I say that as far as that subject is concerned, the danger is great to America. . . . And I say that any man who called the Alger Hiss case a "red herring" isn't fit to be President of the United States. I say that a man who like Mr. Stevenson has pooh-poohed and ridiculed the Communist threat in the United States—he said that they are "phantoms among ourselves"; he's accused us that have attempted to expose the Communists of looking for Communists in the Bureau of Fisheries and Wildlife—I say that a man who says that isn't qualified to be President of the United States. And I say that the only man who can lead us in this fight to rid the Government of both those who are Communists and those who have corrupted this Government is Eisenhower. . . .

The public response to this speech was so overwhelmingly positive that from a political point of view Eisenhower would have been a fool to drop him from the ticket even though he was perhaps inclined to do so. Checkers didn't have much to do with it. Nixon had identified one of those great chasms between American public opinion and the attitudes of the intellectual elites. "Do the American people really 'understand' about Hiss and about the profound implications of the Hiss case?" wrote the anonymous author of a *Time* cover story about Nixon. "On this question the man of ordinary common sense may be less confused than many an 'intellectual.' There is no question that Communists did infiltrate the Government of the U.S., and exercised influence there as well as elsewhere in American life. It is part of Nixon's job to show that if Americans want to rid themselves of Communism and left-wingism at home, they must throw the Democrats out." The essay could have been written by Whittaker Chambers, and certainly reflected his influence on his old magazine. By the time of the "Checkers Speech," *Witness* had for several months been in the hands of members of the Book-of-the-Month Club and was selling briskly in bookstores.

It is difficult to imagine a best-seller that could have been of greater aid to Eisenhower's campaign, or more threatening to Adlai Stevenson's, in 1952. (Stevenson had been among the large, impressive, and bipartisan cohort of blue-ribbon witnesses to Alger Hiss's good character.) That there were important Democrats who didn't "understand" what had happened in the Hiss case is almost too banal a point to argue. As late as *1956*, in Stevenson's second losing campaign, former president Harry Truman, campaigning on Stevenson's behalf, appeared in a televised round-table discussion. Truman (1) denied that he had ever called the Hiss investigation a "red herring"; (2) said that, nevertheless, it *was* a red herring, adding (3) that Hiss was innocent of espionage and that his prosecution on charges of perjury had nothing to do with the fact that the statute of limitations for espionage had expired and everything to do with the "fact that they couldn't prove anything."

The temptation to indict Congressman Nixon of HUAC for high crimes and misdemeanors committed by President Nixon of Watergate twenty-five years later is perhaps irresistible. Few commentators on the Hiss case have even tried to resist. In fact, at its outset, service on the House Committee on Un-American Activities offered Nixon more risks than opportunities. The committee had a bad reputation, and a crook for a chairman. He knew it could be a career-ender as easily as a career-maker, and he took up his assignment to it rather in the spirit that a man with an unconvincing recipe for lemonade might view a crate of lemons. It is true that on the committee he exploited opportunity and avoided unnecessary scruple. In that, he emulated many of his peers in both parties. What actually distinguished him as a member of HUAC was his competence and careful preparation. He believed Chambers and doubted Hiss, when most of his congressional fellows were inclined to do just the opposite, because he alone among them seems to have listened attentively to the early testimony. It was Nixon who bagged the prothonotary warbler.*

As Nixon wrote some years later in *Six Crises*, he too felt like a David facing a Goliath: little Whittier College and Duke Law, against Johns Hopkins and Harvard Law. Chambers was certain—then, and to the end of his life—that powerful forces had wanted to "bury" the Hiss case. The two men were on the same wavelength of suspicion. Chambers naturally responded positively to Nixon's confidence in him. These factors were the basis of a growing personal friendship and the source of much retrospectively embarrassing praise of Nixon in *Witness*. Though Nixon did personally admire Chambers, one may perhaps question just how disinterested his championing of the man was. Once he had committed himself, he was defending his own probity as well as that of Chambers. He did so ferociously and effectively. In one of his satirical poems, Ovid recommends that for greater effect the lover climb the wall and make his entry through the girl's bedroom window even if the front door is unlocked and unguarded. There was more than a touch of such scripted drama in the revelation of the Pumpkin Papers—involving Nixon's emergency return from a vacation cruise on the high seas, to say nothing of the pumpkin itself. Nixon

---

* It must constantly be borne in mind that the first goal of the committee's inquiry was to resolve the contradictory statements by Chambers and Hiss concerning their previous associations. Chambers claimed to have been a close friend of the Hisses as well as a co-conspirator of Alger's, over a period of some years. Hiss at first claimed he had never laid eyes on Chambers, then said he had known him very slightly as a journalist named George Crosley. Chambers had testified in executive session that Hiss was a bird-watcher who had once reported to him the sighting of a prothonotary warbler, a *rara avis* not normally spotted around Washington. When the committee interviewed Hiss privately, Nixon, in a seemingly aimless digression, asked Hiss about his ornithological interests, and in particular whether he had ever seen a prothonotary warbler. He had indeed. The prothonotary warbler, while actually of less probatory value than the apartment he had subleased to Chambers and the car he had given or loaned him, has stuck in the public memory, as it did in the committee's memory at the time.

undoubtedly seized an opportunity, and he played his hand very well. But the discovery that politicians "play politics" is about as astonishing as the discovery that bears have hair and the Pope is Catholic.

Whittaker Chambers was in no sense Richard Nixon's creature. The two men liked and respected one another, and they shared the kind of bond that often joins together those who have shared an agonistic experience. After the publication of *Witness*, Chambers championed Nixon with such a vehemence as to startle even William F. Buckley. But no shred of evidence exists to suggest that the two joined together in an unethical collusion to frame an innocent man. It particularly needs to be said, in the light of some recent revisionist history, that Nixon was passionately convinced of Hiss's guilt. There is a very remote chance that he was in error, but there is no chance at all that he was cynical or indifferent about the matter.

We say that "seeing is believing." It often works the other way around. We see, or hear, what we want or expect to see or hear. There was great excitement among Hiss's defenders, still numerous though by no means legion, when in the last disgraceful days of the Nixon presidency it was discovered that the president's private conversations had been recorded on tape. It seemed possible that Richard Nixon had in unguarded candor made some remarks about the Hiss case, which both he and his enemies regarded as a Copernican moment in his career.

Indeed, the tapes record many revealing statements about the case, one of which, produced in exultation by the Hissites, was that Nixon had said of the Woodstock episode, ". . . we made a typewriter . . ." Any citizen of the republic can be outraged by the content of the Nixon tapes, but a lover of our native tongue will find as well a severe supplementary insult in their form. Here is the mightiest man in the world in intimate discourse with his mighty lieutenants. Yet the vast powers at their command usually fall short of the ability to construct a coherent sentence in the English language. The president in particular seems rarely capable of articulating a complete thought with an identifiable subject properly linked with an identifiable predicate. There is a babble of sentence fragments and free-floating phrases that often have the indeterminacy of the utterances of the Delphic Oracle or the mysterious dying words of the grizzled miner as to the secret location of his stash of gold. It is not surprising that the verbal inkblots of the tapes have constituted a kind of political Rorschach test revealing at least as much of what was on the mind of the decoder as on the mind of the president.

Nixon never said, ". . . we made a typewriter . . ." or anything even vaguely similar. What he seems to have said, according to the most plausible transcription of scholars no friendlier to Nixon than they ought to be, was this: ". . . we had a [?Piper? *lost word*] who . . ." According to this transcription, the verb is not "made" but "had." The "Piper" is uncertain, but a good guess is that Nixon refers to Alger Hiss's lawyer and childhood chum, William Marbury (1901–1988), of the firm Piper, Marbury. He perhaps said, "We had a [Piper lawyer?] who . . ." But the crucial word, undisputed, is "who." It may not be a smoking gun, but it is at the very least a steaming pea-shooter. It is impossible that even such a language-criminal as Richard Nixon ever said "we had/made a typewriter who" was or who did such-and-such. What he may have said was ". . . we had a Piper lawyer who" was or who did such-and-such. In any event, the reference is necessarily to a person, not a thing.

We can never know what the such-and-such was because, as so frequently happens in the president's casual speech, the incipient clause lies inert, stillborn. Context is nonetheless helpful. Nixon was talking about the difficulties he faced in the Hiss case, and the determination needed to overcome obstacles. William Marbury, a most able lawyer of large reputation and unblemished probity, would have been one such obstacle. But nowhere in his many allusions to the Hiss case in the tapes do the speech acts hint that Nixon thought Hiss innocent. He obviously thought Hiss was guilty, and that his own difficult and heroic task was to overcome the powerful interests seeking to prevent Hiss's exposure. He is the David, Hiss the Goliath. He does have a few complete sentences. In one of them he says that his friend J. Edgar Hoover told him that he, Hoover, was under instructions not to cooperate with the committee's investigation of Hiss. Perhaps the *Nation* magazine should look into that one. Who ordered Hoover to lay off Hiss? Who has the power to instruct the head of the FBI in such matters? One good conspiracy theory deserves another.

But even without Dick Nixon to kick around, Chambers's critics would not have been left weaponless. The chief charges against Chambers are three, and they are perhaps not as easily separable as I now must suggest. The first is that Chambers was mentally disturbed. The second is that *Witness* is more fiction than fact. The third is that the office of informer that Chambers willingly embraced is so base as to render valueless the testimony of any man vile enough to fill it.

CHAMBERS THE NUTCASE, CHAMBERS THE QUEER

In a stimulating essay entitled "Why Hiss Can't Confess," the eminent critic of American literature Alfred Kazin summarized the chief categories under which Whittaker Chambers had been discussed up until about 1980. "We know all about Chambers as stinker, messiah, 'informer,' and 'renegade' and pseudothinker." There have been a few more categories added since then. In 1990, for instance, Chambers's judicious biographer, Sam Tanenhaus, published an interesting essay on "Whittaker Chambers: Man of Letters." But the two related theories most relevant to the Hiss defense in 1948 and 1949 were Chambers as psycho and Chambers as queer. These were pursued outside the courtroom in a highly efficient sliming campaign and inside the courtroom through expert psychiatric testimony of a curious kind.

The human mind resists the suggestion of motiveless action, especially when that action is as large, complex, protracted, and consequential as was Chambers's role in the investigation and prosecution of Alger Hiss. Chambers repeatedly explained his motives both in his legal testimony and, at the length of well over a quarter of a million words, in his remarkable *apologia*. If Hiss was indeed guilty, Chambers's stated motives, in part penitential and in part prophetical, are at least plausible. But if Hiss was innocent of the crime for which he was convicted and of the espionage activities of which the perjury charge was a mere outward emblem, those motives crumble into dust and must be replaced by others more responsible and durable.

A good deal of the voluminous "scholarship" on the Hiss-Chambers episode has been devoted to suggesting alternative motives under two broad headings: the political and the psychological. At the top of the "political" list are several variants of a conspiracy theory according to which Chambers, Richard Nixon, J. Edgar Hoover of the FBI, and various others set out to attack, through the surrogacy of Alger Hiss, the legacy of the New Deal, or the Democratic Party, or progressivism generally, or a foreign policy of cooperation with the Soviet Union, and so on. Since the results of the Hiss trials were in fact invoked by some for exactly such polemical purposes, the suggestion can hardly be dismissed out of hand.

One book-length argument is that the whole affair was perhaps the KGB's greatest operational success, for by manipulating Chambers and by supplying the fraudulent technical and documentary evidence that convicted Hiss, Soviet intelligence masterminds sowed chaos, endless recrimination, and division among their enemies. Once again, it is a theory at least consistent with the actual results.

The rumor that Chambers was mentally ill was a persistent part of the pro-Hiss whisper campaign that began in August 1948 and, it might be said, continues to this day. Among the questions read by Hiss into the HUAC transcript—questions he said he would like to see put to Chambers—was the question of whether he had ever been treated for mental illness. The question was raised again, and in brutal fashion, in the cross-examination of Chambers by Hiss's lawyer, Paul Stryker. As always we must try to remember the historical moment. In approaching this subject it is necessary to look backward over six decades of rapid social change. Chambers seemed to many, including several colleagues at *Time,* a crank and a very strange man indeed. He was an ex-Communist. He was moody and lugubrious in a way that might suggest clinical depression. It soon was widely known that his brother had committed suicide. In the popular mind, depression was a moral defect before it was a medical condition. As late as 1972, Thomas Eagleton, the Democratic nominee for vice president, was forced to withdraw from the ticket when it became known that he had been hospitalized for depression. It would probably be a serious impediment for a public figure today. In 1950, it was potentially fatal, as Hiss hoped it would prove. A second and related strand had to do with Chambers's alleged alcoholism, of which there is no actual evidence. But, as usual, the most insidious rumors had to do with sex.

The "mental" aspect fitted in with a generally dim view of the man's physical affect. One of the great appeals of the "Hiss-Chambers affair" to the journalistic mind was the starkness of the contrasts between the two men, now brought together in the oddest of odd couplings. Alger Hiss, in the Indian Summer of his youth, was slim and handsome. At all his public appearances he was invariably well dressed and well groomed in a fashion that announced gravity and professional self-respect rather than affluence or pretension. He looked like exactly what he was: a discreet, distinguished public servant who was now the head of something or other rather important. Whittaker Chambers, though in fact he was only a few years senior to Hiss, looked by contrast like a man over the hill, and perhaps several hills. He was pudgy, not to say seriously overweight. His off-the-rack suits were usually described as "ill-fitting," as though some other cut might better conceal his pear shape. Most fedoras of the period look odd to the contemporary eye. His looks positively sinister. His sallow, fleshy face was generally unsmiling. Above all, perhaps, he was "shifty-eyed." This adjective appears repeatedly in the contemporary commentary. The position he held as a senior editor at *Time*, though in fact highly demanding and responsible, meant little to the general public. To the not inconsiderable extent that the "Hiss-Chambers affair" was a beauty contest, it was—no contest.

Indeed, if Hiss was an innocent victim, the most plausible explanation of the outcome of the case, perhaps its only plausible explanation, is the hypothesis of Chambers's mental illness. But nothing short of a sweeping paranoia will serve. Chambers had actually to believe—in a demented fashion, but no less sincerely—in the fantastic charges he brought against Hiss. He had furthermore to relate them coherently and circumstantially to a full life story that was in part well known to or recoverable by very powerful forces intent on unmasking him. Even this theory may require a conspiracy, as other exculpations of Hiss certainly do.

In the first and still the most elegant book on the "Case," Alistair Cooke's *A Generation on Trial*, Cooke ended with a list of the ten theories that had by then (1950) become canonical. "There are one or two other theories that went the rounds of Washington and New York which, however, so mercilessly intrude into other people's lives that the incompleteness of this report appears a small price to pay for giving everybody so slandered the benefit of a large doubt." Cooke added, sadly and prophetically: "The reader who is most prurient to know about such theories will be the one most apt to hit on them." He alluded, of course, to the widespread rumors that Chambers was queer.

In the 1940s, homosexuality was very widely considered an aberration consistent with, perhaps constituent of, a wider mental abnormality. The Hiss forces put out the word that Chambers was a queer. Indeed, neither homoerotic desire nor homosexual experience was entirely foreign to Chambers. Like his father, he was bisexual. Under the considerable duress of expecting to be "outed" by Hiss's lawyers, he confessed to FBI interrogators in 1948 to an extended "homosexual period" in his life that ran for four or five years, until 1938. "I engaged in numerous homosexual activities both in New York and in Washington, D.C." The essential fact was an open secret. The general attitude of the time was shared by Chambers himself, who viewed his own sexual "tendencies" with horror and disgust, and as evidences of a gross moral failure from which only religion had saved him. Hiss's investigators turned up plenty of suspicion. Sender Garlin, the debunker of Jan Valtin, and the man who had first directed Chambers to a Party meeting, gleefully reported that it had been well known during Chambers's years on *The Daily Worker* that he was a "pervert." Yet for a very particular reason the Hiss forces were unable to exploit this information to the full. The reason was that Timothy Hobson, Alger Hiss's stepson, was gay. Hobson was now twenty-two years old and in rebellion from parental constraints, conducting what he himself recently called "love affairs in New York." The Hiss team could not use a tool that might so easily be turned against them.

For this reason, perhaps, most of the psychologizing explanations for Chambers's perfidy have been grounded in the hypothesis of a sublimated sexual abnormality outwardly evidenced in his literary production. Exhibit number one has been a poem ("overtly homosexual," according to his biographer) about his brother, entitled "Tandaradei."* It is not a very good poem, unless you find sap dripping from a pollarded tree as an apt image of ejaculation. The grim Stryker made Chambers read this poem from the stand. He complied in a barely audible monotone. "The highly charged sexual language, when read in toneless Brooklynese," writes Tanenhaus, "had some spectators smiling." The clear suggestion of the defense was that this was a poem about incestuous homosexuality. Chambers at least affected shock. "It was late in the Hiss Case before any friend summoned the courage to tell me the slander in which the Hiss partisans had involved me with my brother—a story so inconceivable that it seemed to me that only a mind deformed by something more than malevolence could have excreted it."

Discussion of Chambers's homosexuality was for a long time as repressed as the homosexuality itself. With the kind of pendulum swing so

---

* The likely meaning of this poem would probably have been better understood if more medievalists had written books about the Hiss-Chambers case. The title is a learned allusion to a famous lyric poem of Walther von der Volgelweide (fl. 1300) in which a maiden recounts a joyous tumble in the hay, or rather green grass, with a friend. "*Tandaradei*" is a non-verbal expression of lyric delight (of the "la-la-la" genre, as found in one of Carmen's more famous arias). It serves also as a means of evasion. We are not going to learn exactly what happened in the grass. The poem also provides evidence of Chambers's deep immersion in German literature—two birds with one stone.

well known to historians, what was once used to explain nothing is now used to explain everything. Chambers was a bisexual who in important ways loathed and feared his own homoeroticism. In their long and costly investigations Hiss's lawyers must surely have discovered information about Chambers's homosexuality, even supposing that Hiss himself was ignorant of it during the years the men had been friends. Certainly the main "psychological" explanation in the rumor mill was that Chambers's malice was the revenge of a lover scorned. Chambers had fallen in love with Hiss. His love had not been reciprocated, but rejected. Both the sexual approach and its rebuff could have been overt or subliminal. The need to strike back remained the same. Or Chambers was a pedophile whose approaches to young Timmy had been discovered or suspected by the parents.

The odd locus of discussion of this topic is the literary criticism of an offbeat novella by the German writer Franz Werfel, the author of such once famous books as *The Forty Days of Musa Dagh* and *The Song of Bernadette*. The novella, which Chambers had undertaken to translate into English for money, is called *Class Reunion*. Its subject is the mystery of iniquity. In *Class Reunion*, two former classmates meet in an unusual setting: the criminal court in which one is the judge and the other the criminal at the bar. In their youth the two men had been friends. The criminal had been something of a Billy Budd—beautiful alike in his physical and moral natures, full of the brightest promise and hopefulness. Something in the seeming perfection of the man inspired in his fellow, the future judge, an irrational enmity beyond jealousy. There also may well have been—perhaps almost certainly was—a powerful and forbidden sexual desire. So the future judge set about by fraud to destroy the future criminal. Through documentary forgery he accomplished the boy's disgrace and dismissal from school, and thus initiated the social destruction now evidently complete in the man who stood before him.

Well, all this seemed too good to be true to some of Hiss's researchers. If Chambers translated this book, he could have reenacted it. It is but a baby step from the possibility to its actualization. The theory of the psychodramatic reenactment of *Class Reunion* is the subject of one whole book in the Hiss-Chambers literature,* and it plays a prominent role in Meyer Zeligs's psychobiographical *Friendship and Fratricide: An Analysis*

---

* See E. J. Worth's *Whittaker Chambers: The Secret Confession* (London, 1993).

of Whittaker Chambers and Alger Hiss (1967). This second book, though now largely discredited, had for a while a considerable vogue. Readers who might be dubious of the proposition that television violence has an adverse effect on American teens were apparently willing to believe that Whittaker Chambers had ruined his own life and that of Alger Hiss, and produced one of the hugest ruckuses in midcentury American history, because of the internalization of an obscure work of German fiction. When Dr. William Frist appeared to diagnose the condition of Terri Schiavo on the basis of a television clip, most people blinked in incredulity. When Dr. Zeligs made a much more elaborate diagnosis of the long-defunct Chambers even without the aid of television, many people nodded in approving admiration.

The "Werfel hypothesis" of course went back to the days of the whisper campaign, and Chambers had addressed it explicitly in *Witness*. He pointed out the fact obvious to any reader of *Class Reunion* that the person in his own drama who superficially resembled the upright judge basking in a lifetime of recognized professional accomplishment had to be Alger Hiss. The confessed criminal, despised among the upright, was Whittaker Chambers. Mainly, though, Chambers seemed offended by the implication of want of originality, "since it always seemed to me that if I had been bent on ruining Alger Hiss from base motives, the idea might well have occurred to me without the benefit of Franz Werfel." The junk literary criticism was handmaid to the junk science introduced into the first trial by one of Hiss's testimonial experts, the psychiatrist Carl Binger. He was the one who without ever interviewing Chambers had attributed to him "unconscious motivation" and in the second trial assigned him to the category of the "psychopathic personality"—a category he then cheerfully agreed was meaningless.

There is a mental phenomenon that might be called secondary abstraction. The doctrine of the Immaculate Conception of the Virgin Mary became historically necessary because of the currency of another doctrine, never officially dogmatized, concerning the transmission of original sin through human reproduction. In the discussion of the Hiss-Chambers affair, ideas of political conspiracy and the unconscious motivations of a psychopathic personality are the secondary abstractions that flow from the dogma of Alger Hiss's innocence. But a jury of his peers found Hiss guilty, and to abandon the dogma of his innocence liberates us to examine the motives that Chambers himself proposed to explain what he had done. Those motives are strange enough: penitence and patriotism.

CHAMBERS THE FANTASIST: AUTOBIOGRAPHY AND TRUTH (YET AGAIN)

Charles Wright began his May 1952 review of *Witness* in the *Saturday Review* by saying that it was "one of the year's longer works of fiction." The scope of his indictment is clarified by his concomitant statement: "I still believe Hiss was innocent." If Hiss was innocent, practically all of Chambers's account of his underground work for the Communist Party, the larger narrative in which his supposed connection with Hiss is developed, must have simply been made up. While any large autobiography is likely to have a few inaccuracies, this would be wholesale fraud memorializing a sensational if unexposed criminal perjury and the shocking ruin of an innocent man. James Frey's recent pettifogging drug busts would fade into insignificance.

From the very start of the Hiss affair, loud voices proclaimed Chambers to be a "pathological liar." This was hardly a charge that Chambers could dismiss with mere indignation. An underground espionage agent with a string of aliases so long that he himself could not remember them all cannot be a model of transparency. He had testified to his own life of lies. He had cheerfully recounted under oath his own earlier perjury under oath. It is true that Alger Hiss, the man who had in August 1948 most vociferously called Chambers a liar, now had a rap sheet to prove that he himself was one.

How truthful a witness is *Witness*? Every scrap of Chambers's oral testimony was subjected to the hostile scrutiny of Hiss's very able lawyers and their hired investigators. It was further scrutinized by able and knowledgeable journalists. For five decades it has been now and again revisited by historians, some of whom remain unconvinced of the truth of the charges against Hiss. What must seem extraordinary to any dispassionate investigator of all this is just how few and how relatively minor are the actual demonstrable *untruths* of Chambers's autobiography.

Furthermore, the years and decades have revealed considerable evidence—quite independent of Chambers and his book—demonstrating that Alger Hiss was a Soviet agent. This has come from the direct testimony of American ex-Communists, from the decipherment of secret Soviet cables, and from the records of interrogation kept in the files of the Hungarian secret police, among other places. A statute of limitations which once expired in his favor has now expired to his posthumous disgrace. Yet none of this evidence is finally satisfying in assessing the "truth about Whittaker Chambers," a problem strikingly parallel to that of the "truth about Jan Valtin," and one that arises for exactly the same reason. That reason is the status of literary autobiography.

The earlier discussion of Jan Valtin's *Out of the Night* was the occasion for a brief consideration of some modes of interplay between fiction and autobiography. Recent controversies concerning books by Rigoberta Menchú, Vivian Gornick, and James Frey revealed something perhaps more surprising than that autobiographers not infrequently make things up. Critics, reviewers, and perhaps the reading public at large are likely to be more or less indulgent of "fictive autobiography" in direct correlation to their greater or lesser sympathy with what they take to be the author's purposes. *Witness*, too, raises questions about the "truth" of autobiography, but they are somewhat different questions than those already considered.

There are ways quite apart from simple subjective impression by which a reader can conclude that a book is more or less likely to be "true." What the old rhetoricians would have called the "copiousness" of *Witness* makes it nearly certain that the main lines of its narrative, and especially of the history of the Soviet espionage apparatuses and Alger Hiss's participation in espionage, are true. Chambers knew that he was publishing a book that would be minutely examined with great care, patience, and determined skepticism by his numerous and powerful adversaries. It is to be imagined that under these circumstances he would write cautiously. But *Witness* does not give the impression of being a cautious book. Chambers named names literally by the hundred—names of old friends, colleagues, associates—raised in the context of hundreds of specific and often highly detailed anecdotes. He does not make it his business to "unmask" Communists in the sense of mentioning names simply to identify them with Communism, but the number of Communists named is nonetheless very large.

Under these circumstances there were hundreds of opportunities for false or mistaken identifications. Yet so far as I know, the only person in the book named as a Communist actually to claim he was *not* a Communist was Alger Hiss. Several of Hiss's known friends and associates did refuse to answer under oath the question as to whether they were, or had been, members of the Communist Party, on the grounds of the constitutional protection against self-incrimination. In a court of law a judge may warn a jury that no legal inference should be drawn from a witness's recourse to the Fifth Amendment. But the readership of a best-seller is a jury of a different kind, and most people did draw conclusions.

A density of personal reference is not the only level of detail. There are dates. There are places. There are meteorological reminiscences. There are smells, tastes, sounds. The book tends, in anthropological jargon, to "thick description"—carefully observed detail, but within an explicating context. Juliet Poyntz was a patrician American Communist prominent in the Party in the early 1930s. One day in the summer of 1937 she simply disappeared from a New York street, never to be seen again. Chambers reports that in one of his perambulating conversations with his Russian control, Colonel Boris Bykov, Bykov raised her name. "'Where is Juliet Poyntz?' Bykov once asked me when the press had reported her disappearance and it was as clear to Bykov as to me that the G.P.U. had murdered the defenseless woman. 'Gone with the wind,' he answered himself gaily. For he liked to collect topical tags." (p. 439) The "topical tag," of course, is to the blockbuster best-seller of 1936, *Gone With the Wind*.

That is an anecdote that bears either the stamp of truth or the stamp of careful artifice. There are hundreds of such in *Witness*, and most readers found in them the conviction of truth rather than that of art. There are not many prominent intellectuals whose reputations were actually enhanced by the Hiss affair, but among those few is Sidney Hook. In his probing review of *Witness*, he makes the point that the book's very circumstantiality is a powerful testimony to its general authenticity.

However, surprisingly few people have written about *Witness* with a sober critical eye. So great was the hatred of Chambers in the liberal press that there were practically no limits set upon the vituperation or scurrility that might be directed toward him. To test the validity of what may seem an extreme judgment clouded by rhetorical exaggeration, an interested reader could consult an essay by David Cort, "Of Guilt and Resurrection," originally published in the *Nation* on March 20, 1967, and later reprinted by Patrick Swan in his book *Alger Hiss, Whittaker Chambers, and the Schism in the American Soul*. Cort was a younger contemporary of Chambers, knew him at Columbia, and was a colleague of his in the

Luce empire of Time, Inc. He was for much of his career the news editor of *Life*. Like many people who have distinguished careers in journalism, he also published several books. By his own testimony, his animated dislike of Chambers the man was of ancient origin. "My disdain of Chambers at Columbia and then at Time, Inc., was always instinctive, that he was a repellent actor. But I seem to have been nearly alone in that company."

"Of Guilt and Resurrection" is ostensibly a review of Meyer Zeligs's *Friendship and Fratricide*; but that book is the occasion, not the true subject, of the essay. The real subject is the iniquity of Whittaker Chambers, and in particular his apparently pathological lying. According to Cort, Zeligs's book is a useful anthology of Chambers's unmasked falsifications.

For example, Chambers gives in *Witness* a dramatic account of the circumstances of his own birth, a terrible and agonizing trauma for his mother that, in his later analysis, cast a permanent shadow over the relationship between mother and son. The birth is supposed to have taken place in Philadelphia on April 1, 1901. "Snow was falling and soon turned into a blizzard." Cort simply dismissed the meteorological enormity as a big fib. It is probably not impossible through ordinary research methods to find out whether there was snow in the Delaware Valley on April 1, 1901. An April snow would be unusual but by no means unparalleled, as I and millions of others who live there can attest from personal experience.

But that is beside the point as regards the veracity of Whittaker Chambers. Most of us are pretty sure of where and under what circumstances we came into the world, yet our "knowledge" comes not from recollected memory but from what we have been told by people who were there, usually our parents, or at least our mothers. I have more than once heard my son give a spirited report of his own January birth in a hospital in Madison, Wisconsin, which includes the unlikely but nonetheless true detail that the old vehicle that took him and his mother there, having given its last and best effort, then died in the hospital parking lot.

Cort does touch upon the Zeligs book, the central vulnerability of which he recognizes and therefore sidesteps. "It would be easy to find fault with it as literary psychoanalysis; but it is as a compilation of significant data about Chambers and Hiss that the book is important. The Chambers-Hiss case rested above all on the question of the relative honesty and integrity of the two men involved. Dr. Zeligs's facts are so shocking, so consistent, convincing and well documented as to make the psychiatry a mere distraction." According to David Cort, to review the book "as a little exercise in psychiatric techniques . . . is a pedantic enormity—something like reviewing *Othello* without Iago." To review it as Cort did without the psychiatry is more like reviewing *Othello* without Othello. So the April snowstorm is simply a lie along with a thousand others that made up a liar's life. The lies Cort unmasks related to such questions as whether the Hisses did or did not like Shakespeare, whether Priscilla Hiss was a birthright Quaker or a Presbyterian, whether there was a piano in the Hiss residence. There is nothing here about Woodstock typewriters or the titles to Ford automobiles or in fact any of the principal evidence upon which Hiss was convicted after Chambers had been subjected to ferocious questioning by Hiss's lawyers in the presence of the jury that convicted him.

Cort's want of a sense of proportion is founded in a view of the man that is so sinister that Chambers's own one-man conspiracy, by comparison, beggars the conspiracy he pretended to find in Communism. He laid in wait for many years to get Hiss—gathering, watching, planning. But his motive was not homosexual jealousy or a fantasist's role play. "Powerful men and august bodies in this nation received these sleazy lies as significant political truth, at a time when such cobwebs nearly destroyed the American society. For Chambers' enemy was never communism; it was American democracy, you and me. He managed to set America to the task of its own destruction. . . . It is of utmost significance that Chambers did not seek an actual Communist as his prime victim, for there were plenty available. He wanted to bring down the whole structure of democracy. . . . All the people who admired, loved, feared, or even just believed him were pitiably hoaxed. Just to know him was at best an indiscretion."

Cort ended his essay with remarkable intemperance: "Alger Hiss must certainly be vindicated. The wreckage of other reputations is inevitable. And Chambers, with that cute dimpled chuckle and the sly, friendly gleam, is laughing in the grave at his 'friends,' the priceless butts who believed in him." Anyone can make a faulty prophecy, but the rest required fully engaged spleen. It is hardly conceivable that the lawyer for any journal in the country would have let that pass into print concerning any living person; but though a man may laugh from his grave, he rarely files suit from there. And canons of civility and taste are regularly trumped by political certitude.

Of Cort's outburst this much at least may be said. If Hiss was innocent of espionage and perjury—an extremely remote possibility but not yet quite an actual impossibility—then some such plot as he imagines, involving the satanic machinations of an evil genius working over many years with the active or passive collusion of scoundrels or idiots in the offices of government, in the Congress, in the security agencies, and in the grand jury of the Southern District of New York, is the only explanation that will fit the known facts. It would have had to have been a conspiracy of great complexity and nearly endless ramification. It collapses at the first swipe of Occam's razor.

Strictly speaking, the actual truth or falsehood of Chambers's autobiography, as also the actual innocence or guilt of Alger Hiss, are irrelevant to the impact that *Witness* had on American public opinion. But at times "strictly speaking" is simply a form of evasion or pedantry, and this is probably one of them. I owe you my opinion. The book is very convincing in its delineation of the case against Hiss. Chambers's procedure is to reproduce long swatches of the sworn testimony from the committee room and before the jury, though he naturally does so selectively, artfully, and purposefully. It is often said, even today, that Hiss was convicted solely on the testimony of Chambers. That is very far from the truth. No jury would have convicted Alger Hiss on the basis of uncorroborated accusations by Whittaker Chambers. Thomas Murphy, the U.S. attorney who successfully prosecuted Hiss, attributed the conviction to the "immutable witnesses."

By this he referred to very powerful physical evidence that supported Chambers's testimony. There are many books about the Hiss trials, not to mention full transcriptions of the proceedings, and I shall not compete with them now. Some of the more dramatic immutable witnesses were the following: (1) stolen documents and microfilms of documents that Chambers had stashed away in 1939; (2) the actual typewriter, formerly the property of Priscilla Hiss, on which copies of stolen papers had been typed; (3) documentary evidence of a real estate transaction in which Hiss had rented or loaned an apartment to Chambers; (4) an expensive carpet allegedly given by the Soviets through Chambers to Hiss, in gratitude for the latter's work for them; and (5) documentary evidence concerning a Ford car that Hiss had owned and disposed of in a curious fashion. These "immutable witnesses" (and others) dovetailed with the narrative testimony of the possibly mutable witness Whittaker Chambers.

The problem of Chambers's *Witness*, though most certainly a problem of "autobiographical truth," has principally to do not with facts presented in the book, but with the author's interpretation of them. The genre of biography always involves a negotiation between authority and interpretation—what the author can actually find out about the life on the one hand, and on the other the point of view the author brings to the life. Autobiography is a special instance of biography, in which the author's presumed unmatched authority concerning the facts of the life must be weighed against a maximal suspicion of possible bias in the author's presentation of the materials. Let us say that young Augustine's theft of pears was a *fact*. That the theft attested to the total depravity of human nature is an interpretation or a point of view. Few of the facts of *Witness* have been successfully challenged; its interpretations will be debated endlessly.

The texture of autobiography is largely determined by two factors, both of them the exclusive property of the autobiographer. The first is tone. The second is the power of inclusion or exclusion. Much of the more ferocious hostility to *Witness*, even when allegedly centered in the question of Alger Hiss, arose from its recurrent whiffs of sanctimony, personal and political. Nowhere is this more apparent than in Chambers's saccharine accounts of his personal relationships, especially that with his wife Esther, whom he first met as an activist in the radical labor movement. Esther was the friend and roommate of the "Red southern belle" novelist (and later ferocious anti-Communist) Grace Lumpkin. "They were widely known in the Communist movement for their inviolable 'prudery,' which was, in fact, chiefly their way of living uncontaminated by that steaming emotional jungle in which the party had raised promiscuity to a Marxist principle." (p. 265)

This statement ranks somewhere between annoying prissiness and obnoxious hypocrisy in light of information concerning Chambers's own sexual history, unmentioned in *Witness* but available in the FBI files and in Sam Tanenhaus's biography. The motivation for suppressing the names of two earlier Communist "wives," one of whom he bullied into a reluctant abortion, might not be entirely self-serving. The motivation for suppressing any explicit acknowledgment of his own homoeroticism was surely a combination of fear and shame.

Chambers himself records an astute remark of Robert Stripling, the able staff investigator of the House Committee on Un-American Activities. "'I have been reading over your testimony, Mr. Chambers,' he said, 'and one thing about it impresses me. You answer questions readily enough, but I notice that you never volunteer information.'" (p. 709) What his critics have found unsatisfactory in *Witness* is that in it the witness answers only those questions he is willing to put to himself. But this is by definition true of all autobiographies. The "tell-all" memoir is a fantasy of the publishing world.

Thus, quite apart from the question of factual truth there are questions of tone and interpretation. One theory about Chambers, once widely held among liberals but now discarded, was that he was a fantasist in a psychiatric sense. There is a truth, a coherence of texture or plot to the experience of the fantasist, but it differs greatly from the coherence we would experience in his place. The fantasist not merely sees what others do not see; he is scornful of them for their lack of seeing. "'But look, your grace, those are not giants but windmills' . . . 'It is plain to be seen,' said Don Quixote, 'that you have had little experience in the matter of adventures.'"

Chambers saw something that few others at first could see: a Communist conspiracy of espionage successfully infiltrated within the engine of American government. That was no fantasy, but it left a further question unanswered. Was that conspiracy more in the manner of a giant or of a windmill? Here the answer is much less clear. It is not only Chambers's political critics who find in the authorial narrator of *Witness* an unpleasing portentousness, a self-importance, a melodrama, a pomposity—the vocabulary varies, but its drift is steady. Was the pilfering of some confidential cables actual evidence that the republic was in dire peril? Could the timorous perfidies of Harry Dexter White actually give voice to the awful question: who is to rule, God or man?

That was and is very much a question worth asking, and with the luxury of a half century's perspective we might be able to answer it with conviction. But it is more than could reasonably be expected that Chambers would address it in 1947, or even in his book in 1952. In 1947, he was facing the certain ruin of his reputation and domestic tranquility and his probable indictment and prosecution. In 1952, he was trying to justify and if possible to repair a shattered life. What is often called his "paranoia" is in fact a very common phenomenon among other literary anti-Communists. It was a major theme in the work of Solzhenitsyn.

A recurrent topic in the European literature of ex-Communism is the "Cassandra complex." Time and again knowledgeable witnesses report on Soviet famines, purges, concentration camps, mass murders, or simply the absolute awfulness of daily life in Russia only to be pooh-poohed (or much worse) by the guardians of the conventional wisdom in government and in civil life. Recall the reaction of Nina Berberova as she watched the Kravchenko trial: "To see with my own eyes how a former minister, or a world-known scientist, a Nobel Prize laureate, or a Sorbonne professor with the Legion of Honour in his lapel button hole, or a famous writer would take the oath and under oath affirm that there never had been and were not any concentration camps in the U.S.S.R., was one of the strongest impressions of my entire life." Chambers had his own strong impressions.

The testimony of such witnesses as those who stunned Berberova probably should not be considered as perjury. The word many of them later adopted was *aveuglement*—blindness. They were not mendacious. They were blind. Now it is entirely possible that Chambers's *Witness* is a "false autobiography" at the level of authorial interpretation. "I know that I am leaving the winning side for the losing side, but it is better to die on the losing side than to live under Communism." We may now want to judge that a "blind" attitude. But if so, his "blindness" was no more startling than that of those who continue to insist that Hiss was "innocent."

There are some obvious evasions in *Witness*. These are few, but unsettling. The largest, probably, is Chambers's suppression of his bisexual constitution and his homosexual experiences. His motive, however, seems obvious. Two of the very best scholars who have worked on this material— Allen Weinstein and Sam Tanenhaus—come to opposite conclusions as to whether Chambers had made a secret trip to Russia in 1933. If he did not make such a trip, as now seems more likely, why did he scam his friends by having postcards from Russia sent to them? Why the evasiveness (drawn attention to in Hugh Kenner's brilliant essay in the Swan anthology) concerning the extent of his knowledge of the Russian language? The motive here may have been to deflect attention and possible suspicion from his wife. Esther was never, Chambers tells us both early and late in the book, a Communist. If not, one wonders why in their courting days she would have even for a moment taken as authoritative a command from "the party" that she have nothing more to do with Chambers. (p. 267) The discovery of a demonstrable lie, however trivial and motiveless it may seem, must excite a suspicion of others possibly not so trivial. That "point of law" was one that Richard Nixon rather sanctimoniously put to Alger Hiss during his interrogation. Chambers's more serious breach of contract with his reader is also more fundamental.

REBECCA WEST ON CHAMBERS

Five or six years ago, some scholars had the very good idea of gathering into an anthology the more durable essays occasioned by the publication of *Witness* in 1952 or since attracted by the controversy.* It reveals a studied attempt to be "balanced" in terms of establishing some kind of equilibrium between pro-Hiss and pro-Chambers pieces and, in so doing, endorses the notion of unresolved bifurcation and division implied in the word "Schism" in the title. It reprints a number of the more important contemporary reviews, including those of Howe and Hook referred to above. There is much that is intelligent and thought-provoking in this anthology, but a single essay in it seems to me to arise from it like a majestic peak behind foothills, and that is the essay "Whittaker Chambers" by Rebecca West, first published in the *Atlantic Monthly* for June 1952. Rebecca West was one of very few people who have written about Chambers who was as good a writer as he. To aesthetic authority she adds the clarity of a European detachment unavailable to most Americans.

She begins with a singularly original premise: that the Hiss-Chambers affair should be viewed within the context of what she calls "dervish trials," or processes in which the supposed impartiality and reflectiveness of law itself have been strained, distorted, or compromised by the disturbing influences of public opinion or naked political manipulation. Examples she gives include the Dreyfus affair, the burning of the Reichstag, and Stalin's Purge Trials. The startling perspective allows us to see how the legal determination of the case brought so little resolution and why so many later commentators have been able to dismiss so much evidence with such insouciance.

An extraordinary feature of this affair is that Whittaker Chambers perjured himself in his testimony to the grand jury when he brushed off any question that Hiss was involved in *espionage* as opposed to membership in the Communist Party. He states this quite baldly in *Witness*, but in a

* See Patrick A. Swan, ed., *Alger Hiss, Whittaker Chambers, and the Schism in the American Soul* (Wilmington, DE, 2003).

way intended to present a base public action as a private virtue. "The lie," he wrote, "is there for all men to condemn," but he had his reasons. He wanted to expose the conspiracy of the Communists in the government, but on his own terms, minimalist terms that would do as little damage as possible to his old buddy Alger Hiss. It was this lie that made Chambers the "confessed perjurer" to those who sought to discount his amended testimony without, apparently, fully thinking out the implications of their indignation. For here we approach what a medieval logician would have called an "insoluble sentence," as in the famous Liar's paradox: "'Cretans always lie,' said Epimenides the Cretan." For if Chambers were lying when he said that Hiss was not an espionage agent . . . Still, West writes, "it is truly amazing that a man should consent to play a part in an investigation of Hiss's conduct by the law, and then, in order to fulfill what he conceived to be his moral duty toward Hiss, should disregard the understanding on which every trial is founded: that witnesses regard the oath they take as binding. This is an act which is explicable only by reference to the egotism of the mystic." Rebecca West is probably the most intelligent literary reader to have written about *Witness*. It was perfectly obvious to her that he was a "mystic"; that indeed the mystic's search for God is at the center of the book. It is accordingly appropriate to take a moment to consider how a more conventional "mystic" might write autobiography.

We have already had occasion to revisit Augustine's *Confessions*, one of the two or three most influential autobiographies in our literature. It is hardly surprising that Chambers, in writing the history of his own religious conversion, should himself return to that text. We may recall that in the eighth book of his *Confessions*, Augustine narrates the history of his religious conversion, perhaps the most famous in our literature. It is a story implicitly and explicitly linked with several other literary texts, especially the *Life of Saint Anthony*. Augustine, restless with inner spiritual struggle, walks out of the house and into a garden, sits beneath a fig tree with a volume of the Apostle on his lap, and hears from beyond the garden wall the voices of infants, apparently playing a game, saying, *Tolle, lege, tolle, lege*—"Pick it up and read it, pick it up and read it." He finds himself at the closing verses of the thirteenth chapter of the Epistle to the Romans, an urgent invitation to newness of life. With that reading his conversion is instant and definitive. "That day I read no further."

Chambers's conversion to Communism had in a sense been a literary one, and the pattern he presents, I cannot doubt, is that he found in Augustine's *Confessions*. After his drop-out trip to Europe in 1923, he made a second try at Columbia College, but his real reading there was self-directed. He read the Webbs. He read the Christian Socialist R. H. Tawney. He read Hobhouse. He read "the endless volumes in which G. D. H. Cole urged Guild socialism." They were to him all dry theory without "the reek of life." Then, "by sheer chance, there came into my hands a little pamphlet of Lenin's . . . *A Soviet at Work*. . . . The reek of life was on it. . . . This was socialism in practice. This was the thing itself" (pp. 194–95)

Augustine had read in the books of the Platonists that in the beginning was the Word and the Word was with God, and the Word was God. But the reek of life was not upon it. "However, that *the Word was made flesh and dwelt among us*—that I did not read in these books." How was socialism to become incarnate? "Here was the simple statement that terror and dictatorship are justified to defend the socialist revolution if socialism is justified. Terror is an instrument of socialist policy if the crisis was to be overcome."

How many experts in early Christian literature believe that the events in his story "really" happened as described by Augustine? The answer is— about half of them. The other half believe that Augustine's autobiography here truly describes an event as it "spiritually" happened, that he has manipulated literal reality in such a fashion as to make the spiritual reality clearer and more forceful. Several common features of antique rhetorical practice and early Christian scriptural exegesis encourage them in this view.

Chambers eventually became a Christian of sorts, but hardly a medieval one. He was a modern through and through, both romantic and post-romantic, as his onetime master Marx had been. What about *modern* biographical conventions? We found in the response to books by Menchú, Gornick, and Frey a sliding scale of moral outrage. One axis of analysis of autobiography is the measure of its political correctness concerning descents from the literal to the allegorical. In the autobiography of *Witness*, it is the larger *exemplary* pattern that needs to be questioned and often enough challenged. To admit that Alger Hiss was a Soviet agent need not imply the plenary acceptance of a comet's tail of allegorical implication: treason at the heart of the New Deal, the perfidy of all liberals, the historical necessity of Joseph McCarthy, the absolution of Richard Nixon, and various other ideas, some suggested by the author himself, others easily spun from the threads of his text by eager and partisan readers.

CHAMBERS THE INFORMER

We come now to the most abiding revulsion that has stuck to Chambers since Paul Stryker, Hiss's lawyer, likened him to an Algerian leper: "Unclean! Unclean!" It was a revulsion of which Chambers was entirely aware. "The question which first faces every man or woman who breaks with the Communist Party is 'Shall I become an informer against it?'" he writes. (p. 65) In this question lay agony, for "informer" "is a word so hateful that when, years later, in testifying before a grand jury, I came to that word and my decision to become an informer, I could not at once go on." The penumbra of revulsion surrounding the word "informer" fouls the atmosphere surrounding the Hiss case to this very day.

Actually, "informer" is one of the milder English words in a language rich in colorful vituperation of tattle-tales: "snitches," "squealers," "stool pigeons" (or simply "stoolies"), "canaries" (who "sing"), "rats," "finks," and of course the combinatory "ratfink." The hateful rodent provides as well the verb "to rat" on someone. But there is a particular political connotation to "informer," and for twentieth-century intellectuals, who removed the locus of morality from religion to politics, the "informer," like Grendel, bore the wrath of God as well as that of man. The Irish novelist Liam O'Flaherty captured all this brilliantly in one of the great novels of the thirties: *The Informer*.

There is in the concept of the informer an unresolved social tension. Today, as one rides the New York subway, one is surrounded by signs in two languages that say, "If you see something, say something." The particular "something" of the moment is of course "terrorism." Well, Chambers wrote in 1952 that "The Communist Party . . . is a terrorist organization." And though some recent revisionist historians would have us believe that the American Communist Party, at least, was more along the lines of a hyperactive PTA, his judgment is there unimpeachable. Some of our most revered temples of higher learning require that entering students must formally promise as a matter of honor that they will inform the constituted authorities of any acts of cheating they may observe. This system is indeed called an "honor code." There has emerged since Chambers's day a word for a benign informer. That is "whistle-blower," a term drawn from those competitive sports in which a constituted umpire exposes, and sometimes punishes, illegality. The word "cheating" hardly begins to do justice to the criminal operations of the Soviet spy ring in Washington. Yet when Lionel Trilling had the temerity to say that Whittaker Chambers the informer was an "honorable" man, the author of *The Liberal Imagination* found himself nearly buried in liberal outrage.

There is of course honor, and then there is honor, to be adjudicated according to the double standard operative in most political life. Outrage rightly greets the blue wall of silence that sometimes protects misconduct by officers of the New York or Los Angeles Police Department. Disapproval of the Sicilian *omertà* that protects the Mafia don, on the other hand, is moderated by a certain degree of anthropological fascination. By the time we get to political "ratting" before the House Committee on Un-American Activities, all bets are off. Listen to Richard Nixon, as caught on his own White House tapes: "You know the great thing about—I got to say for Hiss. He never ratted on anybody else. Never. He never ratted."

If Richard Nixon could imply a distaste for ratters, we can hardly be surprised by the attitude of Victor Navasky in *Naming Names*, his indictment of the procedures by the congressional inquisitors investigating the supposed Communist infiltration of Hollywood. But neither Nixon nor Navasky can be allowed without challenge to simplify so complex a matter as "informing." For there are at least two quite different attitudes toward "informing" that, roughly speaking, correspond to the two large categories defined by Ivanov in his examination of Rubashov. One places the emphasis of ethical behavior in personal relationships; the other in social duty. The individualist (or perhaps "capitalist") emphasis on private virtue is captured in a frequently quoted apothegm of E. M. Forster. In a passage in *Two Cheers for Democracy*, Forster wrote: "If I had to choose between betraying my country and betraying my friend, I hope I should have the guts to betray my country." In its context in Forster's essay, the idea is perhaps more subtle and ambiguous than it seems in stark citation, but as I have never seen it cited in context, the matter is moot. In at least a half dozen books about the Cambridge spies—Philby, Burgess, Maclean, Blunt—it is presented simply as an admirable moral aspiration.

An alternative attitude toward the informer can rightly be called "socialist." In this conception, personal or familial attachment must surrender to collective need. The Soviets developed within their citizenry to a remarkable degree the patriotic attitude called "socialist vigilance" or "revolutionary watchfulness." Enemies of the state were everywhere. Cunning, devious, fanatical in their counterrevolutionary intentions, they were bent on destroying every spiritual, industrial, economic, and domestic foundation of socialism. They had to be stopped. The state had excellent methods of stopping them, provided only that they had first been discovered and exposed. The verb of official choice for this process was "to unmask." To unmask involves more drama than simply to catch. Who has not seen a film in which the righteous detective must find the villain amid the deceptive chaos of Carnival or a Halloween ball? Though the detective function was specially vested in powerful state organs, discovery and exposure through revolutionary vigilance was the duty of every Soviet citizen. Indeed, failure to exercise due revolutionary vigilance was among the commonest forms of counterrevolutionary "wrecking." Recent revelations from the Stasi files in former East Germany suggest that a sizable proportion of the civilian population there were officially registered informers.

There was a literal poster boy of socialist vigilance, and his name was Pavel Morozov. Though Pavel Morozov has been rather debunked by recent scholarship, and may well never have existed, he was nonetheless a source of inspiration for several generations of Soviet schoolchildren. Young Pavel lived in an agricultural village where "wrecking" and "hoarding" were rife. That is, the peasants in this village attempted to resist the state's confiscation of the grain they had raised in order to have something to eat themselves. Among the miscreants were Pavel's own parents. Their attempts to defeat the social good did not escape young Pavel's socialist vigilance, however, and he reported his mother and father to the police. Their punishment was swift and definitive, but that is not the end of the story. Not all of the other peasants in the village applauded Pavel the Informer. Indeed, a group of them later ambushed and murdered him. The Cheka had to return and sort the whole village out—a task once again performed with efficiency and dispatch. Poor Pavel was dead, but the informer-martyr lived on in song and legend—a legend the medievalist will recognize as a modern and politicized version of the anti-Semitic blood libel of the cult of Saint Hugh of Lincoln, also preserved in Chaucer's "Prioress's Tale." A more contemporary and risible report reaches us from California, where a young boy squealed to investigating authorities that his parents had forced him to get high with them on pot while they all watched *SpongeBob SquarePants*. The police busted the parents; but perhaps the child, having not yet reached the age of reason, had neither arrived at the threshold of treason.

Habitual witnesses to criminal activity are often and unsurprisingly themselves criminals. The expert knowledge they claim and to which they testify must always be tested against powerful suspicions of untruthfulness. Who has not read in truth or fiction that "The only alleged eyewitness was a jailhouse snitch who stood to benefit in his own plea bargain if he told the cops what they wanted to hear"? The people who knew the most about American Communism were, not surprisingly, American Communists. There was a stable of "kept witnesses" or Party-cell snitches like Elizabeth Bentley and Louis Budenz housed in the unsavory precincts of the House Committee on Un-American Activities. There is in the Jan Valtin archive a pathetic letter to Krebs from Ben Mandel, the Communist apostate who for a time was a highly competent factotum with HUAC, in which we get a clear glimpse of the sense of indignity, distaste, dependence, and servility attendant upon an office that all right-thinking liberals thought unclean. Comparatively few apostates from the Communist Party positively desired the alternatives of the Rotary Club or the Southern Baptist Church, though they were often expected to behave as though they did. Whittaker Chambers knew that he now joined such a group. He could do no other. He was privy to a country's fate, which, happily, foreknowing might avoid.

WITNESS AS AN ACT OF PENANCE

The autobiography of the ex-Communist became a minor genre in America. In France, where there were many more Communists among the scribbling classes, it became a major genre. On the basis of a wide reading of this literature one arrives at certain conclusions, among the most prominent of which is that many intelligent and decent people have felt a need to explain how an intelligent and decent person could spend many years as a member of the Communist Party. Such books often are in effect petitions for the "understanding" that is the secular surrogate of religious "forgiveness." This motive is crystal clear in the most famous English anthology of such histories: *The God That Failed*. From one point of view, ex-Communist autobiography might be described as a final, or a definitive, act of "socialist self-criticism." But as the word "God" in the book title suggests, there was in the Communist commitment of many Western intellectuals an element barely if at all different from religious commitment. For the process of inner change described in Chambers's *Witness*, certainly, it is appropriate to use more theological language. Here the operative words would be "repentance" and "confession."

As the impulse to "go public" was maturing in Chambers's mind from nagging suggestion to definite decision, he was working on a major essay: a *Time* cover story about Reinhold Niebuhr. Later, in *Witness*, he offered invitations, both implicit and explicit, to anyone who might be interested in understanding his frame of mind at the time to look carefully at the Niebuhr essay and at other of his roughly contemporaneous writing. His critics have declined the invitation, but we must not. "In many ways, the Niebuhr essay was a statement of my own religious faith at the time," Chambers wrote. "And since, six months later almost to a day, I was to begin to testify publicly against the Communist conspiracy, I believe that it is relevant to quote what I then felt." The eloquent passage from the essay he then quotes is this: "With prayer, with humility of spirit tempering his temerity of mind, man has always sought to define the nature of the most important fact in his experience: God. To this unending effort to know God, man is driven by the noblest of his intuitions—the sense of his mortal incompleteness—and by hard experience. For man's occasional lapses from God-seeking end inevitably in intolerable shallowness of thought combined with incalculable mischief in action." (p. 505)

The idea here expressed is a cliché of Christian thought nowhere more beautifully expressed than on the first page of Augustine's *Confessions*: "You [God] have made us for yourself, and our heart is restless until it rests in you." Augustinian conceptions of inferior and superior loves, indeed, inform many passages in *Witness*. They are the secondary reflexes of Augustine in so much Christian theology, including Niebuhr's. In specific terms, for Chambers the "intolerable shallowness of thought" was the materialist religion of Marxism, the "incalculable mischief in action" his own life of lies devoted to its cause. But the passage is not, as he implies, the opening paragraph of the *Time* essay on Niebuhr, and it is in the actual opening paragraph that we shall most clearly see the relevance to the project of *Witness*: "It was Lent. On Manhattan's Fifth Avenue, a woman and a little girl were stopped by the traffic at a cross street. On the opposite curb stood a young man with an Ash Wednesday mark on his forehead. 'Look,' said the little girl. 'Mustn't point,' said the woman. 'But mother,' asked the little girl, 'why has he got that black mark on his forehead?' 'Hush,' said her mother. 'It's something they do in church, I think.'"

The detail offers a clear signal of the theological point to which Chambers will turn the anecdote. Two close friends of Chambers in New York, Samuel Welles and Robert Cantwell, were active members of the Episcopal Church; they sponsored Chambers in baptism and, later, in his confirmation at the hands of Bishop Manning, at the Cathedral of Saint John the Divine. The elegant dean of the cathedral at that time was the Very Reverend William Dudley Foulke Hughes. Hughes was a serious Anglo-Catholic intellectual and the author of several books. Since the earliest days of the Stalin regime he had been one of the ecumenical leaders in the international campaign against Soviet religious policy.

In 1930, Dean Hughes delivered a widely distributed sermon-lecture on religious persecution in Russia in which he said, among other things, "We are here in this Cathedral not for any political purpose, not to express our views for or against any economic or governmental system. . . . We are here to lift up our voices, in common with believers in God of all faiths, against a power which in its own official organs proclaims itself the enemy of God and of God's laws, which by ruthless persecution is undertaking to stamp out religion and those moral ideals for which religion stands, which seeks to undermine and destroy the free institutions of other nations, and which, let us remember, through many channels, is spreading its teaching of godlessness and immorality here in our own land and throughout the world."

In 1930, Chambers had called himself an atheist and a despiser of "bourgeois morality." Now, nine years later, he aligned himself with Dean Hughes's tract, and as he prepared for baptism he sought out its author as his personal instructor in the elements of the Christian faith. Hughes would certainly have instructed him in such fundamentals as the sacraments of the Church. The sacrament of penance has since the early centuries of the Church been conventionally understood as consisting of three parts: contrition, confession, and satisfaction. As Chaucer's Good Parson puts it, a "perfect penitence" consists of or "stant on three things, Contricioun of Herte, Confessioun of Mouth, and Satisfaccioun." The first of these is internal, the second both internal and external, the third external.

Chambers did not long remain in the Episcopal Church, with its liturgical formalism and sacramental worship. He preferred the unscripted individualism and radical interiority associated with the Quaker meeting. It is nonetheless obvious that *Witness* memorializes and in part performs the pattern of penance in the ancient Christian tradition. The book's spiritual structure is tripartite. He documents his contrition for past errors and iniquities. He makes an agonizing auricular confession before a congressional committee and courts of law, and a stunning written confession in a best-selling book. He is throughout all this aware of the final step, the making of amends for things that cannot be amended, which is the acceptance of the destruction of his life.

What Chambers here calls "an Ash Wednesday mark" was, as he well knew, the sign of the cross left in ash smudge on that place on the forehead earlier signed with a cross in the chrism of baptism. The occasion of the symbolic disfigurement is the solemn liturgy with which the penitential season of Lent commences. Since the finely powdered ash used is the residuum of the burnt palm fronds from the liturgy of the previous Palm Sunday, there is in the "Ash Wednesday mark" a capacious symbolic memorial of the whole "mystery of faith": "Christ has died. Christ has risen. Christ will come again." Yet its focus is on *penance*; the ash is that of "sackcloth and ashes" in the biblical iconography of penance. The anecdote rather brilliantly captures both the idea of penance and the incomprehensibility of the concept to the secular world. "'It's something they do in church, I think.'"

With the idea of *penance* comes the cognate idea of *conversion*. The pattern of the imagery reveals that Chambers is also making an unadvertised allusion to the most famous Modernist invocation of the ideas associated with Ash Wednesday—namely, T. S. Eliot's poem with that title. Its opening line and central image—"Because I do not hope to turn again"—makes fullest sense only to the reader who with Eliot will savor the connection between the English "turn" and Latin *verto*, the etymological source of "verse" itself, of "universe," "version" and "conversion," "convert" and "revert." This, too, is a commonplace thought revealed in the wordplay of the opening paragraphs of Augustine's *Confessions*. Like so much in complex poetry, vivid words and ideas grasped in a moment of happy intuition lose their luster beneath the dull patina of editorial footnotes. Chambers does not *cite* Eliot's "Ash-Wednesday." Instead he makes allusion to its poetic situation (a religious conversion arrived at in penitence) and to its existential imperative (expiation through speaking out). Perhaps the three specific lines in Eliot most relevant to *Witness* are the following:

Because I do not hope to turn again
Let these words answer
For what is done, not to be done again

Here is Chambers's conscious motive in his "testimony," both in the narrow sense of answering questions put to him by investigators and lawyers, and in the much larger prophetic sense of *Witness*. As in Eliot's poem, the motive is expressed within an explicit Anglican economy of penance.

The perception does not in and of itself prove anything about the truth or falsity of the witness, but it at least honors the intelligence and complexity of a carefully crafted work of art. It can also help us see the larger pattern of the book within the life. Perhaps even many journalists are unaware that the so-called six questions of journalism, questions that an adequate news story should answer (Who? What? Where? When? Why? How?) have a medieval literary origin. They derive from the handbooks of penance or "confessors' manuals" that developed as a major literary genre when auricular confession became a widespread practice in the thirteenth-century Church. An expert at "handling sin" (the catchy title of one English manual) had to know all the moral pathology in its particular circumstances in order to apply the specific remedy. From the same source came popular knowledge of the "three parts of penance": contrition, confession, and satisfaction. The penitent must be truly sorry for having committed the sin, must make auricular confession of the sin, and must redress the sin in actual or symbolic satisfaction.

To understand how this tripartite sequence is made articulate in *Witness* requires brief reference to several important narrative episodes so far unmentioned. Very early in the book, Chambers tells the story of a pro-Soviet German diplomat whose spiritual defection was occasioned by his hearing screams, presumably those of NKVD victims, echoing through the streets of Moscow. "He heard screams. That's all. Simply one night he heard screams." Chambers himself had heard the metaphorical "scream" of the purged Dmitri Schmidt, which signaled for him the beginning of the Purge. The essentially emotional reaction to the "screams" is an emblem of contrition. Of explicit auricular confession, the second stage of penance, there are many narrative emblems. In 1939 Chambers, now deeply disillusioned, came into contact with the ubiquitous Isaac Don Levine, to whom he confessed his deep-seated political misgivings. Through Levine he actually met with General Krivitsky, the renegade Soviet intelligence chief, with whom he conducted in German a late night conversation confessional in character. Later Levine arranged a private meeting with Adolf Berle, one of the top aides to President Roosevelt. There he confessed to Berle the existence of a Communist cell—he did not yet identify it as an espionage team—in Washington. (Berle took notes, including the name of Alger Hiss; but nothing more came of it.) His ordeals in committee room, grand jury, and courtroom were thus only the most excruciating of many auricular confessions.

But the most laborious burden of penance is its third stage, "satisfaction." For Chambers, that is the writing of his book itself. A notorious sinner in the Middle Ages might be given some arduous physical penance, corporal punishment, the undertaking of a long and dangerous pilgrimage. To write at a white-hot pace a book of a quarter of a million words, to write it in the isolation of a country cabin, to revise constantly, often to discard pages eked out by a day's strenuous labor, and all, in Koestler's words, "to atone for the guilt of our generation"—this was a penitential "satisfaction" scarcely less grueling. All books are "monuments" to something. *Witness* is a monument to "a broken and a contrite heart."

It is no small achievement to write a complicated and learned book that will be read avidly by a large audience among what we usually call the general public. Such a feat may demand the rarest form of artistry—self-effacing artistry. There is a wonderful line in Ovid, in his account of the sculptor Pygmalion's statue, *Ars latet arte sua*: with his art he disguises his artifice. It is a line that perhaps applies to all deep artistic constructs that achieve a deceptive sense of simplicity. It certainly applies to *Witness*. Chambers had the rare ability to write a very complicated book that found a large popular readership. It is not an unpardonable exaggeration to discuss it in such company as Augustine's *Confessions* or Dante's *Commedia*—books that capture a reader with the hook of an autobiographical narrative sufficient in its mere "story" yet everywhere amplified, extended, and exemplified by a thousand rich, decorative details that reveal themselves only to the curious, the industrious, the learned, or the importunate reader.

His huge audience of "ordinary" Americans was captivated by the "plot." Communists formed an exotic species. Here, in Chambers's account of his early life in the Party, and his literary work at the *New Masses* and *The Daily Worker*, readers found richly textured and often sympathetic portraits of people—many of them "characters" in the colloquial sense of the word—who differed from themselves chiefly in terms of their commitment to a bizarre political fanaticism. In his account of the underground, readers found all of the fascination and satisfaction they usually find in the details of "spy stories"—the techniques of operatives, mail drops, code names, Leica cameras, a whole conspiratorial world at once fascinating in its allure and preposterous in its pretension. Finally, in the long sections of the book devoted to the testimony before HUAC and the two trials of Alger Hiss, they found, expertly edited for Chambers's partisan purpose, "courtroom drama" of a very high order.

That constitutes what we might call the literal sense of *Witness*. But it is obvious that many ordinary readers—in contrast to the more elite audience of academics and intellectuals—also caught its spiritual sense. That was the argument summarized for Chambers in a quotation from Dostoyevsky: "The problem of Communism is the problem of atheism." Koestler had taken as one of his epigraphs another Dostoyevskian gobbet: "Man, man, one cannot live quite without pity." In this and several other places *Witness* and *Darkness at Noon*, two works so different in structure and conception, approach philosophical identity. Chambers's subject here is the relationship of ends and means. As is frequently the case in *Witness,* Chambers advances an argument at least twice—once in a narrative, and once in a philosophical framework. The "narrative" treatment of the "problem of Communism" comes in his account of his Russian intelligence "control," Colonel Bykov. Bykov, he tells us, "was an awed admirer of Nechayev, the nineteenth-century Russian who carried the logic of revolution to its limit teaching (Lenin, among others) that murder, kidnapping, arson, robbery, and blackmail, all crimes, are justified if they serve the socialist cause. From Bykov I first learned the name of Nechayev, who also served Dostoievsky as the terrible prototype of Pyotr Stepanovitch Verkhovensky in *The Possessed*." (p. 438)

Not one in a hundred of the readers of *Witness* will have also read Dostoyevsky's extraordinary novel *The Possessed*, often known under the English title *Demons*. It is unnecessary to know the novel or any of its attending circumstances to understand Chambers's point. But it is almost always better to know something, and the reader who does know something here is at a considerable artistic advantage. Dostoyevsky did indeed model his chief "demon" on Sergey Nechayev, and he learned of Nechayev as so many others did through a famous murder trial of 1871. Nechayev was the leader of a student revolutionary group. Another member of the group, one Ivan Ivanov, withdrew from the conspiracy in protest at Nechayev's dictatorial methods. Nechayev murdered Ivanov, and disposed of the body beneath the ice of a frozen river (the later "Rasputin treatment"). In other words, Nechayev purged Ivanov. He did to him what Jan Valtin was instructed by Getsy to do to the Los Angeles apostate. He did what Chambers believed the Russian organs had done to the apostate General Krivitsky, and what he obviously feared might be done to himself. Among the first victims of the Revolution are the revolutionaries. We recall that Gletkin, the "bad cop" of Rubashov's interrogation, reports without emotion that the "good cop," Rubashov's onetime friend Ivanov, has been shot. The slaughter of the Ivanovs will happen again and again.

The more "philosophical" treatment of the same point comes when Chambers is discussing the preparation of his cover story on Reinhold Niebuhr for *Time* magazine. Niebuhr's theology is not notably other-worldly. It is often called "Christian realism"—meaning that it was a Christian vision liberated from a subservience to antiquated myth systems and responsible to the political realities of modernity. In fact, Niebuhr's recurrent theme—as in his most famous book, *Moral Man and Immoral Society* (1932)—is precisely the meaning of the confrontation of political power with the religious conscience. His critique of Marxism in its religious pretensions was that Marx and Engels had lapsed from realism to idealism in failing altogether to imagine the implications of an overwhelming political power consolidated in the hands of human beings as they actually are, as opposed to what a reckless secular optimism might hope they would become.

That is, Niebuhr maintained two fundamental tenets of orthodox Christianity through the ages: the otherness of God, and the fallenness of men. In his essay on Niebuhr, Chambers quotes a stanza from Tennyson's *In Memoriam*, a stanza that in his mind typified the vagueness of liberal Protestantism, but also "scientific" socialism:

> O, yet we trust that somehow good
> Will be the final goal of ill,
> To pangs of nature, sins of will,
> Defects of doubt, and taints of blood . . .

Swinburne had made fun of this side of Tennyson (expressed even more appallingly in a poem called "The Higher Pantheism") in a memorable satiric couplet:

God, whom we see not, is; and God, who is not, we see:
Fiddle, we know, is diddle: and diddle is possibly dee.

"It was a good deal easier to see that Tennyson was silly than to see that the attitude itself was silly," wrote Chambers. "That was the blind impasse of optimistic liberalism." Against it, he tells us, he marshaled three thinkers whom he regarded as more profound: Søren Kierkegaard, Karl Barth, and Fyodor Dostoyevsky, "whom I am not alone in holding to be one of the great religious voices of our age."

Now this was very clearly to suggest a *theological* explanation for phenomena for which *political* explanations seemed to fall short. It was a suggestion that Americans, in their thousands, were fully able to comprehend. These people were not theologians. They might not even know what "theology" is. They were, however, believers in God. Many of them read the Bible, attended church, lived a life not untouched by the reflectiveness of prayer or the experience of sacramental grace. In the early pages of the "Letter to My Children," Chambers had said what Communism was, and what it was not. Toward the idealism of Communists he was very generous. In like manner he expressed an admiration for Communists' intensity in believing in a cause. "Their power, whose nature baffles the rest of the world, because in a large measure the rest of the world has lost that power, is the power to hold convictions and to act on them." Very clearly Communism was a "faith" to which the actions and activities of individual Communists was a "witness." "It is the great alternative faith of mankind. Like all great faiths, its force derives from a simple vision. Other ages have had great visions. They have always been different versions of the same vision: the vision of God and man's relationship to God. The Communist vision is the vision of Man without God." (p. 9)

It takes no great sophistication to understand what Chambers is saying. Yet none of his sophisticated critics—not even Sidney Hook, who had the very great virtue of taking the religious argument seriously—presented a counterargument of anything like comparable power. It is too much to hope that Chambers more than any other man will practice what he preaches. Rebecca West, as always penetrating and original, pointed to a significant weakness in Chambers's analysis. He gave Communism and Communists too much ethical credit. She scoffs at his examples of Communist altruism and heroic self-sacrifice. She implies that Chambers has, for purposes of his "mystical" argument, created a pseudoreligious straw man. Sam Tanenhaus makes a similar point about Chambers's expressed attitude to Alger Hiss, the lineaments of whose career show no more unwavering commitment to political idealism than they do to more familiar opportunism.

For while it is obviously possible to construct a political vision quite independent of any idea of God, and equally possible to construct a vision of God quite independent of politics, it was nearly impossible to ignore the fact that Communism was a religion in which the dogmas of men had triumphed over the dogmas of God. Hence the insistent return on the part of Chambers's adversaries, then and later, to the question of Alger Hiss. Unfortunately, readers friendly to Chambers were as quick as his adversaries to accept the idea that *Witness* was a book about Alger Hiss, and that everything in it depended upon the innocence or guilt of Alger Hiss. It does not. Chambers came to abandon Communism, and thus to betray the man he claimed was as close a friend as one makes in a lifetime, because he came to believe that Communism was in the power of a godless *Soviet* theocracy.

There is a hypothesis among some ecclesiastical historians to the effect that all of Asia would today be Roman Catholic if only the Popes of the sixteenth and seventeenth centuries had been men of a larger vision. Jesuit missionaries petitioned in vain for a strategic release from certain Eurocentric accidental forms of their religion—clerical dress, the Latin language, and so on—that they might be more lithe, unencumbered, and supple in their evangelism. Similarly, American Communism might have thrived the better without its Muscovite millstone. But whether in Italy or America—or most sensationally, Tito's Yugoslavia—indigenous national "Communisms" were opposed by Soviet orthodoxy.

Some revisionist historians have asserted, though without demonstration or documentation, a kind of rugged, independent American Communism untouched by the tarbrush of totalitarian excess. The fact is that at least from the time of the purgation of the "Lovestonites," the American

Communist Party was a wholly owned subsidiary of Moscow.* The Western Communists who remained in the Party through the purges and the
Hitler-Stalin Pact had to possess a very particular mind-set. In the United
States and Britain (as opposed to France and Italy), Cold War Communists
were in fact a vanishing breed. In one of her short stories ("The Day Stalin Died"), Doris Lessing gives in cameo a satirical portrait of a die-hard
British Communist of the immediate postwar period who might as easily
have lived in Brooklyn as in Bayswater. "Comrade Jean had left her husband when he became a member of the Labour Party at the time of the
Stalin-Hitler Pact, and ever since then had been living in bed-sitting rooms
on bread, butter, and tea, with a portrait of Stalin over her bed."

Most historians who have dealt with the American political history of
the 1930s have either known little or cared little about the complex relationships between politics and religion in the period. This perhaps explains
why the religious theme in *Witness*—its principal ideographic theme—has
so often been ignored or trivialized. The religious opinions of George W.
Bush, and of the so-called religious right—the only religious ideas likely to
be invoked—are nearly irrelevant to Chambers and the nature of his witness. Several of his critics have accused Chambers of adopting an "apocalyptic" worldview. They have perhaps been encouraged by the fact that
one of his greatest admirers, Ronald Reagan, once mused in public about
relationships between the United States and the Soviet Union in terms of
Armageddon. In fact, the word "apocalyptic" has been so debauched as to
mean nearly anything a user wants it to mean, but if it responsibly refers to
an eschatological theory founded in the exegesis of the Book of Revelation,
few things could be further from Chambers's mental universe.

Even in its journalistic connotation—meaning something like "characterized by belief in a dramatic confrontation of good and evil"—it
hardly represents the center of Chambers's thinking. In moving from a
materialist to a providential philosophical viewpoint, Chambers was abandoning "apocalypticism." An "apocalyptic" reading of history, a marginal

---

* Jay Lovestone (1897–1990) was an early leader of the American Communist Party who (with
his followers) was expelled from the Party in 1929 for his association with the "right-wing
deviationism" of Nikolai Bukharin. This purge of course reflected developments in the Soviet
Union, where Stalin was consolidating his power. Bukharin was definitively purged by the show
trial in 1938. Lovestone eventually became a determined anti-Communist.

and aberrant feature of modern Christian thought, was at the dogmatic center of Marxism-Leninism and, to the extent that Marxism-Leninism remains ambulatory, still is. The doctrine that social redemption requires as its indispensable prolegomenon a violent revolution and a "struggle to the death" is an apocalyptic doctrine. The practical results of the doctrine as applied in the Soviet Union, in China, in Cambodia, can be quickly reviewed in the statistical tables of the *Black Book of Communism*.

The Religious Climate of the Thirties

On the other hand, Chambers's ideas are naturally connected to the thought of his own day, and these ideas show a remarkable range and complexity. There was a large political spectrum even within organized religion. A wit said that Father Charles Coughlin, who developed along the not untypical trajectory from anti-capitalist populism to anti-Semitic Fascism, was "Protestant America's favorite Catholic priest" during Roosevelt's early years. His colleague Gerald L. K. Smith was an ordained minister. The complex political tendencies in American Catholicism arise from the long history of relationship with the ethnic groups that were its historical base. Italian-American Catholics were prominent in the agitation over the Sacco-Vanzetti case. As recently as the 1970s, the terrorist IRA commanded wide support among American Catholics of Irish extraction. Dorothy Day, now a candidate for canonization, was nearly indistinguishable from the Marxist labor activists with whom she so often cooperated. By no means all of the former Communists who converted or reverted to Catholicism abandoned leftist political views. The rightward drift of many ex-Communists was often a more or less desperate effect of the "Cassandra complex." They kept moving on until they found a community who would believe them.

Unfortunately, much American liberal thought joined in with a more hateful strain of nativist anti-Catholicism at the time of the Spanish Civil War. Though the Spanish religious scene was complex, the Church was overwhelmingly allied with Franco, and the forces of the Republic were overwhelmingly anti-clerical. Even without their propagandistic exaggeration, the atrocity reports of the widespread murder of priests and religious—not one or two murders but several thousands—and the ubiquitous photographs of destroyed and desecrated churches had a profound impact on American public opinion. Louis Fischer could attribute the defeat of the Republic to a "Catholic lobby" in several countries, particularly the United States, which enforced the policy of "non-intervention" that for many leftists was the equivalent of active Fascist collaboration. Shortly before he died in 1939, the radical, crusading journalist Heywood Broun became a Roman Catholic. His conversion mystified and appalled many of his left-wing friends—"especially after Spain," as one of them who had uncomfortably attended his huge funeral in St. Patrick's Cathedral in New York put it in a memoir.

The immediate postwar period in America was one of considerable religious vitality, and the persecution of religion in Eastern Europe had a large effect on American public opinion. Alger Hiss's was by no means the only drama of the year 1948. Among several other episodes, the well-publicized case of Cardinal Mindszenty in Hungary dramatized the hostility of Communism to religious liberty, the second of Roosevelt's celebrated "four freedoms" from the State of the Union address in 1941. Mindszenty, we may recall, was the persecuted churchman, a potential martyr, who retired to a protracted asylum in the grounds of the American Embassy in Budapest.

The idea of "godless Communism" that became current in the vulgar anti-Communism of the 1950s was as shallow as most popular political clichés. Particularly absurd, perhaps, was the linkage of unmasking Reds with religious virtue. But it is not fair to judge anti-Communism by its crudest manifestations and anti-anti-Communism by its most responsible. To Gus Hall, the hapless leader of a Party on its deathbed, was attributed a fantastic "quotation" that, like the cardboard figure of Pavel Morozov, derived eventually from the ancient anti-Semitic "blood libel." Pseudo-Gus began by looking forward to that happy day "when the last Congressman [*sometimes* businessman] will be strangled with the guts of the last preacher." This sentiment summarized the Red threat to church and state alike, as viewed by certain patriots, with a wonderful economy. Its style was embraced by Jerry Falwell, and perhaps by Ronald Reagan.

The idea that Christians in general found a natural congruence between Christianity and capitalism is another vulgar error. In 1925, Bruce Barton, an advertising executive, published a widely admired book called *The Man Nobody Knows*. In it he presents Jesus as the very model of a successful and innovative businessman. Had the Lord not said, after all, "I must be about my Father's business" (Luke 2:49)? Jesus, giving inspired leadership to his twelve vice presidents, builds an effective "organization." The book had a certain vogue, even as today there is an audience for the "preachers of plenty" and their "prosperity gospel." Jesus the Rotarian was, however, an extraordinary novelty unrecognized by serious theologians.

In Europe there were numerous serious Christian interventions in the political dialogue. In England there were many Christian connections to the radical movement. Alumni of the dissenting academies had been among the greatest agitators for Reform. It is hardly an exaggeration to say that British socialism, as an actual political force as opposed to an intellectual enthusiasm, was born within the bosom of Methodism. Similarly, there was a definite radical streak, at the pastoral level, in Anglo-Catholicism. The essays in *Christianity and the Crisis* (1933), edited by the Anglican scholar Percy Dearmer, commanded a wide and respectful reading in Britain. Another Anglican, Archbishop William Temple, made several public "political" interventions in accord with widely accepted ideas of Christian social justice. In France Maurice Thorez, who became the Communist Party leader in 1930, had articulated the policy of the "extended hand" toward Catholics. This policy was endorsed if not initiated by his Soviet masters, who in their own country were simultaneously following a policy that, had it been given a name, might be called the "smashing fist." (Stalin had declared that the final solution to the religious problem—the extermination of religion—would coincide with the first Five Year Plan). There was in the texture of French Catholicism a distinct radical strand that antedated even the Revolution and was not entirely effaced even in the post-revolutionary reaction. With this tradition we may associate Charles Péguy, whom Chambers cites with approval. Péguy, we recall, was the spiritual master of Georges Izard (Kravchenko's lawyer), and the founder of the politically radical Christian journal *Esprit*. There were French Catholic intellectuals willing to take the "extended hand" in an attempt to find common ground for possible common action in facing the social crisis of the Great Depression. One result was *Le Communisme et les Chrétiens* (*Communism and the Christians*), a collection of essays by eminent hands under the editorship of François Mauriac (1937).

Among several brilliant essays there is one by Nicholas Berdyayev ("The Human Person and Marxism"). In it the powerful Orthodox thinker summarizes but also extends the critique he had begun in his book

Christianity and Class War (1933), the dedication to which reads thus: "I dedicate this book to the memory of Karl Marx who was the social master of my youth and whose opponent in ideas I have now become." One somehow doubts that this book came to the attention of the ex-seminarian in the Kremlin. It is perhaps not surprising that the deep critique made of Marxism by Christian theologians was balanced by no deep critique of Christianity made by Marxists. But Whittaker Chambers, who had read some Mounier as well as his Marx, did not shrink before the task of discussing the "problem of Communism" with a certain theological sophistication.

Niebuhr's distinction between the individual and society, and his theory that the consistency of ethical virtue achievable by and demanded of individuals can never characterize the behavior of political states, directly confronts all millenarian and apocalyptic political suggestions, particularly those (like the "withering away of the state") so prominent in Marxism. The tentative or reluctant attitude toward political power in Niebuhr's "Christian realism" thus roughly corresponds in Augustinian theological terms to the attitude of Koestler's Yogi rather than that of his Commissar. It also put him in opposition to the major current of liberal Protestant thought in the 1930s.

Among the most vociferous of Western Sovietophiles of the 1930s were prominent members of the Christian clergy. Dr. Hewlett Johnson, the "Red Dean" of Canterbury Cathedral, was so keen in his devotion to the Soviet Union that he defended the Hitler-Stalin Pact even while Great Britain was in a state of war with Germany! He traveled extensively in Russia in the thirties, seeing and hearing no evil, and certainly speaking none upon his return. He typified a long generation of European intellectuals whom we call visionaries, prophets, innocents, useful idiots, or Communist dupes, according to political inclination. On the faculty of Union Theological Seminary in New York, Niebuhr's chief rival for the public ear was the Reverend Harry F. Ward. It is possible that Ward was an actual secret member of the Communist Party; but the question is nearly irrelevant for readers of *In Place of Profit: Social Incentives in the Soviet Union* (1933) or *The Soviet Spirit* (1944). He was a man who believed that the Kingdom of God could be achieved on earth by political means and that the paradox of its agency—a militantly atheistic "revolutionary" political party—was no more astonishing than any other religious paradox. Union Theological Seminary was in this period one of the most prestigious centers of advanced theological thought in what had been Christendom. The "debate" between Ward and Niebuhr arose from its vital center. When Whittaker Chambers raised the question that so scandalized Irving Howe—is man to rule, or God?—he was entering on the "Niebuhrian" side of an ancient yet ferociously contemporary dispute. Intellectual fairness demands respect for the question even if it rejects his answer.

It is true that Chambers's posture became increasingly pessimistic, and hence traditional and conservative. Christian orthodoxy has ever maintained that human nature is wounded and human beings alienated from God. "We were by nature the children of wrath," writes Saint Paul. This is the "historical situation" in which God entered history in the Incarnation. What a wounded human nature cannot on its own achieve, grace can. The mission of Jesus Christ was one of rescue and repair. The very etymology of the word "religion"—*re+ligare*, "to tie together again"—archives this belief. Such are the broad assumptions Chambers found in Niebuhr and that, he tells us, represented his own religious views as he began his witnessing.

Chambers, Hiss, and the New Deal

We have now perhaps gained the detachment to see that this famous matter of Alger Hiss and Whittaker Chambers has been troubled by two cognate literary misprisions. The first is the misapplication of the Sherlock Holmes principle; and the second is premature allegorization. The evidence for Hiss's guilt is very convincing, so convincing, in fact, as to raise the question of why it has been so stoutly resisted. It has been so stoutly resisted because of a misapplication of the Sherlock Holmes principle: "Once you have eliminated the impossible, whatever remains, no matter how improbable, must be the truth."

Hiss has been held to be innocent because innocence was what was left if guilt were *impossible*. And guilt was impossible because he denied guilt, because he had clerked for Oliver Wendell Holmes, because he had had a distinguished career in government service, because Felix Frankfurter and Dean Acheson thought he was a fine fellow, or—taking the negative approach—because his chief accuser was a shifty-eyed homosexual who was a great pal of Richard Nixon and an enabler of Joseph McCarthy.

Now, while all those things might make a man's guilt seem improbable or unpalatable, none makes it *impossible*.

Second, the entire episode suffered from premature allegorization. The rather mundane matter of law—whether the individual Alger Hiss did or did not commit perjury—was overwhelmed by grand designs. Right from the start, observers no less than agonists searched for a "larger meaning." Alistair Cooke's book bears the title *A Generation on Trial*, and it typifies the thrust of many others. Chambers had encouraged the search for "larger meaning" himself: "The simple fact is that when I took up my little sling and aimed at Communism, I also hit something else. What I hit was the forces of that great socialist revolution, which, in the name of liberalism, spasmodically, incompletely, somewhat formlessly, but always in the same direction, has been inching its ice cap over the nation for two decades." (p. 741) Chambers is here alluding to the New Deal, of course, and to "creeping socialism"; and it is this statement, as amplified in several following paragraphs in *Witness*, that has most enraged his liberal critics. For he claimed that "it was the forces of this revolution that had smothered the Hiss Case (and much else) for a decade, and fought to smother it in 1948."

Within the economy of *Witness*, this remark, which Ronald Reagan once cited with approval, may seem a gratuitous partisan slur among so many others. It has more than once been cited by Chambers's enemies as evidence that the "reactionary" who would emerge fully only in his association with *The National Review* was already animating his autobiography. However, his interpretation, though it is not inevitable, is in its historical context hardly remarkable. Defenders of Alger Hiss and Harry Dexter White, the most controversial government figures linked by Chambers to Soviet espionage, are wont to exculpate them by saying that they were "simply" New Dealers, as though being a New Dealer was wholly incompatible with radical politics, let alone turpitude. Historians who write about the New Deal today generally speak of it in mild-mannered terms as a package of essentially moderate policies tending in the direction of augmented social justice in public health and social welfare, agrarian reform, "price control," artificially stimulated state-sponsored employment, and the inspired patronage of the collaboration of Chambers's close friend James Agee with Walker Evans in *Let Us Now Praise Famous Men*. But this, like most more or less settled historical judgments, is a privilege of hindsight. And if there is no very concrete meaning to the term "New

Deal" today, there was probably even less during the first two terms of the Roosevelt presidency when, depending upon one's point of view, the "New Deal" was being implemented, imposed, or improvised. Was the so-called New Deal simply the achievement of socialism by other means? There were those who thought so, and they were not all Republican reactionaries, Ku-Kluxers, or fundamentalist preachers.

What did the New Deal look like in 1938, around the time of Chambers's break with the Communist Party? There surely is the potential for revolution in the phrase itself, taken from the world of poker playing, and meaning a completely fresh redistribution of resources. Many American radicals saw it precisely in those terms. There is an instructive notice in one of the final numbers of *The Modern Quarterly*, edited by the prominent non-Communist Marxist V. F. ("George") Calverton, among the most humane in the great tradition of American radicals. He is explaining why his magazine, which had begun as a quarterly but then speeded up to a monthly, faced serious retrenchment:

> The consolidation of the New Deal and the consequent change in attitude of a number of radical groups and many thousands of individuals who had formerly thought themselves part of the left-wing movement, has seriously curtailed the field of active supporters for an independent radical journal. These erstwhile radical groupings and their supporters have either openly or tacitly abandoned their radicalism and sworn allegiance to the Roosevelt program. Many of them can no longer allow themselves in good faith to either read or support such a journal as *The Modern Quarterly* which continues to insist that the New Deal is an extension of old-line capitalism in new form and with a different nomenclature, and that its object is to protect capital-investment and discourage the working-class from adopting a socialist ideology.

Calverton makes his own view of the matter clear, certainly. But let us hear also what he is saying about those "many thousands of individuals" in the "erstwhile radical groupings" who eagerly supported a Marxist journal. They did not think the New Deal was another name for "capitalism." Indeed, many early New Dealers claimed that the administration had achieved, wholly or in part, the workable "planned economy" that Stalin sought through more drastic measures.

There is further evidence in the literary career of John Dos Passos, as well as in his own "New Deal" novel, *The Adventures of a Young Man* (1939), in which Paul, an American Communist returning from an extended residence in Russia, amazes his friend Glenn Spottswood with his account of the horrors of Stalinist life, and adds, "the New Deal's got the five-year plan knocked for a row of red squares as a social experiment. . . . The revolution's happened; kid, it's all over. " The revolution here referenced, of course, is the *American* socialist revolution.

Martin Dies, along with some of his colleagues and successors, had been saying for years that the New Deal bureaucracy was riddled with Communists, and that the leaders of the Democratic Party were culpably myopic in pooh-poohing the Communist presence. This was not particularly fair, but it did little for their case in the court of public opinion when Nathan Silvermaster, a real Communist and a real Soviet espionage agent, proclaimed in indignation: "Because I have never attempted to conceal my strong advocacy of the rightness of all New Deal principles, I have been constantly harassed by groundless accusations of disloyalty." The Communists, no less than their bitterest enemies, were happy enough to claim the mantle, protective or deceptive, of the New Deal. The anti-Communist, Silvermaster continues, "regards as traitors those who supported Franklin Delano Roosevelt in his magnificent policy of complete unity with our wartime allies."

During the political campaign of 1950 in which Nixon defeated the liberal superstar Helen Gahagan Douglas for a Senate seat, he was able to portray his opponent as "pink down to her underwear" simply because she was so closely associated with the New Deal enthusiasms for economic planning and centrally organized social welfare. This would not have been possible had there not been a fairly widespread belief that a Communist was "a liberal in a hurry."

THE DOMESTICATION OF AMERICAN COMMUNISM

The books of Arthur Koestler, Jan Valtin, and Victor Kravchenko chiefly exposed the iniquities of the Soviet state in its inner workings and in its projection of international skulduggery through the Comintern. The struggles of Jan Valtin had taken place in 1942 and 1943. That was at the very apogee of the "popularity" of American Communism. America's top Communist, Earl Browder, was successfully marketing the idea of an anti-Fascist coalition that continued the idealism of the period of the Spanish Civil War. Browder realized that for most Americans there was already something indelibly sinister in the phrase "the Party." Indeed, before he was purged, he hoped to achieve a triumph of public relations that might "mainstream" and democratize American Communism by dropping the name "Party" altogether, and relaunching it as the "American Communist Association." A decade later, when *Witness* was published, the American Communist Party was a ragged and persecuted remnant of what it had once been. As for *international* Communism, American public opinion was by now implacably fearful and hostile. Hence the historical role of Chambers's anti-Communist manifesto was rather different from that of Koestler, Valtin, or Kravchenko. His role was in a sense to revive in the American consciousness the reality, or at least *a* reality, of American Communism.

One of the remarkable features of Chambers's book, which surely appealed to the literary instincts of readers who find fascination in true crime stories, is that he presents so many of his onetime Communist friends and acquaintances as interesting and appealing people, often quirky and gently risible. This he does without surrendering so much as a single square inch of his anti-Communism. He is rather better than Augustine at drawing sharp distinctions between sins and sinners. Some of the Russians were pretty desperate types, but even they seem a couple of cuts above the population of the rogues' gallery of Comintern agents as we meet them in *Out of the Night*. Most of the Americans, on the other hand, are domesticated and socially acceptable. Take Sender Garlin, for example, the scourge of *Reader's Digest* and debunker of Jan Valtin. Garlin had been the man who introduced Chambers to the "Party" way back at the beginning of it all.

In seeking about for some way in which he might give the socialism that he now accepted in theory some concrete expression, Chambers notes, "I remembered that there had once passed across the Columbia campus a high-strung, red-headed boy from an upstate college. He had slept overnight on the bare floor of a friend's room in one of the residence halls. He talked incessantly in a voice like a teletype machine, and what he talked about was the Soviet Union and Communism." (pp. 196–97) Later

Chambers was Garlin's colleague on *The Daily Worker*, and he records affectionate reminiscences of him.* This generosity is all the more remarkable, as Chambers was not unaware that at the time of the Hiss affair Garlin was busy stoking the rumor mill that Chambers was a "pervert." One has a sense of interesting people living in interesting times. It is perhaps ironic that one fellow Communist whom he cannot make interesting, except to the degree that an enigma always arouses curiosity, is Alger Hiss. But that, as we have seen, was not for want of trying, as he is extravagant in his praise of the man's character and capacities.

Many of Chambers's Communists did not fit the stereotype of Hoover's "masters of deceit," nor even hirsute professors, let alone of trench-coated aliens with sinister accents. He gave several portraits of patrician Communists—Harvard graduates, Yale graduates. One of the prominent Red aristocrats on the Washington scene, Henry Collins, was a Princeton graduate, for heaven's sake! Before *Witness* was in print, the world had come to know that these people really and truly were Communists. There were a number of Commie matrons and *grandes dames*. He tells the amusing story of two Red bluebloods who showed up at a relative's house like a pair of Mafia goons to pass on the message that Chambers better shut up if he knew what was good for him.

What Chambers was intending here was an attack on the "Marbury syndrome." William Marbury was Hiss's old chum and his lawyer in the first trial. Chambers could not forgive him for being so competent as nearly to prevail. In his mind, Marbury represented the most potent weapon of the Communist conspirators, which was the inability of so many proper people to believe there could possibly be a Communist conspiracy. In light of the avalanche of documentary evidence, "I used to wonder . . . how a man of Marbury's acute mind and long legal experience could possibly continue to believe sincerely in Hiss's innocence. Of course, he did not have to believe in it. From the first Marbury *knew* that my charges could not be true because he himself was not a Communist and Communists simply could not occur in the social and professional worlds that were

---

* Garlin was not without his fans. On May Day, 1943, David Greenglass, future "atom spy" and supersnitch who would put his sister and brother-in-law (Ethel and Julius Rosenberg) in the electric chair, wrote to his wife from Army Machinists School: "By the way darling I read and enjoyed your letter and also the clippings from PM you had put in. I'd like to see some clippings from the Daily Worker too. Something like Mike Gold or Sender Garlin or the 'Veteran Commander.' I really miss them."

his own. Hiss could not be guilty because he was Marbury's friend and belonged to both those worlds." (p. 731)

But the fact that Chambers was domesticating American Communists made them from a certain perspective not less but more alarming. The uncontested narrative of *Witness* strongly suggested a dangerous and perhaps a criminal laxness in the government's attitude to an active conspiracy. It probably never occurred to Chambers that there were those who would find his story, in a word, incredible. He knew it was true. Don Levine believed him, and the government official to whom Chambers went with Levine gave him every reason by his deportment to think that he believed him, too. When nothing came of his intervention, the evidence seemed to leave only two possibilities. The first was that the Roosevelt administration thought that Communist penetration of the apparatus of government was a trivial matter of no practical concern. The second was that people in high places were actively covering the revelations up.

An analogy occurs from our more recent history. In August 2001, certain FBI agents in the Minneapolis office began to pay serious attention to Zacarias Moussaoui, a French jihadist with a lapsed visa, a suspicious bankroll, and an interest in trying to learn how to fly (but not take off or land) large jet passenger planes. The *9/11 Commission Report* calls him "an al Qaeda mistake and a missed opportunity." He was an al-Qaeda mistake because he incompetently drew suspicion upon himself. The opportunity missed was the possibility of nipping the World Trade Center and Pentagon plot in the bud, since that would have been the likely result of a search of Mr. Moussaoui's hard drive. The Minneapolis agents, who very much wanted to conduct such a search, were unable to gain the necessary permission to do so until after nearly three thousand people had been murdered by Mr. Moussaoui's friends and colleagues, by which time the confirmation of their suspicions was of greater archeological than practical import.

The 9/11 commissioners, who prided themselves on eschewing the blame game, simply reported this "missed opportunity." But when the report of the insufficiently attended "Minneapolis memo" became widely known, public indignation was great, as in the press and on talk radio. We can imagine, perhaps, the feelings of Whittaker Chambers in 1939. Chambers was suffering from a bad case of the guilty conscience as the Spanish Civil War came to its disastrous end. Then he had been told by Krivitsky that Stalin was trying to make a deal with Hitler—an astonishing claim that staggered the mind of any anti-Fascist. Then, in late August, the Germans and the Russians jointly announced the pact that Krivitsky had predicted. Under these circumstances, in fear and trembling, Chambers decided that he must inform the federal police of the secret Communist cell of which Alger Hiss was a member.

He acted through Isaac Don Levine, the indefatigable and ubiquitous anti-Communist who had secured his introduction to Krivitsky. It is a testimony less to Chambers's naïveté than to the simpler world of seventy years ago that Chambers at first insisted that he could reveal his secret only to President Roosevelt personally. That was not possible, but Levine could arrange something almost as good. The Office of Homeland Security did not exist in President Roosevelt's time, but Adolf Berle was in effect the president's director of Homeland Security. Levine arranged a lengthy, leisurely dinner meeting at Berle's house. Berle listened. He took notes. (The notes were headed "Underground Espionage Agent," suggesting that he understood the subject under discussion.) He raised the matter with the president, who profanely dismissed it as nonsense. The immediate effect of the meeting of Chambers with the Director of Homeland Security was precisely nothing. Nearly a decade later, Adolf Berle faced rather heavy weather trying to explain this nothingness to the grand jury that indicted Alger Hiss.

Nor was Berle the only intermediary through whom Levine was trying to get through to Roosevelt. He approached the gadfly radio news personality Walter Winchell, who had access to the White House. Winchell got nowhere with the story. He fed the story to William Bullitt, the former ambassador to the Soviet Union, and by then an implacable anti-Communist who makes a cameo appearance in many "episodes" of our history, including the campaign to save Jan Valtin.* Bullitt too got nowhere.

There are perfectly plausible explanations why the "Minneapolis memo" was not effective in getting legal access to Moussaoui's computer. There are perhaps plausible reasons why Franklin Roosevelt couldn't be

---

* There are two William Bullitts in the "Chambers story," and they get confused in the index to *Witness*. They are William Marshall Bullitt (1873–1957), onetime Solicitor General and a prominent Kentucky Republican; and William Christian Bullitt (1891–1967), the diplomat, ambassador successively in Moscow and Paris, and the husband of Louise Bryant, widow of John Reed.

bothered with reports that Alger Hiss was a member of a Communist cell in his government. But if there were, nobody had then, or indeed has yet, made them public. Chambers could think of only sinister ones, and he took a large swath of the country with him. "No feature of the Hiss Case is more obvious, or more troubling to history," Chambers wrote rather bitterly, "than the jagged fissure, which it did not so much open as reveal, between the plain men and women of the nation, and those who affected to act, think and speak for them." (p. 793)

WITNESS AND THE EMPIRE OF FEAR

One theme in *Witness* was in strict harmony with the national mood, and that was the theme of the *fear* of Communism. It is a fearful book about a usually fearful man. It came into a country in which schoolchildren were drilled in "duck and cover" exercises against the prospect of nuclear attack. In 1947, Lionel Trilling published *In the Middle of the Journey*, among the most widely admired "political" novels of the century. When the book was reissued in 1976, Trilling added a preface in which he revealed that the novel's central character, the ex-Communist Gifford Maxim, was modeled on Whittaker Chambers, whom he had known since student days. He seemed less interested in the development of Maxim as a "character" than in dramatizing the dilemma of onetime or would-be political radicals. In another place he later wrote that his intention had been to illuminate "the clandestine negation of the political life which Stalinist Communism has fostered among the intellectuals of the West." Yet in one particular respect the fictional treatment of Maxim is most revealing of the factual situation of Chambers, and that is in the character's fearfulness. Maxim is seized by a polymorphous fear, only the most obvious aspect of which is fear for his life. Hiss's psychological experts concluded that one part of Chambers's mental pathology was a "paranoid" strain.

One sees the theme of fear repeatedly in *Witness*. In the first place Chambers is fearful that in the great scheme of things, the Communists are winning, and that his "conversion" thus adds the ironic to the quixotic by removing him from the winning to the losing side. From the hindsight of history, his alarmism may seem quaint, but it was very common among ex-Communists staggered by what they took as their contemporaries' nonchalance in the face of the "Communist threat." Read Solzhenitsyn's *Warning to the West*, published *twenty-five years* after Chambers sat down to write *Witness*. Of course Chambers did fear also for his own life, and for the safety of his family. The Communist apparatus could indeed operate effectively in the West, and could destroy even the most wary, as the fate of Trotsky so dramatically attested. Communist assassination of renegade agents in the United States was rare but not unknown. We recall its central role in the history of Jan Valtin. Chambers was quite convinced, with excellent reason, that the disappearance of the American Communist Juliet Poyntz in 1937 had been a "wet job," to use the term of art for murder used by GPU assassins themselves. It was in connection with Poyntz's disappearance that Chambers related the anecdote of Colonel Bykov's literary witticism in saying that Poyntz was "gone with the wind." One can understand how such ghoulish levity might have seemed ominous to Chambers, who was even then flirting with defection from the Party.

His anticipatory fear of informing the authorities about the penetration of major sectors of the American government by Soviet spies long paralyzed him, but he was at last moved to action by his disgust at the Hitler-Stalin Pact. It took every ounce of courage he had to give his report to Adolf Berle. He then retreated, the psychological equivalent of a wrung-out dishrag, awaiting an explosion, the scream of sirens in the streets of Washington, shocking headlines in the national press. What he got was—absolutely nothing. Now one fear replaced another. So great was the conspiracy that the conspirators had successfully thwarted even its explicit exposure. Chambers here almost certainly was dignifying mere incompetence as diabolical omnipotence, but given the nearly heroic efforts made by men of power to disbelieve or ignore him, now and later, one cannot judge the man severely. At the beginning of 1941 he was reading and reviewing *Out of the Night*, and reading articles in his and other magazines about the possible dangers to Valtin's life from a special perspective. "For a year I lived in hiding, sleeping by day and watching through the night with gun or revolver within easy reach. That was what underground Communism could do to one man in the peaceful United States in the year 1938." (p. 541)

His fear perhaps reached its apogee with the strange death of Walter Krivitsky in a Washington fleabag in February 1941, less than three weeks after the publication of his laudatory review of *Out of the Night*. Krivitsky's importance may have been slightly exaggerated in the title of his sensational book. In America it was called *In Stalin's Secret Service*; his identification as "head of Stalin's Secret Service" was prominent on the jacket. His conversations with Chambers, arranged through the ubiquitous Isaac Don Levine, had had an important role in Chambers's decision to go to the security authorities. The two men did become friends. Krivitsky had decided that he wanted to be baptized, and Chambers was trying to help him with his old sponsors at the Cathedral of Saint John the Divine. Krivitsky's death appeared to be a suicide, and may have been one. Gary Kern, who wrote an excellent book on the episode, believes it probably was. But Krivitsky had assured his wife that should he ever turn up a "suicide," she should know that he had in fact been assassinated.

Koestler, Chambers, Krebs, and doubtless many others were sure it was a KGB murder. Here the evidence of the fear under which Chambers had been living is compelling. His family was rusticating for several months in Florida—hiding out rather than vacationing. "The news of Krivitsky's death reached my wife through the newspapers before I could write to her," says Chambers. "She was overcome by panic and terror . . . knowing that I saw Krivitsky frequently, she was afraid that I also had been killed, or would be." (p. 486) Chambers doubted that he himself was slated for attack, but he did fear for Krivitsky's widow and son. He spirited them—obviously with the knowledge and perhaps help of the FBI—to be with his wife in Florida. Later they stayed on the Maryland farm for a time.

Historians of the Hiss affair who have theorized that Chambers was a fantasist ignore the Krivitsky episode, which exposes the melodrama and totalitarian ruthlessness of an espionage world beyond fantasy, the world in which Chambers had moved, and from which he had caught his greatest fear: the fear that he would not be believed. If Western intelligence had been less myopic, Krivitsky's information could probably have closed down the Cambridge spy ring of Kim Philby and his friends in 1940. Unfortunately, one of the spies, Anthony Blunt, a sort of British Alger Hiss, whose extraordinary distinction and public reputation made the very thought of his disloyalty impossible, was one of the foxes overseeing the operations of the MI5 henhouse. The attacks on Krivitsky in the Western liberal and fellow-traveling press, in which a decorative anti-Semitism is an incidental but persistent presence, today make for incredulous reading. It was the recurring fate of ex-Communist whistle-blowers to be called liars by liars.

That had been the fate of Krivitsky, who ended up with a bullet in his brain. Chambers repeatedly went to the security officials without result. One president of the United States is said to have rejected his testimony "with an expletive." A second publicly described the case he was making as a "red herring." Even paranoids have real enemies.

AFTER *WITNESS*

Chambers was prepared to be despised by old Communists and fellow travelers, but he appears to have been strangely blindsided by the obloquy now heaped upon him by the liberal press. He had for years been saying that many liberals were dupes, yet he appeared amazed when they were duped by Hiss. The real or imagined war between the "American people" and the "mainstream media," which is so lively a topic in the current blogosphere, is adumbrated in the Hiss-Chambers case. Several of the giants of liberal journalism, such as James Reston, could scarcely rein in a nearly visceral revulsion for their colleague from *Time*. To revisit their pages today does little credit to their reputations for perspicacity or even fairness. The countervailing and unseemly glee in the conservative press, which often made hardly a feint in the direction of presuming Hiss's innocence, was no better. Chambers was hardly one who naively believed in "objective" news. His early training had come from *The Daily Worker* and the *New Masses*, and he openly boasts of turning the political "line" of *Time* in a generally anti-Communist direction. Yet before he was a professional witness or a professional anti-Communist Chambers was a professional journalist of great energy and ability, and his ostracism from the guild wounded him grievously.

Even more shocking to him was the fact that Hiss's conviction, which should have been for him a vindication, seemed to count for so little. Legal victory and social acceptance are often strangers. As Hiss was on his way to federal prison, Dean Acheson, Truman's secretary of state, said in so many words, "I will not turn my back on Alger Hiss." It was a comment extorted from him by importunate journalists, and even in those days before personal honor had been quite banished from public discourse it was, from the political point of view, a reckless indiscretion. But Chambers was incapable of seeing it for what it was—a spontaneous expression of friendship and loyalty not unlike the friendship and loyalty that had for so long paralyzed his own intellectual political will. Recall that when testifying to the New York grand jury, Chambers had withheld the not insignificant fact that in addition to being a Communist, Hiss had been a spy. This evasion was later to prove nearly fatal to his cause. But when he reflected on matters as he wrote *Witness*, he vehemently denied that Acheson's remark might "be reviewed merely in those terms of personal feeling that I of all men must be the first to understand, for I shared that feeling. . . . You will look in vain in history for anything comparable to it." No. It was part of a pattern that had included the appearances of two justices of the U.S. Supreme Court as character witnesses on Hiss's behalf.

When asked what he thought he was doing in opening up the Hiss case, Chambers replied, "I am destroying myself." He repeats that idea several times in *Witness*. To advertise one's self-destruction is a rhetorical gesture so extravagant and self-indulgent that it can be justified by one thing alone: the truth. For Chambers did in truth quite knowingly destroy himself. *Witness* was published in 1952, and what might be called the brouhaha surrounding it raged or simmered or gestated for two or three years, by which point its author had only five or six years left to live. He was once again affluent, and he once again denied it by retiring to the pumpkin patch from which he had once commuted to his highly remunerated job in New York.

There is a political pattern typical of ex-Communists. Former revolutionaries become doctrinaire conservatives. It is not invariable, but the pressures, which are perhaps more social than spiritual, are powerful. Chambers had won the undying hatred of several generations of American liberals, but he had suddenly gained numerous previously unknown friends. He was an instant expert on the "Communist conspiracy in America," and the sort of people who thought in such terms sought him out. The brief ascendancy of Senator Joseph McCarthy began immediately following Hiss's conviction and lasted during the period of the writing and publication of *Witness*. According to Chambers's biographer, McCarthy was "awed" by the man, so to the historical burden of admiring Nixon Chambers has added the historical burden of being admired by McCarthy.

A man who calls himself a witness and writes a best-selling book called *Witness* could hardly fail to be summoned to Washington now and again to help dignify the questionable activities of congressional investigators.

Chambers was expert in a form of journalism for which we invoke the French term *haute vulgarization*—the serious, elevated, high-class popularization of complex subject matter. To write for a very broad readership a responsible essay on the theology of Reinhold Niebuhr or the historical theories of Arnold Toynbee, and to write it in such a way as to make reading it a pleasure, is no small skill. The term *haute vulgarization* could be used for many parts of *Witness*, which so successfully places a particular individual life within a complex intellectual and political context unfamiliar to most of its readers.

Chambers's arena of activity and personal connection contracted dramatically. His health, none too good to begin with, certainly must have been taxed by the long, exhausting, sedentary months spent writing *Witness*. He suffered one nearly fatal heart attack before actually succumbing to a second. His friendship with William Buckley is memorialized in a collection of striking letters, many of which are remarkable alike for mental agility and a kind of all-consuming political pessimism that Buckley once rightly characterized as "Spenglerian gloom." They are emblems of a mind exhausted, or perhaps seduced to self-indulgence, by the contemplation of the probable demise of Western society. Buckley very much wanted Chambers to join *The National Review*, which for a time he did. But Chambers's relationship with the magazine was by no means easy or uncomplicated. He was embarrassed by its continuing connections with doctrinaire strands of conservatism that he considered cranky and (his term) "crackpot." He also thought it was frequently intellectually flimsy. He obviously would have preferred to see in it the kind of depth that characterized the cover stories in *Time*—particularly, one imagines, those written by himself. In *The National Review*, Chambers published a few memorable pieces—memorable and perhaps surprising, such as his devastating review of Ayn Rand's *Atlas Shrugged*. If we can believe his letters to Buckley—as Buckley clearly did—Chambers continued to work hard as a writer, indeed dangerously hard in light of his health, but expended most of his energy on multiple drafts and rewrites, most of which were eventually discarded.

Random House continued to hope for a book that somehow might be a "sequel" to *Witness*, as though either author or publisher could have actually imagined such a thing. At various times Chambers had proposed an enormously ambitious trilogy, of which *Witness* would be but one part. Years passed without much progress on it, and it is hard to believe he ever really engaged with it. His intellectual biography was unfinished at his death—unfinished, and in some ways still unformed. The fragments were gathered together and published posthumously under the title *Cold Friday*. This book is perhaps as surprising as everything else about the man. "Cold Friday" is actually a topographical name, an old field on an old farm in Maryland. There is indeed some intellectual history in the book, an aging conservative's lament for an intellectually and spiritually misspent youth, but its best parts are "nature writing" of a high order. It is the kind of book that inevitably attracts comparison with Thoreau, but the comparison is not in fact absurd. One recalls some remarks in the astonishing essay by Rebecca West first published as an article in 1952, in which she very surprisingly identifies Chambers's sense of locality as one of the great achievements of his book: "We see through his eyes the miraculous quality of the American landscape which touches and astounds all European visitors." The best parts of *Cold Friday* are mainly devoid of political content, unless so ostentatious a retreat from the political field is itself a political statement. The book's central metaphor is inescapably bleak: the onset of an early winter from which no early relief is to be expected.

It is perhaps enough that a man should play as much of a role in the history of nations as did Whittaker Chambers. Yet his final years suggest that for all his roles—spy, journalist, witness, and enigma—he may have missed his calling. He was probably cut out to be a sort of no-holds-barred intellectual, a college professor of history or of literature, as he indeed had once planned to be. He was a quirky and reclusive intellectual whose considerable pedagogical skill did not necessarily imply a much wider social competence or congeniality. In *Witness* he spoke, utterly unconvincingly, of a friendship with Alger Hiss "as close as a man ever makes in his life." Not that he was, as sometimes characterized by his enemies, "friendless." The early chapters of *Witness* contain many passages of writing of that wistful poignancy so frequently the product of the meeting of youth and death. His brother's suicide was less a blow than a reproach to one so leaden as to persevere in living in a world so cruel and rough. Our literature contains few more haunting treatments of youth's bafflement in the face of death than James Agee's *A Death in the Family*, published posthumously in 1957. In a book teeming with the proper names of colleagues, acquaintances, co-conspirators, and adversaries, Chambers himself used the word "friend" infrequently. He didn't have many friends. But "friend" is the

word always used of Agee, his fellow political radical and his fellow introspective Christian. He found such friendship again in his last years of life,
with William Buckley, another intellectual constrained by the importuni-
ties of his popular audience. His correspondence with Buckley—published
by Buckley after Chambers's death—has the flavor of the shared intimacies
of erudite old friends in the common room or faculty lounge.

Reflection upon an episode of his post-*Witness* life can serve to end
this section and this book. In the summer of 1959, Chambers and his wife
made a trip to Europe. Chambers had been once to Europe, to Germany,
in 1923. He was at that time a Columbia drop-out, and he traveled with
Columbia friends. His wife Esther had never traveled abroad but always
wanted to.* So, flush with capital gains from shrewd stock investments,
they decided to go. They were in Paris briefly, then took off for the Austrian
Alps, where Arthur Koestler had invited them to visit him in his mountain
chalet. The journey was rendered adventurous by a landslide that made
it difficult to reach Koestler by road, even in a jeep. Intense public and
literary anti-Communism linked the two men, but in another world they
might conceivably have been soul mates even without that bond.

Among other surprises with which Koestler hoped to delight Chambers was the company of Margarete Buber-Neumann, who was rusticating in the same Alpine village. As Koestler introduced her to Chambers,
it would perhaps be a good idea to reintroduce her to readers of this
book. Buber-Neumann (1901–1989) was the German Communist and
anti-Communist who was married to the son of the famous Jewish theologian, Martin Buber. She divorced her husband to become the "Communist
wife" of Heinz Neumann, second in command of the German Communist Party. When Hitler came to power, the couple fled to Moscow. Heinz
Neumann disappeared in the Great Purge. A little later, Margarete herself
was thrown into the Gulag. At the time of the Hitler-Stalin Pact she was
among the German Communists taken out of the Russian prisons to be
transported directly to German prisons.

After the war, she published one of the more remarkable concentration camp memoirs, titled in English *Under Two Dictators*. She is related
to the anti-Communist masterpieces that are the subject of this book in

---

* This assumes that the "trip to Russia" of 1933 was an unexplained fabrication possibly related to
underground work.

the following ways. She was Arthur Koestler's friend and, especially, the friend of Koestler's great friend Willi Münzenberg, her brother-in-law. She was of course in prison while Koestler was writing *Darkness at Noon*, but they became good friends after the war. Richard Krebs had worked closely with Heinz Neumann, who was, in fact, as violent and ruthless a Communist terrorist as those who killed him in Russia. We may forgive his wife for omitting this information from an autobiography already sufficiently crammed with engrossing detail. In the Jan Valtin Papers in Princeton there is a folder in which Krebs filed information concerning Buber-Neumann. In 1949, she electrified the auditors at the Kravchenko libel trial not merely by her testimony that concentration camps did indeed exist in Russia, but that on the whole Hitler's camps were to be preferred to Stalin's. She spoke of course with a unique authority. Thus, when she shook hands with Whittaker Chambers in June 1959, she was completing a circuit that joined the authors of the four most important anti-Communist books of the mid-twentieth century.

This meeting was memorialized in a letter that Chambers wrote to Buckley. After explaining briefly who was this woman whose life story "makes the Odyssey, for all its grandeur, somehow childish," Chambers added a wistful reverie: "So there we sat, and talked, not merely about the daily experiences of our lives. Each of the two men had tried to kill himself and failed; Greta was certainly the most astonishing and hardy of the three. Then we realized that, of our particular breed, the old activists, we are almost the only survivors." He himself would not long be a survivor. He died three years later.

The idea of a bond of sympathy between Arthur Koestler and William Buckley is one to test the elasticity of historical irony. Yet on the occasion of Chambers's death, Arthur Koestler sent to *The National Review* a telegram of condolence, which surely must give the last words to any attempt to describe the life and work of Whittaker Chambers: "I always felt that Whittaker was the most misunderstood person of our time. When he testified he knowingly committed moral suicide to atone for the guilt of our generation. . . . The witness is gone, the testimony will stand."

A NOTE ON THE TEXTS

Each of the four books dealt with here was an American bestseller. Three were Book-of-the-Month Club selections. Two were partially serialized in mass market magazines. Two of them were bestsellers in their French translations. Although the discussion does not involve bibliographical fine points, I have used and cited the editions in which the large majority of their American readership first encountered them. One implication of the large printing runs of their original success is that, although long since out of print, they are still readily and cheaply available in the secondhand book market and in eBay auctions. The list below identifies the editions used and gives partial bibliographical descriptions sufficient for our purposes of identification by the aspiring collector of our nation's important intellectual antiques.

Arthur Koestler, ***Darkness at Noon*** (New York: Macmillan, 1941)
Darkness at Noon / by / Arthur Koestler / *Translated by* / Daphne Hardy.
NEW YORK / THE MACMILLAN COMPANY / 1941
267 pages.
This book has since been published in numerous other formats, several of which are in print.

Jan Valtin [pseudonym of Richard Krebs], ***Out of the Night*** (New York: Alliance, 1941)
OUT OF / THE NIGHT / By JAN VALTIN / [Alliance logo] / NEW YORK / ALLIANCE BOOK CORPORATION
On the verso of the title page: "Copyright 1941 by Alliance Book Corporation"

749 pages.

The true first edition of this book has 841 pages and bears the publication date of 1940 (although its appearance was actually delayed until January 1941). The earlier of the mass printings is 9.5 inches tall, with a zombielike figure on the jacket. Later printings were slightly smaller, with a circular geometrical design on the jacket. (The jackets seldom survive.) I have not consulted a recent reprint.

Victor Kravchenko, *I Chose Freedom* (New York: Scribner's, 1946)
I CHOSE FREEDOM / *The Personal and Political Life of a* / *Soviet Official* / by / VICTOR KRAVCHENKO / *New York* / CHARLES SCRIBNER'S SONS / 1946
496 pages.

The boards of the true first edition are brownish in color, gold stamped. The original edition was as usual extended by reprinting. The reprint is usually in violet cloth. There is no current edition available.

Whittaker Chambers, *Witness* (New York: Random House, 1952)
Witness / Whittaker / Chambers
On verso of fly leaf: RANDOM HOUSE / NEW YORK
On verso of title page: Copyright, 1952, by Whitaker Chambers
808 pages.

The original mass printing has black boards, marked only on the spine. "Witness" in white at the top, "Whittaker Chambers" in gold, two lines just beneath the title, and at the very bottom in a single line "RANDOM HOUSE." Chambers's book has remained almost continuously in print in one form or another.

ACKNOWLEDGMENTS

Most books are made out of other books. Certainly *The Anti-Communist Manifestos* is. Hence my first and warmest thanks must go to the librarians who enable all that scholars do. It has been my privilege during a long career as a medievalist to work in many of the famous collections of Western Europe and America, but my greatest debt has always been to the professionals at the fabulous Firestone Library in my home institution of Princeton University. It was the wholly unexpected discovery of the Jan Valtin papers housed in the Division of Rare Books and Special Collections there that rendered the idea of this book an actual possibility. In that same place are preserved the records of Scribner's relevant to the publication of Kravchenko's books. The University archives, housed in the Seeley Mudd Library a few hundred yards away, hold important papers relating to Roger Baldwin, Louis Fischer, and others who play supporting roles in my book. The papers of Isaac Don Levine, a treasure-trove for the historian of anti-Communism, are expertly preserved in the Manuscript, Archives, and Rare Book Library of Emory University in Atlanta. The Tamiment Collection in the Bobst Library of New York University has many items relating to the history of radicalism in America that are not easy to find in one place elsewhere. I enjoyed the expert help of librarians at all these places, and also at the Bibliothèque Nationale and the American Library in Paris.

I am grateful also to some scholars from whose advice I have benefited, two of whom need special mention. One of them is the Soviet expert Gary Kern, the author of important books including, most recently, a deeply researched study of the "Kravchenko case." The other is my old friend and colleague Samuel Hynes, a great expert on the literature of the

1930s, whose encouragement allowed me to undertake this project in the first place. I explain my general approach to my sources in the Introduction, but I should here mention three very recent books that appeared too late for me to use in this study but will be of interest to readers of *Witness*: namely, *Alger Hiss and the Battle for History* (Susan Jacoby), *The Conservative Turn* (Michael Kimmage), and *Spies* (John Earl Haynes, Harvey Klehr, and Alexander Vassiliev).

I have been richly blessed in my nuclear—but fortunately only occasionally ballistic—family. All its members have made significant contributions to the project, and especially, by inspiration, the two able historians to whom it is dedicated. My anthropologist son Luke came up with the perfect title when I myself could think of nothing very smart, and my travel-writer son Richard, expert as he is on the last surviving bastion of Communism in the West, set me a challenging standard. My children encouraged me to practice myself what I had so long preached to them, to set off in new directions, to try new things, to test the strength of my convictions. My life partner Joan, an unusually lucid reader and writer who in a distant early life was a professional editor, spent long hours improving the prose. A former student, Katy Flynn of the Princeton class of 2002, quite innocently set in motion a chain of events that led me to my delightful agent, Julia Lord. Ms. Lord sold the book to W. W. Norton—or rather "placed" it there, as during the whole process, she allowed no mercantile vocabulary to sully her lips or disturb my illusion that what was actually a rather ordinary commercial transaction was on my part a display of *virtù* and on the part of the publisher an enthusiastic act of cultural altruism in the service of the nation. It must have been by beginner's luck that within the Norton offices the project fell under the supervision of Starling Lawrence, who, according to those who know, turns out to be one of the legendary editors in New York publishing. He and his *aide de camp*, Nydia Parries, have been unfailingly helpful. Yet another superb professional, Ann Adelman, copyedited the submitted manuscript with extraordinary scrupulosity. My friend Eli Schwartz helped me with further proofreading. If any still is justly offended by such of my errors and infelicities as remain, I can but be very glad that that person did not see the book in its "before" state.

Such are some of the special debts requiring special mention. Perhaps only those who have shared my privilege of living and working within a great university will understand my felt need to give a much more generalized thanks for the stimulation, enthusiasm, and example, over many years, of colleagues and students too numerous to mention. It is only in retirement that I have fully absorbed the remarkable fact that for decades somebody was actually paying me to do what coercive force or large bribes alone could have prevented me from doing for nothing: that is, to live in a world of books and ideas. This little miracle has no unique relevance to the strivings of Communists and anti-Communists in the time of my infancy; but it certainly merits acknowledgement, and where better than in a section headed "Acknowledgments"?

INDEX